D1033936

William Blake and the Language of Adam

William Blake and the Language of Adam

ROBERT N. ESSICK

CLARENDON PRESS · OXFORD
1989

Oxford University Press, Walton Street, Oxford OX2 6DP
Oxford New York Toronto
Delhi Bombay Calcutta Madras Karachi
Petaling Jaya Singapore Hong Kong Tokyo
Nairobi Dar es Salaam Cape Town
Melbourne Auckland
and associated companies in
Berlin Ibadan

Oxford is a trade mark of Oxford University Press

Published in the United States
by Oxford University Press, New York

British Library Cataloguing in Publication Data
Essick, Robert N.
William Blake and the language of Adam.
1. Poetry in English. Blake, William, 1757–1827—Encyclopaedias
I. Title
821'.7
ISBN 0–19–812985–8

Library of Congress Cataloging in Publication Data
Essick, Robert N.
William Blake and the language of Adam/Robert N. Essick
p. cm.
Bibliography: p. Includes index
1. Blake, William, 1757–1827—Language. 2. Blake, William, 1757–1827—Knowledge—Language and languages. 3. Language and languages in literature. 4. Adam (Biblical figure) in literature. 5. Semiotics and literature. I. Title.
PR4148.L33E87 1989 821'.7—dc19 88-18816
ISBN 0–19–812985–8

Phototypeset by Dobbie Typesetting Limited, Plymouth, Devon
Printed in Great Britain
at the University Printing House, Oxford
by David Stanford
Printer to the University

Acknowledgements

I am grateful to the National Endowment for the Humanities for a Research Fellowship that allowed me to complete this book during the 1986–7 academic year. For permission to reproduce works of art in their collections, I thank the Glasgow Museums and Art Galleries, Stirling Maxwell Collection, Pollok House; the Henry E. Huntington Library and Art Galleries; the Fogg Art Museum, Harvard University, Grenville L. Winthrop Bequest; and the Victoria and Albert Museum.

I have been blessed with the help of several friends and fellow students of Blake in the course of writing this book. Conversations with Morris Eaves, Paul Mann, Jerome McGann, W. J. T. Mitchell, Eleanor Shaffer, John Villalobos, and Joseph Viscomi helped sharpen my view of Blake and expand my knowledge of linguistic history. Several colleagues at the University of California, Riverside, including Steven Axelrod, Bruce Campbell, Ralph Hanna, and John Steadman, made helpful suggestions during early stages of this project. I am particularly indebted to Morton Paley and Gunnel Tottie for reading and commenting on the first two chapters. James McKusick generously read the entire book at a late stage in its development and gave me many excellent suggestions. Valuable assistance has also been rendered by the staffs of the University of California, Riverside, and the Huntington libraries. My considerable indebtedness to Hazard Adams, Robert Gleckner, and Nelson Hilton, three scholars whose studies of Blake's language stimulated my own, is indicated in my frequent references to their works. To Kim Scott Walwyn of the Oxford University Press I owe much for her initial interest in this project and her expert guidance of its development from manuscript to print. My greatest debt, as always, is to Jenijoy La Belle.

Contents

List of Plates

Following page 22

Note on Texts

All quotations of Blake's writings are taken from *The Complete Poetry and Prose of William Blake*, newly revised edn., ed. D. V. Erdman (1982), hereafter cited as E followed by page number. Reference is also made (K followed by page number) to *Blake: Complete Writings*, ed. G. Keynes (1966).

Blake's paintings and drawings are catalogued and reproduced in M. Butlin, *Paintings and Drawings of William Blake* (1981), hereafter cited as 'Butlin' followed by volume and page or catalogue entry number.

Introduction

THE most important development in our understanding of William Blake, over the last twenty years or so, has been the emergence of Blake the Artist as an equal companion to Blake the Poet. The shift in interest has not been a simple matter of substitution or displacement, for our knowledge of Blake's poetry has had a profound effect on our perception of his visual art. That influence has been both unavoidable and generally salutary, particularly in the iconographic study of Blake's illuminated books as composite visual/verbal forms. One traditional area of art-historical scholarship, the study of an artist's materials and techniques, might seem relatively safe from the incursions of the literary mind. Yet even here, at least in the study of Blake's prints, the artist's writings have provided guiding principles for investigators of his graphic processes.[1] The portrait of Blake generated by these media-oriented endeavours is not that of an other-worldly visionary, but rather of an artist fully conscious of his materials and methods of production, the ways they determine the images they convey, and the historical and quotidian engagements their use entails. This book is an attempt to complete the circle of influence by returning to Blake's writings and bringing to the study of their language a perspective informed by what we have learned from the study of his graphics and the media-consciousness they have raised.

There is already a well-stocked shelf of books that deal, at least in part, with Blake's techniques as a poet, the many voices in his tradition that shaped his poetry, and the way his style as a writer changed over the years. Although this book will touch on these topics, its main course will run in a different direction. The history of poetry and the study of stylistics will be less important to my

[1] The relationships between Blake's theories of art and the physical properties of graphic media are a central issue in M. Eaves's prize-winning essay, 'Blake and the Artistic Machine', *PMLA* 92 (1977), 903–27; rept. in N. Hilton, ed., *Essential Articles for the Study of Blake* (1986), 175–209. These same relations are a less explicit, but no less important, presence in R. N. Essick, *Blake Printmaker* (1980). The literary influence on the study of Blake's printmaking methods might be anticipated from the vocations of those who have written at any length on the subject: the poet Ruthven Todd and three English teachers—Eaves, J. Viscomi, and myself.

purposes than the history of linguistics and the study of semiotics. Nor will specific sources and influences be as important as general intellectual affinities and the history of ideas. I begin with, and frequently return to, the nature of the linguistic sign as that was understood in Blake's time and as I understand it as a theme in his writings. From that issue springs a host of others as the sign is perceived in relationship to what it signifies and to those engaged in its production and consumption. Such a study runs the risk of a double hermeticism: the special vocabulary of Blakean myth that can all too easily dominate the work of its expositors when attempting ventriloquism, and the technical arcana of modern semiotics and post-structuralist theories. Further difficulties can arise from the nature of language itself as a meta-medium from which it is impossible to escape (as we can from painting or engraving) and thereby deal with as an object distinct from the operations of our discourse about it. My awareness of these hazards has prompted the attempt in what follows to situate Blake within the history of language theory and to generate a hermeneutic on the basis of that history. This strategy in turn leads to a double perspective. Even within single paragraphs, I often move from general statements about 'signs' to more specific comments on 'words' or 'language'. This shifting about between the semiotic and the linguistic is a response less to a modern critical agenda than to the eighteenth-century habit of placing the study of language origins within broader theories of signs—human, animal, and divine. Similarly, I have not separated into distinct categories Blake's concepts of language and his practices as a writer. To do so would be to disguise the reciprocal relationships between theory and practice, conception and execution, as each gives rise to the other within the daily labours of a poet self-consciously aware of the what and the how of his making. These intersections between language performance and language ideology are the interpretive nexus of this book.

A useful point of departure for a study of Blake's linguistic concepts is Robert F. Gleckner's essay, 'Most Holy Forms of Thought: Some Observations on Blake and Language', first published in 1974.[2] Midway through this brief but wide-ranging and spirited work, Gleckner poses three related questions that have prompted my own research:

[2] *ELH* 41 (1974), 555–77; rpt. in Hilton, *Essential Articles*, pp. 91–117.

(1) What was Blake's conception of the language of Eternity, the ur-linguistic condition so to speak?
(2) What are the linguistic implications of the fall from this condition and how does Blake present 'fallen' language other than merely using it himself?
(3) How does he conceive of the redemption of language, the reassumption of the reality and primacy of the Word, the reintegration of Babel into not merely one language but into that language that requires no temple, no building to signify it? (p. 564)

My attempts to answer these questions, and to open to inquiry their implications about theories of language current in Blake's time, have contributed much to the structuring of this book. In the first, preliminary chapter, I use four of Blake's paintings to introduce my titular subject (or, more accurately, leitmotif) and several types of signs, both ideal and fallen. This anatomy of signs is followed by their history, from Plato to Wilhelm von Humboldt, organized around the ideal of a motivated sign as the origin and telos of language. The eighteenth-century linguistic concepts explored in the second chapter provide a context for understanding Blake's use of natural signs, primarily in his earlier poetry, and his later rejection of them and of rationalist sign theory. In this third chapter, I begin to test the limits of Gleckner's heuristic exaggeration that 'everything Blake says about Man, the Universe, society, imagination and the senses—in fact, everything that he says about anything—is translatable into a comment upon language, words, the poet's task, poetry' (p. 563).

Gleckner's second question shifts his emphasis from 'Blake's conception' of language to modes of presentation. The fact that Gleckner had already addressed this issue in a separate essay may be symptomatic of a sense of conflict between idea and form, a theme put forward in some recent studies as a fundamental problematic in Blake's work.[3] By grounding the linguistic features of this debate in Blake's production practices, I have tried in the fourth chapter to reconceive the relationship of language ideal to language

[3] Gleckner, 'Blake's Verbal Technique', in A. H. Rosenfeld, ed., *Blake: Essays for Damon* (1969), 321–32. For some general thoughts on how 'artistic form is both conveyor of and barrier to meaning', see E. Larrissy, *Blake* (1985). Perhaps the first version of the content/form debate was the charge that Blake, as a pictorial artist, could conceive but could not execute, first raised during Blake's lifetime and vigorously rebuffed by him in the *Public Address* of *c.*1810 (see esp. E 582, K 601–2).

performance as symbiosis rather than disjunction. To do so requires some admittedly speculative excursions into Blake's practices linking oral composition and graphic production, the spoken word and the printed book. In these discussions I am more than a little guilty of adopting Blake's own beliefs as a self-justifying way of judging his art, but I have tempered this methodological romanticism by refusing to repress the inescapable materiality of communication that Blake himself stresses through the uncompromising physicality of his publications.[4]

Gleckner's final question assumes that the perfection of language requires its annihilation—or at least the elimination of its physical side, its 'temple' or 'building'. These architectural metaphors recall Blake's reference to 'English' as the 'rough basement' for his building of Jerusalem 'as a City & a Temple' in *Jerusalem*,[5] but the thrust of Gleckner's question saps these material foundations. His construction of a transcendentalizing perspective, one that finds the ideal of language in the utter otherness of silence, is buttressed by his observation that 'any image (or set of images), any words, by their very nature, would compromise its [Eternity's] imaginative (or mental) reality'.[6] But a year before Gleckner published his essay, Hazard Adams had already pointed to a contrary view: 'We can only make a world with a language, indeed *in* a language. There is nothing imaginable independent of a medium to imagine *in*.'[7] My discussion, in the final chapter, of Blake's imagining of a post-apocalyptic language traces its lineage to Adams's comment

[4] For a 'materialist' perspective on Blake's relief etchings, see R. N. Essick, 'Blake, Hamilton, and the Materials of Graphic Meaning', *ELH* 52 (1985), 833–72; and Essick, 'How Blake's Body Means', in N. Hilton and T. A. Vogler, eds., *Unnam'd Forms* (1986), 197–217.

[5] Pls. 36, 84; E 183, 243, K 668, 729.

[6] 'Most Holy Forms of Thought', p. 564. In 'Blake's Moving Words and the Dread of Embodiment', *Cithara*, 15 (1976), 75–85, A. Taylor carries Gleckner's view far beyond his formulations of it by arguing that 'imagination is betrayed by language and form, as it is betrayed by the body' (p. 83). Blake's supposed attempts to escape his media find their most recent expression in L. Damrosch, Jr., *Symbol and Truth in Blake's Myth* (1980); see esp. p. 73 ('. . . behind the words he [Blake] sees a divine vision to which they point, and has little interest in words for their own sake') and p. 362 ('The peculiarities of Blake's language derive, then, from a determination to make us break through language, a refusal to accept it as the structure in which we think and exist.').

[7] 'Blake and the Philosophy of Literary Symbolism', *New Literary History*, 5 (1973), 146. See also E. Benveniste, *Problems in General Linguistics* (1971), p. 56: 'Linguistic form is not only the condition of transmissibility, but first of all the condition for the realization of thought. . . . that is to say that the question of whether thought can do without language or skirt it like an obstacle emerges as meaningless . . .'.

and to Blake's own observation, in his annotations of *c.*1788 to Lavater's *Aphorisms*, that 'it is impossible to think without images of somewhat on earth' (E 600, K 88). Like several recent studies of particular features of Blake's poetry,[8] I replace transcendence with incarnation, sublimation with immanence, and questions about how far even an ideal language can become a transparent medium of something other than itself with questions about how far that other is a reified projection of the medium. The phenomenological view of language I introduce in the fourth chapter finds its correlative in Blake's own shift from the structuralisms of eighteenth-century linguistics to the power of language to create a community of speakers that, in its ideal expansions through the last plates of *Jerusalem*, includes all of being.

—But before approaching these epic complexities, we must begin like a good storyteller at the beginning, with Adam and the animals in Eden.

[8] For example, A. Fogel, 'Pictures of Speech: On Blake's Poetic', *Studies in Romanticism*, 21 (1982), 217–42; N. Hilton, *Literal Imagination* (1983); and many of the essays in Hilton and Vogler, *Unnam'd Forms*.

1. *Adam Naming the Beasts* and its Companions

IN 1799, William Blake began to draw and paint illustrations to the Bible for his new patron Thomas Butts. By the end of his life, Blake had produced more than 135 of these pictorial responses to the most important text in his cultural heritage. Many designs were executed in watercolours, but over fifty were painted in a medium Blake called 'fresco', apparently a mixture of carpenter's glue, whiting, and pigments.[1] Most of these 'tempera' paintings, as they are now generally called, produced before 1805 have darkened badly and are now in a sad state of decay beneath overlays of restoration. Blake seems to have been aware of the limitations of his medium, for in the *Descriptive Catalogue* of his 1809 exhibition he admitted that his 'experiment' pictures had been 'molested continually by blotting and blurring demons' and 'bruized and knocked about, without mercy' (E 546, 548, K 581, 583). By the next year, Blake began to alter his technique, working up his designs with a less viscous mixture, applying it more thinly, and perhaps preparing the ground in a better manner.[2] Thus the temperas of 1810 and subsequent years are in a reasonably good state of preservation and reveal the crisp outlines now absent from the earlier examples. Among these later works is *Adam Naming the Beasts*, now at Pollok House, Glasgow (Plate 1). The limb of the tree, upper right, bears a simple scratched-out inscription, 'Fresco by Willm Blake 1810'.

The frontal bearing of Adam's head, the symmetry of his features, and his hypnotic gaze give to the portrait the hieratic values of a Byzantine icon. Yet, in spite of the other-worldliness of this face, it is a visage which was long familiar to Blake, for it is an idealized

[1] For early descriptions of the process, perhaps based on information supplied by Blake, see J. T. Smith, *Nollekens and his Times* (1828), 2: 480–2; and F. Tatham's manuscript *Life of Blake* (*c.*1833), printed in G. E. Bentley, Jr., *Blake Records* (1969), 515–17. Smith's account is reprinted in *Blake Records*, p. 472.

[2] Butlin, 1: 318, 549, dates Blake's reformation of his tempera technique to the early 1820s, but the paintings of *c.*1810–11 (Butlin nos. 667–70, 673) exhibit some of the physical stability and technical refinements Blake developed further in the final temperas (Butlin nos. 803–9).

version of his own. A monochrome wash portrait of Blake, unsigned but perhaps attributable to John Linnell, reveals the similarities. This portrait (Plate 2) seems to have been influenced by one of Blake's own pencil 'Visionary Heads', *The Man who Taught Blake Painting in His Dreams*, itself an idealized self-portrait. At the very least, these visages share a number of significant features, and thus the wash drawing embodies something of Blake's own self-conception.[3] Blake's face in the portrait is more elongated than Adam's, but the mouths are nearly identical and the broad forehead, almond-shaped eyes drawn out to a short line at their outer edges, perfect arch of the eyebrows, curled bow forming the lower outline of the nostrils, and rounded chin are unmistakably related. Even the hair, with its residual tufts above the centre of the brow in the wash drawing, suggests that we are seeing the same face in youth and in middle age. Blake as bard, as the inventor of so many names in his mythological poems, is adumbrated by the physiognomy of his Adam.

We do not know what title, if any, Blake gave to this painting. *Adam Naming the Beasts* is the invention of William Michael Rossetti, author of the first catalogue of Blake's drawings and paintings.[4] We should not accept Rossetti's title without question, particularly since he suggests, in a note appended to his catalogue entry, that the painting has the same 'subject' as Blake's frontispiece (Plate 3) to the 1802 *Designs to a Series of Ballads, Written by William Hayley*. The engraving illustrates a passage from William Cowper's *The Task*, quoted in part beneath the design, which makes no reference to naming the beasts.[5] As Hayley accurately noted in a letter to John Johnson of 16 May 1802, the frontispiece represents Adam merely 'surrounded [by] animals' and not giving them names.[6] Does the tempera represent the same subject, thereby making Rossetti's title a misnomer?

[3] *The Man who Taught Blake Painting in His Dreams* is now in the Keynes Collection, Fitzwilliam Museum (Butlin no. 753); there are also a counterproof and a replica, the latter perhaps by Linnell, in the Tate Gallery (Butlin nos. 754, 755). For a discussion of this head as a self-portrait, see G. Keynes, *Complete Portraiture of Blake* (1977), 24–5, 131–3. For the attribution of the wash portrait to Linnell and its relationship to the Visionary Head, see M. Butlin, 'A New Portrait of Blake', *Blake Studies*, 7 (1975), 101–3.

[4] 'Annotated Lists of Blake's Paintings, Drawings, and Engravings', in A. Gilchrist, *Life of Blake* (1863), 2: 205, no. 36.

[5] *Poetical Works* (1934), bk. 6, 'The Winter Walk at Noon', pp. 232–3, ll. 601–30. An earlier passage, ll. 352–60, describes how the animals 'pass'd' before Adam to 'confess his sway' over them prior to the fall, but even here Cowper makes no mention of naming.

[6] For the excerpt from Hayley's letter, see Bentley, *Blake Records*, p. 95.

Adam's hands direct us to the answer. In the engraving, his left hand is extended upward with an open palm and fingers slightly spread. The gesture draws our attention outward to the whole composition, as though Adam's hand were the visual embodiment of a courteous command: 'Behold!' In the painting, his right hand is similarly raised but very differently formed, with forefinger and thumb extended and the other fingers curled over the palm. This arrangement fits comfortably into a large and various family of gestures with a particular meaning that remained essentially unchanged over many centuries. Quite simply, a figure with one or two pointing fingers and the others folded over the extended or raised hand is visually saying, 'I am speaking', even when his mouth is closed. This chirological image can be traced back at least to early fifth-century AD illuminated manuscripts, including some that illustrate classical texts and are very probably based on much earlier models.[7] The two-finger variety predominates in these early representations, but the twelfth-century York Psalter contains one-finger versions as well.[8] Blake would have needed no access to such rarities to encounter the gesture, for the examples in paintings, architectural sculpture, and printed book illustrations are legion from the Middle Ages through the eighteenth century. Of more significance is the persistence of the motif in portrayals of Adam naming the beasts. We find both the one- and two-finger gestures in some of the earliest renderings of the scene in illuminated manuscripts from the eleventh through the fourteenth centuries.[9] Graphic examples

[7] For example, the Vatican Virgil (Vatican Library codex lat. 3225), fo. 73[v], showing the Trojans in council; the *Iliad* in the Ambrosian Library, Milan (codex F.205), Illus. 37, showing Patroclus addressing Nestor; and the Roman Virgil (Vatican Library codex lat. 3867), fo. 1[r] and 100[v], showing Meliboeus addressing Tityrus and Dido and Aeneas in conversation. For reproductions, see K. Weitzmann, *Late Antique and Early Christian Book Illumination* (1977), Pls. 4, 10, 11, 13. Roman sculptures of much earlier periods, such as the Augustus of Primaporta (*c.*20 BC; Vatican Museum), show the gesture, but the lack of a textual context makes the precise meaning less than certain.

[8] MS. U.3.2, Hunterian Museum, Glasgow University. See for example the Virgin addressing St John, reproduced in T. S. R. Boase, *York Psalter* (1962), Pl. 4. Blake uses the 2-finger gesture in *Sabrina Disenchanting the Lady* among his illustrations to Milton's *Comus* in the Huntington Library (*c.*1801; Butlin no. 527.7).

[9] Eleventh-century Octateuch, Seraglio Library, Istanbul, MS 8, fo. 42[v] (2 fingers); 11th-century bestiary, BM Add. MS 11283, fo. 11[v] (1 finger); 12th-century bestiary, Bodleian Library, Ashmole MS 1511, Illus. 1 (1 finger, with a scroll inscribed 'HIC DAT NOMINA BESTIIS ADAM'); late 12th-century bestiary, Aberdeen University Library, fo. 5[r] (2 fingers); early 14th-century Psalter and bestiary, Corpus Christi College, Cambridge, MS 53, fo. 195[v] (1 finger). These illuminations have not been published, but photographs are accessible through the Princeton Index of Christian Art.

from later times range from Pieter Van Der Borcht's engraving of 1582 to numerous illustrated folio Bibles of the later eighteenth and early nineteenth centuries (Plate 4).[10] While not a major subject for the more fashionable historical painters in the England of Blake's era, Adam naming continued to appear in large-format (if rather crude) engravings and paintings in which the artists seem to be appealing to their audience's love of animals—the more the merrier—rather than religious concerns (see Plate 5). All these renditions during a span of nine centuries contain the significant hand and finger position. Indeed, I have not found any pictures of Adam *naming* the beasts, as distinct from the related subject of Adam *among* the beasts, without some version of the gesture. Its presence in Blake's painting testifies to the appropriateness of Rossetti's title and its textual basis in verse nineteen of Genesis chapter two: 'And out of the ground the Lord God formed every beast of the field, and every fowl of the air; and brought them unto Adam to see what he would call them: and whatsoever Adam called every living creature, that was the name thereof.'

The lines from Genesis have been cited with great frequency, beginning no later than the first century AD,[11] in discussions of the origin of language and the characteristics of the first language. These passing references and more extended exegeses centre on the link between Adam's language and God's, the Bible's claim that all men spoke the same language (presumably Adam's) until its fragmentation at the Tower of Babel (Genesis 11: 1–9), and the foundation of this universality in a special relationship between the words of Adam's tongue and the things they designate.[12] Adam gives to each beast '*the* name', not just any collection of sounds selected at random which by fiat became associated with the animal. While this last theory was questioned by some speculators in language

[10] For other typical illustrations close in date to Blake's tempera, see the amateurish engraving in *The Christian's Complete Family Bible* (1808), with 1 finger extended; and the title-page vignette in *The Holy Bible* (1811), with 1 finger extended, the others only slightly curled inward.

[11] See the references to Philo Judaeus in ch. 2. I have made no attempt to trace the exegesis of Adam naming the beasts in earlier Hebrew commentaries.

[12] For a useful historical overview of these concepts, see S. E. Fish, *Surprised by Sin* (1971), 107–30, 'Language in Paradise'. In *After Babel* (1975), G. Steiner very briefly characterizes the 'Adamic vernacular' as one which 'enabled all men to understand one another, . . . bodied forth, to a greater or lesser degree, the original Logos', and, because of this 'direct divine etymology, . . . had a congruence with reality such as no tongue has had after Babel . . .' (p. 58). For similar but even briefer comments, see M. Foucault, *Order of Things* (1973), 36.

origins, those who held to it defined the essential structure of Adamic language as a real, material or causal, bond between words and things, whereas all languages after Babel manage as best they can with a merely conventional (and hence weak) link between word and world. To couch the matter in terms provided by modern semiotics, the linguistic Adamists proposed a sign with a 'motivated', rather than 'arbitrary', relationship between 'signifier' and 'signified'.[13] The longevity of this ancient ideal is indicated by Thomas Scott's note on Genesis 2: 19–20 in what was probably the most consulted annotated Bible from the 1790s to the end of the next century: 'Adam seems to have been vastly better acquainted, by intuition or immediate revelation, with the distinct properties of every creature, than the most sagacious observers, since the fall, by study. When, therefore, the power of God brought the several species before him, he gave them names expressive of their distinct natures or exterior forms.'[14]

The textual source for Blake's tempera implicates its iconography in issues of language origin and language structure at the heart of the exegetical tradition extending from that source. *Adam Naming the Beasts* thereby becomes a painting about language. By so emphatically foregrounding Adam, Blake stresses the man-centred event rather than the diversity of nature overwhelming Adam in other illustrations of the scene (Plate 5). Adam's closed lips diminish the importance of physical utterance and thus emphasize the mental processes essential for the act of naming. The prominence of the serpent, gently touched on the head by Adam's left hand, suggests that we are witnessing the naming of that beast. In most portrayals, Adam points toward whichever beast is being named, or at least toward the general assembly. The verticality of Adam's right hand in Blake's version would seem to indicate the Creator of the animals, much as in the old Jewish legend 'that all the creatures, marveling at Adam's greatness, prostrated themselves before him, taking him

[13] I take the quoted terms in this statement from F. de Saussure, *Course in General Linguistics* (1966). Whether one defines the 'signified' as a thing independent of the signifier or (following Saussure) as a concept wholly dependent upon the presence of the signifier, the essential phenomenon of motivation remains intact as an ideal proposition.

[14] *Holy Bible . . . with . . . Marginal References by Thomas Scott* (1811). On the popularity and authority of Scott's commentary, see T. R. Preston, 'Biblical Criticism, Literature, and the Eighteenth-Century Reader', in I. Rivers, ed., *Books and their Readers in Eighteenth-Century England* (1982), 97–126.

to be their creator; whereon he pointed upward to God, exclaiming: "The Lord reigneth, He is clothed with majesty!" '[15] This may be the meaning of Adam's raised left hand and the light streaming from above in Plate 5. But Adam may also be signalling the divine source of his onomastic skills both in the print and in Blake's painting. The gesture itself reinforces a bond between God's power and Adam's, for versions of this hand appear with remarkable consistency in pictures of God creating the world and its inhabitants—most famously in Michelangelo's Sistine fresco of God creating Adam.[16] This shared gesture points toward—indeed, participates in—the commonality between God's Word, which brings the universe into being, and Adam's words, which give that universe its names and thereby make the world available to human consciousness. God moves from Mind to things through the Logos; Adam returns things to mind through names.[17] In both movements of the cycle, language is the medium of existence. On Plate 28 of his *Milton*, Blake expands upon an allusion to Theseus's description of the poet in *A Midsummer Night's Dream* to dramatize this symbiosis between naming and being:

> Some Sons of Los surround the Passions with porches of iron & silver
> Creating form & beauty around the dark regions of sorrow,
> Giving to airy nothing a name and a habitation
> Delightful! with bounds to the Infinite putting off the Indefinite
> Into most holy forms of Thought: (such is the power of inspiration)
> They labour incessant; with many tears & afflictions:
> Creating the beautiful House for the piteous sufferer.
>
> (E 125, K 514–15)

The architectural metaphor in this passage builds, for the modern reader, an associative link with Martin Heidegger's contention that

[15] I. Singer, ed., *Jewish Encyclopedia* (1910), 1: 176, citing the Pirke Rabbi Eliezer, a midrashic commentary on Genesis composed shortly after AD 833.

[16] The presence of the gesture in scenes of God creating, where it is as pervasive as in scenes of Adam naming, is indicated by the hundred or more examples taken from illustrated Bibles, 15th to the early 19th century, and used to extra-illustrate vol. 1 of the Kitto Bible in the Huntington Library. The 2-finger version is commonest in the earlier examples, but with God's hand raised (as in Blake's *Adam Naming*) rather than pointing horizontally (as is Adam's hand in most portrayals of his naming the beasts).

[17] The linguistic nature of the first half of this movement finds its most extreme pictorial representation in the engraved Genesis illustrations by Marten de Vos (1531–1603). Throughout, God never appears in human form but simply as His words surrounded by rays of light.

'language is the house of Being' since 'the word alone gives being to the thing'. And much as Blake gives special powers to the Sons of Los, Heidegger grants to the poet 'entrance into the relation of word and thing. This relation is not, however, a connection between the thing that is on one side and the word that is on the other. The word itself is the relation which in each instance retains the thing within itself in such a manner that it "is" a thing.'[18] But we need not leap to our own century to find expressions of the constitutive power of language. Blake's contemporary, the great philologist Wilhelm von Humboldt, wrote in much the same vein: 'Just as no concept is possible without language, so no object is possible without it for the psyche, since even external ones receive their intrinsic substance only through language. . . . Man surrounds himself by a world of sounds in order to take into himself the world of objects and operate on them.'[19] Humboldt's and Heidegger's sense of the quasi-divine potency of the language of man finds further resonances with a slightly later passage in *Milton*:

> As the breath of the Almighty. such are the words of man to man
> In the great Wars of Eternity, in fury of Poetic Inspiration,
> To build the Universe stupendous: Mental forms Creating
>
> (Pl. 30; E 129, K 519)

When viewed from a perspective offered by these contexts, Blake's painting reveals an Adam-*cum*-Godlike poet bestowing on the beasts the names, the mental forms, from which they originated in the Mind of God and through which they take on their being for man. Blake, a son of Adam who inherited his visage, indicates through that physical similarity the continuity between Adam's language and the words of the inspired poet-prophet Blake claimed to be.

I have been able to pursue this high-minded, perhaps even high-handed, commentary on *Adam Naming the Beasts* by ignoring a few salient features. The background trees are bare, as though the fall had already occurred and autumn had come to Eden. The acorn-bearing oak framing the upper right margin and top of the design

[18] *On the Way to Language* (1971), 62, 66. The absorption of such concepts into the canonical texts of modern Blake criticism is indicated by N. Frye's statement, in *Fearful Symmetry* (1947), 114, that 'an object that has received a name is more real by virtue of it than an object without one. A thing's name is its numen, its imaginative reality in the eternal world of the human mind.'

[19] Humboldt's general 'Introduction' to his study of the Kawi language, 1830–5, *Humanist without Portfolio* (1963), 293–4.

may seem perfectly innocent at first glance, like the one 'the old folk' sit under in 'The Ecchoing Green' (E 8, K 116) and the oaks 'laughter sat beneath . . . & innocence sported round' in Night the Sixth of *The Four Zoas* (E 350, K 317). But the ivy, evinced by two pointed leaves, clinging to the trunk warns of something more restrictive than protective, for stylized versions of such leaves appear in *Songs of Experience* as the counter-topos to the lovingly entwined vines and trees of *Songs of Innocence.*[20] In poems Blake wrote in the same period he painted *Adam Naming*, the oak becomes a very sinister emblem. *Jerusalem* leads us into 'the Oak Groves of Albion' where 'Human Sacrifices' take place in 'Druid Temples of the Accuser of Sin' (Pl. 98; E 258, K 746). The connection between oaks and Albion's early inhabitants reminds us that Blake claimed in his *Descriptive Catalogue*, published the year before the date inscribed on the tempera, that 'Adam was a Druid' (E 542, K 578). Is the naming we witness in the painting in some sense a fall, a sacrifice of living creatures to 'Druidical Mathematical Proportion of Length Bredth Highth' (*Milton*, Pl. 4; E 98, K 484)?

The most disturbing motif is of course the serpent. He is a very Miltonic beast, with a 'Crested' head, 'Carbuncle' eye, and 'Burnisht Neck of verdant Gold.'[21] While Genesis is the primary text for *Adam Naming the Beasts*, *Paradise Lost* would seem to be an important secondary influence. The event in question unfolds in Book Eight:

> Not only these fair bounds, but all the Earth
> To thee and to thy Race I give; as Lords
> Possess it, and all things that therein live,
> Or live in Sea, or Air, Beast, Fish, and Fowl.
> In sign whereof each Bird and Beast behold
> After thir kinds; I bring them to receive
> From thee thir Names, and pay thee fealty
> With low subjection; understand the same
> Of Fish within thir wat'ry residence,
> Not hither summon'd, since they cannot change

[20] Compare the tree trunk with ivy in the frontispiece to *Songs of Experience* with the sheltering canopies of entwined trees and vines in the frontispiece to *Songs of Innocence* and 'The Lamb'. The long tradition of these contrary images of fruitful union and destructive embrace is explored, without reference to Blake, in P. Demetz, 'The Elm and the Vine', *PMLA* 73 (1958), 521–32.

[21] For Milton's description, see *Paradise Lost*, 9. 494–510. Quoted here from Milton, *Complete Poems* (1957), 390. Subsequent quotations of Milton's work are from this edition.

Thir Element to draw the thinner Air.
As thus he [God] spake, each Bird and Beast behold
Approaching two and two, These cow'ring low
With blandishment, each Bird stoop'd on his wing.
I [Adam] nam'd them, as they pass'd, and understood
Thir Nature, with such knowledge God endu'd
My sudden apprehension: . . . (lines 338–54)

Milton makes no specific reference here to the snake, but the sinuous meekness of Blake's serpent would seem to express the same 'fealty' and 'subjection' demonstrated by the creatures in Milton's poem. Yet even if we think of the snake as still benign and unalloyed with Satan, it is impossible to avoid prolepsis. The association between the serpent and the fall of man is so powerful that his prominence in *Adam Naming the Beasts* casts over it the shadow of that impending event. Much the same serpent appears in Blake's two series of watercolour illustrations to *Paradise Lost* he executed only two or three years before the tempera.[22] In one version of *Satan Watching the Endearments of Adam and Eve* (Butlin no. 529.5), Satan caresses with his left hand the head of his serpentine self, entwined about his still human body, in a way very similar to the location and configuration of Adam's left hand. This intimacy between the serpent and Adam can only increase our suspicions about the latter's activities.

Language plays a key role in the temptation and fall. The snake is the only talking beast in *Paradise Lost*, and it is through the arts of language that he seduces Eve in Milton's account and in Genesis.[23] Blake begins *The Book of Urizen* (1794) with a material creation that is simultaneously a fall. He repeats and extends this collapse of two events into one in *The Four Zoas*, *Milton*, and *Jerusalem*, and thus the notion that the birth of human language is also its fall is well within the conceptual parameters of Blake's art in 1810. Adam's left arm is already within the serpent's coils; the ivy is already wrapped about the oak. Beginning in *The Four Zoas*, Blake frequently describes Adam as the 'Limit of Contraction' (E 338, K 304), and in the *Laocoön* inscriptions he is called 'only

[22] See 7 of Blake's 12 *Paradise Lost* designs of 1807 (Huntington Library) and 6 of the dozen designs in the 1808 series (Boston Museum of Fine Arts); Butlin nos. 529 and 536.

[23] In Paradise Lost *and the Genesis Tradition* (1968), 275, J. M. Evans points out that 'the serpent's seeming command of the "Language of Man" is the key to the whole temptation . . .'.

The Natural Man & not the Soul or Imagination' (E 273, K 776). Is Adam's language, even at this moment of origin in Eden, a further contraction of the Word into words, of infinite spirit into finite nature?[24] The serpent's ability to lie to Eve has its structural foundation in the power of language to call to mind that which is not present. Adam provides the groundwork for that (mis)use of words by translating the stately progression of the animals into a sequence of words, which here, on this page at this moment, records their literal absence from letters: a ram, three oxen, a sheep with at least one goat behind, a leaping stag, a wolf or wolfhound behind a horse, a lion, a rabbit. This line of words may parallel in its ordering the animal's line of march; but it is independent of them, may be reproduced endlessly even in the void left by their absence, and has its own laws of grammar and indefinite articles. Josephus claims that Adam gave names to the animals 'according to their respective species', thereby suggesting that the primal act of naming was also a generalization into taxonomic categories.[25] This descent from Logos to logic will lead, through further abstracting processes, to a parade of terms moving only through the landscape of language: genera, families, orders, classes, phyla. If this is the nature of the language brought into the world by Adam, then his Eden has already fallen under the dominion of Urizen, Blake's creator of bondage, abstraction, generalization, law, the indefinite, the void. With this language Adam names what he looks out upon so intently—our world after the fall. He is the first to commit what T. S. Eliot has called 'the natural sin of language'.[26]

The serpent, the oak, and the ivy have led us to a concept of language far from the dream of a motivated sign and far from the companionship of Humboldt and Heidegger. Painting, drawing, and engraving are also implicated in this fall into the signifying order, for like language they are used to produce signs radically different

[24] In what may be a preliminary sketch for the tempera, a few horizontal lines suggest a serpent wound round Adam's torso (McGill University; Butlin no. 686^{v}), thus underscoring the themes of restriction and fall. An even slighter associated drawing, showing only a figure with left hand raised, is in the National Gallery of Art, Washington (Butlin no. 539^{v}).

[25] *Works of Josephus*, (*c.*1785), p. [7]. Blake engraved 3 plates appearing in this edition.

[26] 'The Post-Georgians', *Athenaeum*, no. 4641 (11 April 1919), 171. For brief comments on *Adam Naming* as pessimistic as the ones I offer here, see Damrosch, *Symbol and Truth in Blake's Myth*, p. 90. Damrosch sums up his view in a footnote: 'to name the beasts at all is to testify to the fact of the Fall. The fawn in *Alice* [actually in Lewis Carroll's *Through the Looking-Glass*] flees from her in terror when they emerge from the wood where things have no names.'

in their matter and form from the things to which they refer. We have now carried Blake's painting into the company of Nietzsche, Sartre, and Derrida, the philosophers of absence and difference, of language as their trace, of 'the origin of the sign' as 'the breaking of immediacy'.[27]

A distinguished Blake scholar has warned us that interpretations of Blake's designs 'according to which mutually exclusive meanings are seen as equally valid are not likely to be helpful'.[28] Yet I can see no easy way of eliminating one of the two opposing interpretations of *Adam Naming the Beasts*, nor do I feel any great compulsion to do so. Artists may present images without imbedded interpretations of a unitary and single-minded sort. Since we are dealing with an artist profoundly interested in 'the Two Contrary States of the Human Soul' (title page to *Songs of Innocence and of Experience*, E 7, K 210), it is not too surprising that he would produce a picture containing motifs calling to mind two contrary views of language, one associating it with the creation of life, the other with the fall into death. And these perspectives may not be mutually exclusive but intertwined aspects of the same phenomenon, much as Derrida claims that it is 'simultaneously true that things come into existence and lose existence by being named'.[29]

Some of the acts of naming in Blake's poetry prompt yet a third perspective on Adam and the serpent. At the end of *The Book of Urizen*, the 'children of Urizen' begin their exodus from 'the pendulous earth' by giving it a name: 'They called it Egypt, & left it' (Pl. 28; E 83, K 237). When in *The Four Zoas* 'The Saviour' gives the name of 'Satan' to 'the Limit of Opacity', and 'Adam' to 'the Limit of Contraction', he begins to exercise a measure of control over 'Eternal Death' necessary for salvation (E 337–8, K 304). In both cases, naming in itself gives an identity 'to Falshood that it may

[27] J. Derrida, *Of Grammatology* (1976), 234. For associations among this comment, Nietzsche, Sartre's sense of naming as a loss of innocence, and naming in Blake's *Milton*, see T. A. Vogler, 'Re: Naming in *MIL/TON*', in Hilton and Vogler, *Unnam'd Forms*, pp. 143–5.

[28] M. D. Paley, *Continuing City* (1983), 118.

[29] 'Edmond Jabès and the Question of the Book', *Writing and Difference* (1978), 70. See also *Order of Things*, p. 104, where Foucault points out that the 'arbitrariness' of language and 'its profound relation with that which it names . . . are absolutely indispensable to one another, since the first gives an account of the substitution of the sign for the thing designated and the second justifies the permanent power of designation possessed by that sign'.

be cast off for ever' (*Jerusalem*, Pl. 12; E 155, K 631). These examples suggest that the serpent's presence in the tempera does not necessarily throw an evil pall over Adam's linguistic activities. By naming the serpent, by identifying it as such, Adam initiates a structure that promotes life by defining its enemies.

Although *Adam Naming the Beasts* may seem sufficiently capacious in its linguistic suggestiveness, we can find an even more inclusive sense of language origins and language history by grouping this single painting with three others. *Eve Naming the Birds* (Plate 6), *The Virgin and Child in Egypt* (Plate 7), and *Christ Blessing* (Plate 8) share several physical features with *Adam Naming*. All are in the same tempera medium painted on linen or fine canvas, all are frontal head and torso portraits of figures who fill a considerable proportion of the pictorial space, all have a vertical major axis, and all are very close in size.[30] Each design contains vegetation—a large tree or trees in all but *Eve Naming the Birds*—framing the dominant human form. *The Virgin and Child in Egypt* bears a scratched-out signature and a date on the trunk of the palm identical to those on the oak in *Adam Naming*. Similarities in style and format indicate that the two uninscribed works were also produced in about 1810. Parallels and contrastive pairings in motif and format interlink all four paintings within the straightforward chronological sequence. In the first two designs, male and female are separately pictured, but in the third picture the sexes are combined in a portrayal of the new Eve (a traditional epithet for the Virgin) and Jesus Christ, the new Adam (as He is suggested to be in Romans 5: 19). The women's hand and arm positions reflect each other in the two central designs, while the arm positions of Adam and Christ are similar enough in the first and last paintings to evoke comparison. All four works were originally sold by Blake to Thomas Butts and were probably intended to be companion pieces. Taken together, they form a polyptych on the theme of language. As far as I can determine, the history of art offers no precedents for a series of paintings or prints so directly focused on this subject.

As with *Adam Naming*, it is Rossetti who gave the title of *Eve Naming the Birds* to the second painting in the series.[31] In the Bible,

[30] See Butlin, nos. 667–70, and his comment (1: 483) that the 4 paintings 'form an interrelated group'.

[31] In Gilchrist, *Life of Blake*, 2: 205, no. 37.

Adam names 'every fowl of the air', and thus many illustrations of Genesis 2: 19 contain a large number of birds (Plates 4–5). Further, Eve is not created until Genesis 2: 22—at least in the 'Jahwehist' layer in the text, of which the naming episode forms a part. Given these clear statements in the Bible, my inability to find any other design or text on the subject of Eve naming birds may not be due to inadequate scholarship. Although other examples may be hiding somewhere in the history of the arts, I think we have sufficient cause to suspect Rossetti's title.

Neither of Eve's hands resembles Adam's gesture signalling speech. Her left hand is poised almost identically to Adam's 'behold' gesture in the *Ballads* frontispiece (Plate 3). Her right hand is in much the same position turned to show its back. Together, Eve's gestures express pleasant surprise, admiration, and attention.[32] The open beaks of all three birds indicate what she is attending to. The slight tilt of her head to her right also suggests that Eve is listening to the birds, not naming them. While *Adam Naming the Beasts* points to the divine origins of language, Eve and the birds lead us to a natural source. In his more than a little scornful summary of theories of language origin, the nineteenth-century philologist Max Müller grouped many of them into two types: the 'bow-wow' school of thought, which held that man learned to speak by imitating, and gradually improving upon, the sounds of animals; and the 'pooh-pooh' advocates, who held that speech evolved from man's own emotive cries.[33] Eve would seem to be dramatizing the first of these theories. Although versions of it can be traced back as far as Democritus,[34] the idea had particular currency during the eighteenth century as part of the general substitution of naturalistic for divine theories of origin. References to birds are a common feature of these

[32] T. Page, *Art of Painting* (1720), 40: '. . . in admiration we hold the hand up bent somewhat backward with all the fingers closed'. Compare Eve's gesture to the more dramatic versions, with arms raised above the head, exemplified by the 2 women in Blake's *Raising of Lazarus* (*c.*1805; Butlin no. 487) and by the Virgin in *Christ Returns to His Mother* among Blake's *Paradise Regained* illustrations (*c.*1816–20; Butlin no. 544.12). For a discussion of the gesture in these 2 watercolours as a traditional expression of 'Admiration and Astonishment', see J. A. Warner, *Blake and the Language of Art* (1984), 66–7.

[33] *Lectures on the Science of Language* (1861), 1: 344–55.

[34] Plutarch, *Moralia* (1957), 12: 407, 'Whether Land or Sea Animals are Cleverer', sec. 20: 'Yet perhaps it is ridiculous for us to make a parade of animals distinguished for learning when Democritus declares that we have been their pupils in matters of fundamental importance: of the spider in weaving and mending, . . . of the sweet-voiced swan and nightingale in our imitation of their song . . .'.

eighteenth-century presentations, such as Lord Monboddo's contention that the first men 'were led to the discovery' of speech 'by the imitation of the articulate animals, . . . particularly birds, which utter sounds that may be called truly articulate . . .'.[35]

Birds and their songs play generally happy roles in Blake's poetry and designs. They soar through eleven illuminations in *Songs of Innocence* and sing in four of its poems ('The Little Girl Lost', 'The Ecchoing Green', 'The School Boy', 'Laughing Song'). The nightingale begins 'the Song of Spring' and the lark 'leads the Choir of Day' on Plate 31 of *Milton* (E 130, K 520). The 'trill, trill, trill, trill' of this lark, whose 'every feather | . . . vibrates with the effluence Divine', plays a crucial role in the poem as a source of its inspiration. Blake's spiritualized birds were probably influenced by Milton's lark in 'L'Allegro', pictured by Blake as a winged human in his illustrations to the poem (*c.*1816–20; Butlin no. 543.2) and described as 'an Angel on the Wing' in his notes on the design (E 682, K 618). In Night the Seventh of *The Four Zoas*, Vala hears 'sweet voices in the winds & in the voices of birds' (E 367, K 340), much like Eve in the tempera. But Vala is a nature goddess who, like Eve, is intimately associated with the fall: only a few lines earlier, Tharmas accuses her of 'Sins' which 'have lost us heaven & bliss' (E 366, K 339). Nature, as source or guiding principle, is consistently denounced by Blake. As he writes in *Milton*:

> . . . every Natural Effect has a Spiritual Cause, and Not
> A Natural: for a Natural Cause only seems, it is a Delusion
> Of Ulro: & a ratio of the perishing Vegetable Memory.
>
> (Pl. 26; E 124, K 513)

Eve's identification with the 'Vegetable' world is underscored in the tempera by the entanglement of the fingers of her right hand in her hair, the luxuriant curls of which complement the frilly leaves and twisting vines in the top corners of the painting. Milton's description of how Eve's 'wanton ringlets wav'd | As the Vine curls her tendrils' (*Paradise Lost*, 4. 306–7) may have prompted Blake to picture a visual equivalent of this simile. The outline of Eve's left arm and hand repeats the sinuous curve of the vine immediately to the right. A language based on a similar imitation of such a world could

[35] Lord Monboddo, *Of the Origin and Progress of Language* (1774), 1: 492.

never reach beyond the seemingly pleasant but 'hard restricting condensations' of 'Vegetable Nature' (*Jerusalem*, Pl. 73; E228, K 713). It would be a medium only for the 'natural or organic thoughts' of natural religion, the instrument of those 'Who pretend to Poetry that they may destroy Imagination; | By imitation of Natures Images drawn from Remembrance'.[36]

Like *Adam Naming the Beasts*, the tempera of Eve and the birds intimates contrary views of the language produced in the scene of origin represented. But Eve also suggests, through her hand gestures, an example of Müller's 'pooh-pooh' cluster of theories, as important as the 'bow-wow' group in eighteenth-century semiotic speculations. Monboddo argues that 'gestures' and 'inarticulate cries . . . are common to us with the brutes'. Both are '*natural* signs' because they can be 'understood by every animal, without any previous compact or agreement'.[37] In his comments on gestures, Lord Kames similarly treats 'these external appearances or signs' as a 'universal language' expressing 'to all beholders emotions and passions as they arise in the heart'. Kames also makes a distinction between 'natural' gestures like Eve's, an immediate product of feelings, and 'arbitrary' gestures developed through social custom, a category which would presumably include Adam's 'I am speaking' hand sign.[38] Even if taken to be simply a pointing gesture directing us heavenward, Adam's gesture remains essentially referential rather than directly expressive of his emotions. Erasmus Darwin explains the link between 'Internal passions' and natural 'external signs' as a product of 'Association's mystic power'. He further proposes that 'From these dumb gestures first the exchange began | Of viewless thought in bird, and beast, and man.' 'On this slender basis', Darwin states, 'is built all human language'.[39] These representative views claim for natural gesture

[36] *There is No Natural Religion*, ser. a (E 2, K 97); *Milton*, Pl. 41 (E 142, K 533).

[37] *Of the Origin and Progress of Language*, 1: 461–2. The idea that language developed from emotive cries can be traced back at least to Epicurus; see his 'Letter to Herodotus' in Diogenes Laertius, *Lives of Eminent Philosophers* (1950), 2: 605–7.

[38] Lord Kames, *Elements of Criticism* (1785), 1: 426, 428, 434. Kames is quoted at length and with approval in one of the standard books on the use of gesture in oratory: G. Austin, *Chironomia* (1806). Austin, p. 475, cites J. B. Dubos, *Réflexions critiques* (1719) for a similar distinction between 'natural' and 'instituted' visual signs.

[39] Darwin, *Temple of Nature* (1803), 112 n., 113 (canto 2, ll. 355–8). Darwin's reliance on a mechanistic theory of association was indebted to D. Hartley's *Observations on Man* (1749). Blake was probably familiar with Darwin's works of versified science, for he was a member of the circle of artists and writers working with Darwin's publisher, Joseph Johnson, and engraved plates for Darwin's *Botanic Garden*, first in 1791 and again in 1799.

nothing less than the attributes of a secularized language of Adam: primacy, universality, and motivation.

The two varieties of 'natural' signs Blake portrays through his painting of Eve form the mimetic and expressive poles of eighteenth-century theories of language origin. The birds pour forth their feelings into song; man learns significant utterance by imitating their habits. But primal man need not copy the beasts to share in their power of signification. He too can give direct expression to emotion through cries or, like Eve, through gesture. In the first case, motivation is located primarily in animals and in man only through imitation. In the second proposition, motivation resides in the causal relationship between man's own inner being and its expression through the body, as in physiognomy, or through sounds. In both the mimetic and expressive theories, man is defined as an entirely natural creature whose semiotic propensities require neither the intervention of God from above nor a divine soul within.

As we have seen, Blake was profoundly suspicious of any theory of man and his endeavours based on copying nature, but his attitude toward the external expression of internal substance was far more positive, as is indicated by his annotation to Lavater's *Aphorisms* that 'substance gives tincture to the accident & makes it physiognomic' (E 596, K 81). Like most artists of his generation, Blake represented emotions in his designs along lines set forth in standard handbooks of facial expressions and bodily gestures.[40] His art continually involved Blake in Eve's visible language, and he entreated viewers of his *Last Judgment* painting to 'attend to the Hands & Feet to the Lineaments of the Countenances they are all descriptive of Character' (E 560, K 611). A poet who held that 'No man can think write or speak from his heart, but he must intend truth', that 'the voice of honest indignation is the voice of God', and that 'Passion & Expression is Beauty Itself' shares common ground even with a secular version of expressive theory.[41] In *A Vision of the Last Judgment*, composed in the same year as the tempera series, Blake situates his own concept of the emotions within what was for him a larger realm of spirit:

[40] For example, C. Le Brun, *Method to Learn to Design the Passions* (1734); and G. Smith, *School of Art* (1765), based on Le Brun's works. Blake's use of such guides is amply documented in Warner, *Blake and the Language of Art*; see also n. 32 above.

[41] *All Religions are One* (E 1, K 98); *Marriage of Heaven and Hell*, Pl. 12 (E 38, K 153); annotations to Reynolds's *Discourses* (E 653, K 466).

'Men are admitted into Heaven not because they have curbed & governd their Passions or have No Passions but because they have Cultivated their Understandings. The Treasures of Heaven are not Negations of Passion but Realities of Intellect from which All the Passions Emanate Uncurbed in their Eternal Glory' (E 564, K 615). This statement would seem to be the best guide to a positive interpretation of Eve's gesture and the birds' song, for it locates the ultimate origin of both in the same heavenly intellect pointed to by Adam in the companion painting.

Blake's *Virgin and Child in Egypt* (Plate 7) is in many respects a conventional Madonna and Child with obvious indebtedness to its many Renaissance and Baroque forebears. Mary's haloed head, turned slightly to her left, and downcast eyes are traditional expressions of reverence and veneration, while her hands are just enough different from Eve's to eliminate surprise and emphasize admiration, according to standard guides.[42] The Child's fingers are arranged like His Mother's but His hands extend outward like the Son's more dramatic gesture in *Christ Offers to Redeem Man*, included in both series of Blake's *Paradise Lost* illustrations (Butlin nos. 529.3 and 536.3). In these watercolours, the posture clearly foreshadows the Crucifixion, and perhaps that sacrifice is gently intimated in the tempera as well. The palm tree along the left margin bears both large dates and traditional emblematic associations with strength, the Virgin's Immaculate Conception and fruitfulness, Christ's entry into Jerusalem (John 12: 12–13), and His final victory over death.

The cluster of walls, towers, and a dome in the left background are representative of the 'Eastern' architecture displayed in several of Blake's designs.[43] The sphinx (a union of animal and man that parodies Christ's union of God and man), obelisk, and two great pyramids of Giza on the right provide the titular setting for the repose of the Holy Family in Egypt, a subject of two other, compositionally unrelated, designs (Butlin nos. 405, 472). Blake

[42] See Anon., *School of Raphael* (c.1800), p. 39 and Pl. 40.1 ('Reverence'); Le Brun, *Method to Learn to Design the Passions*, p. 27 and Fig. 6 ('Veneration . . . which requires our Faith'); J. Bulwer, *Chirologia* (1644), Pl. following p. 150, Fig. D ('Admiror'). Dirk Bouts (1400–75) gives to the Virgin a very similar combination of facial expression and hand gesture in his painting of *The Annunciation*, now in the Getty Museum, Malibu, Calif.

[43] See M. D. Paley, 'The Fourth Face of Man: Blake and Architecture', in R. Wendorf, ed., *Articulate Images* (1983), 184–215, esp. the reference to *The Virgin and Child in Egypt*, p. 189.

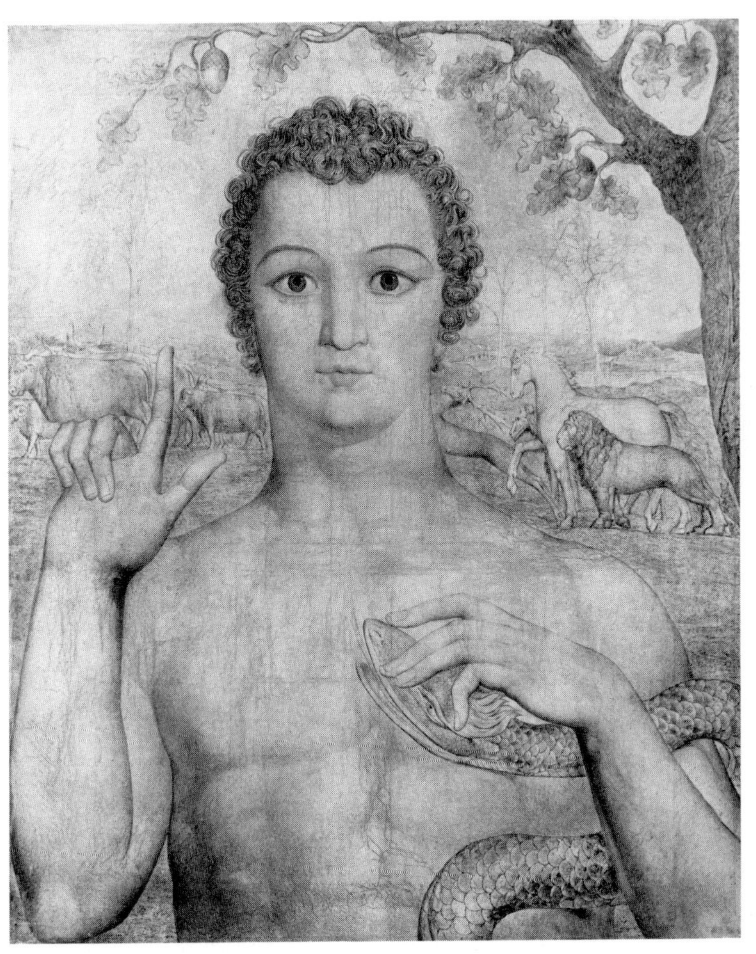

1. Blake, *Adam Naming the Beasts*.

2. Portrait of William Blake.

Their strength, or speed, or vigilance, were givn
In aid of our defects. In some are found
Such teachable and apprehensive parts.
That man's attainments in his own concerns
Matchd with th'expertness of the brutes in theirs
Are oft times vanquishd and thrown far behind.
Cowpers Task
Book VI.

3. Blake, *Designs to a Series of Ballads*, frontispiece.

Adam in Paradice. Genesis Chap.II. ver. 19.
Read also Milton's Paradice lost, who sing, the Sixths Day Creation in Book 7. line 449 to 549.
I
And out of the Ground the Lord God formed every Beast of ye Field, and every Fowl of ye Air; & brought them unto Adam to see what he would call them; and whatsoever Adam called every living Creature, that was ye Name thereof.
Figures Design'd by Gravelot Landskip by Chatelain.
Publishd April 19. 1748. According to Act of Parliament.
G. Scotin Sculp

4 Scotin after Gravelot and Chatelaine, *Adam in Paradice*

5. *Adam Naming the Creation*, published by T. Kelly.

6. Blake, *Eve Naming* [or *Listening to*] *the Birds*.

7. Blake, *The Virgin and Child in Egypt.*

8. Blake, *Christ Blessing*.

considered Egypt as a particularly hellish portion of the fallen world of mathematical abstraction, materialism, slavery, and death.[44] But of more significance to the role of this painting within the linguistic theme of the whole series are Blake's hints about the kind of language he associated with Egyptian culture. In the aphoristic *Laocoön* inscriptions, he proclaims boldly that 'Israel deliverd from Egypt is Art deliverd from Nature & Imitation' (E 274, K 776). This deliverance must also lead away from a language based on the imitation of nature, the foundation of one of the two main theories of language origin evoked by the painting of Eve. Blake's image in *Jerusalem* of Egypt as a 'perverted' Eden in the brain of the Covering Cherub includes the perversion of Adam's universal language into the 'many tongued | And many mouthd' (Pl. 89; E 248, K 734). This connection between Egypt and the multiplication of tongues at the Tower of Babel is reinforced by Blake's comments, in a letter to Butts of 6 July 1803, on a painting of 'the Riposo' representing 'the Holy Family in Egypt' (perhaps Butlin no. 405, now lost). This work contained 'in the background a building which may be supposed the ruin of a Part of Nimrods tower which I conjecture to have spread over many Countries . . .'.[45] This odd spreading of fragments of the tower about the world offered Blake a picturable metaphor for the wide dispersal of Babel's many tongues.

The linguistic form traditionally identified with Egypt is of course the hieroglyph, and much of the eighteenth-century literature on that form of writing would have bolstered Blake's sense of Egypt as a fallen state of consciousness. It was generally believed that hieroglyphs began as natural signs, like those we found in Eve among the birds, but these were usurped by priests and converted into a mysterious code. Thus Egypt, like Babel, was the place of a fall from a motivated into an arbitrary mode of signification. Blake probably read in Jacob Bryant's *New System . . . of Ancient Mythology* about the consequent division of sign and meaning as the Egyptians and other ancient peoples 'adhered to the letter, without considering the

[44] For a survey of Egypt as a symbol in Blake's art and poetry, see A. S. Roe, 'The Thunder of Egypt', in Rosenfeld, *Blake*, pp. 158–95.

[45] E 729, K 823–4. That the Tower of Babel was erected at the Tyrant Nimrod's behest is not altogether clear in the Bible, but Josephus states as much (*Antiquities of the Jews*, bk. 2, ch. 4) and the association had become proverbial by Dante's time (see *Inferno*, 31. 76–8).

meaning: and acquiesced in the hieroglyphic, though they were strangers to the purport'.[46]

The contrast between the signifying systems evoked by the Egyptian setting and the Christ Child could not be greater. While the linguistic themes of the first two paintings in the group evolve out of the dispositions and implied actions of the figures, the semiotic nature of Christ inheres in His very being. As the Word made flesh (John 1: 14), Christ returns us to the language of Adam—and goes beyond it. There is no need for external reference, for Adam's pointing finger to indicate invisible speech or an absent God. The idea of the Son's incarnation in Jesus finds its semiotic equivalent in the incarnational sign—that is, a sign which is one with its referent. The motivated relationship defining Adamic words and Eve's expressive gesture is in Christ collapsed into the union of body and spirit and the immanence of the transcendental signified within the material signifier. Blake traces the evolution of this sign on plate 42 of *Jerusalem*:

> . . . the Saviour in mercy takes
> Contractions Limit, and of the Limit he forms Woman: That
> Himself may in process of time be born Man to redeem
> But there is no Limit of Expansion! there is no Limit of Translucence.
>
> (E 189, K 670)

Out of the language of Adam, a contraction of the Logos even before the fall, the Son creates a further contraction into the natural signs of Eve so that in time they will give miraculous birth to a sign that expands to contain its referent and thereby becomes translucent, the exemplar of unmediated semiosis. Christ is for the true believer what Derrida has called, in a context more secular than Blake's, 'an impossible sign, which belongs neither to nature nor to convention . . . , a sign giving the signified, indeed the thing, *in person*'.[47]

[46] Bryant, *New System* (1774–6), 2: 533. Most of the plates for Bryant's 3 volumes were engraved in James Basire's shop during Blake's apprenticeship to that master, and Blake refers directly to Bryant's book in the *Descriptive Catalogue* of 1809 (E 534, K 578). For studies of Bryant's influence on Blake, see R. Todd, 'Blake and the Eighteenth-Century Mythologists', in *Tracks in the Snow* (1946), 29–60; K. Raine, *Blake and Tradition* (1968), *passim*; Roe (see n. 44 above). For 18th-century theories about hieroglyphs, see the discussion of Warburton, ch. 2.

[47] *Of Grammatology*, p. 234. Such a sign is an impossibility for Derrida because it would erase *differance*, his term for the difference between signifier and signified intrinsic to all signs by definition. By way of contrast, see Heidegger's sense of a sign which 'retains the thing

In the final painting, *Christ Blessing* (Plate 8), a single pyramid with a broken top remains as a reminder of the fallen world. A contrastive mode of architecture and its attendant state of consciousness, the 'Living Form' of Gothic Art,[48] are introduced through the embroidery decorating the neckline and sleeves of the garment worn by Christ, the living Word. He is framed by large laurel or olive trees, emblems of victory, plenitude, and peace.[49] To the incarnational sign of Christ's very presence Blake has added gestures inviting comparison with Adam's. Christ's left hand rests not on the serpent but over His heart to indicate the indwelling spirit and His heartfelt concern for the audience He gazes out upon. But it is the raised right hand of Christ that provides the painting with its titular subject and most important addition to the variety of signs presented in the tempera series.

The gesture of Adam's right hand is indicative, referential, and—as an 'I am speaking' emblem—arbitrary and conventional. Christ's hand, with palm turned outward, is equally conventional in its reference to the idea of blessing, and even recalls naturally expressive signs by being nearly a mirror-image of Eve's left hand. But, for the Christian, to receive from Christ a blessing in word or gesture is to be blessed in fact. John Bulwer, writing in 1644, hints at the special redemptive nature of Christologic gesture by claiming that the '*naturall Language of the Hand* . . . had the happiness to escape the curse at the confusion of Babel: so it hath since been sanctified and made a holy language by the expressions of our Saviours *Hands*; whose gestures have given a sacred allowance to the naturall significations of ours'.[50] Christ's hand becomes a kerygmatic or 'performative' gesture because it does what it signifies.[51] The

within itself', quoted earlier, and S. A. Handelman, *Slayers of Moses* (1983), 120: 'Jesus is the essential link between signifier and signified because with the incarnation, the substance and its representation are one and the same.'

48 *On Homers Poetry* [and] *on Virgil*, E 270, K 778. The juxtaposition of Gothic and Egyptian design in *Christ Blessing* parallels the contrast between Gothic form and the 'Mathematic Form' of Grecian art in this text of *c.*1820.

49 Blake's insufficient pictorial distinction between laurel and olive makes their discrimination uncertain. Compare, for example, the foliage in the portrait of Spenser in the *Heads of the Poets* series, identified by Butlin as olive (no. 343.9), with the 'bay or laurel' in the portrait of Dryden (Butlin no. 343.12).

50 *Chirologia*, p. 7.

51 I extrapolate this concept of performative gesture from J. L. Austin, 'Performative Utterance', in *Philosophical Papers* (1961), 220–39. Strictly speaking, a performative must enact its own referent, but I have extended this meaning to include signs for which this enactment must

structure of this sign is not dyadic (signifier/signified) but triadic, requiring for its completion the signifier (physical gesture or sound), the signified (blessing), and the recipient believer whose condition is changed by his inclusion within the signifying process.[52] The sign's motivation lies not in the signifier/signified relationship but in the causal connection between them and the recipient. Thus we can include Christ's gesture of blessing within that larger category Blake calls 'Visionary forms dramatic' (*Jerusalem*, Pl. 98; E 257, K 746), for His hand is a visible and spiritual form which not only refers but acts. For the theologian Rudolf Bultmann, this dramatic sign, reaching out to include its perceiver, lies at the heart of Christianity: 'God as acting does not refer to an event which can be perceived by me without myself being drawn into the event as into God's action, without myself taking part in it as being acted upon.'[53]Christ's kerygmatic signs avoid the solipsism of pure self-referentiality by extending incarnation to the community of faithful recipients. It thereby approaches the power of the Logos: although it does not create the recipients as objects or give them organic life, it creates them as blessed souls, gives them spiritual life, and binds them together in the community of Christians. As we learn in the Gospel of St John, 'The hour is coming, and now is, when the dead shall hear the voice of the Son of God: and they that hear shall live. For as the Father hath life in himself; so hath he given to the Son to have life in himself; . . .' (5: 25–6).

be provided by the recipient. If he refuses, then the sign is not completed. Performatives of this type are the secular cousins to the theological concept of kerygmatic speech, the words of the preacher that proclaim his faith and move others to share in it. Christ's words are of course the ideal paradigm for kerygma. For the role of kerygma in modern religious thought, see R. W. Funk, *Language, Hermeneutic, and Word of God* (1966). In all cases of the performative sign, as I define it here, its power is not diminished through representation unless the recipient believes it to be so diminished. That is, if a Christian believes he is in fact blessed by Christ when beholding a picture of Him blessing, or when receiving that blessing through the agency of a priest, then the sign's kerygma remains unshaken.

[52] My sense of the triadic nature of performative signification is based in part on C. S. Peirce's analysis of all signs as triadic. His concept of the 'interpretant' fulfills the same function within signification as my 'recipient', but the two cannot be equated in other respects. Peirce's interpretant is another sign, whereas my recipient is a human response necessarily included within the performative sign to complete it as such. Since this response need not be semiotic, the ideal performative can bridge the gap between language and the extra-linguistic. The 'direction' of motivation is the same as with God's Word and the reverse of most characterizations of the Adamic sign (i.e., word motivates world rather than world motivating word). For the briefest and clearest definition of his triadic sign, see Peirce, *Semiotic and Significs* (1977), 31, 81. Peirce at least once compares his triad to the 'Christian trinity'; see *Writings of C. S. Peirce* (1982), 1: 503.

[53] *Jesus Christ and Mythology* (1958), 68.

The final design of the tempera series has added yet another species of sign to what has become a considerable list, one which begins with Logos and now includes Adamic, mimetic, expressive or physiognomic, arbitrary or conventional, incarnational, and kerygmatic or performative signs. I am tempted to test at once the utility of this taxonomy as the basis for a semiotic approach to Blake's texts, but I am restrained by a sense that I have skipped rather quickly over some very complex issues and jumbled together concepts from the first century AD to yesterday within a predominantly synchronic methodology. History beckons, for we need to situate the double perspective on language evoked by Blake's series of paintings, and in particular by *Adam Naming the Beasts*, within the theories shaping language concepts and practices in his time. To do so will require a more detailed (albeit selective) survey of speculations on the origin and nature of language, concentrating on English materials of the seventeenth, eighteenth, and early nineteenth centuries. The purpose of such an overview is not to uncover sources for Blake's works, but to delineate the landscape of intellectual possibilities available in his age. In turn, the second chapter will provide an historically based hermeneutic for an understanding of the central issue in the remainder of this book, the interactions within Blake's poetry between theological and rationalist, constitutive and differential, views of semiosis.

2. In Pursuit of the Motivated Sign

THE task I have set myself is more than a little daunting. Much has been written in recent years on the history of linguistics, and even the more limited subject of seventeenth- and eighteenth-century concepts of language origins has received a good deal of attention.[1] We need a major theme, or at least a leitmotif, to guide us through several centuries of competing theories, interpretations, and wild-eyed notions. Underlying the various sign types intimated by Blake's tempera series and listed near the end of the first chapter is the myth of the motivated sign, the word or gesture or image bearing more than an arbitrary relationship to its referent. This concept has not been adequately examined within the context of English linguistic thought, nor has its relevance to romantic ideas of the symbol been given sufficient attention.[2] By tracing the history of the motivated sign and some related ideas, we will encounter most of the important theories needed to begin a study of Blake's language concepts and practices. Even though this background material will lead us into some odd byways, their relevance will become clear in subsequent chapters as we try to understand how an early nineteenth-century English poet might endeavour 'to Restore what the Ancients calld the Golden Age' (*Vision of the Last Judgment*, E 555, K 605).

The basic division between the motivated and the arbitrary sign was first established by the pre-Socratic Greek philosophers. Parmenides

[1] Useful modern studies emphasizing 17th- and 18th-century British thought include the works by Aarsleff, Allen, Cohen, Cornelius, De Mott, Knowlson, Land, Michael, Salmon, Slaughter, and Stam listed in the Bibliography. Many of these works, and in particular Aarsleff's two books, are much concerned with the genealogy of ideas and the influence of one school of thought on another. My emphasis here falls mainly on representative texts that most clearly express linguistic concepts helpful in understanding Blake's language ideas and practices.

[2] The single previous study to centre on the history of the motivated sign is G. Genette, *Mimologiques* (1976). Genette considers many of the same basic issues I treat here, but he emphasizes works by a number of Continental figures (such as Charles de Brosses, Antoine Court de Gébelin, and Charles Nodier) of little importance to my British-oriented perspective. The final third of Genette's book deals with 19th-century and 20th-century writers (Mallarmé, Valéry, Sartre, *et al.*) beyond the chronological scope of this chapter. In spite of their titles, neither N. J. Jacob's potpourri of linguistic trivia and speculation in *Naming-Day in Eden* (1958) nor R. A. Fraser's witty and idiosyncratic *Language of Adam* (1977) bears more than a tangential relationship to my subject.

and the Eleatic school took the conventionalist view that names are arbitrary designations enforced by habit, while Heraclitus believed in a natural or real link between words and their referents.[3] Both views find expression in Plato's *Cratylus*. In the dialogue, Hermogenes the conventionalist argues against the theory of a natural bond between objects and their names put forward by Cratylus. Socrates, although as usual the master of the interrogative mode, devotes most of his attention to investigating and developing his own hypotheses about motivation. The thrust of his rhetoric at times suggests satire; but whatever his intentions, Socrates does offer an extended exposition of naturalist, anti-conventionalist theory. He leads Hermogenes through a series of etymological analyses to demonstrate how names are compounds or derivatives of roots to which they are related both in sound and sense. Further, these roots are expressive of the qualities of the person, action, or thing named. Yet no matter how ingenious or convincing Socrates may be in these activities, his reasoning is inevitably limited to the realm of language itself. Etymology can never show how words are causally connected to the extra-linguistic objects or events they refer to, and thus it cannot solve the problem of origin—that is, how words began before there were any root terms to build on. Like its frequent ally, punning, etymology constitutes a form of *secondary* motivation, perhaps paralleling within language structures the phenomenon of *primary* motivation between things and signs but never one with it. Socrates himself raises this difficulty at a fairly late stage in the dialogue and begins to consider the sources of roots, those 'primary names which precede [etymological] analysis'. He proposes a primitive language of visual signs that 'imitate the nature of things' and then extends this mimesis or isomorphism to those vocal signs, and finally even single letters, beyond which etymology cannot proceed.[4] Significantly, Socrates does not propose that this first language imitated appearances, but rather that it somehow shared in the same

[3] T. Taylor discusses these pre-Socratic views in the introduction to his translation of the *Cratylus*; see *Cratylus . . . of Plato* (1793), pp. xvi–xvii. For a much clearer summary, see J. C. McKusick, *Coleridge's Philosophy of Language* (1986), 4–5 and notes thereto.

[4] *Cratylus*, sec. 422–3, *Dialogues of Plato* (1937), 1: 211–12. In contrast, Aristotle takes a strong conventionalist position. See *De interpretatione*, sec. 16a. 26 ('the limitation "by convention" was introduced because nothing is by nature a noun or name . . .') and sec. 17a. 1 ('Every sentence has meaning not as being the natural means by which a physical faculty is realized, but, as we have said, by convention.'); *Basic Works of Aristotle* (1941), 40, 42.

'nature', the same metaphysical ground, as its referents. A theory of Platonic essences lurks behind the linguistics of the *Cratylus*.

In the last section of the dialogue, Socrates turns his attention to finding weaknesses in the absolute motivation of all signs propounded by Cratylus, thereby leaving uninvestigated how motivation between the essential nature of things and root signs corresponds with or evolves into etymological motivation, the process whereby a great many new terms are constructed out of the roots. As Genette points out in his chapter on the *Cratylus*, the 'central difficulty' in the dialogue is 'the delicate juncture between direct [what I call "primary"] and indirect [i.e., secondary] motivation.'[5] As we shall see, that juncture—or its troubling absence—will haunt linguistic speculation for many centuries after Plato.

At two points in the *Cratylus*, Socrates introduces the possibility that primary, motivated names were given to things by 'the Gods'. He also suggests that 'the original forms of words may have been lost in the lapse of ages' through changes made by accident or by speakers unaware of the real connections between the original forms and their referents.[6] As I briefly suggested in Chapter 1, the stories of Adam naming the beasts and of the Tower of Babel in Genesis became the joint nexus for these related themes of origin and loss. The first century AD philosopher Philo Judaeus initiated the basic combination of Cratylean linguistics and Biblical exegesis continued and augmented by later Christian theologians, including Eusebius and Thomas Aquinas. These authorities, perhaps relying on the statement in Genesis that God brought the beasts together to see 'what he [Adam] would call them' (2: 19), granted to the first man what Vico would later call 'divine onomathesia'.[7] Philo is typical in his claim that the names Adam gave the beasts 'were fully apposite, for right well did he divine the character of the creatures he was describing, with the result that their natures were apprehended as

[5] *Mimologiques*, p. 46 (my translation). My distinction between primary and secondary motivation is much the same as C. S. Peirce's theory of two types of 'iconicity' of signs: the 'imagic', in which the sign resembles its referent; and the 'diagrammatic', in which the systemic relationships among signs replicate the relationships among their referents. See Peirce, *Collected Papers* (1932), 2: 247, 277–82. For a brief structural analysis of secondary motivation, see S. Ullman, 'Natural and Conventional Signs', in T. A. Sebeok, ed., *Tell-Tale Sign* (1975), 103–10. Ullman's proposal that all such 'morphological' motivation falls into just two types, the metaphoric and the metonymic, is too rigid.

[6] *Cratylus*, sec. 421, 425 (*Dialogues of Plato*, 1: 210, 214).

[7] G. Vico, *New Science* (1968), 127.

soon as their names were uttered'.[8] Such statements establish a double bond between minds and signs: the insight into essences is embodied in words that transparently reveal those essences. In his *Questions and Answers on Genesis*, Philo adds an affective, Orphic or proto-kerygmatic, dimension to Adam's powers through the supposition 'that the giving of names was so exact that so soon as he gave the name and the animal heard it, it was affected as if by the phenomenon of a familiar and related name being spoken'.[9]

One of the more charming versions of Edenic language was the notion that all the animals could speak to each other and to man before the fall. The pseudepigraphic Book of Jubilees makes passing reference to this belief, but Philo gives a more detailed account of a story 'to be found in the writings of the mythologists, telling of the days when all animals had a common language'. In their communal pride, the beasts asked for immortality, but as punishment for their 'audacity' their 'speech at once became different, so that from that day forward they could no longer understand each other, because of the difference of the languages into which the single language which they all shared had been divided'.[10] Blake seems to have known something of these legends, perhaps through William Warburton's *Divine Legation of Moses* or the brief reference in Josephus,[11] for in Night the Sixth of *The Four Zoas* he describes Urizen's attempt to communicate with the beasts. But in their fallen condition, 'His voice to them was but an inarticulate thunder for

[8] 'Allegorical Interpretation of Genesis II', *Philo* (1929), 1: 119 (bk. 1, sec. 150). For Aquinas's brief comments on Adam's tongue, see *Summa Theologica*, question 94, art. 3, 'Whether the First Man Knew All Things'.

[9] *Questions and Answers on Genesis* (1953), 1: 12.

[10] 'On the Confusion of Tongues', *Philo* (1932), 4: 13 (sec. 6). For the passage on talking animals in Jubilees, see R. H. Charles, ed., *Apocryphya and Pseudepigrapha of the Old Testament* (1913), 3: 28.

[11] *Divine Legation* (1741), 2: 90–3; Josephus, *Antiquities of the Jews*, p. 8, in Maynard's translation. Warburton distinguishes between fables '*that Beasts and Men* had a common Language' and those in which the animals 'had a Language, but a Language of their own' (2: 92). He even suggests '*that Trees spoke in the first Ages of the World*' (2: 91) in order to mock such fancies. In a footnote to Josephus' statement that 'there was one common language among animals in general', the editor (apparently Edward Kimpton) explains that 'it appears from thence, that Josephus thought several of the brute animals, besides the serpent, could speak before the fall'. J. G. Herder makes passing reference to 'man here [in Eden] in conversation with the brutes' in *The Spirit of Hebrew Poetry* (1833, first pub. 1782–3), 1: 128, but it is unlikely that this book had any direct influence on Blake since it was not translated into English until after his death.

their Ears' and 'no one answerd every one wrapd up | In his own sorrow howld regardless of his words, nor voice | Of sweet response could he obtain . . .'. Urizen tries to 'stand & question a fierce scorpion' and converse with a lion, but all in vain, 'in vain the Eloquent tongue'. Both man and beast have lost those 'Climes of happy Eternity | Where the lamb replies to the infant voice . . .' (E 347–8, K 315).

By the sixteenth and seventeenth centuries, the motivated character of Adam's speech had become a commonplace among both Biblical exegetes and secular speculators on the original language. It was a particularly popular topos among the mystically minded, such as Agrippa von Nettesheim, for whom Adam's words 'contain in them wonderfull powers of the things signified', and Jacob Boehme, who held that 'When God had created the Beasts, he brought them to *Adam*, that he should give them their Names, every one according to their Essence and Kind'.[12] But the theme also entered into academic debate through the works of reformist divines such as John Webster, who held that Adam 'was made in the out-spoken word' of God and 'so lived in, understood, and spoke the language of the father'. When the animals were brought before him, Adam knew their 'internal and external signatures' and thus could give them names 'agreeing with their natures'.[13] The language of Paradise and its oneness with essences were even fit topics for sermons. As Robert South preached at St Paul's on 9 November 1662, Adam 'came into the world a philosopher, which sufficiently appeared by his writing the nature of things upon their names; he could view essences in themselves, and read forms without the comment of their respective properties'.[14] Eighteenth-century linguists relied less on Biblical authority than their more theologically minded forebears, but they often repeat the Adamic myth as a requisite gesture even as they question it. William Massey, for example, considered the language of Eden as a subject of pure speculation, but none the less points out that Adam 'had the wonderful capacity of giving names to all creatures; which names, according to the opinion of some learned

[12] Agrippa von Nettesheim, *Three Books of Occult Philosophy* (1651), 153; Boehme, *Three Principles of the Divine Essence*, in *Works* (1764), 1: 57 (ch. 9, para. 6).

[13] Webster, *Academiarum examen* (1654), 29.

[14] Quoted in H. Aarsleff, *From Locke to Saussure* (1982), 59. For the full context, see South, *Sermons* (1842), 1: 30–1.

men, were expressive, in the *original language*, of their natures and qualities'.[15]

South's comment hints at the belief that Adam's motivated signs were not limited to the gestural and vocal but extended even to his supposed writings. John Evelyn, citing early Christian authorities as precedents, attributes to Adam the invention of letters and links their first forms with the antediluvian invention of engraving.[16] In his *Arca Noë* of 1675 and *Turris Babel* of 1679, Athanasius Kircher discusses the motivated nature of Adam's letters and their use in books written before the flood.[17] Blake may have been attracted to such beliefs, particularly because of Evelyn's association of Adamic inscriptions with engraving. Blake's tantalizingly brief comment in *A Descriptive Catalogue* that his own theories about the early history of man 'are written in Eden' (E 543, K 578) suggests his knowledge of the myth of Adamic writing. Yet his most explicit comment on the divine origin of letters adheres to the competing theory that Moses was the first to learn alphabetic writing when he (Exodus 34: 27–8) or God (Exodus 31: 18) inscribed the tablets of the decalogue.[18] As Blake states on the third plate of *Jerusalem*, God 'in mysterious Sinais awful cave | To Man the wond'rous art of writing gave' (E 145, K 621).

The story of Nimrod's ziggurat (Genesis 11: 1–9) required little elaboration to demonstrate its relevance to the dissolution of the original language. Most commentaries, from Philo's allegorical reading in *De confusione linguarum* to Kircher's *Turris Babel*, assume that the Adamic unity of word and world was not lost until the confusion of tongues, but a few texts suggest that the linguistic division was contemporaneous with the fall of man. Du Bartas, for example, claims that Adam's 'Fit sense-full Names' would still be known 'had that fall of thine | Not cancell'd so the Character divine'.[19] But

[15] *Origin and Progress of Letters* (1763), 14.

[16] *Sculptura* (1662), 11–12. See also Massey, *Origin and Progress of Letters*, pp. 18, 38, 44.

[17] *Arca Noë* (1675), bk. 3, pt. 3; *Turris Babel* (1679), 148, 166, 168. For brief summaries of Kircher's views, see P. Cornelius, *Languages in . . . Imaginary Voyages* (1965), 7–8.

[18] See Massey, *Origin and Progress of Letters*, p. 35: 'Some have *supposed*, that the writing of the Ten Commandments, on the tables of stone, was the first writing by *letters* and *words* that was in the world, and that the knowledge of them was of divine original; *Moses* being inspired by God to instruct the people in the use, in the pronunciation, in the reading, and writing of them.'

[19] *Du Bartas His Divine Weekes and Workes* (1611), 170. For Kircher's views, see *Turris Babel*, p. 194. For a comprehensive survey of commentaries on Babel, see A. Borst, *Der Turmbau von Babel* (1957–63).

however the sequence of language changes is aligned with Biblical narrative, Genesis offers an answer to the argument between Cratylus and Hermogenes by historicizing their positions. In the beginning, language consisted of motivated signs, but the sins of man led to a fall from that ideal condition and into language composed of arbitrary signs. This linguistic feature of the more general 'fall into Division', lamented by Blake at the beginning of *The Four Zoas* (E 301, K 264), introduces some new questions into the debate. What were the characteristics of Adam's language in addition to motivation? Are any remnants of it still extant in known tongues? Is it possible, through either philosophical or historical investigations, to reclaim or reinvent motivated semiosis and thereby achieve, at least in the world of signs, a 'Resurrection to Unity' (*The Four Zoas*, E 301, K 264)?

Attempts to answer these and related questions about the origins of speech and writing found a natural ally in the study of Eastern languages. Perhaps one of them was Adam's. Hebrew, the language of the Old Testament, was the obvious choice for most early scholars, including St Augustine (*City of God*, bk. 16, ch. 11), whose view remained the majority opinion well into the eighteenth century. Yet Hebrew words seemed no more motivated than any others, and thus it was difficult to reconcile the selection of Hebrew as the first language with one of the special characteristics attributed to the Adamic sign. Two solutions were possible: either Hebrew had over the centuries (or suddenly at the Tower of Babel) degenerated into an arbitrary system, or fallen man had lost the ability to perceive the motivation still present in the language. The first position is represented by John Wilkins, who found so many 'defects and imperfections' in Old Testament Hebrew that 'it may be guessed not to be the same which was con-created by our first Parents, and spoken by *Adam* in *Paradise*'.[20] The second view led to attempts at rediscovering the hidden, motivated essence of Hebrew. One of the more elaborate practitioners of this type of analysis was

[20] *An Essay towards a Real Character, and a Philosophical Language* (1668), 5. For surveys of 16th- and 17th-century opinions on Hebrew as the first language, see D. C. Allen, 'Some Theories of the Growth and Origin of Language in Milton's Age', *Philological Quarterly*, 28 (1949), 5–16; and Cornelius, *Languages in Imaginary Voyages*, pp. 10–22. The latter is particularly helpful in sorting out the various theories on the relationships among Hebrew, Chaldean, and Syriac, and on the loss of the archaic form of Hebrew—or, as Kircher calls it, the *Lingua Humana*—during the Babylonian captivity.

Franciscus Mercurius who, in his treatise of 1667, uncovers a mimetic relation between the positions the tongue assumes when pronouncing the Hebrew alphabet and the meanings of the sounds produced.[21] Kircher dealt more directly with the graphic forms of Hebrew letters and found that some, when combined into words, became schematic representations of the qualities of the things designated.[22]

Kircher's efforts typify the seventeenth-century tendency to concentrate on the written forms of languages rather than their vocal utterance. But alphabetic writing can be forced only with difficulty into visually mimetic programmes since each letter stands for a sound, not a thing. Thus, writing composed of pictographic or ideographic characters seemed to offer more fruitful ground for finding motivated signs. Francis Bacon believed that the peoples of China 'and the Kingdomes of the High *Levant*' wrote 'in *Characters reall*, which expresse neither *Letters, nor words* in *grosse*, but *things* or *Notions*'.[23] A more popular choice for investigation was the hieroglyphic writing of ancient Egypt, both because of its pictorially mimetic features and its possible influence on, or interference with, Hebrew culture. The hieroglyph and the emblem were often compounded into a single form in Renaissance theories of pictorial symbolism, as is demonstrated by the *Hieroglyphica* of Horapollo, an emblem book purporting to reveal the true meanings of Egyptian writing.[24] Marsilio Ficino suggested that such ancient symbols were not simply representational images but that they somehow embodied, and thus bore a motivated relationship to, abstract concepts such as time.[25] Neoplatonic symbology like Ficino's tended to combine

[21] F. Mercurius, *Alphabeti verè naturalis Hebraici* (1667). Boehme's similar theory, but one based on divine 'signatures' rather than direct mimesis, will be discussed later in this chapter.

[22] See for example Kircher's analysis of the Hebrew word for 'horse' in *Turris Babel*, p. 168 (quoted in Cornelius, *Languages in Imaginary Voyages*, p. 11). For other versions of alphabetic mimesis, see Genette's chapter on 'Mimographismes', *Mimologiques*, pp. 71–83.

[23] *Two Bookes of Francis Bacon* (1605), bk. 2, fo. 59^r. Blake probably owned a copy of this, the first edition of the *Advancement of Learning*; see G. E. Bentley, Jr., *Blake Books* (1977), 683.

[24] First pub. by Manutius, Venice, 1505. The confusion of the two forms was perpetuated by the very title of F. Quarles's emblem book of 1638, *Hieroglyphikes of the Life of Man*. See also Bacon, *Advancement of Learning*, bk. 2, fo. 59^v: 'For as to *Hierogliphickes*, (things of Ancient use, and embraced chiefely by the *Aegyptians*, one of the most Ancient Nations) they are but as continued *Impreases* and *Emblemes*.'

[25] For Ficino's beliefs, see E. H. Gombrich, 'Icones Symbolicae', *Journal of the Warburg and Courtauld Institutes*, 11 (1948), 163–92, esp. pp. 172–3. In *The Myth of Egypt and its Hieroglyphs* (1961), p. 46, E. Iversen writes that Plotinus believed that hieroglyphs 'revealed to the initiated contemplator a profound insight into the very essence and substance of things', but this claim is not substantiated by the passage in the *Enneads* Iversen cites (bk. 5, 8. 5–8. 6).

(or perhaps confuse) the pictographic and the ideographic, finding in the emblem/hieroglyph both visual mimesis and a form of incarnational motivation between the sign and transcendental ideas.

In spite of the apparently motivated nature of hieroglyphs, they remained stubbornly resistant to decipherment. How could signs be immediately intelligible as images of things, and yet create a mystery when systematically arranged together? The most sophisticated attempt to answer this question was William Warburton's *Divine Legation of Moses*, a work received by its eighteenth-century readers as an exemplar of antiquarian scholarship. This comprehensive and diverse work, first published in three volumes between 1738 and 1741, is itself resistant to easy summary. Most of Warburton's philological investigations are concentrated in the second volume. There he states his intention to show 'how one of the simplest and plainest Means of Instruction that ever was contrived, came to be converted into one of the most artificial and abstruse'.[26] To demonstrate this fall from nature to artifice, Warburton was led to a detailed consideration of Egyptian and Near Eastern cultures, not just to the formal properties of their writings. As I briefly noted in Chapter 1, his basic thesis was that hieroglyphs developed as an abridged form of pictographic writing and thus originally had a basis in mimetic motivation. Alphabetic writing was a further evolution toward refinement, abridgement, and abstraction. The history of these forms, however, was not one of simple progression, but a kind of historical chiasmus. To hide the written record of their rituals and beliefs from the laity, the Egyptian priests developed ever more arcane forms of hieroglyphic. At the same time, the newer form of alphabetic characters, even though further from the motivational source than hieroglyphs and first invented as a secret method of writing, came into general use. The Jews found it a particularly useful medium for preserving their own beliefs and countering the Egyptian polytheism couched in hieroglyphs. By this means the Hebrew alphabet evolved and its meanings were preserved.

As my brief overview suggests, Warburton's narrative detaches writing from speech. To repair this breach, Warburton offers a

[26] *Divine Legation of Moses*, 2: 96. Warburton deals with many other non-philological matters, including (as his subtitle states) 'The omission of the Doctrine of a future state of reward and punishment in the Jewish dispensation'.

history of oral rhetoric which, in its development from mimesis to figuration, parallels the history of writing. He posits a primitive form of communication through gestures and other actions dramatically imitating the objects and concepts signified. This 'Method of *expressing* the Thoughts by Actions perfectly coincided with that of *recording* them by Picture' (2: 87). The next stage, corresponding to the development of hieroglyphs, was a combination of actions and energetic speech filled with visual imagery.[27] This mode is exemplified by the Hebrew prophets. Their extravagant deeds, such as those of Isaiah and Ezekiel Blake describes in *The Marriage of Heaven and Hell*,[28] were in their culture perfectly acceptable accompaniments to their rhetoric and use of '*Fable*; a kind of Speech which corresponds, in all Respects, to writing by *Hieroglyphics* . . .' (2: 91–2). For Warburton, 'the old *Asiatic* style so highly figurative, seems likewise, by what we find of its Remains in the Prophetic Language of the Sacred Writers, to have been evidently fashioned to the Mode of the ancient *Hieroglyphics*'.[29] Indeed, 'the Prophetic Style seems to be a speaking Hieroglyphic' (2: 152), and thus to contain remnants of the original motivated form of signification through actions. But even among the Hebrews the use of signifying actions decreased and was replaced by a verbal equivalent—the imagery, similes, and metaphors constituting figures of speech.

Warburton's work marks an important development in the study of language origins and changes. He refers in passing to Adam naming the beasts, but dismisses it 'as groundless as any' other speculation on how speech began (2: 82). Similarly, he denies the notion that alphabetic writing was given by God to Moses on Mt. Sinai (2: 139). For these tales of sudden and transcendental origin Warburton substitutes gradual evolution, and in place of divine inspiration as the source of primary motivation he offers pictorial

[27] These observations are Warburton's development of Bacon's comment, in *The Advancement of Learning*, bk. 2, fo. 59^{v}, that 'as for *Gestures*, they are as *Transitorie Hierogliphickes*, and are to *Hierogliphickes*, as *Words spoken* are to *Wordes Written*, in that they abide not; but they have evermore as well, as the other an affinitie with the thinges signified'.

[28] 'I also asked Isaiah what made him go naked and barefoot for three years? . . . I then asked Ezekiel. why he eat dung, & lay so long on his right and left side' (E 39, K 154). See Isaiah 20: 2–3; Ezekiel 4: 4, 6, 12.

[29] *Divine Legation of Moses*, 2: 153. On this point, Warburton was anticipated by Sir Isaac Newton, who wrote that 'the language of the Prophets, being Hieroglyphical, had affinity with that of the Egyptian priests and Eastern wise men'. See Newton's manuscript, 'The Language of the Prophets', printed in part in Newton, *Theological Writings* (1950), 120.

mimesis.[30] Further, he replaces human pride and divine wrath as the causes of language change with the complex interactions of cultural forces. These extra-linguistic phenomena affecting language are not always subject to man's conscious will, and thus Warburton characterizes the 'Birth and Continuance' of writing as the products of '*Nature* and *Necessity*, not *Choice* and *Artifice*' (2: 81). William Warburton, Bishop of Gloucester, thoroughly secularized the genesis and exodus of language. Yet the underlying direction of language change remains the same: an original motivated form becomes, or is replaced by, an arbitrary sign system. For Warburton, this movement indicated the progress of language and letters toward ever more abstract, concise, and useful methods of signification.

We must now turn our attention from attempts to rediscover motivated signs to seventeenth-century schemes for reinventing them. John Webster, writing in 1654, clearly states the contemporary desire to go beyond antiquarian research and improve on the past: 'What a vast advancement had it been to the Re-publick of Learning, and hugely profitable to all mankind, if the discovery of the universal Character (hinted at by some judicious Authors) had been wisely and laboriously pursued and brought to perfection?'[31] Attempts to answer Webster's implied intellectual challenge had already been launched by Francis Lodowyck, in his *Common Writing* (1647) and *Ground-Work* (1652), and others were soon to follow, including Cave Beck (*The Universal Character*, 1657), George Dalgarno (*Ars signorum*, 1661), and John Wilkins (*An Essay towards a Real Character, and a Philosophical Language*, 1668).[32] The 'characters' sought by these language projectors were written signs which, as Beck's and Wilkins's titles suggest, reclaimed the two main features defining the Adamic word: universality, and a 'real' or motivated

[30] It is of course possible to question the supposed motivation, the 'real' similitude, between an object and its pictorial (or even mental) image, but I find no hint of such doubts in 17th-century and 18th-century language theory concerned with mimesis as the basis of semiotic motivation. For some modern conventionalist views of imagery, see N. Goodman, *Languages of Art* (1976); and W. J. T. Mitchell, *Iconology* (1986). For a theory of auditory mimesis, based on a musical theory linking objects and the sounds used to name them, see M. Mersenne, *Harmonie universelle* (1636–7).

[31] *Academiarum examen*, p. 24.

[32] All these projectors were anticipated by Comenius, who visited England in 1641–2 while he was working on his scheme for a universal language, the *Via Lucis*. This work, not pub. until 1668, may have influenced British scholars while still in manuscript. See V. Salmon, *Study of Language in 17th-Century England* (1979), 131. For a summary of Leibniz's interest in an ideal language based on universal grammar, see S. K. Land, *From Signs to Propositions* (1974), 135–9.

relationship to the referent. A system based on such signs could, in Webster's words, repair 'the ruines of *Babell*' and, according to Seth Ward, offer man a 'naturall Language' that 'would afford that which the *Cabalists* and *Rosycrucians* have vainely sought for in the Hebrew, and in the names of things assigned by *Adam*'.[33]

Wilkins's general comments on how he intended to accomplish the high goal of a universal and real character are typical of all such mid-seventeenth-century projects:

If to every thing and notion there were assigned a distinct *Mark*, together with some *provision* to express *Grammatical Derivations* and *Inflexions*; this might suffice as to one great end of a *Real Character*, namely, the expression of our Conceptions by *Marks* which should signifie *things*, and not *words*. And so likewise if several distinct *words* were assigned for the *names* of such things, with certain invariable *Rules* for all such Grammatical *Derivations* and *Inflexions*, and such onely, as are natural and necessary; this would make a much more easie and convenient Language then is yet in being.

Wilkins's first sentence makes it clear that the relationship between his 'marks' and 'every thing and notion' will be purely arbitrary, although once fixed in a logical grammar the 'assigned' bond will be distinct and invariable. But how can such marks achieve the motivated status of 'real' characters? In his next paragraph, Wilkins indicates how his scheme, somewhat more sophisticated than those of his predecessors, will address this question:

But now if these *Marks* or *Notes* could be so contrived, as to have such a *dependance* upon, and relation to, one another, as might be sutable to the nature of the things and notions which they represented; and so likewise, if the *Names* of things could be so ordered, as to contain such a kind of *affinity* or *opposition* in their letters and sounds, as might be some way answerable to the nature of the things which they signified; This would yet be a farther advantage superadded: by which, besides the best way of helping the *Memory* by natural Method, the *Understanding* likewise would be highly improved; and we should, by learning the *Character* and the *Names* of things, be instructed likewise in their *Natures*, the knowledg of both which ought to be conjoyned.[34]

[33] Webster, *Academiarum examen*, p. 24; Ward, *Vindicae academiarum* (1654), 22.
[34] *Essay towards a Real Character*, p. 21.

Significantly, this statement makes no reference to any form of primary motivation, whether the result of divine inspiration, or the sharing of Platonic essences, or visual mimesis. The motivation in Wilkins's system will be entirely secondary, depending like Cratylean etymology on an isomorphism between the relationships among things in nature and the relationships among the elements of the signifying system. This type of semiosis is essentially allegorical, for it is based on the one-to-one matching of physical entities with conventional terms and their functional similitude within discrete systems that have a similar structure, but never a common identity or metaphysical ground. A third domain must come into play in such a scheme: the mind, capable of perceiving the natural order of things and reinstituting it in a signifying order of marks. For Wilkins and his fellow projectors, the common denominator to all three realms is logic, a rational schema implanted by God in 'every thing and notion' and by man in the grammar of an ideal language.

The details of seventeenth-century ideal languages need not detain us, but their intellectual allegiances and semiotic implications are most important. Webster, whose use of the word 'signatures' shows the influence of Boehme, writes with apparent religious enthusiasm about the Logos and its revelation in the language of nature.[35] Yet his major goal is educational reform along Baconian lines, and his chief enemy is the heavy weight of scholasticism he believes is still burdening the academies of learning. Most language projectors refer to Adam's naming of the beasts or to the Tower of Babel, but these attempts to set their efforts within traditional theological contexts are little more than conventional auxiliaries to their secular and rationalist pursuits.[36] They looked back to Francis Bacon as a forefather because of his concern with 'the false appearances, that are imposed upon us by words' and the need to 'imitate the wisedome of the *Mathematicians*, in setting downe in the verie beginning, the

[35] *Academiarum examen*, pp. 27–29. For 'signatures', see the comments from pp. 26, 29 quoted above.

[36] On this point I am in substantial agreement with Salmon, *Study of Language in 17th-Century England*, esp. pp. 129–31, 153 n. 4, where she argues against De Mott's view that ideal language schemes were prompted by theological concerns. See B. De Mott, 'The Sources and Development of Wilkins' Philosophical Language', *Journal of English and Germanic Philology*, 57 (1958), 1–13. For another perspective on this debate, but one that basically supports Salmon's position, see J. Knowlson, *Universal Language Schemes* (1975), 85–91.

definitions of our wordes and termes'.[37] Inventors of philosophical languages also shared an implicit belief in the spatial logic developed by Peter Ramus and applied to the study of language by the universal grammarians of Port-Royal.[38] Wilkins in particular sought to arrange his 'marks' into a taxonomy of signs and their referents much as natural scientists like Linnaeus would soon be organizing the species, families, and phyla of the animals.[39] Dalgarno, for example, divides all ideas into seventeen classes, each designated by a letter from the Latin or Greek alphabet. The absence of primary motivation and the importance of abstract logical categories in the systems proposed by the language projectors of seventeenth-century England have the same fundamental semiotic orientation as my negative or ironic interpretation of Blake's *Adam Naming the Beasts* presented in Chapter 1.

The historical contacts between the British linguists we have been considering and the Royal Society point to important intellectual affinities. Wilkins was one of the founders of the Society and his *Essay towards a Real Character* was published under its aegis.[40] Sir Isaac Newton was probably aware of Dalgarno's work, or other such treatises, when he composed his own plan for a universal language in about 1661.[41] Like Bacon, who branded the 'studie of words, and not matter' as 'the first distemper of learning',[42] the rationalist language projectors were allied with their scientific associates in programmes of linguistic Puritanism. Both were interested in systems of pure signification devoid of the ambiguity and figuration that cluttered spoken languages with merely decorative

[37] *Advancement of Learning*, bk. 2, fo. 57^{r}. See also Salmon, *Study of Language in 17th-Century England*, pp. 144–45.

[38] The *chef-d'oeuvre* of the Port-Royal grammarians is A. Arnauld [and C. Lancelot], *Grammaire générale* (1660). For the influence of Ramus on 17th-century grammar, see A. Richardson, *Logicians School-Master* (1629).

[39] M. M. Slaughter, *Universal Languages and Scientific Taxonomy* (1982), offers a convincing and thorough demonstration of the thesis stated here and implied by her title.

[40] T. Sprat, *History of the Royal-Academy* (1667), 53, points out that it was 'some space after the end of the Civil wars at *Oxford*, in *Dr. Wilkins* his Lodgings, in *Wadham College*, which was then the place of Resort for Vertuous, and Learned Men, that the first meetings were made, which laid the foundation of all this that follow'd'. Wilkins knew Dalgarno and wrote the prefatory letter (signed 'N.S.') for Ward, *Vindicae academiarum*, a reply to Webster.

[41] R. W. V. Elliott, 'Isaac Newton's "Of An Universall Language" ', *Modern Language Review*, 52 (1957), 1–18. Elliott's essay includes a transcript of Newton's manuscript, now in the University of Chicago Library. Newton attempted to create a spoken, as well as written, language based on a taxonomy of ideas.

[42] *Advancement of Learning*, bk. 1, fo. 18^{v}.

and potentially misleading verbiage. Webster praises chemical and mathematical symbols as models for a philosophical language, and Wilkins criticizes the actual languages of men for their '*Equivocals*' (that is, words that have 'several significations'), their 'ambiguity of words by reason of *Metaphors*', their '*Synonymous* words, which make Language tedious', and their '*Anomalisms* and Irregularities in Grammatical construction'.[43] The same attitudes toward language were, according to Thomas Sprat, basic to the principles of the Royal Society, whose members 'have indeavor'd, to separate the knowledge of *Nature*, from the colours of Rhetorick'. 'Who can behold', asks Sprat, 'without indignation, how many mists and uncertainties, these specious *Tropes* and *Figures* have brought to our Knowledge?'[44] Such 'superfluities', as Wilkins calls the figures of rhetoric, must be eliminated to attain Sprat's goal of 'bringing all things as near the Mathematical plainness as they can' (p. 113). These values were projected into the past to form a sense of the original language, one characterized by Sprat as having 'primitive purity, and shortness, when men deliver'd so many *things*, almost in an equal number of *words*.'[45] Sprat also praises the French Academy for its successes in preserving the language of its country from 'the corruptions of speech' (p. 39)—a comment indicating that the taxonomic ideal required a complete dissociation from spoken language, with its spontaneity and propensity for whimsical changes, and the establishment of the hegemony of the visual over the auditory image in all conceptions of nature, mind, and sign systems. The final *reductio ad absurdum* of these narrowly reformist attitudes is offered by Swift's 'School of Languages' in the 'grand Academy of Lagado' where the most advanced projectors have launched 'a Scheme for entirely abolishing all Words whatsoever' and 'expressing themselves by *Things*' which they carry in great bundles on their backs.[46]

Taxonomic logic from Aristotle to Wilkins and Linnaeus shared the same semiotic ground with the atomistic and mathematical logic

[43] Webster, *Academiarum examen*, pp. 25–6; Wilkins, *Essay towards a Real Character*, pp. 17–18.

[44] *History of the Royal-Society*, pp. 62, 112.

[45] *History of the Royal-Society*, p. 113. The longevity of this view is indicated by D. Hartley's claim 'that the language, which *Adam* and *Eve* were possessed of in paradise was very narrow, and confined in great measure to visible things', and was probably 'monosyllabic in great measure'. Hartley, *Observations on Man* (1791), p. 176. Blake engraved the frontispiece for this edition.

[46] J. Swift, *Gulliver's Travels* (1959), 'A Voyage to Laputa', ch. 5, pp. 179, 185–6.

of Bacon and Newton. To this considerable group we can add the name of John Locke, whose *Essay concerning Human Understanding*, first published in 1690, continues and extends rationalist linguistics even as it denies the possibility of a motivated semiotic. Locke claims, at the very beginning of his chapter 'Of the Signification of Words', that they are 'arbitrarily' related to their referents 'by a voluntary Imposition'.[47] This elimination of primary motivation would still permit a universal language project like Wilkins's, but in his next chapter Locke argues that '*it is impossible, that every particular Thing should have a distinct and peculiar name*' because 'it is beyond the Powers of Human Capacity to frame and retain distinct *Ideas* of all the particular Things we meet with' (3. 3. 2). The acceptance of this position would effectively demolish the one-to-one matching of things and signs basic to taxonomic linguistics.

In spite of his denial of at least one requirement for a 'philosophical' language, Locke vastly increases the importance of another of its elements. In my earlier remarks on universal language schemes, I introduced the 'third domain' of the logical mind, the presence of which is necessarily assumed by seventeenth-century British projectors although seldom an issue in their works. One of the few exceptions is Wilkins's discussion of the mental image: 'That *conceit* [i.e., idea] which men have in their minds concerning a Horse or Tree, is the Notion or mental Image of that Beast, or natural thing, of such a nature, shape and use. The *Names* given to these in several Languages, are such arbitrary *sounds* or *words*, as Nations of men have agreed upon, either casually or designedly, to express their Mental notions of them'.[48] This nascent mentalism—the theory that words refer to ideas or mental functions, not things—becomes an essential presence in Locke's linguistics. '*Words in their primary or immediate Signification, stand for nothing, but the* Ideas *in the Mind of him that uses them*' (3. 2. 2). Some of these ideas are 'particulars', brought to mind by specific objects or events presented

[47] Locke, *Essay concerning Human Understanding* (1975), bk. 3, ch. 2, para. 1. In his annotations to Reynolds's *Discourses*, Blake noted that, 'when very Young', he read 'Locke on Human Understanding & Bacons Advancement of Learning' (E 660, K 476), but it is not known which edition of Locke's *Essay* he used. For other references and possible allusions to Locke, see Hilton, *Literal Imagination*, p. 63.

[48] Wilkins, *Essay towards a Real Character*, p. 20. Locke has often been credited as the first to express these views, clearly but briefly noted by Wilkins 22 years before the publication of Locke's *Essay*.

to the senses, but others are 'essences', including many which are purely 'nominal' abstractions without existence outside the semiotics of the mind (3. 3. 18–20). Words and ideas should be closely knit together, according to Locke, so that their logical arrangement into propositions will embody knowledge. But words 'interpose themselves so much between our Understandings, and the Truth, which it would contemplate and apprehend, that like the *Medium* through which visible Objects pass, the Obscurity and Disorder does not seldom cast a mist before our Eyes, and impose upon our Understandings' (3. 9. 21). The remedy for these obfuscations lies not in the discovery or invention of a motivated system, but in the right use of the words and propositions available in man's familiar, arbitrary languages. Linguistic motivation is situated in the ideal concord between mental functions and grammatical and syntactic structures. Like Sprat, Locke projects his linguistic ideals into an image of the original tongue, finding that Adam's power 'of affixing any new name to any *Idea*' and his ability to form 'complex *Ideas*' according to the 'Pattern' of 'his own Thoughts' were the same as those available to 'all Men ever since' (3. 6. 51). The first man may have been made in God's image, but the history of linguistics from Philo to Locke demonstrates how Adam's language has been continually remade according to man's shifting theories of ideal methods of meaning.

The senses rescue Locke from absolute mentalism. Since all simple or 'particular' ideas are images of things or events, the senses play a crucial role in the progression from world to mind to signs to other minds. The study of language 'may also lead us a little towards the Original of all our Notions and Knowledge, if we remark, how great a dependence our *Words* have on common sensible *Ideas*; and how those, which are made use of to stand for Actions and Notions quite removed from sense, *have their rise from thence, and from obvious sensible* Ideas *are transferred to more abstruse significations*, and made to stand for *Ideas* that come not under the cognizance of our senses; v.g. to *Imagine*, *Apprehend*, *Comprehend*, *Adhere*, *Conceive*, *Instill*, *Disgust*, *Disturbance*, *Tranquillity*, etc. are all Words taken from the Operations of sensible Things, and applied to certain Modes of Thinking' (3. 1. 5). In spite of his practical criticisms of object-based language projects, Locke has come full circle, returning words to things through the (ideally transparent) medium of the senses. But absolute sensibilism is avoided, in the famous passage from the beginning of Book 3 quoted above, because Locke does not claim that words referring to 'modes of thinking' are the mechanical products of sense experience. Rather, he states that they are merely 'transferred' from the 'cognizance of our senses', and this transferral implies that the mind has its own powers independent of the senses but capable of manipulating ideas arising from them. Locke in effect divides words into two large classes—those that name things or events and their 'real' qualities, and those that arise from and refer to mental functions. The first group leads to a sensibilist theory of reference and sign origins, while the second requires a mentalist theory.[49]

The competing claims made by these two views of reference became a central issue in eighteenth-century language theory. But both theories tended to deny the concept of primary motivation in which sign and referent share a common essence, at once both ontological and semiotic. The linguistic sign becomes a double entity of signifying image (visual or auditory) and a signified image (mental or physical), with the gap between them bridged only by arbitrary representation. Motivation is at best secondary, relegated to the grammatical, syntactic, or etymological relationships among signifiers.

In his annotations of *c.*1808 to Sir Joshua Reynolds's *Discourses*, Blake offers a direct criticism of Locke's idea of words. Reynolds complains that 'our judgement upon an airy nothing, a fancy which has no foundation, is called by the same name which we give to our determinations concerning those truths which refer to the most general and most unalterable principles of human nature; to the works which are only to be produced by the greatest efforts of the human understanding. However inconvenient this may be, we are obliged to take words as we find them; all we can do is to distinguish the THINGS to which they are applied.'[50] Perhaps Sir Joshua's reference to 'human understanding' reminded Blake of the *Essay*

[49] In *From Locke to Saussure*, pp. 42–69, Aarsleff concentrates on Locke's mentalism, but the sensibilist elements of his linguistics have considerable historical import, as the theories of Condillac (*Essai sur l'origine des connaissances humaines*, 1746) and Blake's contemporary H. Tooke (discussed below) amply indicate.

[50] *Works of Reynolds* (1798), 1: 199. The edn. annotated by Blake. In their editions of Blake, neither Erdman nor Keynes quotes enough of Reynolds's paragraph to give the full context of Blake's annotation.

concerning Human Understanding, for Blake's typically energetic retort is to Locke as much as it is to Reynolds: 'This is False the Fault is not in Words. but in Things Lockes Opinions of Words & their Fallaciousness are Artful Opinions & Fallacious also' (E 659, K 474). We should not of course expect a full argument against Locke's *Essay* in a marginal note, but Blake is clearly critical of the sensibilist position that limits words to object-reference. The fault lies in an erroneous metaphysics to which Locke has, in Blake's view, bound his semiotics. Locke then brands as fallacious any linguistic extensions outside the referential system. From Blake's critique we can extrapolate some hints toward a concept of language he would agree to, one that celebrates the word capable of calling new thoughts, images—perhaps even worlds—into being. God's Word was not limited to the representation of that which already existed. Why should man's?

Blake's brief response to Locke via Reynolds calls to our attention a tradition of linguistic thought opposed to the rationalist school. We have already encountered, in the comments on Adam's language by Philo and Agrippa von Nettesheim, a transcendental version of primary motivation, dependent not on mimesis but on the divine (or at least divinely inspired) origin of Adam's language. Even Webster and the rationalist language projectors could accept this notion as long as it was safely ensconced in the prelapsarian past so as not to conflict with the Baconian version of the present. But others were less reluctant to extend the Adamic sign beyond the fall, beyond Babel. The attempt to uncover divine motivation hidden within extant languages—or to find, in Blake's words, 'the Divine Revelation in the Litteral expression' (*Milton*, Pl. 42; E 143, K 534)—defines the mystical tradition of linguistic thought.

The Hebraic tradition of Cabbala (or 'Kabbalah') and associated midrashic texts offer one of the oldest repositories of mystical attitudes toward language. According to Gershom G. Scholem, the Cabbalists held that 'letters and names are not only conventional means of communication. They are far more. Each one of them represents a concentration of energy and expresses a wealth of meaning which cannot be translated, or not fully at least into human language.' Further, there are causal links and formal similitudes between the 'process of Creation' and 'the process that finds its expression in divine words and in the documents of Revelation, in which the divine language is thought to have been reflected'.[51] Such views prompt the establishment of canonical writings as 'incarnational signs', as I have defined the term in Chapter 1. That is, certain texts, and even individual letters forming them, are taken to embody motivated signs and their divine meanings immanent within the arbitrary signs and their literal meanings.

The influence of Cabbala on Christian thought is a complex issue, but certainly the two traditions touched and intermingled in seventeenth-century England. Robert Fludd's *Mosaicall Philosophy* includes, as part of its potpourri of alchemical and mystical lore, a single omnibus sentence demonstrating one such point of contact:

> And there are some that will not shrink to say, that all the Species or kinds of creatures, were expressed in and by the 22. Hebrew letters, not those external ones which are vulgarly painted out with Ink or Art, which are but shadows; but the fiery formall and bright spirituall letters which were ingraven on the face or superficies of the dark hyles, by the fiery word of the eternall Speaker in the beginning, and therefore they are tearmed originally *Elementa quasi Hylementa*, or Elements; as engraven in the forehead of the dark abysse or Hyle, and by reason of the essence of that divine Word, which received the mystery of the Typicall creation, and did trace it out after the Archetypicall patern, and delineated it in characters of formall fire the language which was framed out of it was called *Lingua Sancta, a language* (I say) much spoken of by the learned *Rabbies* of our age, but little known or understood by them, and yet of an infinite importance, for the true enucleation as well of sacred Mysteries, as of all true Cabalisticall abstrusities.[52]

Fludd jumbles together, and thus in his own way forms a continuum among, God as the Word, the *Lingua Sancta* engraved in the very being of living creatures and the elements, and at least one of the languages of man. The common essence of their being, the 'Archetypicall patern', is semiotic. We have seen how the philosophical language projectors and (according to Blake) even Locke shaped their sense of words according to their sense of things. For these rationalist and sensibilist theorists, metaphysics is the ground

[51] *On the Kabbalah and its Symbolism* (1965), 36. See also Scholem, *Major Trends in Jewish Mysticism* (1941), esp. pp. 17–18. For some parallels between cabbalistic thought and Blake's, see A. A. Ansari, 'Blake and the Kabbalah', in Rosenfeld, *Blake*, pp. 199–220; Raine, *Blake and Tradition*, esp. 2: 210–13.

[52] *Mosaicall Philosophy* (1659), 161.

of semiotics. Fludd offers the reverse of this formula. The 'dark hyles', or undifferentiated matter, have existence independent of the Word, but all form and life are based in the universal extensions of divine semiosis. Conversely, all that is created by God's Word is itself a sign ultimately referring back to the Word. As Blake states in his annotations to Lavater's *Aphorisms*, 'every thing on earth is the word of God' (E 599, K87). Thus such notions as speaking trees, scorned by Warburton, have a serious basis in Cabbalistic linguistics. So too perhaps in the works of a poet for whom 'aged trees utter an awful voice' and 'roots . . . cry out in joys of existence'.[53]

Fludd's brief description of 'Cabalisticall abstrusities' serves as an apt introduction to the language theories presented, in repetitious bits and pieces, in the writings of the German mystic Jacob Boehme. It is probable that Blake became familiar with Boehme's works through the so-called 'Law's edition', published in four volumes between 1764 and 1781. Blake claims, in *The Marriage of Heaven and Hell*, that 'Any man of mechanical talents may from the writings of Paracelsus or Jacob Behmen, produce ten thousand volumes of equal value with Swedenborg's' (Pl. 22; E 43, K 158). In a letter of 12 September 1800 to John Flaxman, Blake included 'Behmen'—the Anglicized spelling used in Law's edition—in a group of people he had known either in person or through their writings (E 707, K 799). Twenty-five years later, in his conversations with Henry Crabb Robinson, Blake called Boehme 'a divinely inspired man' and praised 'the figures in Law's transl^{n}. as being very beautiful'. Frederick Tatham, who inherited many of Blake's possessions after Mrs. Blake's death in 1831, claimed in 1864 that he 'possessed books well thumbed and dirtied' from Blake's library, including 'a large collection of works of the mystical writers, Jacob Behmen, Swedenborg, and others'.[54] In the context of the present study, Boehme's writings clearly make special claims on our attention.

Comments on the signifying properties of God's creations permeate most of Boehme's works. But if we define 'language' somewhat more narrowly and limit it to sign systems consciously used by God or man, *The Mysterium Magnum*, in which Boehme weaves a history

[53] *French Revolution*, E 297, K 145; *Four Zoas*, Night the Ninth (E 401, K 373).

[54] Bentley, *Blake Records*, pp. 313 (Robinson's Diary, 18 October 1825), 41 n. 4 (Tatham's letter to F. Harvey, 8 June 1864). For a general study of possible influences, see B. Aubrey, *Watchmen of Eternity* (1986).

of language through a commentary on Genesis, stands out as a key text. Boehme begins conventionally with Adam naming '*all Things*, . . . each from its Property' and the '*one Language*' spoken before 'the Flood'.[55] Boehme immediately identifies this original speech with 'the Language of Nature' (35. 8) invested both in the 'Spirits of the Letters' (35. 13)—that is, in man's spoken and written language—and in the creations of God's Words. Unfortunately, 'of such a Gift (as the understanding of the Language of Nature) Mankind was *deprived* of at *Babel*' (35. 14). Yet for Boehme this fall from original vision does not mean that nature has totally lost its 'Language of Sense', for 'the Birds in the Air and the Beasts in the Fields understand it according to *their Property*' (35. 59). As he explains at length in the *Signatura rerum* (volume 4 in Law's edition), the internal 'signatures' are still present in all things. Similarly, the original and spiritual meanings of words have been lost only to our understanding, not to the words *per se*. These meanings manifest themselves in the physical acts of articulation—the position of the tongue and the movement of the breath, 'whether through the Teeth, or above, or with open Mouth' (35. 56). And it is here that Boehme situates the Adamic, motivated sign still in the languages of man, for 'as the *Word* was formed, so is also the *Thing* in its Form and Property, which is named by the Word' (35. 56). Since all human languages contain hidden remnants of the original divine and natural language, Boehme can use his native German as the basis for his linguistic theories, much as Blake's English served as 'the rough basement' (*Jerusalem*, Pl. 36; E 183, K 668) for his attempts at universal myth. In *The Aurora* (volume 1 in Law's edition), Boehme offers detailed analyses of individual German words according to a system of correspondences among the physiology of articulation, the sounds produced, and the alchemical properties of substances.[56] This approach would seem to depend on mimesis as its form of motivation, but Boehme tries to avoid such

[55] *Mysterium Magnum*, in *Works*, 3: 188–9 (ch. 35, para. 7, 12); hereafter cited by ch. and para. only. The relationships between Boehme's concepts of language and earlier linguistic theories, particularly those of Paracelsus and the Cabbalists, are set forth in W. Kayser, 'Böhmes Natursprachenlehre und ihre Grundlagen', *Euphorion*, 31 (1930), 521–62; French trans., *Poétique*, 3 (1972), 337–66.

[56] For an explication, perhaps a little clearer than Boehme's own, of this alchemical linguistics, see S. A. Konopacki, *The Descent into Words* (1979). Konopacki becomes so enmeshed in the details of Boehme's system that he fails to consider the larger linguistic implications.

dependency in *Mysterium Magnum* by erecting his system on the foundation of God's '*Verbum Fiat*' (16. 27), the semiosis underlying both signs and their referents. Utterance need not copy objects, for when rightly understood, both are part of the same universal 'Language of Nature' emanating from God. Whoever 'has the Understanding . . . of the *Spirits of the Letters*' and the 'framing of the Word, when [it] is formed or brought forth to Substance' in the mouth, is also 'able to understand the *sensual* (natural or *essential*) Language of the *whole* Creation, and understand *whence Adam gave Names unto all Things*' (35. 57). Much as we have seen in Fludd's commentary, Boehme finds a subtle bond between God's performative utterances that brought forms and properties into being, and the utterances we use to name them. Indeed, the whole mystical tradition in linguistics offers, in effect, a complex but resoundingly affirmative answer to the question asked by Albertus Magnus in his *De modis significandi* of *c.*1240: 'Are the modes of signification, of understanding and of being the same?'[57]

Boehme carries his history of motivated signs well beyond Babel. The 'Holy Spirit has spoken by the sensual Tongue in the *holy Penman* of the Scripture' (35. 63), and there the truly learned may read the original 'Language of Sense' (35. 59). The failure to understand this language has led to a conception of God as 'something with Form' but no substance, and thus 'dwelling apart from' man and his language (35. 65). Rather than seeing 'the holy God in the sensual Language' (36. 67) of their own tongue, men have treated their language as only an '*outward* contrived Vessell, and understood not the *Word* in its own proper Language of *Sense*; they understood not that God was *in* the speaking Word of the Understanding' (35. 68). Apparently in reference to written Hebrew, Boehme also claims that the loss of 'the *five* Vowels in the Alphabet' (36. 42) indicates the loss of 'the great holy Name of JEOVA or JESUS (*viz.* the living Word)' from our language (36. 43). 'The literal Form in the sensual Tongue is now the evil Beast', but the return of 'the Spirit of the five Vowels, *viz.* the Name JEHOVAH (which with the *H* has breathed the JESUS thereinto)' will destroy the beast and return language to its true form (36. 48). Christ '*rests* in the five Vowels *in his Grave*, viz. in the mental Tongue, which died in

[57] Quoted in R. H. Robins, *Ancient & Medieval Grammatical Theory in Europe* (1951), 80.

Adam' (36. 75). When Christ rises, and the vowels are returned to language, 'then he opens *all the Treasures of the heavenly Wisdom* in the sensual Tongue; so that Man does far more clearly understand the Spirits of the Letters' (36. 75). A resurrection within language will reveal the now hidden incarnation of spirit in language. For Boehme, linguistics and theology, the destiny of the soul and the history of language from Adam to Christ, are thoroughly intertwined.

Although couched in rhetoric both ponderous and enthusiastic, Boehme's linguistics touches on matters of continuing interest. His idea of fallen language includes both the Biblical multiplication of tongues and an internal division between substance and form, letter and spirit. Yet this divided condition is a creation of the beholder's eye—or his fallen theory of signs that separates them into a substance (signifier), an idea (signified), and an abyss between. When seen aright, letters and words are motivated signs uniting the mental and sensual tongues in a linguistic equivalent of the Devil's proclamation, in Blake's *The Marriage of Heaven and Hell*, that 'Man has no Body distinct from his Soul for that calld Body is a portion of Soul discernd by the five Senses' (Pl. 4; E 34, K 149). Boehme's distinction between language in its material presentations and the internal 'signatures' on which all understanding depends is a precursor to Saussure's division between *parole*, as language performance, and *langue*, the immaterial structure giving communicable meaning to the performance.[58] Boehme's similarity to Saussure on this point is particularly apparent at the beginning of *Signatura rerum*: 'For though I see one to speak, teach, preach, and write of God, and though I hear and read the same, yet this is not sufficient for me to understand him; but if his Sound and Spirit out of his Signature and Similitude enter into my own Similitude, and imprint his Similitude into mine, then I may understand him really and fundamentally, be it either spoken or written, if he has the Hammer that can strike my Bell' (1. 1). But the differences between Boehme and Saussure offer even more insight into the mystical tradition. While Saussure insists that 'in language there are only differences *without positive terms*',[59]

[58] See Saussure, *Course in General Linguistics*, esp. ch. 4, 'Linguistics of Language and Linguistics of Speaking', pp. 17–20.
[59] *Course in General Linguistics*, p. 120.

words and even individual letters and sounds are positivities, even substances, for Boehme. In this sense, Boehme is a linguistic materialist, in spite of his obvious dedication to transcendental meanings. This combination of spirit and matter, or meaning and linguistic act, with the former immanent within the latter, defines the incarnational sign. And whereas Saussure takes the distinction between *parole* and *langue*—and its companion difference between signifier and signified at the level of the individual sign—as fundamental to all semiosis, Boehme holds that these are the very divisions that must be overcome for true understanding. This conversion of the differential into the incarnational sign requires a great deal from its audience, even extending to an abnegation of self to merge with the sign. As Boehme writes in *Signatura rerum*, 'he that is born from within out of the speaking Voice of God in God's Will-Spirit, he goes in the Byss and Abyss everywhere free, and is bound to no Form; for he goes not in Self-hood, but the Eternal Will guides him as its Instrument, according as it pleases God: but he that is born only in the Letter, he is born in the Form of the expressed Word, and goes on in Self-hood, and is a self-ful Voice; for he seeks what he pleases, and contends about the Form, and leaves the Spirit which has made the Form.'[60] In *A Vision of the Last Judgment*, Blake asks for a similar responsiveness from the viewers of his pictorial signs: 'If the Spectator could Enter into these Images in his Imagination approaching them on the Fiery Chariot of his Contemplative Thought if he could Enter into Noahs Rainbow or into his bosom or could make a Friend & Companion of one of these Images of wonder which always intreats him to leave mortal things as he must know then would he arise from his Grave then would he meet the Lord in the Air & then he would be happy' (E 560, K 611). By giving up independent 'Self-hood'[61] and entering into incarnational signs, man can become a companion to their immanent meanings, arise like Boehme's Christ from '*the Death* of the Letters' (*Mysterium*

[60] 15. 22. In this context, 'Form' means the visual or auditory shape of the sign, not some transcendental form or immaterial system.

[61] I take this term from *Signatura rerum*, but Blake made it his own, using it 22 times in his writings. See the discussion in ch. 4 of Blake's sense of Selfhood in its relationship to textual production. Although my observations here do not depend on sources or verbal echoes, it would seem that Boehme's sense of how intelligible signs 'enter into' the auditor's consciousness (*Signatura rerum* 1.1, quoted above) is the complementary mirror-image of Blake's hope that the spectator will 'Enter into' the visual signs of the artist.

Magnum, 36. 49) to return them to their original significance as covenants with God's Word, and overcome the multiple dualities dominating the fallen vision of language—signifier and signified, *langue* and *parole*, spirit and matter, artist and audience, man and his signs.

Blake's comparison between Boehme and Emanuel Swedenborg, quoted earlier, supplies a not altogether unfair critique of the latter's linguistic concepts. Instead of harkening back to Adam in Eden as the main historical precedent for an ideal language, Swedenborg shifts to the language of angels.[62] In several works, Swedenborg stresses the vast difference between angelic and human language; as he states in *The True Christian Religion*, 'the angels spoke . . . spiritually, and spiritual language embraces thousands of things which natural language cannot express, and, what is wonderful, which cannot even fall into the ideas of natural thought'.[63] Swedenborg rises even further toward the ineffable in the *Arcana coelestia* when he claims that angels do not use words at all but converse in 'the universal of all languages, by means of ideas, the primitives of words'.[64] The two modes, human and heavenly, can 'communicate with each other only by correspondences'—that is, by reading the lower, more limited language as an allegory of the greater.[65] These views are antithetical to the concept of the incarnational sign, so important in Boehme's linguistics, but elsewhere Swedenborg describes the words of angels and of the Bible as material signifiers with immanent spiritual meanings. In *A Treatise concerning Heaven and Hell*, he develops a variation of Boehme's theme of prelapsarian Hebrew. Swedenborg receives from the angels 'a little paper . . . on which were written some words in Hebrew characters, and it was told me that every letter contained some secrets of wisdom, nay the very flexures and curvatures of the letters, and the sounding of them from thence'. This is no ordinary Hebrew,

[62] For a bizarre 16th-century precursor to Swedenborg's theorizing, see D. C. Laycock, *Complete Enochian Dictionary* (1978).

[63] *True Christian Religion* (1915), 1: 494, sec. 386.4. Blake annotated 3 of Swedenborg's books and probably read a good many others; see Tatham's statement about Blake's library, quoted earlier. For a general study of Swedenborg's influence on Blake, see M. D. Paley, ' "A New Heaven is Begun": Blake and Swedenborgianism', *Blake: An Illustrated Quarterly*, 13 (1979), 64–90.

[64] *Arcana coelestia* (1928), 2: 268, sec. 1641.

[65] *Angelic Wisdom concerning the Divine Love and the Divine Wisdom* (1915), 156, sec. 295.

but a special form known only to angels, although once it 'also was the manner of Writing by the most ancient inhabitants of our earth, before the invention of letters; and . . . afterwards translated into [conventional] Hebrew characters, which were all inflexed formerly, and not terminated by spaces, as at present: hence it is, that the Word contains divine and heavenly secrets, even in it's jots, tittles, and points.'[66] But the ideal of angelic language does not mean that man can dispense with literal meanings when reading the Bible. He comes to know 'the Lord by means of the Word because He is the Word'. Within the literal 'sense of the letter . . . there is a spiritual and celestial sense; and the angels are in these senses, the angels of the Lord's spiritual kingdom in the spiritual sense of the Word, and the angels of His celestial kingdom in its celestial sense' (*True Christian Religion*, sec. 234). The literal cannot be discarded, for 'the Word in the sense of the letter . . . protects the spiritual sense, which lies hidden within, as the wall does a city and its inhabitants'.[67] Even though 'it appears as if the literal sense vanishes or dies through the internal sense . . . it does not vanish, still less dies; but through the internal sense it lives' (*Arcana coelestia*, sec. 8943). Like Boehme, Swedenborg indicates that the perception of the 'spiritual sense' requires special qualities in the reader. He must be 'enlightened by the influx of the light of heaven' to 'see truths in their connexion and thence in their form; and the more he so sees them, so much the more interiorly is his rational mind opened' (*Apocalypse Revealed*, sec. 911). Boehme asks the true believer to give himself over to the spirit of the letters; Swedenborg requires his followers to be inspired before they can find the spirit in the letters. In both cases, the sign requires for its completion the active participation of its perceivers to close the gap between letter and spirit. The incarnational sign thereby approaches the triadic condition of the kerygmatic or performative sign. 'Motivation', in its special semiotic sense, merges with the motivation, the desire, of man to marry his words with the Word of God. The process is circular, and avoids solipsism only for

[66] *Treatise concerning Heaven and Hell* (1784), 148–9, sec. 260. This edn. annotated by Blake. See also sec. 236, where Swedenborg explains the motivated character of the angels' spoken language, one in which 'the sound of the voice corresponds to the affection, and the articulations of that sound, or words, to the ideas of the thoughts . . .'. Thus their language 'may be called a sounding affection, and a speaking thought'.

[67] Swedenborg, *Apocalypse Revealed* (1949), 1: 331, sec. 898.

those who have faith in a transcendental power, arising from within or descending from above, that makes possible a language without a difference between what it *is* and what it *means*—a language the very existence of which is denied by those who, from Locke to Saussure and Derrida, are equally convinced of the differential nature of all linguistic signs.

The almost sacrilegious invocation of the author of *An Essay concerning Human Understanding* is enough to jolt us out of mystical realms and back to the rationalist linguistics of the eighteenth century. Locke established the terms of several leading debates over the nature and origin of language. Perhaps his most important contribution was to make an explicit principle what the universal grammarians and language projectors had only assumed—that the study of language was a branch of philosophy, not theology. Conversely, the very presence of an entire section 'Of Words' in an essay on human understanding indicates the impossibility of disengaging philosophical propositions from the medium of their execution. 'When I first began this Discourse of the Understanding', Locke confesses, 'and a good while after, I had not the least Thought, that any Consideration of Words was at all necessary to it. But when having passed over the Original and Composition of our *Ideas* [in bk. 2 of the *Essay*], I began to examine the Extent and Certainty of our Knowledge [bk. 4], I found it had so near a connexion with Words, that unless their force and manner of Signification were first well observed [bk. 3], there could be very little said clearly and pertinently concerning Knowledge: which being conversant about Truth, had constantly to do with Propositions' (3. 9. 21). For Locke, the relationship between ideas and language was often one in which the latter prevented the clear expression of the former, an attitude that assumes a conceptual difference between the two, at higher levels of philosophical insight, even if they are interdependent in practice. The very title of J. D. Michaelis's *Dissertation on the Influence of Opinions on Language and of Language on Opinions* (1760, English translation 1769) implies the same distinction. Other eighteenth-century treatises indicate an increasing sense of the unity of idea and sign, knowledge and proposition. In his highly influential *Essai sur l'origine des connaissances humaines* (1746), Condillac describes how, in the early history of man, the use of 'signs insensibly enlarged and improved the operations of the mind, and on the other hand these having acquired such improvement, perfected the signs, and rendered the use of them more familiar'.[68] Given such reciprocal improvement, Monboddo could find that, 'from the study of language, if it be properly conducted, the history of the human mind is best learned'.[69] Mutuality grows even closer to unity in Herder's *Ursprung der Sprache* of 1772. The 'invention of language', Herder proposes, is 'as natural to man as it is to him that he is man'. Reflection itself, the focusing of mind on a particular image, requires a 'distinguishing mark' to indicate 'that this object is this and not another'. With this mental mark, 'human language is invented!'[70] Herder gives to consciousness itself a semiotic character, an intra-subjective language corresponding in its mode of operation to the visual or auditory systems of intersubjective communication. Friedrich Schlegel, in the *Philosophie des Lebens* (1828), brings this line of thought to its logical conclusion: 'For as speech must be regarded as a thinking outwardly projected and manifested, so, too, thinking itself is but an inward speaking and a never-ending dialogue with oneself.'[71] Accordingly, 'what is a fact of all human language is of course a fact of all human consciousness', as Coleridge claimed.[72] These correspondences form a secular parallel to Boehme's theology of language, with the internal discourse of human consciousness replacing the Logos.

Arguments for the unity of mind and language depend in part on the 'mentalist' view of reference, discussed earlier as one of two competing theories of signification in Locke's *Essay*. But he was hardly the first to consider the psychological basis of linguistic structures, for this approach can be traced back through medieval grammatical theory to the Greek Stoics.[73] Nor was Locke the major representative of mentalism for eighteenth-century England. That distinction goes to James Harris's *Hermes: or, a Philosophical*

[68] *Essay on the Origin of Human Knowledge* (1756), 173–4.
[69] *Of the Origin and Progress of Language*, 1: 574.
[70] J. G. Herder, *Essay on the Origin of Language* (1966), 115–16.
[71] *Philosophy of Life, and Philosophy of Language* (1847), 388. For a surprising anticipation of Continental thought on the unity of language and consciousness, see D. Defoe, *Mere Nature Delineated* (1726), 38–9: 'Words are to us, the Medium of Thought; we cannot conceive of Things, but by their Names, and in the very Use of their Names; . . . we cannot muse, contrive, imagine, design, resolve, or reject; nay, we cannot love or hate, but in acting upon those Passions in the very Form of Words.'
[72] *Logic* (1981), 82.
[73] See Robins, *Ancient & Medieval Grammatical Theory*, pp. 25, 75.

Inquiry concerning Language and Universal Grammar (1751), arguably the most important contribution to its subject between Locke's *Essay* and Horne Tooke's *Diversions of Purley* (1786). For Harris, the existence of 'general or universal ideas' proves that there are 'Forms intelligible, which are truly previous to all Forms sensible'.[74] The Platonism of his argument becomes clearly evident in Harris's claim that 'the whole visible World exhibits nothing more, than so many *passing* Pictures of these *immutable Archetypes*' (pp. 383–4). The priority of mind over the senses and their objects leads Harris to conclude that ' 'tis of these comprehensive and permanent Ideas, the genuine Perceptions of pure Mind, that Words of all Languages, however different, are the Symbols'.[75] Thus we are once again presented with universal and transcendental signifieds not so very different from Boehme's formulations of spiritual reference.

The distinction between mentalist and sensibilist theories would seem to provide a convenient paradigm for understanding the course of eighteenth-century linguistics. Yet what we usually find in the texts of the period is an uneasy mingling of both views. Harris offers a particularly clear case of this tendency, for in direct conflict with his avowed mentalism, he claims 'that the *first Words* of Men, like their *first Ideas*, had an immediate reference to *sensible Objects*, and that in after Days, when they began to discern with their *Intellect*, they took those Words, which they found *already* made, and transferred them by metaphor to *intellectual* Conceptions' (p. 269). Harris's point here, and even his use of 'transferred', echoes the passage from Book 3 of Locke's *Essay*, quoted earlier, often cited as a fundamental statement of sensibilist principles. Given such contradictory compounds, the separation of mentalism and sensibilism into mutually exclusive doctrines is at best a useful simplification.[76] Further, the inherent conflicts between the two

[74] *Hermes* (1751), 350, 381.

[75] P. 372. By 'Symbol' Harris means arbitrary sign, as distinct from 'Imitations' (see pp. 331–2, 336).

[76] I believe that this is also true of Land's attempt, in *From Signs to Propositions*, to define 18th-century linguistics as a shifting of emphasis from the sign/referent structure to the relationships among signs in propositions. This perspective produces some important insights, but is no more accurate as a general observation than D. E. Wellbery's contrary contentions that, 'within the representational paradigm of knowledge characteristic of the Enlightenment, the notion of the sign plays an essential, organizing role', and that 'the sign in eighteenth-century thought is inextricably bound up with a primordial act of naming'. Wellbery, *Lessing's Laocoon* (1984), 2, 19.

positions devolved, like so many philosophical issues in the eighteenth century, into a question of origins—specifically, whether the noun or the verb was the radical from which all other parts of speech evolved.[77] This chicken-or-egg argument became the eighteenth-century focus for the Adamic debate, for whichever grammatical form came first raises the issue of primary motivation and relegates all others to the secondary motivations internal to language. The mentalist position would logically tend toward the verb as primary, since it can signify thought processes such as naming, while the sensibilist view should be more comfortable with the noun, the name given to perceived objects. Condillac, for example, follows his sensibilist inclinations when he claims that 'language was a long time without having any other words than the names which had been given to sensible objects'. 'The first verbs were contrived' out of 'names' and used 'only to express the disposition of mind, when we either act or suffer'.[78] Herder, as part of a complex argument not easily labelled either sensibilist or mentalist, directly disputes Condillac's view. Although the act of naming is primary for Herder, the action rather than the object shapes the original form of speech. 'The thought of the thing itself was still hovering between the actor and the action: The sound had to designate the thing as the thing gave forth the sound. From the verbs it was that the nouns grew and not from the nouns the verbs. The child names the sheep, not as a sheep, but as a bleating creature, and hence makes of the interjection a verb.'[79] We also find a mingling of theories in *Hermes*. In spite of his mentalism, Harris leans toward the noun as the first form, but finds 'to be', the verb substantive, as a useful middle position—a strategy later employed with much more sophistication by Coleridge in his *Logic*.

Once the original part of speech, noun or verb, was established, the 'progress of language', as Monboddo called it, was usually characterized by eighteenth-century philosophical grammarians as a process of substitution, refinement, abbreviation, and abstraction

[77] For an overview of this debate, including its roots in Plato and Aristotle, see McKusick, *Coleridge's Philosophy of Language*, pp. 34–38.

[78] *Essay on the Origin of Human Knowledge*, pp. 238–9. For Condillac's theory on how verbs developed out of adjectives, see pp. 245–7.

[79] *Essay on the Origin of Language*, p. 132. Monboddo is more directly assertive of the verb's priority, at least in Greek and Hebrew; see *Of the Origin and Progress of Language*, 2: 188, 211, 219.

as language evolved ever further from its root forms. Condillac again provides a useful example. 'Abstract substantives', he claims, are the product of a 'decompound[ed]' noun and adjective; hence, the general concept of 'greatness' was derived from phrases such as 'great King'.[80] Analyses of this type support the view expressed succinctly by one of Monboddo's chapter headings: 'The progress of abstraction and generalization deduced from the progress of language'.[81] Such progress could not of course occur without the proliferation of new words and grammatical categories. This necessity seems to have prompted David Hartley's surprising reinterpretation of the fragmentation of Adamic speech. Rather than the products of a tragic diminution in man's linguistic powers, 'the new languages' after Babel 'far exceeded the old common one in the number and variety of words'. Thus 'the confusion of tongues was by this means a beneficial gift and blessing to mankind' which 'does also both help the invention, and correct false judgments' (*Observations on Man*, p. 181). Whatever its primitive form may have been, language had progressed sufficiently to allow Harris to define it as 'A System of articulate Voices, the Symbols of our Ideas, but of those principally, which are general or universal' (*Hermes*, p. 349).

Sensibilists and mentalists shared a common sense of the teleology of language even as they disagreed over origins. The destiny of signs was to become ever more abstract. In Hartley's opinion, this movement leads to 'the abstract terms of logicians, metaphysicians, and school-men' which 'have spiritualized men's understandings, and taught them to use words in reasoning, as algebraists do symbols' (*Observations on Man*, p. 181). In terms of the internal structure of signs, the signifier, as a physical presence, is suppressed as much as possible in the pursuit of the transparent revelation of spirit as the final, transcendental signified. This 'effacement of the signifier', as Derrida calls it, provides the linguistic complement to the progress of Enlightenment 'science' as 'the movement of idealization: an algebrizing, de-poetizing formalization whose operation is to repress—in

[80] *Essay on the Origin of Human Knowledge*, pp. 244–5. See also J. Beattie, *Theory of Language* (1788), 128, on the derivation of 'Abstract Nouns . . . by abstracting, or separating, from any natural or artificial substance, either real, or imaginary, certain qualities, and making those qualities the subject of meditation or discourse'.

[81] *Origin and Progress of Language*, 1: xi. See also 1: 573 for Monboddo's sense of the development of language and mind from lower to higher levels of abstraction.

order to master it better—the charged [i.e. motivated] signifier or the linked hieroglyph' (*Of Grammatology*, p. 285).

Derrida's sweeping generalization achieves much of its power by repressing an important counter-movement. Theorists interested in the first forms of language, including Condillac and Herder, had to work back from the sophisticated languages of their age to discover the less abstract and more sensate precursors. This deconstructive method was elevated into an essential principle by Horne Tooke in Ἔπεα πτερόεντα*: Or, the Diversions of Purley*, the first volume of which appeared in 1786. Tooke accepts the need for abstracted and abbreviated signs in discourse, but finds that the processes by which they were invented are 'productive of error'.[82] Equating meaning with origin, Tooke wishes to cast off the obfuscations of philosophical grammar and return to the source of all words in nouns or verbs denoting sense experiences. Accordingly, Tooke directly attacks Harris and calls for a return to the principles of Locke's *Essay*—or at least to those that support Tooke's sensibilist position. Reversing Harris's concept of mental archetypes, Tooke finds that there are no 'ideas, but merely *terms*, which are *general* and *abstract*' (1: 37). These terms have given rise to the chimerical impression that there are general ideas existing only as mental categories. Tooke's sensibilism is so complete that he even chides Locke for occasional slips into mentalism and claims that 'the business of mind, as far as it concerns Language, . . . extends no farther than to receive Impressions, that is to have Sensations or Feelings' (1: 51).

Etymology is the instrument Tooke uses to pry into the original meanings of abstract terms. The parts of speech generally thought not to have extrinsic reference, such as conjunctions and prepositions, receive particular attention in the first volume of the *Diversions of Purley* to demonstrate how even they can be traced back to their sources in sense experience. In the second volume, not published until 1805, Tooke even carries etymology below the level of words and into morphemes, claiming that 'all those *common* terminations, in any language, of which all Nouns or Verbs in that language equally partake (under the notion of *declension* or *conjugation*) are

[82] *Diversions of Purley* (1798), 1: 25. Although couched as a dialogue, the speaker denominated as 'H' presents Tooke's ideas; his interlocutors do little more than offer leading questions. For a comprehensive study of Tooke's ideas and influence, see H. Aarsleff, *Study of Language in England* (1967), chs. 2 and 3.

themselves separate words with distinct meanings' (2: 432). Such analyses bear a structural parallel to the mystical interpretation of individual letters of the alphabet, even though the meanings revealed could not be more different. Much as Boehme's linguistics can be described as a form of verbal alchemy, William Hazlitt claimed that 'Mr. Tooke . . . treated words as the chemists do substances; he separated those which are compounded of others from those which are not decompoundable'.[83]

By Tooke's era, etymology had received considerable praise from philosophers and grammarians as a route to linguistic and epistemological knowledge, although the technique was never applied with his single-minded thoroughness. Locke's brief comments on the derivation of terms 'from the Operations of sensible Things', quoted earlier, provided the spark for Tooke's far more ambitious investigations. Michaelis expresses a common view of etymology when he describes it as 'a treasure of sense, knowledge, and wisdom' and as a reservoir of 'truths which most philosophers do not see into'.[84] Etymology could also serve the purposes of an antiquarian mythographer like Jacob Bryant, who found that 'the only way of obtaining insights' into the origins of culture 'must be by an etymological process, and by recurring to the primitive language of the people, concerning whom we are treating' (*A New System*, 1: xiv). The growing interest in etymology through the eighteenth and into the nineteenth century provided an historicizing counterbalance to theories of linguistic progress toward abstraction. Etymological derivations, from the *Cratylus* to modern dictionaries, operate on the level of the signifier: words are joined through shared sounds or (more rarely) spellings. Unlike modern etymologists, who make extensive use of simple sound shifts, eighteenth-century practitioners freely manipulated words through a variety of figural dislocations, such as punning, synecdoche, and metonymy, which allegedly changed one word into another over time. Just as Harris claimed that words denoting '*sensible Objects*' were 'transferred [from] them by metaphor to *intellectual* Conceptions', Tooke and like-minded

[83] *Spirit of the Age* (1825), 125. My comparison of Tooke and Boehme accords with Aarsleff's observation (*Study of Language in England*, p. 54) that Tooke's philosophy 'contains the germs of a very romantic and nearly mystical notion of language'.

[84] *Dissertation on the Influence of Opinions on Language and of Language on Opinions* (1769), 12.

etymologists tried to reverse the engines of metaphor and recover original meanings. Although his goal was to reduce all words to literal forms of reference, the method deeply engaged Tooke in the figurative. We have seen how the universal grammarians of the seventeenth century tried to establish language on the basis of a taxonomic matrix. But 'in order to go back to the origins', as Tzvetan Todorov has observed, 'we rely on the tropic matrix'.[85]

Near the beginning of the *Diversions*, Tooke notes that, during his trial for seditious libel in 1777, he was 'made the miserable victim of—*Two Prepositions and a Conjunction*' (1: 74). This combined legal and grammatical issue prompted Tooke to write his disquisition on the word 'that', first published in *A Letter to John Dunning*, a pamphlet of 1778. The motivation for Tooke's etymological deconstructions is but one indication of the more general and more important connections between linguistics and radical politics at the end of the eighteenth century.[86] It is an age that demonstrates Julia Kristeva's observation that 'the traversing of the system' of signs 'coincides with the moment of social rupture, renovation and revolution'.[87] In Tooke's *Diversions*, such 'traversing' takes the form of an attack on mentalism, abstraction, and their attendant cultural values. Michaelis offers a typical example of these values when he observes that 'every language, before it has gone through philosophic hands, must of necessity be wanting in proper terms for denoting such objects which do not come within the senses, and especially metaphysical ideas' (*Dissertation*, p. 5). The proper development of language is granted to an intellectual élite who can purge language of its grosser forms and add to its powers of abstraction. This implicit class-consciousness becomes explicit in Samuel Johnson's Preface to his great *Dictionary*. When he began his work, Johnson found 'our speech copious without order, and energetick without rules'. Not surprisingly, it is the 'duty' of the good Tory 'lexicographer to correct or proscribe' these free-wheeling 'improprieties and absurdities', including those created by the 'casual

[85] *Theories of the Symbol* (1982), 231.

[86] For a general study of this subject, see O. Smith, *Politics of Language* (1984). My observations here are in accord with Smith's general thesis 'that late eighteenth-century theories of language were centrally and explicitly concerned with class division and that they cannot be entirely understood without their political component being taken into account' (p. viii).

[87] 'Signifying Practice and Mode of Production', *Edinburgh Magazine*, 1 (1976), 64; first pub. as the intro. to Kristeva, ed., *La Traversée des signes* (1975).

and mutable' diction of 'the laborious and mercantile part of the people'.[88] In short, linguistic freedoms must be tamed by those educated in the mastery of words; speech must be corrected by the stabilizing powers of writing. Tooke's etymologies are attempts to counter this expropriation of language by returning it to sense experiences available to all social classes. With its emphasis on the history of the signifier, etymology asserts the value of the material body of signs that all may perceive. At the same time, it tends to devalue the abstract meanings attributed to signs by the ruling classes as an instrument of intellectual, moral, and political power. By reducing the ethical terms 'right' and 'law' to their supposed roots as past participles in Latin and Anglo-Saxon respectively, Tooke shows how 'Participles and Adjectives, not understood as such, have caused a metaphysical jargon and a false morality, which can only be dissipated by etymology' (2: 18). As Michaelis had pointed out long before, but without the reformist zeal of Tooke, 'language is a democratic state' in which 'etymology is the voice of the people' (*Dissertation*, pp. 12, 73).

Tooke's avowed intentions illuminate the political implications of earlier linguistic programmes. The ideal languages invented by seventeenth-century projectors like Wilkins would, if instituted as a general means of written communication, affect the forms of political and legal discourse as much as scientific publications. A truly universal language would tend to lessen the strength of linguistic/political divisions that arose at the Tower of Babel. Comenius, one of the forerunners of the rationalist projectors of England, even gives an apocalyptic dimension to language reform with his belief that only through a 'language absolutely new, absolutely easy, absolutely rational, in brief a Pansophic language' could 'the commonwealth of men, now torn to pieces, be restored, a single speech granted again to the world, and the glory of God increased by so splendid a method'.[89] While the seventeenth century provides some precursors to Tooke's use of linguistic speculation as an agency of social change,

[88] Johnson, Preface, *Dictionary of the English Language* (1755), 1: [1, 8].

[89] *Way of Light* (1938), 8, 188. Knowlson, who quotes these lines from Comenius, further contends that 'most projects of universal language in the seventeenth century do, in fact, refer at some point to the confusion of tongues at Babel, their authors often claiming that the new character of language would in itself provide a remedy for this curse' (*Universal Language Schemes*, p. 9).

we can find among his contemporaries evidence of his influence on the rhetoric of political discussion. In *The Rights of Man*, Thomas Paine attacks aristocratic titles as dangerous abstractions that have left us 'immured within the Bastille of a word'. Like an etymologist tracing a word to its origin in natural sensation, Paine sets out to 'trace the rights of man to the creation of man'.[90] This same perspective, and even something of the tone of Tooke's *Diversions*, is continued by Jeremy Bentham in his discussion of titles and the class distinctions they enforce: 'Amongst the instruments of delusion employed for reconciling the people to the dominion of the one and the few, is the device of employing for the designation of persons, and classes of persons, instead of the ordinary and appropriate denominations, the names of so many abstract fictitious entities, contrived for the purpose.'[91]

Although there is no direct evidence for Blake having read the *Diversions of Purley*, it seems more than likely that he was familiar with Tooke's views on language. The *Diversions* was highly regarded in its day for revolutionizing the study of language, and its author was one of England's most famous radical politicians. In the 1790s, Blake was at least on the fringes of the circle of artists and writers associated with Joseph Johnson, the publisher of the first and second editions of the *Diversions*. Blake's friend of many years, George Cumberland, knew Tooke well and wrote a biography of him.[92] In 1798, Cumberland designed a new frontispiece for the second volume of the *Diversions* and, in a letter to Tooke, recommended the 'true son of Freedom Mr Blake' as its engraver.[93] The design was not used, but Cumberland's appellation for Blake hints at political sympathies shared by all three men. Finally, in about 1855, John Linnell wrote a list of events and persons important in Blake's life, apparently as an *aide-mémoire* during discussions with Gilchrist about his forthcoming biography of Blake (1863). 'Godwin, Paine,

[90] *Rights of Man* (1791), 45, 67.

[91] *The Constitutional Code*, in *Works of Bentham* (1841), 9: 76.

[92] The unpublished manuscript, 'Anecdotes of, and Letters from, John Horne Tooke', is described in G. E. Bentley, Jr., *Bibliography of Cumberland* (1975), 85–92. According to Bentley, the 'Anecdotes' contain brief references to Tooke's linguistic interests. E. Darwin, whose *Botanic Garden* contains engravings by Blake (see ch. 1 n. 39), appended to his *Temple of Nature* (1803), a 14-page note on 'The Theory and Structure of Language' that praises and briefly summarizes Tooke's theories.

[93] Bentley, *Bibliography of Cumberland*, p. 92.

H. Tooke' appear in this list, along with the names of Stothard, Fuseli, and others Blake knew well.[94] Blake would have had a hard time avoiding familiarity with Tooke's political and philological ideas, if not the man himself.

Blake's belief in the spiritual nature of man and his artistic productions places Blake in direct conflict with Tooke's Lockian programme of reducing all words to roots naming sense experiences in the physical world of objects and events. Indeed, the long-awaited appearance of Tooke's second volume in 1805 may have been one of several texts prompting Blake's declaration in *Milton* (*c.*1804–8) that 'every Natural Effect has a Spiritual Cause, and Not | A Natural' (Pl. 26; E 124, K 513). However, other theories and methods in the *Diversions* are companionable with Blake's. Tooke's attack on general, abstract terms and their ability to mask original meanings is echoed by Blake's contentions that 'General Knowledge is Remote Knowledge' and 'To Generalize is to be an Idiot'.[95] Nor was Blake any less aware than Tooke of the political uses of abstraction—how, for example, a 'Priesthood' had 'enslav'd the vulgar by attempting to realize or abstract the mental dieties from their objects'.[96] Even though Tooke limits mind to a receptacle for sensations, his methodology assumes a firm bond between idea and sign. Thus, the manacles that he believes have been forged by abstract words are close companions to the 'mind-forg'd manacles' Blake hears 'in every voice' of London's citizens (E 27, K 216). To free us from the conceptual and linguistic restraints of general ideas, Blake asks that we 'Consult Particulars' and 'Labour well the Minute Particulars',[97] much as Tooke seeks original meanings by focusing on individual morphemes.[98] Tooke's etymological treatment of these semantic units seizes on their figural relationships as traces of

[94] Linnell's list is known only from a transcript made by his son; see Bentley, *Blake Records*, pp. 318–19 n. 2.

[95] *Vision of the Last Judgment*, E 560, K 611; annotations to Reynolds, E 641, K 451.

[96] *Marriage of Heaven and Hell*, Pl. 11; E 38, K 153. Tooke refers to the judges who made him 'the miserable victim' of three abstract terms as 'officiating Priests' (*Diversions*, 1: 74).

[97] Annotations to Reynolds (E 645, K 456); *Jerusalem*, Pl. 55 (E 205, K 687). See also Blake's response to Reynolds's appeal to 'a rule, obtained out of general nature': 'What is General Nature is there Such a Thing what is General Knowledge is there such a Thing (*Strictly Speaking*) All Knowledge is Particular' (E 648, K 459).

[98] Blake's 'particulars', however, are not the same as Tooke's 'particles' (1: 19), a term used by 18th-century grammarians for words without apparent reference, such as conjunctions and prepositions.

real, motivated, historical connections among words. By tracking these connections to their sources, Tooke tries to reclaim the literal. Converting analysis to synthesis, a 'literal realist of imagination'—as Yeats so accurately dubbed Blake[99]—might try to create figural patterns with etymological motivation—that is, patterns on the level of the signifier revelatory of truths on the level of the signified. As Nelson Hilton has demonstrated, much of Blake's wordplay operates in this Tookean manner, revealing truths within the context of Blake's thought even when not 'etymological' (i.e., historical) outside the boundaries of his poetry.[100] We will have occasion in later chapters to return to these connections between the figural matrices of the etymologist and of the poet.

Neither clever etymologies, operating through regressive figuration, nor universal grammar, operating through the logic of progressive schematization, extends beyond the limits of secondary motivation to explain how radical forms had first come into being. Questions about primary motivation—the cause of human language outside and prior to human language—had been answered for centuries by Genesis, but the desacralizing philosophers and grammarians of the eighteenth century were no longer convinced by the *deus ex machina* of the Biblical exegetes. We have already seen this change in Warburton's *Divine Legation of Moses*, but even those who continued to believe in the divine origin of language tended to follow Locke in denying the special character of Adamic speech. Thomas Stackhouse is typical in this respect. After blandly accepting the notion that 'it was God . . . alone who was truly the Author of the first Tongue', he then questions the concept of linguistic motivation. Genesis 2: 19 'does not in the least signify that the Name express'd its [the beast's] Nature; and those that understand this Passage in this Sense, would in my Opinion, find in it a meaning which it no wise has'.[101] But in the midst of questioning the expressive 'Energy'

[99] W. B. Yeats, 'Blake and his Illustrations to *The Divine Comedy*', *Savoy*, no. 3 (1896), 45. Marianne Moore paraphrases Yeats's comment ('literalists of | the imagination') in her famous poem 'Poetry'; in turn, Frye used yet a third version ('A Literalist of the Imagination') as the title for the 4th chapter of *Fearful Symmetry*.

[100] *Literal Imagination*. The claim that Tooke's etymological methods and Hilton's critical premises are interrelated is mine, not Hilton's. Like Tooke, some of Hilton's analyses take morphemes to be referential terms; see for example his discussion of 'me-/-tals', pp. 250–1.

[101] *Reflections on the Nature and Property of Language* (1731), 23, 31. This book is based in part on J. Frain du Tremblay's *Traité des langues* (1709), trans. into English by 'M.H.' [i.e., M. Halpenn] as *A Treatise of Languages* (1725).

of Hebrew, Stackhouse suggests a way back to primary motivation: 'For I cannot comprehend that one simple Word shou'd express the Nature of a Thing, otherwise than by reason of the accidental [i.e., arbitrary and conventional?] Union of the Idea of that Thing to that Word. For if it were so, the Words which constitute that *Tongue*, wou'd be so many Natural Signs, and have a necessary Connexion with the Thing it self, which we cannot see to be any way possible' (p. 30). In spite of Stackhouse's doubts, the discovery and description of 'Natural Signs' as the source from which the arbitrary signs of known languages were derived became major themes in eighteenth-century philosophical linguistics. Having discarded the Adamic sign, rationalist philosophers found it necessary to invent a secular substitute, a way of generating conventions out of nature without recourse to God.

Eighteenth-century concepts of natural signs, both mimetic and expressive, have been illustrated in Chapter 1 by Blake's painting of Eve and in this chapter by Warburton's theory of a language of gesture. Here we need only consider the link between primary and secondary motivation through the evolution of arbitrary out of natural signs. Onomatopoeia offers a rather obvious possibility;[102] but even if the first words were imitative in this way, the naming of things without an identifiable auditory presence would still require explanation. To overcome such difficulties with a mimetic approach, Condillac turns to expressive theory and suggests a simple process of associative transference from 'cries of the passions' to the indicative use of the same cries when the motivating passion is not present but only recollected. When the 'memory' of primitive men 'began to acquire some sort of habit, they were able to command their imagination as they pleased, and insensibly they learned to do by reflexion what they had done merely by instinct. . . . For example, he who saw a place in which he had been frightened, mimicked those

[102] Condillac, *Essay on the Origin of Human Knowledge*, p. 181, claims 'that the first names of animals probably were made in imitation of their cries: a remark which is equally applicable to those that were given to winds, to rivers, and to every thing that makes a noise'. Vico, *New Science*, p. 150, states that 'articulate language began to develop by way of onomatopoeia, through which we still find children happily expressing themselves'. See also C. de Brosses, *Traité de la formation mécanique des langues* (1765), in which words are etymologically reduced to root sounds somehow imitating the non-auditory things they name. For informative summaries of de Brosses and his follower, A. C. de Gébelin, see Genette, 'Peinture et dérivation' and 'L'hiéroglyphe généralisé', in *Mimologiques*, pp. 85–148.

cries and movements which were the signs of fear, in order to warn the other not to expose himself to the same danger.' The next step was to utter a variety of sounds at random and, on the basis of the habitual patterns developed through the use of natural signs, gradually to associate each sound with a particular referent. Men 'articulated new sounds, and by repeating them several times, and accompanying them with some gesture which pointed out such objects as they wanted to be taken notice of, they accustomed themselves to give names to things'.[103]

Several theorists of the natural sign show a considerable interest in the difference between inarticulate and articulate utterance. This topic has received little attention from modern historians of eighteenth-century linguistics, perhaps because it would seem to relate to a merely mechanical contingency. Yet the difference was taken to be crucial by Condillac and Monboddo, for articulation marked the transition between direct expression of present emotion and the ability to join sounds together to express related ideas and thereby form propositions. Monboddo refers to the sounds of 'articulate animals' in Book 3 of his treatise on *The Origin and Progress of Language* (1: 492), but in Chapter 14 of Book 1 he takes great pains to show that articulation is not even natural to man, but must be learned. The acquisition of this skill is, for Monboddo, one with the early proliferation of vocal signs that in turn necessitated the development of grammatical structures. Without articulation, man could not have developed language out of the emotive utterances common to animals and pre-linguistic man. As we shall see in Chapter 5, Blake developed eighteenth-century theories of articulation into an important motif in his later poetry.

The companion distinctions between natural and arbitrary signs, and between inarticulate and articulate sounds, place the interjection in the earlier and more primitive part of each division. Harris, in his anatomy of grammatical categories, established the common eighteenth-century opinion that 'Interjections coincide with no Part of Speech' and are 'Voices of Nature, rather than Voices of *Art*, expressing those Passions and natural Emotions, which spontaneously arise in the human Soul, upon the View or Narrative

[103] *Essay on the Origin of Human Knowledge*, pp. 173–4. Monboddo, *Origin and Progress of Language*, 1: 318–26, presents a similar argument, but with less clarity and precision.

of interesting Events' (*Hermes*, pp. 289–90). Even Tooke follows Harris on this point, devoting a chapter to 'the Article and Interjection' and claiming that 'the brutish inarticulate *Interjection* . . . has nothing to do with speech' (*Diversions of Purley*, 1: 60). For Tooke, 'The dominion of Speech is erected upon the downfall of Interjections'; they are now used voluntarily only 'when the suddenness or vehemence of some affection or passion returns men to their natural state' (1: 62–3). Herder describes the interjection—'those howling and wailing tones'—in the 'elegies' of 'the oldest Oriental languages' as 'a continuous interjection of the language of nature' (*Essay on the Origin of Language*, p. 91). The presence of interjections in written language harkens back to the pre-grammatical and pre-articulate origins of utterance, a fragment of nature within the conventions of art. This rather obscure point in eighteenth-century grammatical theory may not be irrelevant to the language of a poet who used the interjection 'O' 555 times.[104]

The concept of natural signs and the theory that language evolved from them found common cause with the study of so-called primitive languages. They would presumably contain lexical structures only one or two steps removed from natural signs and thus reveal something about the origins of language and culture. Monboddo, for example, makes frequent reference to the language of the Huron Indians to support his concepts of how the first language began. The interests of philosophical grammarians and etymologists intersected with those of antiquarians to form the eighteenth-century beginnings of philology and cultural anthropology. Because of its clear and immediate connections with literary concerns, this tradition in linguistic thought is a particularly important context for the study of Blake's language.

Mimetic theories of natural signs—Müller's 'bow-wow' group—imply that the first languages would in some sense be close to nature; the expressive or 'pooh-pooh' theories suggest that they would be highly emotive. Both criteria were used as touchstones for determining what constituted a primitive language. Not too surprisingly, the languages thereby discovered (or invented) corroborated these

[104] See D. V. Erdman, ed., *Concordance to the Writings of Blake* (1967), 2: 2181, 'Index Words in Order of Verse Frequency'. Among the words included, only 'all' appears more frequently in Blake's poetry.

criteria. Close contact with nature was evinced by a wealth of natural imagery, while the emotive sources of primitive languages gave rise to energetically figurative modes of speech. As Rousseau asserts in his *Essai sur l'origine des langues*, first published in 1781, 'man's first motives for speaking were of the passions', and hence 'his first expressions were tropes'.[105] For Hugh Blair, even the limitations of the first speakers contributed to their figural richness because 'the want of proper and precise terms for the ideas they would express, obliged them to have recourse to circumlocution, metaphor, comparison, and all those substituted forms of expression, which give a poetical air to language'.[106] As etymologists like Tooke were busy showing, figuration—everything from simple sound homologies to elaborate types of substitution—was a form of secondary motivation; and Condillac, Monboddo and others had demonstrated the transformation of primary into secondary motivation through the theory of natural signs. If the first linguistic structures to develop out of natural signs were tropological, then the figural matrix evolved before logical and grammatical forms. This would seem to be the line of reasoning behind such statements as Condillac's that 'the style of all languages was originally poetical' (*Essay on the Origin of Human Knowledge*, p. 228) and Rousseau's that 'at first only poetry was spoken; there was no hint of reasoning until much later' (*Essay*, p. 12). And if the first form of speech was poetic, then all poetry might contain at least fragmentary intimations of the original, motivated forms of language. As Herder comments in *The Spirit of Hebrew Poetry* (first published 1782–3), 'among all nations, who are not wholly savage, a feeble echo at least is still heard respecting the blissful golden age of their ancestors. The poets, always the most uncorrupted and susceptible of impressions among a people, . . . have seized upon these traditions.'[107] Poetry, rather than a decorative feature superadded to language, was viewed by Blair, Rousseau, Herder, and many other theorists as superior to

[105] *Essay on the Origin of Languages* (1966), 12. See also H. Blair, *Lectures on Rhetoric and Belles Lettres* (1783), 2: 322–3, for similar opinions.

[106] *A Critical Dissertation on the Poems of Ossian* (1763), 2. See also Vico, *The New Science*, p. 153, for how 'poetic language . . . was born entirely of poverty of language and need of expression.'

[107] *The Spirit of Hebrew Poetry*, 1: 123. A. W. Schlegel continues this line of thought in his comments on wordplay in poetry as an attempt to 'restore the lost resemblance between the word and the thing'. *A Course of Lectures on Dramatic Art and Literature* (1846), 366.

logical discourse because of its contact with origins. By the last few decades of the eighteenth century, the pursuit of the motivated sign had become an aesthetics of primitivism. When Adam named the beasts he composed a poem, not a taxonomy. The poets, not the philosophers or theologians, would lead man—or at least his language—back to 'the blissful golden age'.

In the foregoing paragraph I have condensed a very complex group of historical developments into a single argument. It may be a further simplification to claim that this summary constitutes a theory, or even an 'episteme',[108] but something like this medley of interrelated ideas shaped attitudes toward signs, origins, and poetry held by many of the writers and readers of Blake's generation. The sensibility and poetics of this period have received a good deal of attention from modern scholars; their observations on primitivism, the interest in comparative mythology, and the taste epitomized by James Macpherson's Ossianic forgeries need not be reiterated here.[109] But to continue a history of the motivated sign, we need to consider the concepts of signs implicit in late eighteenth-century aesthetics and some of the byways of linguistic speculation in the period.

According to primitivist theory, the tropes of poetry recall a linguistic condition only once removed from natural signs. To this historical recapitulation, Lessing added a further connection between the primary motivation of natural signs and the secondary motivation of figuration: 'It [poetry] . . . has a means of elevating its arbitrary signs to the status of natural signs, namely metaphor. For, since the forcefulness of natural signs consists in their similarity with things, poetry introduces—instead of this similarity, which it doesn't possess—another similarity which the signified object has with a second object.'[110] Linguistic signs, with the exception of

[108] See *The Order of Things*, pp. 30–2, where Foucault implicitly defines his now famous term as designating 'the epistemological configuration' of an historical 'period' which underlies and determines what will be recognized as 'knowledge' in that period.

[109] The classic study remains M. H. Abrams, *The Mirror and the Lamp* (1958); see particularly ch. 4, part 3, 'Primitive Language and Primitive Poetry'.

[110] G. E. Lessing, *Anti-Goeze* (1778), quoted in Wellbery, *Lessing's Laocoon*, p. 195. Wellbery makes many salient observations in his section on 'Poetry as Natural Sign' (pp. 191–203), but my arguments here about the differences between the natural and the poetic sign, particularly the direct referentiality of the former and the non-referential indirections of the latter, disagree sharply with Wellbery's attribution of 'transparency' to poetic language (p. 233). For another discussion of Lessing's concepts of motivation, see Todorov, *Theories of the Symbol*, ch. 5, 'Imitation and Motivation', pp. 129–46.

onomatopoeic words, cannot become natural signs. To overcome this limitation in the referential capabilities of the vast majority of words, the poet (like the primitive speakers of the first language) must substitute relational parallels: one word will relate figuratively to another in a manner isomorphic with the relationships between the things named. This type of secondary motivation, when stated in Lessing's very general, structural terms, bears some similarities to the taxonomic programmes of seventeenth-century ideal language projectors, but with the crucial substitution of the figural for the grammatical matrix as the ground on which the relationships between terms will be constructed. And while a taxonomic system requires exclusive and direct correspondences between signifiers and their signifieds, the figural system requires that the signifier be freed from its arbitrary bondage to a single signified so that its manifold relationships with other signs can become apparent. Only then can language replicate the complex interrelationships among things—assuming, of course, that nature is organized tropologically, not logically.

The emphasis on the signifier and the freedom granted to it are among the most important features of the linguistic and poetic theories of the eighteenth century that have become associated with, or seen as precursors to, romanticism. Polysemy and connotation—the 'exuberance of signification' Johnson complains about in the Preface to his *Dictionary* (p. [6])—were welcomed as ways of overcoming the limitations of arbitrary and univalent reference. Like figuration, they also establish multiple relations among terms and extend their emotive range. What was described by rationalist grammarians as the 'progress' of language toward higher forms of abstraction and concision was seen by the aestheticists as a fall from its original essence. 'The more ossified and urbane customs become', Herder wrote, 'and the more passions cease to have much influence in the world, the more will language lose its natural objects. . . . Perhaps language becomes more perfect but it also loses its true poetic character.'[111] The non-referential or multi-referential powers of language replaced direct and exclusionary reference as its most valued functions. 'That which can be made Explicit to the Idiot is

[111] *Über die neuere deutsche Litteratur* (1767), quoted in J. H. Stam, *Inquiries into the Origin of Language* (1976), 112.

not worth [Blake's] care' because explicit signification leaves out so much that 'rouzes the faculties to act' in response to the full potency of signs (Blake's letter to Trusler, E 702, K 793). The semantic surplus of the poetic sign, its energetic escape from the logical paradigms of reference to suggest more than it literally signifies, was not viewed as an encumbrance or threat but as evidence of creative potential, a remnant of the Word's original plenitude.[112] Since this semantic surplus, this invitation to add meanings beyond the literal, can be realized only through the active engagement of the reader's 'faculties', the poeticized sign reaches toward the triadic condition of the kerygmatic sign as its ideal form. The figural density of poetic discourse, its twists and turns and unwillingness to reveal transparently a single meaning, became a resource rather than an impediment. When these characteristics were allowed to flourish, words could become the vehicles of 'genius' and 'sublimity', both also redefined in the late eighteenth century as the exceeding of conventional and referential limits. These semiotic freedoms were the natural allies and expressions of individual liberties in the political arena. To borrow from Blake's 'Proverbs of Hell', linguistic 'Improvement makes strait roads, but the crooked roads' of poetry 'are roads of Genius'. These are the 'roads of excess' in semiotic activity that lead 'to the palace of wisdom' and to the 'Exuberance' that 'is Beauty' (E 35, 38, K 150, 152).

We can find in the prose poems of Ossian some of the stylistic features that were in part created by Macpherson in response to, and in part helped to shape, the primitivist and aestheticist theories of language I have summarized in general terms. The repetitiousness of these works—itself an indication of their supposedly ancient character—allows me to use the beginning of *Fingal* to exemplify the whole:

Cuchullin sat by Tura's wall; by the tree of the rustling leaf.—His spear leaned against the mossy rock. His shield lay by him on the grass. As he

[112] A theory of semantic surplus can be traced back at least to J. Addison's concept of the 'Secondary Pleasure of the Imagination' and the way 'A Description often gives us more lively Ideas than the Sight of Things Themselves'. See *The Spectator*, no. 416 (27 June 1712), in D. F. Bond, ed., *Spectator* (1965), 3: 559–60. See also T. Weiskel, *Romantic Sublime* (1976), 24, on how 'any excess on the part of the object cancels the representational efficacy of the mind . . .'. To restore its balance, the mind reconstitutes 'the very indeterminacy' into which it has been thrown 'as symbolizing the mind's relation to a transcendent order'.

thought of mighty Carbar, a hero whom he slew in war; the scout of the ocean came Moran son of Fithil.

Rise, said the youth, Cuchullin, rise; I see the ships of Swaran. Cuchullin, many are the foe: many the heroes of the dark-rolling sea.

Moran! replied the blue-eyed chief, thou ever tremblest, son of Fithil: Thy fears have much increased the foe. Perhaps it is the king of the lonely hills coming to aid me on green Ullin's plains.

I saw their chief, says Moran, tall as a rock of ice. His spear is like that blasted fir. His shield like the rising moon. He sat on a rock on the shore: like a cloud of mist on the silent hill.—Many, chief of men! I said, many are our hands of war.—Well art thou named, the Mighty Man, but many mighty men are seen from Tura's walls of wind.—He answered, like a wave on a rock, who in this land appears like me? Heroes stand not in my presence: they fall to earth beneath my hand. None can meet Swaran in the fight but Fingal, king of stormy hills. Once we wrestled on the heath of Malmor, and our heels overturned the wood. Rocks fell from their place; and rivulets, changing their course, fled murmuring from our strife.[113]

Even in this alleged translation of a poem into prose, repeated syntactic units of approximately the same length carry the language forward in a stately, if monotonous, quantitative cadence. Smaller clusters are knit together with alliteration: 'fears have much increased the foe,' 'many mighty men', 'walls of wind'. Both characteristics speak to the supposed musicality of the first language, which, according to Rousseau, 'would be sung rather than spoken' (*Essay*, p. 15). In the earliest cultures, music, poetry, and their gestural expression through dance had not yet split into different forms. This was the thesis announced by the title of John Brown's *Dissertation on the Rise, Union, and Power, the Progressions, Separations, and Corruptions, of Poetry and Music*, in which the author commends the 'naturall Alliance of these three *Sister-Graces, Music, Dance, and Poems*, which we find moving Hand in Hand among the savage Tribes of every Climate'.[114] The unity attributed to the natural sign and its referent is matched by the unity of the media in which such signs—and their figural successors—first arose. It was also widely held that the earliest poems were oral compositions. Thomas Blackwell introduced this idea in his *Inquiry into the Life and*

113 *Fingal* (1762), 1–3.

114 *Dissertation* (1763), 28. Condillac, *Essay on the Origin of Human Knowledge*, p. 178, was one of the first to suggest the common origins of language, a 'dance of gesture', and harmony.

Writings of Homer (1735), Robert Lowth speculated briefly on the original oral delivery of the Biblical prophecies and their subsequent scribal transmission in his verse translation of Isaiah (1778), and John Pinkerton described the characteristics of what we would now call oral-formulaic poetry in his essay 'On the Oral Tradition of Poetry' appended to his edition of *Scottish Tragic Ballads* (1781). Macpherson was well aware of Blackwell's views, later developed by Robert Wood in *An Essay on the Original Genius and Writings of Homer* (1769). In his Dissertation prefatory to *Fingal*, Macpherson claims that the 'species of composition' exemplified by the poems of Ossian 'was not committed to writing, but delivered by oral tradition' (p. xiii). The simple rhythmic patterns, so evident in the passage from *Fingal* quoted above, indicate its supposed source in oral composition. As Macpherson points out, the musical and formulaic nature of the verse aided memorization, for 'each verse was so connected with those which preceded or followed it, that if one line had been remembered in a stanza, it was almost impossible to forget the rest' (p. xii). The repeated structures also establish metonymic associations and evoke the parallelism of the Bible, a technique first brought to light by Lowth in *De sacra poesi Hebraeorum* (1753).

The presence of alliteration and absence of rhyme also suggest the antiquity of *Fingal*; as Pinkerton explains, 'alliteration was before the invention of rime greatly used'.[115] But it is the poem's grammatical and figural structures that most clearly indicate the qualities identifying the first languages, including their relative proximity to natural signs. All the imagery is drawn from nature. Persons are given the attributes of nature through similes ('Moran, tall as a rock of ice') and natural objects are animated with emotions and will ('rivulets, changing their course, fled murmuring from our strife'). The poet and his culture have not yet arrived at that state of language and consciousness placing them in opposition to nature. Thus Ossian evokes the 'naïve' as that term was defined by Friedrich Schiller in *Über naive und sentimentalische Dichtung* (1795–6). A few adjectives and adverbs appear, but the language remains stark, with an emphasis on unmodified nouns and verbs, the forms of speech claimed by Condillac, Monboddo, and others to be the first to develop out of natural signs. Some adjectives ('mossy', 'stormy')

[115] 'On the Oral Tradition of Poetry', in *Scottish Tragic Ballads* (1781), p. xxi.

are clearly made from nouns; others ('many are the foe') are placed syntactically in the position of noun subjects. Both features point to the theory that adjectives first evolved from names. Participles used as adjectives ('rustling leaf', 'dark-rolling sea', 'blasted fir') indicate the alternative view that modifiers evolved out of verbs. Rousseau claimed that the first language would have 'few . . . abstract names for expressing . . . relationships' but 'would have many augmentatives, . . . composite words, [and] expletive particles'. It 'would deemphasize grammatical analogy for euphony, . . . and would represent without reasoning' (*Essay*, p. 15). Rousseau may have had Ossian's poems in mind, for we find in *Fingal* no abstractions, very few terms to indicate relationships between parts of the narrative, and the use of 'composite words' as formulaic modifiers ('dark-rolling sea', 'blue-eyed chief'). The specific has preference over the general, even to the extent of using far more definite than indefinite articles.

Similes, sometimes three in immediate succession, are the most prominent form of figuration. The presence of 'like' or 'as' standing between the compared terms establishes their separate identity at the same time it proclaims similitude. We are thereby placed at an inchoate stage in the development of language when the competing claims of the figural and grammatical matrices, of unity and logical discrimination, are particularly evident.[116] The relative paucity of connective terms between syntactic units also tends to reinforce their semantic separateness. As Blair notes, converting an absence along the signifying axis into an opportunity along the affective axis, Ossianic poetry contains 'no artful transitions; nor full and extended connection of parts, . . . leaving several circumstances to be supplied by the reader's imagination' (*Dissertation*, p. 18). In many passages, the only indication of temporal sequence, much less relationships of cause and effect, is the actual sequence of the clauses. Thus, to read *Fingal* as a story of consecutive events, we assume a parallel between syntax and the arrangement of events in time. The individual signifiers are arbitrary, but their ordering has the mimetic motivation of a natural sign. As Stackhouse explained in 1731, 'All the Rules

[116] Warburton, in his genealogy of tropes, states that the apologue or fable was the first form, subsequently abbreviated into simile and finally into metaphor (*Divine Legation of Moses*, 2: 93–4).

then, which regard the Order of our Ideas, are so Essential to Discourse, that they depend not on the Caprice or Fancy of Men, but are as Natural to a Language, as it is for Fire to produce Smoak' (*Reflections*, p. 26). Later in the century, Lessing extended this concept of syntactic motivation from the order of ideas to the order of things: 'Thus, even if the words are not natural signs, their sequence can still possess the forcefulness of a natural sign. Namely in cases when all the words follow upon one another exactly like the things they express.'[117]

The enormous celebrity of Macpherson's Ossian was probably due in part to the way these poems both confirmed and stimulated theories of primitive language and their concomitant political principles. In this sense, Ossian's language, covertly subversive of mid-eighteenth-century concepts of linguistic progress, is a forerunner to Rousseau's natural man and Tooke's democratic revolt against abstraction. *Fingal* and its companions appeared to their contemporary admirers to have a more than usual level of motivation—linguistically, in their proximity to natural signs, and psychologically, in their performative ability to stimulate 'the reader's imagination', as Blair claimed. The cadences and tropes evoke emotional intensity, but we are given few directives toward general or abstract meanings because of the paucity of relational terms. We are thrown back on discrete noun and verb units that, like Adamic naming, are but one step removed from the pre-linguistic particularity of things and actions themselves. As when confronted by a lofty cliff, we are invited to inscribe our own meanings on it in proportion to our heightened emotions, including an initial sense of deprivation or disorientation. It is difficult for us now to think of the poems of Ossian as anything more than notorious fakes, but in their day they seemed to many readers to have a sublime voice like one of nature's own.

In 1826, Blake confessed himself 'an admirer of Ossian equally with any other Poet' and a believer that what Macpherson and Thomas Chatterton 'say is Ancient, Is so'. In these same annotations to Wordsworth's *Poems* of 1815, Blake also noted that 'Natural

[117] *Laokoon* (1880), 431 (quoted in Wellbery, *Lessing's Laocoon*, p. 198). For a more detailed discussion of syntactic motivation, or 'mimésis phrastique', see Genette, *Mimologiques*, pp. 183–226.

Objects always did & now do Weaken deaden & obliterate Imagination in Me' (E 665–6, K 783). These apparently contradictory comments can be reconciled if we shift from a sensibilist to a mentalist approach to the language of Ossian, a perspective that posits the origin and ideal form of signs not in mimetic but in expressive motivation. We may then observe in *Fingal* not objects but a mind in its elemental linguistic engagement with objects through acts of naming, comparing, and attempting to find order in the flux of events. The emphasis now falls more on the medium in which signs come into being than on their referents, more on the nature of linguistic phenomena than on the phenomena of nature. This interpretive focus, the offspring of a union between an 'Ancient' poem and eighteenth-century linguistic theory, will be worth considering again when we confront one of Blake's similarly ancient texts, such as *The* [*First*] *Book of Urizen*.

The interest in Northern European languages and cultures produced theories as well as poems exploring their motivated origins. Some of these speculations are the forebears of nineteenth-century discoveries about the Indo-European family of languages, but others recall the Adamic myths and mystical theories of an earlier era. In the 1760s and 1770s, a small group of highly imaginative etymologists looked to Celtic and English as keys to the original, motivated language. Rowland Jones was the first to set out along this path in *The Origin of Language and Nations* of 1764, a title that suggests the common late eighteenth-century proclivity for using language derivations to prop up more general theses about cultural history. Jones's preface, however, reads like a return to sixteenth- and seventeenth-century themes: he begins with Adam naming the beasts according 'to the property and qualities thereof' and proceeds to the bold anti-Lockian proposal 'that language ought not to be considered as mere arbitrary sounds, or any thing less than a part, at least, of that living soul, which God is said to have breathed into man'. Through the etymological study of Celtic, 'the first speech of mankind', Jones hopes to recover 'those primary signs transmitted from Adam amongst his posterity, and preserved at all times in some corner of the world, whereby such as once lost their language at Babel, might again recover a rational scheme of speech'.[118] Jones has given a Celtic accent to some very old tunes.

[118] *Origin of Language and Nations* (1764), Preface, [2–4]. Blake may have learned about

Jones repeats and extends his ideas through a series of four more short tracts: *Hieroglyfic* (1768), *The Philosophy of Words* (1769), *The Circles of Gomer* (1771), and *The Io-Triads* (1773). In the second of these, he argues specifically against Locke's theory of knowledge and proposes his own 'Universal Philosophical Language' based on English, which he believes is a derivative of ancient Celtic.[119] By analysing English into its 'primitive particles' (roughly equivalent to morphemes or single letters), Jones hopes to reconstruct the original 'hermetic language' in which the 'letter forms' had a 'hieroglyfic nature' (pp. 6, 41, 42). His more than a little obtuse, but thankfully brief, demonstrations indicate that by 'hieroglyfic' he means both auditory and visual mimesis as the basis of motivated signs having a 'natural connection with things'. A language built out of such signs 'must be far preferable, as well as more practicable, than the arbitrary real characters of Dr. Wilkins and others' (p. 11). Here again, Jones steps out of the mainstream of linguistic thought of his age and joins an earlier tradition, attempting to succeed where the language projectors of the previous century had failed by treating the letters of our familiar alphabet in the same way Cabbalistic writers analysed Hebrew or Boehme manipulated German.

Jones continues his plans for a motivated language in *The Circles of Gomer*. In this volume he treats English as 'the best Celtic dialect' and claims 'that no other language can make so near an approach to the first universal language, and to natural precision and correspondence with ideas and things, as the English in the form and mode it has been here introduced as an universal language; for in short the author has discovered the first language'.[120] Jones admits that most languages have fallen into the arbitrariness described by Locke, but he believes that English has preserved much of its original, motivated root forms or 'hieroglyfic and argrasic [i.e., acrostic] prototypes' (p. 30). Jones offers long lists of comparisons between English and Hebrew words—with some Greek, Latin, and Gallic tossed in for good measure—to show that they share the same

the literature of Celtic lore from William Owen (or William Owen Pughe), the great enthusiast for the Welsh language and culture. For Blake's contacts with Owen, see Bentley, *Blake Records*, pp. 226, 399–400; and G. E. Bentley, Jr., 'The Triumph of Owen', *National Library of Wales Journal*, 24 (1985), 249–61.

[119] *Philosophy of Words* (1769), 12.

[120] *Circles of Gomer* (1771), 30, 41.

linguistic 'prototypes' of an ancient Celtic culture.[121] Place names are particularly important in Jones's system, for they 'consist of certain lines or chords, springs, circles, semicircles, surfaces, sides, divisions or parts, figures and letters, which as symbols and articulate sounds or voices, describe and represent the elements and parts of nature'.[122] Eden, Eden in North Wales, and Ederington in Suffolk all have the same source, while Babel and Babingley in Norfolk both derive from a prototype meaning 'spring water place' (pp. 17, 70). Many of Jones's roots and hieroglyphic letter forms refer to water or parts of the body, including 'the sea and river, the vulva and penis, and the mouth and tongue' (p. 30). The letter *t* 'hieroglyfically represents man's legs and thighs close together with the toes outwards' (p. 4). Although the tradition of anthropomorphized letter shapes extends back at least to the Middle Ages, Blake may have had something like Jones's symbolism in mind when he drew several small figures in rigid or contorted postures on page 74 of his *Notebook*. As Erdman has noted, several of these human forms seem to be 'stylized into letters of the alphabet and similar shapes'.[123]

John Cleland, of *Fanny Hill* fame, is an unexpected contributor to Celtic studies. In *The Way to Things by Words* (1766), he attempts to recover ancient Celtic, a language that exhibits the original 'harmony of words and things'.[124] Cleland claims that his etymological reductions will also aid 'in disembroiling the chaos of the antient mythology' of the Greeks (p. ii), a task later undertaken by Jacob Bryant in his *New System, or, an Analysis of Ancient Mythology* (1774–6). Yet whereas Bryant traces the names of the gods to Near Eastern roots, Cleland finds that 'the heathen mythology had a Celtic original' (p. v) in the rites of the Druids. When the Romans conquered Britain, 'their mythology could not . . . but be matter of the greatest scorn and derision to the Druids, whose invention it can be demonstrated to have been, purely in

[121] The notion that Hebrew and Celtic have much in common was first noted by 17th-century scholars; see for example C. Edwards, *Hebraismorum Cambro-Britannicorum specimen* (1675), in which cognates in the two languages are arranged in columns to show how they 'sing in symphony'.

[122] 'An Universal English Grammar', p. 1, appended to *Circles of Gomer*.

[123] *Notebook of Blake* (1977), 74 and facing commentary. Blake also sketched a few Hebrew letters composed of human bodies on the back of a drawing for *Tiriel Denouncing His Sons and Daughters* (Butlin no. 199, where 'some such works as Peter Flötner's alphabet of *c.*1535–40' are suggested as a model).

[124] *Way to Things by Words* (1766), p. iv.

allegorical, but never in a theological sense. Thence it came, that the names of those fabulous Deities, Jupiter, Mars, Mercury, &c. so often used in allegory and astrology, must have been as familiar in Britain and in Gaul, as in Rome, Athens, or Egypt' (p. 109). Cleland implies that the names of gods had indicated, in their original Celtic forms, the qualities attributed to each figure within allegorical fables. Later cultures, including the Greeks, forgot the motivated meanings of these names and transformed poetic personifications into deities.

In *An Essay toward an Investigation of the Origin and Elements of Language and Letters* (1772), L. D. Nelme pays little heed to Celtic lore, but proposes that 'English-Saxon' preserves elements of the original language in which '*sounds* or *symbols* [i.e., letters], must bear such a likeness of the idea or object to be represented, as to obtain the concurrence and assent of the person to whom the *sound* or *symbol* is offered'.[125] Since the 'roots' of the '*radical* language . . . still exist in most languages, and especially in the English' (p. xiii), Nelme treats letter shapes as directly 'expressive of Ideas' through visual analogy, much as in Jones's system. Two forms, the vertical line and the circle, play the most important roles. The latter represents 'the boundary of sight, or horizon' (frontispiece), much as Blake's pictorial representations of Urizen—probably a play on both 'your reason' and 'horizon' or its Greek root—are frequently dominated by circular forms. Nelme's interests were not limited to the merely antiquarian, for like the seventeenth-century projectors he believed that 'one primordial set of *Ideas*, *Symbols* and *Sounds*, were once common to all; and, that some one set of *Sounds* or Language, shall again become universal, and probably be a means of an universal uniformity in religious worship' (p. x). For Nelme, this millennial recuperation of original linguistic and religious unity can be prefigured, perhaps even assisted, by revealing the motivated foundations of English.

The antiquity of the Druids and related themes were continued into the next century by Edward Davies's *Celtic Researches, on the Origin, Traditions & Language, of the Ancient Britons* (1804). In the last section of his book, an 'Essay on the Celtic Language', Davies offers a surprisingly cogent summary of the concept of natural signs,

[125] *Essay* (1772), pp. ii, 3–4.

including gestures, and theories of how languages evolved from them. His claims for Celtic are far more restrained than those of his predecessors. Rather than proposing Celtic as the original tongue, Davies groups it with Hebrew as one of several ancient languages he subjects to etymological analysis to demonstrate how their 'sounds may have appropriate relations to the ideas, which the mind intends to convey'.[126] 'Material accidents and changes' have 'affected elementary sounds, and characters' (p. 390) in most languages, including Hebrew, but the ancient Celts conserved at least remnants of the original, natural signs. In Davies's view, this premiss is supported by the language and poetic tales of 'our primitive order of *Druids*, and their successors, the *Bards of Britain*' (p. 370).

Several modern commentators have claimed that Blake was a latter-day 'Bard of Britain' who continued Druid lore in his epics *Milton* and *Jerusalem*.[127] His statements that 'Adam was a Druid' and that 'All things begin & end in Albions ancient Druid rocky shore' lend unmistakable support to this general thesis.[128] Given his interest in the Druids, Blake would have found it difficult to avoid the concepts of language origins and motivated signs that were a part of so many Celticist studies. When read within the context of Nelme's tract, *All Religions are One*—Blake's title for what is probably his first illuminated book—suggests an equivalent unity of languages, while the theories of Jones and Nelme about the priority of Celtic/English offer an etymological and historical rationale for Blake's habit in *Jerusalem* of referring to the locations of ancient events 'by their English names: English, the rough basement' (Pl. 36; E 183, K 668). For our present purposes, however, specific parallels are less important than the crucial role theories of motivated signs played in the eighteenth-century study of Anglo-Celtic culture. By considering the history of words as part of their signification, and by appreciating the way extra-linguistic forces such as migrations and conquests shaped that history, eighteenth-century Celticists and mythographers

[126] *Celtic Researches* (1804), 368.

[127] The best exposition of this thesis, with particular reference to Jones and Davies, is A. L. Owen, *Famous Druids* (1962), esp. pp. 179–92, 224–36. On Blake's possible knowledge of Davies's book and its influence on Blake's writings after 1804, see also Frye, *Fearful Symmetry*, pp. 173–5.

[128] *Descriptive Catalogue*, E 542, K 578; *Milton*, Pl. 6 (E 100, K 486). Blake's description of his painting, *The Ancient Britons* (now lost), in *A Descriptive Catalogue* includes his most explicit and detailed account of 'the Druidical age' (E 542–3, K 577–8).

could elevate etymology nearly to the status of primary motivation. For Jones, Nelme, Cleland, and Davies, the genealogies of cultures were one with the etymologies of their words. Accordingly, we should be alert to the linguistic corollaries implied by Blake's statements about subjects such as mythology, religion, and the visual arts.

The British Celticists were not alone in using language as a key to cultural history and identity. In the first volume of *The Origin and Progress of Language* (1773), Monboddo proposes that language could not have been invented before men banded together in social groups. Although he argues against it, Monboddo also offers the converse proposition 'that there could be no Society without Language'.[129] The mutual interdependence of language and society became an increasingly important assumption in the historical study of languages, such as Sir William Jones's work on Sanskrit and other Asiatic languages, but it is in Germany that this working hypothesis was elevated into a general philosophy of language.[130]

As those major eighteenth-century issues, the structure of signs and propositions and the origin of language, began to lose their preeminence for Herder, Friedrich Schlegel, and others, they turned to the activity of discourse and the relationships it establishes among speakers as phenomena that define what language does and what it is. This perspective informs Herder's celebration of communication in *The Spirit of Hebrew Poetry*: 'How great a mystery is involved in the fact, that the soul thinks, the tongue speaks, and the hand executes; that our soul thinks, others understand and listen to it merely by means of the breath of the mouth. To God himself, nothing could be ascribed, it would seem, more powerful than a word, a breath' (1: 164–5). These bonds among speaking, hearing, and understanding receive their finest exploration in the works of Wilhelm von Humboldt, beginning with 'Latium and Hellas' in 1806, extending through his 1812 'Announcement' of a study of the Basque language and the essay on comparative linguistics of 1820, and concluding with the general introduction to his unfinished study of the Kawi language, 1830–5.

[129] *Origin and Progress of Language*, 1: 279. Monboddo attributes this idea to Rousseau.

[130] I am here skipping over many complex developments in order to summarize basic concepts. For information on Jones, F. Schlegel, and the contributors to the 'New Philology', see Aarsleff, *Study of Language in England*, pp. 115–61.

Humboldt's performative or phenomenological approach to language is founded on an almost mystical sense of communication as a continual reenactment of primal unity. 'Language everywhere mediates first between infinite and finite nature, then between one individual and another. Simultaneously and through the same act it makes union possible and itself originates from it. The whole of its nature never lies in singularity but must always be guessed or intuited from otherness.'[131] Here and elsewhere in Humboldt's work, the binary structure of the sign (sign and referent, or signifier and signified) is supplemented by the field of interchange between two parties, speaker and auditor, necessary for language to be a medium of communication. To the ideal union of word and world, represented by the Adamic or motivated sign, Humboldt adds a vision of humanity's original unity granted by the very act of exchanging words no matter what their referents. 'It [language] is the brightest trace and the surest proof of the fact (leaving out for the moment the celestial relatives of mankind) that man does not possess an absolute segregated individuality, that "I" and "Thou" are not merely interrelated but—if one could go back to the point of their separation—truly identical concepts, and that there exist, therefore, only concentric circles of individuality, beginning with the weak, frail single person who is in need of support and widening out to the primordial trunk of humanity itself' (p. 236).

While the single sign disappears as the nexus of motivation for Humboldt, the concept spreads everywhere through his comments on the reciprocal relations among self, other, and the medium that joins them. He wishes to disabuse his readers of the dominant eighteenth-century ideas on the natural origins of language and its evolution into a system of conventions. 'Only one must free oneself of the notions that language . . . is a product of reflection and agreement, an agreed-upon code, as it were, or in fact that it is any work of man at all (in the common sense in which one takes that phrase), not to mention the work of some individual' (p. 236). But rather than returning to traditional arguments for the divine origin of language, Humboldt posits 'the indivisibility of human consciousness and human speech', of which 'the mutual interdependence

[131] 'Announcement of an Essay on the Language of the Basques', *Humanist without Portfolio*, pp. 235–6. All further quotations of Humboldt's works are taken from this anthology.

of thought and word' is but one expression.[132] When he turns from the psychological to the referential dimension—that is, from the mind/word relationship to the word/referent relationship—Humboldt similarly dismisses the eighteenth-century emphasis on language as representation, the word as 'an image of the thing which it designates' or as 'a mere intimation that this thing is supposed to be thought by reason or represented in imagination. It is differentiated from an image by the possibility inherent in it and in us to imagine the thing according to the most various points of view and in the most various ways; it is different from a mere intimation in that it has its own definite, sensuous form.'[133] For some words, the personal and cultural associations that arise to consciousness as soon as they are uttered are so strong that 'the sound of the word attunes the soul in a manner befitting the object' (p. 247). Thus language—'a universe which lies midway between the external, phenomenal one and our own inwardly active one'—is essentially performative in its promotion of 'the analogical relation between man and the world in general' (p. 249). Humboldt's sense of language as a grand synthesis of the subjective and objective realms grants to even the simplest conversation something of the motivated and motivational intensity we have previously encountered only in ideal forms of semiosis such as Boehme's union of the spiritual and sensual tongues, the unity of body and spirit in Christ's incarnation and His kerygmatic gestures, and the co-presence of conception and execution in the Logos.

Humboldt extends the psychological affectivity of language to its institution of speech communities. This view finds its fullest expression in the general introduction to Humboldt's study of the Kawi language, a long and enthusiastic essay in which he argues that 'the spiritual characteristics and the linguistic structure of a people stand in a relationship of such indissoluble fusion that, given one, we should be able to derive the other from it entirely' (p. 277). Indeed, 'one might just as well consider the intellectual characteristics of a nation the product of its language, as the other way around. The truth is that both simultaneously and in mutual agreement emerge from unfathomable depths of human psychic constitution' (p. 273). This 'fusion' of the individual and the communal indicates

[132] 'On Comparative Linguistics', pp. 240, 246.

[133] 'Latium and Hellas', p. 247.

to Humboldt that his linguistic investigations should not begin with a taxonomy or grammar—the 'dead artifice of scientific analysis' (p. 280)—but must 'proceed from the point at which language is connected to the general configuration of the national spirit' (p. 252). While this hermeneutic initiates Humboldt's work as a comparative linguist, it always remains a part of his sacramental sense of language. For even though a word has 'a sensuous form borrowed from nature, it makes possible an idea which is beyond all nature'.[134] As individual expression, language 'must be considered an unconscious, involuntary emanation of the spirit'; as a communal phenomenon, 'language is deeply enmeshed in the spiritual development of mankind'.[135] Language thereby becomes the memory of a culture, a permanent record of its history and aspirations. Although the individual speaker 'is limited by' his language, he is also 'enriched, strengthened, and stimulated by the deposits of countless generations. . . . Everything that has once been expressed in words shapes that which has not, or prepares the way for it.'[136]

Humboldt comes very close to equating the history of language, inscribed in the etymology of its words, with the history of consciousness, for 'man thinks, feels, and lives within language alone and must be formed by it'.[137] And since 'language is not a work (*ergon*) but an activity (*energeia*)', its speakers are continually adding to its storehouse of memories, while at the same time drawing upon those memories not only as 'means for representing already known truths' but as 'instruments for discovering previously unrecognized ones'.[138] With these statements, Humboldt claims for language itself, in its phenomenal totality, the capacities Blake gives to his Bard, 'Who Present, Past, & Future sees' (Introduction to *Songs of Experience*, E 18, K 210), and embodies in 'the City of Golgonooza', the city of art where 'all that has existed in the space of six thousand years' remains

[134] 'Latium and Hellas', p. 248.

[135] Introduction to the study of Kawi, pp. 254–5. A complete but inelegant translation of the Introduction appears in Humboldt, *Linguistic Variability & Intellectual Development* (1971).

[136] 'On Comparative Linguistics', pp. 241, 251.

[137] 'On the National Characteristics of Languages', a fragment written in 1822; p. 298.

[138] Introduction to the study of Kawi, p. 280; 'On Comparative Linguistics', p. 246.

Permanent, & not lost not lost nor vanishd, & every little act,
Word, work, & wish, that has existed, all remaining still
In those Churches ever consuming & ever building by the Spectres
Of all the inhabitants of Earth wailing to be Created:
Shadowy to those who dwell not in them, meer possibilities:
But to those who enter into them they seem the only substances
For every thing exists & not one sigh nor smile nor tear,
One hair nor particle of dust, not one can pass away.

(*Jerusalem*, Pls. 13–14; E 157–8, K 634)

Humboldt's phenomenology of language serves as a chronologically and conceptually appropriate conclusion to our pursuit of the motivated sign through the history of linguistics to Blake's time. We must, however, return to a theme first encountered in the theory and imitation of supposedly primitive forms of poetry. As the natural sign began to disappear from philosophies of language near the beginning of the nineteenth century, it found a new role within theories of poetic diction, finally to reappear in the guise of the romantic symbol. We can trace the main course of this development in England through the writings of just two authors, William Wordsworth and Samuel Taylor Coleridge.[139]

In the 1802 Appendix to the Preface to *Lyrical Ballads*, Wordsworth repeats some typical features of eighteenth-century theories positing an original language composed of natural signs and such arbitrary signs that developed directly from them. 'The earliest poets of all nations generally wrote from passion excited by real events; they wrote naturally, and as men: feeling powerfully as they did, their language was daring, and figurative.'[140] For Wordsworth, our decline from this original ideal was not occasioned by abstract grammarians, but by a far more fraudulent class—'Men ambitious of the fame of Poets' who 'set themselves to a mechanical adoption' of the 'figures of speech' of the earliest poets and 'applied them to feelings and thoughts with which they had no natural connection whatsoever' (1: 160). Thus, Wordsworth constructs his own version of the familiar story of original motivation, both psychological and linguistic, and fall into arbitrariness. Fortunately, a return is made

[139] For a study of similar developments on the Continent, see Todorov, *Theories of the Symbol*. Todorov's quotations from French and German authors constitute a most useful anthology of 18th- and 19th-century contributions to his subject.

[140] *Prose Works* (1974), 1: 161. Further quotations of Wordsworth's prose are from this edn.

possible by a substitution of space (and social class) for time that allows Wordsworth to locate a motivated language not just in the primitive past but in the present countryside. In the words of the 1800 Preface, men of 'low and rustic life' speak 'a more permanent and a far more philosophical language than that which is frequently substituted for it by Poets' who 'indulge in arbitrary and capricious habits of expression' (1: 124). To call the language of rustics 'philosophical' may seem oddly perverse, but when juxtaposed to 'arbitrary' the word recalls its use in the seventeenth century to indicate a system of signs with at least secondary motivation, as it does in Wilkins's title of 1668, *An Essay towards a Real Character, and a Philosophical Language*. The utterances of men in daily contact with nature and natural signs are in this special sense more philosophical, more motivated, because they are closer to the origins of speech than the sophisticated language of city-dwellers. Similarly, Wordsworth addresses the babe in the 'Intimations' ode as 'Thou best Philosopher' because of his soul's proximity to its origin.[141]

In his *Essay on the Origin of Language*, Herder associates the expressive powers of the 'language of nature' with 'children, with those who live through their senses, with women, with people of sensitive feelings, with the sick, the lonely, the sorrowful' (p. 98). This list could serve as a catalogue of ennobled and ennobling figures we meet in Wordsworth's poetry whose utterances and demeanour take on the character of natural signs. Even the illiteracy of such classes helps preserve their contact with origins; as Rousseau points out, 'it is not possible for a language that is written, to retain its vitality as long as one that is only spoken'.[142] To return the primary and seemingly unmediated powers of speech to poetry, Wordsworth asks that we attend less to the actual language of country folk than to its origin in natural forms which for Wordsworth constitute a

[141] 'Ode: Intimations of Immortality from Recollections of Early Childhood', *Poetical Works* (1947), 4: 282. Further quotations of Wordsworth's poems are from this edn., except as noted otherwise.

[142] *Essay on the Origin of Language*, p. 22; see also Rousseau's comment that writing substitutes 'exactitude for expressiveness' (p. 21). Rousseau's sense of the secondariness of writing, discussed at length in Derrida's *Of Grammatology*, was a very common 18th-century opinion based on the simple observation that 'a word is an audible and articulate sign of thought: a Letter is a visible sign of an articulate sound' (Beattie, *Theory of Language*, p. 108).

'language' of nature.[143] This metaphoric strategy makes nature itself semiotic, as in Boehme's system, thereby transforming the problematic relationship of the linguistic to the extra-linguistic into a question of translation theory. But in some poems, natural signs, as defined in the more limited eighteenth-century sense, play an important role as transitions between the language of nature and the language of the poet. In 'The Tables Turned', the 'Friend' addressed in the poem is urged to quit his concentration on written language and to listen, like Eve in Blake's painting, to the 'woodland linnet' and to 'how blithe the throstle sings' (4: 57). This return to primary sources receives one of its more extreme expressions through the adventures of Johnny, himself a 'natural' or fool, in 'The Idiot Boy'. He becomes confused about time and species, both products of logical and linguistic distinctions beyond his ken, but retains a primal responsiveness to natural signs:

> 'The cocks did crow to-whoo, to-whoo,
> And the sun did shine so cold!'
> —Thus answered Johnny in his glory,
> And that was all his travel's story.
>
> (2: 80)

In diction, tone, and other elements of style, 'The Idiot Boy' and its companions in *Lyrical Ballads* differ greatly from the poems of Ossian, the harsh criticism of which in Wordsworth's 1815 *Poems* elicited Blake's defence noted earlier. Yet, in their linguistic or semiotic orientation, Wordsworth's early poems and Macpherson's inventions are both consonant with much the same belief in natural signs as the origin of speech and the same desire to regain contact with that origin to revitalize an attenuated written language and give it once again 'a power like one of Nature's'.[144]

[143] See M. H. Abrams, *Mirror and the Lamp* (1958), 110: 'In Wordsworth's theory the relation between the language of "Tintern Abbey" and the speech of a Lake Country shepherd is not primarily one of lexical or of grammatical, but of genetic equivalence.' Aarsleff, *From Locke to Saussure*, pp. 372–81, argues against Abrams's views on Wordsworth's primitivism and points to the influence of Locke, Condillac, and Destutt de Tracy on Wordsworth's concepts of language. Although Wordsworth may have agreed with the French *Idéologues* on the arbitrary character of actual words, he still turns to the natural, motivated sign as an ideal. Further, Condillac's own description of the origin of language depends upon the primordial presence of such signs.

[144] Wordsworth, *Prelude* (1959), 472–3 (bk. 12, line 312, of the 1805 version). For a study of 'The Idiot Boy' and *Peter Bell* in relation to theories of education and the origins of language and memory, see A. J. Bewell, 'Wordsworth's Primal Scene', *ELH* 50 (1983), 321–46.

In the third of his *Essays upon Epitaphs*, written in 1810 but not published until 1876, Wordsworth supplements his ideal of words as 'the pure emanations of nature' with a sense that 'expressions' should be to 'thoughts' not 'what the garb is to the body but what the body is to the soul'.[145] This 'metaphor' of 'incarnation', as Wordsworth calls it, would seem to lead beyond mimetic or expressive theories of natural signification to an ideal sign in which the signifier and signified are not joined like a cause to its effect, or an imitation to the original, but like man and God in Jesus. A similar progression toward a unity transcending the bonds of nature and logic, and at the same time a return to a mystical ideal, find expression in Coleridge's theory of symbol.

Coleridge's views on language were shaped in large measure by Locke and his contemporary advocate, Horne Tooke.[146] We must, however, turn to a very different tradition in linguistics to trace the concept of the motivated sign through Coleridge's scattered comments on language. In 'The Destiny of Nations' of 1796, he hints at a desire to discover a common ground for ontology and semiosis similar to Boehme's doctrine of signatures:

> For all that meets the bodily sense I deem
> Symbolical, one mighty alphabet
> For infant minds; . . .[147]

Four years later, in a letter to William Godwin, Coleridge questioned 'how far . . . the word "arbitrary" ' is a 'misnomer' in reference to 'signs' and expressed the desire, underlying all schemes for the recovery of primary motivation, 'to destroy the old antithesis of *Words & Things*'. This he hoped to do by 'elevating, as it were, words into Things, & living Things too',[148] much as Boehme had treated words as substances subject to alchemical transmutation to recover the linguistic equivalent of gold. Tooke and Boehme tend to reinforce each other in the use of the auditory materials of language to investigate etymologies. We can see the influence of both theorists

[145] *Prose Works*, 2: 84. For the connections between this important passage and Wordsworth's other comments on the powers and limits of language, see F. Ferguson, *Wordsworth: Language as Counter-Spirit* (1977), esp. pp. 1–34; and J. Wordsworth, 'As with the Silence of the Thought', in L. Lipking, ed., *High Romantic Argument* (1981), esp. pp. 50–65.

[146] See McKusick, *Coleridge's Philosophy of Language*, esp. pp. 33–52.

[147] *Complete Poetical Works* (1912), 1: 132.

[148] Letter of 22 September 1800, *Collected Letters* (1956), 1: 625–6.

in Coleridge's reference to 'the identity of *nomen* [name] with *numen*, that is, invisible power and presence' in many Biblical passages, including the naming of the beasts in Genesis 2: 19.[149] Perhaps we can also sense the incorporation of Boehme's views in Coleridge's admonition in the *Biographia Literaria* not 'to overlook the important fact, that besides the language of words, there is a language of spirits'. The second half of this sentence—'that the former is only the vehicle of the latter'[150]—leaves intact the hope that one can recover the spirit hidden in that vehicle.

The annotations Coleridge wrote over many years, beginning in 1808, in his copy of Law's edition of Boehme offer the clearest indication of what he found so compelling in the mystic's theory of language and what he could not accept. 'Even in the most startling [paragraphs], those on the correspondency of Letters, and syllables, to the universal sense of words', Coleridge sensed 'an important Truth hidden in the seeming Blunder of its exemplification'.[151] To explain this disparity between intuitive principle and the fanciful parsing of German words to find Adam's, Coleridge proposes a 'way of saving Behmen's credit' by supposing 'that he had seen the truth as to the *Ideal* of Language—and had in his ordinary state confounded the spiritual, perhaps angelic, language with the poor arbitrary & corrupted Languages of men as they actually exist' (1: 629). In short, Boehme had not paid sufficient heed to the fact of man's fall, that 'fundamental postulate of the moral'—and linguistic—'history of Man' (*Table Talk*, p. 65).

Boehme's failure to resurrect Adamic speech left as an alternative the rationalist tradition of language reformation. It at least recognized the limitations of contemporary languages. But the substitution of secondary for primary motivation could not satisfy Coleridge's philosophical instincts, nor perhaps his needs as a poet. His rejection of the taxonomic view of language is implicated in his criticism of its necessary twin, the taxonomic view of nature, in his annotations to Johann Friedrich Blumenbach's *Über die natürlichen Verschiedenheiten*. 'The fault common to the Systems & Systematizers of Natural

[149] *Aids to Reflection* (1839), 168–9. See also Coleridge's comment of 13 March 1827 that 'a Pun will sometimes facilitate explanation', which he then exemplifies with an English pun and a Hebrew etymology. *Table Talk* (1923), 43.

[150] *Biographia Literaria* (1983), 1: 290.

[151] *Marginalia* (1980), 1: 591. Further quotations of Coleridge's annotations are from this vol.

Hystery' is not, in Coleridge's view, 'the falsehood nor even the unfitness of the guiding principle', but rather the 'forgetting that Nature may pursue a hundred Objects at the same time' (*Marginalia*, 1: 536). As we have seen, the logical systematizers of language required the elimination of polysemy and connotation. They are blind to the 'living powers' of 'Words'[152] much as the taxonomists are blind to Coleridge's proto-evolutionary sense of nature's protean dynamics.

Confronted with the narrowness of rationalist theories of language, Coleridge clung to the essential features of the transcendental position in spite of Boehme's demonstrative blunders. Coleridge's strategy was to preserve the ideal of primary motivation by constructing a sign defined in counterdistinction to the mechanical matching of taxonomic linguistics. The relevant passages in *The Statesman's Manual* are well known, but it is sometimes forgotten that Coleridge's definition of a 'symbol' unfolds in the context of a book about the uses of the Bible, not secular literature. The key term is introduced as 'a system of symbols, harmonious in themselves, and consubstantial with the truths, of which they are the conductors'.[153] This 'system' fulfills the requirement that the words of an ideal language should be properly related to each other. The basis of these relationships in a concept of the 'harmonious' suggests neither figuration nor logical grammar but an organic form of secondary motivation encompassing both. Coleridge next moves his system beyond intrinsic harmony among signs to propose a unity of signs and their referents, the former 'consubstantial with'—that is, one with the same substantial reality as—the latter. Such a sign, which 'always partakes of the Reality which it renders intelligible' (p. 30), is not consubstantial with things but with 'truths'. Coleridge implicitly accepts Locke's insight that signs refer to ideas, not things,[154] and is able to substitute 'truths' for 'ideas' because he is considering only ideas in the Bible.

[152] Coleridge, *Essays on his Times* (1978), 2: 249.

[153] *The Statesman's Manual*, in *Lay Sermons* (1972), 29.

[154] For Coleridge's explicit acceptance of Locke's position, combined with a suggestion of Harris's mentalism, see Coleridge's letter of 22 October 1826 to James Gillman: 'For (as I have long ago observed to you) it is the fundamental Mistake of Grammarians and Writers on the philosophy of Grammar and Language [to assume] that words and their syntaxis are the immediate representatives of *Things*, or that they correspond to *Things*. Words correspond to thoughts; and the legitimate Order & Connection of words to the *Laws* of Thinking and to the acts and affections of the Thinker's mind' (*Letters*, 6: 60; see also 6: 817).

This higher mode of signification is contrasted to allegory, a product of 'the mechanical understanding' that translates 'abstract notions into a picture-language which is itself nothing but an abstraction from objects of the senses' (p. 30). Coleridge's terminology here might seem to refer only to a poetic mode, but it refers also to a method of reading the Bible and, by implication, to those ideal language schemes which I earlier called allegorical because they propose the alignment of the order of words with the order of things, those 'objects of the senses' to which the Baconian logician matches his arbitrary signs.

With his definition of the symbol, Coleridge proposes nothing less than a sign in which being and meaning share the same ontological/ semiotic ground. The precursors of such a sign are found in the mystical tradition of linguistic motivation exemplified by Boehme, although perhaps it would be unfair to say of Coleridge's theory what he said of Schelling's 'System': 'it is little more than Behmenism, translated from visions into Logic and a sort of commanding eloquence' (to C. A. Tulk, 1818; *Letters*, 4: 883). The transcendental nature of Coleridge's symbol is indicated by his use in *The Statesman's Manual* of 'consubstantial', a term generally applied to the interrelationships of the Trinity, and by the example of the symbolic he offers from Ezekiel 1: 20. Significantly, Coleridge does not take the language of the Biblical passage as itself symbolic; that could fall into the same blunders with English or Hebrew that Boehme fell into with German. Rather, Coleridge indicates that Ezekiel's vision of the eyed wheels was the exemplary moment when 'the truths and the symbols that represent them move in conjunction and form the living chariot that bears up (for *us*) the throne of the Divine Humanity' (*Statesman's Manual*, p. 29). Coleridge does not, indeed could not, claim that the actual languages of man after Babel are the same as the motivated language of Adam and of divine revelation. Only when we 'suppose man perfect' can we claim that his 'organic Acts' are 'faithful symbols of his spiritual Life and Cognition' (annotations to Boehme; *Marginalia*, 1: 634). That perfection can be restored through transmundane visions like Ezekiel's, but only then is there a 'translucence of the Eternal through and in the Temporal' (*Statesman's Manual*, p. 30). Unlike Boehme, Coleridge does not forget the fall, standing between sign and referent, signifier and signified, as it stands between Eden and England, Ezekiel's wheels and Coleridge's words.

As several critics have pointed out, no one has been very successful in discovering Coleridgean symbols in secular literature.[155] The reason for this becomes clear when we consider the type of primary motivation Coleridge attributes to the symbol from the perspective of prelapsarian or divine language, the only media in which it can be fully embodied. Any account of the symbolic experience will itself fall short of that ideal. Coleridge's symbol is not an instrument of a practical poetic or hermeneutic. It is, rather, what Coleridge might call the 'Hypopoēēsis' or 'subfiction'[156] of a general but transcendental semiotic. The explication of that semiotic always takes the form of an allegory in which the transcendental descends into the rhetorical and the symbolic degenerates into the synecdochic. This linguistic recapitulation of the fall happened even when Coleridge attempted to offer a mundane example of a symbol. In a lecture on *Don Quixote* delivered in 1818, he states that 'The Symbolical cannot, perhaps, be better defined in distinction from the Allegorical, than that it is always itself a part of that, of the whole of which it is the representative.—"Here comes a sail,"—(that is, a ship) is a symbolical expression.'[157] A sail, as a physical object, is consubstantial with the ship of which it is a constitutive part, but the word 'sail' no more 'partakes of the Reality it renders intelligible' through synecdoche than does any other sign. The problem is not one of alternative tropes, rhetoric, or grammar, but the crucial difference between an arbitrary mode of signification and a transcendental ideal of primary motivation.

Given the inherently transcendental nature of Coleridge's symbol, it should be no surprise that he turned to theological texts and

[155] See for example R. Wellek, *History of Modern Criticism* (1955), 2: 175: 'In his practical criticism Coleridge rarely uses the term "symbol".' The point has been most recently reiterated by J.-P. Mileur, *Vision and Revision* (1982), 21–2. Mileur characterizes P. de Man's view (the validity of which I argue for here) that there are no true symbols in 'any actual act of Romantic figuration', but (quite rightly) questions de Man's conclusion that 'the notion of the symbol was a self-deceiving mystification'. See de Man, 'The Rhetoric of Temporality', *Blindness and Insight* (1983), 187–228.

[156] *Notebooks* (1973), 3: 3587. J. Christensen further defines and uses 'Hypopoesis' [*sic*] as 'the necessary artifice' and 'enabling figure that makes fiction as well as philosophy conceivable' in *Coleridge's Blessed Machine of Language* (1981), 19.

[157] *Miscellaneous Criticism* (1936), 99. For a study of Coleridge's distinction between symbol and allegory that takes much the same sceptical view I am proposing here, see J. A. Hodgson, 'Transcendental Tropes', in M. W. Bloomfield, ed., *Allegory, Myth, and Symbol* (1981), 273–92. As Hodgson states, 'beneath the false issue of synecdochic [symbolic] versus metaphoric [allegoric] tropes there lay a genuine, significant crux, that of determined [i.e., motivated] versus arbitrary figuration, the true and inescapable issue for any rhetoric that would strive to be transcendental' (p. 292).

contexts for its definition. The need for grounding the symbolic in the divine is intimated as early as some fragmentary notes on Shakespeare Coleridge wrote *c.*1812. He claims that 'the language of Shakespeare (in his *Lear*, for instance), is a something intermediate' between the 'pure arbitrary modes' of human discourse and the motivated 'language of nature'.[158] The latter, however, is not defined in the secular terms common to eighteenth-century advocates of natural signs, but as 'a subordinate *Logos*, that was in the beginning, and was with the thing it represented' (*Shakespearean Criticism*, 1: 185). Similarly, when Coleridge defines the symbol making/perceiving faculty—the 'imagination'—in the *Biographia Literaria*, he describes it as a 'repetition in the finite mind' of a divine utterance, 'the infinite I AM' (1: 304). He thus grants to the mind of man traces of the infinite, situating in the psychological realm what Boehme claimed could still be uncovered in the physical presence and performance of actual languages.

In a *Notebook* entry of 14 April 1805, Coleridge adumbrates the reciprocal relationship between imagination and symbol, between inner and outer manifestations of divine semiosis, when he describes the production of symbols as a projection of something within the subject:

> In looking at objects of Nature while I am thinking, as at yonder moon dim-glimmering thro' the dewy window-pane, I seem rather to be speaking, as it were *asking*, a symbolical language for something within me that already and forever exists, than observing any thing new. Even when the latter is the case, yet still I have always an obscure feeling as if that new phaenomenon were the dim Awakening of a forgotten or hidden Truth of my inner Nature. (2: 2546).

Such a 'Truth' depends not on a mode of signification, a 'language' in any structural or performative sense, but on a faith in the divine and in man's ability to participate in divinity. Coleridge's parenthetical interjection and emphasis ('for *us*') in his description of Ezekiel's vision in *The Statesman's Manual* hint at this necessary ingredient: the

[158] *Shakespearean Criticism* (1960), 1: 185. As J. Coulson points out in *Newman and the Common Tradition* (1970), 22, Coleridge's 'original concern was with religious language, and . . . his account of poetic language must always be interpreted as a derivative from a more fundamental enquiry'. See also S. Prickett, 'The Living Educts of the Imagination', *Wordsworth Circle*, 4 (1973), 105: 'For Coleridge, . . . personal assent is an essential part of the function of a symbol.'

Biblical passage is symbolic for faithful Christians, but not for non-believers. Accordingly, in one of his last descriptions of the symbolic, Coleridge finds it in the dramatization of faith through those Christian rituals 'of the same kind, though not of the same order, with the religion itself—not arbitrary or conventional, as types and hieroglyphics are in relation to the things expressed by them; but inseparable, consubstantiated (as it were), and partaking therefore of the same life, permanence, and intrinsic worth with its spirit and principle' (*Aids to Reflection*, p. 15). With Coleridge's symbol we witness a resacralization of linguistic motivation, but one limited finally to acts and utterances that have transcendental truths as both ground and referent. Thus the archetype of the symbolic is the incarnate Word and His kerygmatic words; it is only Christ who can say with truth that '*My words . . . are spirit*: and they (that is, the spiritual powers expressed by them) *are truth*;—that is, very being' (*Aids to Reflection*, p. 309). Those without faith in this '*truth*' uniting being and meaning remain at best with Shakespeare's *Lear* in that 'intermediate' realm of secondary motivation between the fully arbitrary and the fully motivated.

Coleridge's concepts of allegory and symbol offer an appropriate context for considering Blake's use of 'allegory' and terms he sets in opposition to it. Allegory, as a mode for positing meanings, has resoundingly negative associations throughout Blake's poetry. The false idea of 'Eternal life' in *Europe* (1794) is 'an allegorical abode where existence hath never come' (Pl. 5; E 62, K 240). In *Jerusalem* (1804–20), 'the Falshood which | Gwendolen hid in her left hand' becomes 'a Space & an Allegory' (Pls. 84–5; E 243, K 729–30). A few plates later, Blake describes another concealment—but this time of a truth (Jerusalem) within a false container (the Covering Cherub)—as an 'allegoric delusion' (Pl. 89; E 249, K 735). In all three examples, allegory is essentially a projection of a lie or an evil into a falsifying system that hides or replaces truth. Yet, when Blake characterizes his own poetry in a letter to Butts of 6 July 1803, he does not abandon the word 'allegory' but only modifies it. Blake claims that he has completed a 'Grand Poem' (perhaps *The Four Zoas*, or some ur-version of *Milton* and *Jerusalem*) containing, or based on, 'a Sublime Allegory' (E 730, K 825). Fortunately, Blake defines what he means by the key adjective: 'Allegory addressd to the Intellectual powers while it is altogether hidden from the

Corporeal Understanding is My Definition of the Most Sublime Poetry.'

It is all too easy to conclude that Blake makes, in his letter to Butts, a distinction equivalent to Coleridge's between allegory and symbol—that is, between an arbitrary and a motivated system of reference. There are, however, several features of Blake's statements that thwart this conclusion. False allegory, as described in Blake's poems, is an act of concealment, but this is also a function of sublime allegory when it hides itself from 'the Corporeal Understanding'. The two forms are not distinguished by the mode of their operation but rather by what is revealed (truth or falsehood) and from what it is concealed (intellectual powers or corporeal understanding). Blake's failure to use a word other than 'allegory' to name his own method of signification shows both honesty and insight. Unlike Coleridge, Blake does not attempt to construct an ideal difference in kind where none exists in actual practice. The sublimity of Blake's allegory resides in to *what*, not *how*, it is 'addressd'—in the sense of both reference and audience. As I have tried to demonstrate in my remarks on Coleridge's symbol, it also depends ultimately on what is signified (transcendental truths) and who is addressed (true believers). By engaging the intellectual powers, arousing them to action and thus bringing them into phenomenal presence, Blake's allegory establishes the ground of its motivation in the relationship between sign and recipient. Sublime allegory, like Humboldt's general sense of language performance, posits a triadic structure (sign, referent, recipient) based in turn on the community of speaker, audience, and the medium joining them. But nothing in the letter to Butts claims for Blake's poems anything inconsistent with the Lockian principle that signs are arbitrarily related to their referents.

Blake offers a further characterization of allegory in *A Vision of the Last Judgment* he wrote in his *Notebook* in 1810:

> The Last Judgment is not Fable or Allegory but Vision Fable or Allegory are a totally distinct & inferior kind of Poetry. Vision or Imagination is a Representation of what Eternally Exists. Really & Unchangeably. Fable or Allegory is Formd by the Daughters of Memory. Imagination is Surrounded by the daughters of Inspiration who in the aggregate are calld Jerusalem Fable is Allegory but what Critics call The Fable is Vision itself (E554, K 604)

The implicit distinction in the letter to Butts (allegory/sublime allegory) here becomes the more explicit and seemingly more categorical difference between allegory and vision. Yet once again I find it difficult to extrapolate from Blake's words any claim that the superiority of 'Vision or Imagination' depends on their mode of signification. Blake clearly states that they are a 'Representation', a word reminding us that he is describing the representational images of his painting. At this basic semiotic level, vision is not distinguishable from allegory, for the latter must also depend on representation. The difference lies once again in *what* is represented and whether the viewer takes this representation literally or figuratively. As we have seen in the letter to Butts, allegory is a false representation (in that sense, a 'Fable') of something that does not exist outside that falsification. Vision represents what really exists and thus deals in truth, not lies. Allegory misleads by transforming the first order representation of vision into a second order of figuration in which reality is treated as though it were merely a system of signs (in that sense, a 'Fable or Allegory') pointing toward what that system posits as real—but which Blake believes is actually the reification of a lie. The distinction between vision and allegory depends on where they situate the real and the true, not on how they represent them. Thus, Blake can claim, without contradicting his initial equation of allegory and fable, that the latter 'is Vision itself', for the images of his *Last Judgment* painting represent what really exists and are not to be taken as signs of signs, representations of images which are in turn 'Allegories . . . that Relate to Moral Virtues' (E 563, K 614). It also follows that 'Fable or Allegory is Seldom without some Vision' (E 554, K 604) because allegorical meanings often have as their vehicles the images of true and existing acts and beings. For example, 'the Greek Fables originated in Spiritual Mystery & Real Vision', but 'are lost & clouded in Fable & Alegory'.[159] The allegorist's error is in not stopping with the individual images seen in the imagination—those 'Mental Things' that 'are alone Real' (E 565, K 617)—but taking them as figures for general and abstract concepts.

[159] E 555, K 605. This descent from vision into allegory through abstracting processes of figuration is much the same as the decline from the animating faculties of the 'ancient Poets' to the 'system' used by the 'Priesthood' to 'abstract the mental dieties from their objects' on Pl. 11 of *The Marriage of Heaven and Hell* (E 38, K 153).

Blake asks us to believe in the literal existence of his vision of the Last Judgment and to refuse its conversion into a trope. But he also equates the literal with imagination and opposes it to memory, thus inverting the more conventional association of imagination with the figural and the description of memory as a repository of real events. The result is a double reversal or chiasmus: that which is usually taken to be imaginary, in the sense of unreal, is for Blake the only reality; that which is usually taken literally as the real is for Blake an allegory of the memory and the fallen senses. The literalization of figuration can be revelatory, as it is when 'Eternal Forms' are incarnate 'in the Divine body of the Saviour the True Vine of Eternity The Human Imagination' (E 555, K 606), or a tragic mistake, as when the Druids turned 'allegoric and mental signification into [a] corporeal command' to commit 'human sacrifice' (*Descriptive Catalogue*, E 543, K 578). The issue is once again, as it was with Coleridge, the relationship of ontological faith to semiosis, the question of where one finds the real and the true within the phenomenon of signification. For Blake and Coleridge, the chain of signs, arbitrary or motivated, must begin and end somewhere, and for both this point of origin and ultimate reference is the immutable truths of religious conviction.

Blake's modern readers have devoted a good deal of energy to making a distinction between the language of 'myth', as a narrative extension of 'symbol', and the eighteenth-century mode of personification allegory of the very sort Blake's early fragment, 'then She bore Pale desire', so insistently exemplifies. But Blake's own comments on allegory offer no practical way of making such a discrimination on the basis of grammatical or rhetorical configurations. Even 'then She bore Pale desire', no less than *Jerusalem*, may contain 'Fable' or 'Vision' constitutive of a reality. Either work becomes 'a totally distinct & inferior kind of Poetry' when its visionary (i.e., literal) presence is converted into a signifier that empties its own reality into an abstract signified. This fall away from vision can happen to texts themselves when figurative meanings are substituted for original and literal ones during transmission from one culture to another. Thus, Blake writes in *A Vision of the Last Judgment* that 'Apuleius's Golden Ass & Ovids Metamorphosis & others of the like kind are Fable yet they contain Vision in a Sublime degree being derived from real Vision in More Ancient Writings' (E 556, K 607). But even in these cases, the error lies principally in the realm of interpretation, as a production of general meanings, and not in the realm of composition as the production of specific signs.

Blake's definitions of sublime allegory and vision do not constitute a theory of primary motivation. Nor is it very helpful to claim that poems such as *The Four Zoas*, *Milton*, and *Jerusalem* do not contain allegorical structures unless we are willing to ignore Blake's own description of the texts of his illuminated books as 'Poetical Personifications & Acts' (letter of 1818; E 771, K 867) and abandon a great deal of what we have learned about these poems as 'Representations' (to borrow Blake's word) of a host of philosophical concepts and historical events. If most allegories contain some vision, it would seem that most visions turn into allegories as soon as Blake or his critics start to interpret them.[160] But the presence of allegory does not exclude secondary motivation among the terms constituting the fable. Indeed, Blake's location of the real and the true in the fable emphasizes the values of the signifier, in its manifold and literal relationships to other signifiers, over the general or transcendental (in counterdistinction to incarnated) signified.[161]

Blake also made use of two systems of correspondences, typology and physiognomy, that claim for themselves forms of primary motivation. In his 'Visionary Portraits', Blake appears to have drawn upon the methods set forth in J. C. Lavater's *Essays on Physiognomy* (1789–98), a work for which Blake engraved four plates.[162] In a general sense, all of Blake's pictures of the human form and face are physiognomic, as he suggests by asking 'the Spectator' of his *Last Judgment* painting to 'attend to the Hands & Feet to the Lineaments of the Countenances they are all descriptive of Character'

[160] Frye, *Fearful Symmetry*, p. 117, argues that allegorical interpretations of Blake's poems are 'neither very helpful nor very interesting', but I fail to see how Frye's own explications and charts of correspondences (pp. 277–8) avoid allegorical structures. As Damrosch has pointed out, Blake's 'poems are indeed allegorical in any useful sense of the term' (*Symbol and Truth in Blake's Myth*, p. 94). For some insightful comments on how a tendency to privilege symbol over allegory has skewed our perception of Blake's theory and use of the latter mode, see G. Pechey, '1789 and After: Mutations of "Romantic" Discourse', in F. Barker, ed., *1789: Reading Writing Revolution* (1982), 52–66.

[161] As noted earlier in connection with Tookean etymology, Hilton in *Literal Imagination* has demonstrated Blake's use of puns and other sorts of wordplay at the level of the signifier.

[162] See A. K. Mellor, 'Physiognomy, Phrenology, and Blake's Visionary Heads', in R. N. Essick and D. Pearce, eds., *Blake in his Time* (1978), 53–74. See also Blake's comment, in his annotations to Lavater's *Aphorisms*, that 'substance gives tincture to the accident & makes it physiognomic' (E 596, K 81).

(E 560, K 611). Blake's illustrations to the Bible and to *Paradise Lost* show a distinct awareness of typological patterns in those works. Although he never uses the term 'typology' in his writings, the 'Divine Analogy' Blake names in *Jerusalem* would seem to be at least a similar structure since he grounds it in time and contrasts it to the spatial orientation of allegory.[163] But however extensive Blake's use of these systems may be, both are fundamentally extrinsic to language. Typology claims a divinely motivated relationship between events or persons, not between them and the words used to name them or their relationship. Similarly, physiognomy asserts a causal link between personality and visage but makes no claims about the language used to describe them or their connections. Both typology and physiognomy can be the basis for metaphoric patterns, particularly parallelism, in a text, but as such they become a form of secondary motivation among semantic units.

My brief pursuit of primary motivation as a linguistic principle in Blake's work has been rather unproductive, and has even taken on something of the character of a deconstruction—not of Blake, but of readings of his poems based on notions about the romantic symbol and its ability to transcend arbitrary signs even as it makes use of them. But one further avenue remains unexplored. In his recent study, *Philosophy of the Literary Symbolic*, Hazard Adams anatomizes the romantic symbol into two types.[164] The first is a secularized variety of, or closely related to, the 'miraculous' religious or incarnational sign. Coleridge's symbol is, in my view, of this type, an ideal based fundamentally on religious beliefs that collapses back into synecdoche or some other rhetorical figure in actual practice. Adams's second variety is only 'emergent . . . in romanticism because a ground is never quite fully articulated for it' (p. 18). He associates

[163] Pl. 85; E 243, K 730. In *Biblical Tradition in Blake's Early Prophecies* (1982), 86–123, L. Tannenbaum argues for the 'typological content and structure of Blake's imaginative vision in all his works' (p. 88). Recently, R. F. Gleckner has questioned Tannenbaum's extensive claims for Blake's use of typology; see Gleckner, *Blake and Spenser* (1985), 308–10. Gleckner quite rightly points out that typology is, broadly speaking, a form of allegory, but this does not *ipso facto* mean that Blake either did not use it or did not believe in its claims for divine motivation. Further, as Blake intimates in his reference to 'Divine Analogy', it is possible to make a distinction between figural modes (such as typology and metonymy) that are based on a temporal/syntagmatic sequence and those that are based on a spatial/paradigmatic matrix (for example, calling a lion the King of Beasts because he occupies the same position in the order of animals as a king in the hierarchy of men).

[164] *Philosophy of the Literary Symbolic* (1983). See esp. pp. 17–19 for an introductory overview of the concepts I summarize here.

this with Blake's concept of the 'prolific' in *The Marriage of Heaven and Hell*, and thus with 'symbolic activity' (p. 19) rather than structure. The next step—one that Adams never fully takes—would be to give up the symbol, 'romantic' or otherwise, for the constitutive proliferations of language-as-performance. That route, which I intend to pursue in this book, has already been mapped out for us by Humboldt, who abandons referential signification to the arbitrary and preserves motivation everywhere else within a phenomenological view of language. The performative, including the activities of the reader, is also hinted at by Blake's sense of sublime allegory as *addressing* the intellectual powers and engaging them in the completion of the allegory. If 'Thought is Act', as Blake proclaims in his annotations to Bacon's *Essays* (E 623, K 400), then words, whether conceived of as identical to thoughts or as their vehicles, are also actions.

If the phenomenological perspective on Blake's language I am advocating is to be something more than an abstract doctrine and come to grips with actual linguistic performances, it must be developed either within the context of Blake's methods of producing the words he communicates to us in his writings, or within the context of readers' responses to those writings. The development of these approaches must, however, await Chapters 4 and 5, when we will consider the arbitrary and the motivated as they pertain to Blake's theories and actual processes of conception, composition, publication, and reading.

The conceptual biases of the foregoing historical overview are more than sufficient to indicate, in general terms, where I wish to situate Blake's language in the landscape of possibilities. Indeed, we would not need much in the way of background information to place him with those who, like the mystics, the Celticists, and the romantic etymologists and symbolists, believe that words are individual positivities, not empty counters within a logic of differences, and find within language at least traces of original motivation. But when we put aside broad categorical distinctions and focus on Blake's practices as a writer, the situation becomes less clear-cut. Students of Blake's pictorial art have found that he sometimes borrowed motifs from artists he clearly disliked in order to criticize or improve on their work.[165] We should be alert to similar possibilities in Blake's handling of his linguistic medium. His profession as a copy engraver implicated Blake in techniques and commercial systems he criticized—explicitly in his writings on the graphic arts, and implicitly in his inventions of processes antithetical to the dominant tastes of his time. Similarly, Blake's texts are unavoidably built out of 'the stubborn structure of the Language', its rules of grammar and syntax, even if they constitute one of the 'Systems' he is 'Striving with . . . to deliver Individuals from those Systems'.[166] Much of Blake's poetry is devoted, on the thematic level, to the fallen condition of man and nature. We should expect Blake's equal involvement in less than ideal forms of discourse as a way to dramatize a fallen state of consciousness in the very texture of his medium. But the fall of language is predicated on an original condition that is not fallen. Eighteenth-century theories of the natural sign offer just such a story of motivated origins and the evolution of language away from them. How Blake used these theories in his poetry to intimate the prelapsarian condition of language, and how for him they led finally to false and fallen conceptions of what language is, will be our next concern.

[165] A good case in point is Blake's *Laocoön* engraving of *c.*1820 in which he carefully pictures the restored statue but, in the accompanying inscriptions, criticizes it as a Hellenistic copy and tries to return it to its original Hebraic meanings. For Blake's use in his writings of ideas he disapproved of, see M. K. Nurmi, 'Negative Sources in Blake', in Rosenfeld, *Blake*, pp. 303–18.

[166] *Jerusalem*, Pls. 11, 36; E 154, 183, K 630, 668.

3. Natural Signs and the Fall of Language

BLAKE'S evocation of natural signs begins with a conventionality belying their complexity and significance in his mature poetry. At the end of 'King Edward the Third', first published in the *Poetical Sketches* of 1783, Blake suspends the dialogue of his Shakespearian fragment to introduce a 'Song' by a 'Minstrel'. These words alone should prepare us for entry into the poetic world of the ancient bards, as loosely defined by eighteenth-century speculations on the origins of language and poetry. The first two lines do not disappoint these expectations:

> O Sons of Trojan Brutus, cloath'd in war,
> Whose voices are the thunder of the field, . . .
>
> (E 437, K31)

Our tendency to read such propositions as implied metaphors reducible to similes (the voices are *like* thunder) should not blind us to the copular structure intimating the incomplete emergence of human articulation from the greater world of natural sounds. This naturalization of the human leads us to the same undifferentiated semiosis as an anthropomorphic figuring of nature, as in 'shady mountains | In fear utter voices of thunder' (*The French Revolution*, E 286, K 134). The Ossianic precedents for this primordial condition would seem to be poised at a slighly later stage of linguistic development, in part because of the reliance on simile, as in 'pleasant is the noise of arms: pleasant as the thunder of heaven before the shower of Spring' (*Fingal*, p. 6).

This kind of imagery was of course the stock-in-trade for late eighteenth-century poets attempting a primitive sublimity, and its implications about language origins do not rise into thematic self-reflexivity in 'King Edward the Third'. But by tracing the image of thunder as it is related to voice through several of Blake's poems, we can observe its movement beyond mere stylistic imitation and an increasing emphasis on its linguistic character. In the next work in *Poetical Sketches*, a 'Prologue, Intended for a Dramatic Piece of King Edward the Fourth', we find the equation of thunder and voice couched as the poet's desire for a return to that original condition: 'O For a voice like thunder, and a tongue | To drown the throat of war!' (E 439, K 33). While this appeal admits a distinction between natural and human utterance in the very act of calling for their recombination, its initial 'O' has already brought to voice the pre-linguistic—an expressive fragment from 'the language of nature', as Herder called the interjection. But something is still lacking in the poet's articulate language needed to counter another product of the human 'throat', the sounds of war. To achieve the requisite bardic force, his speech must reclaim its origin and take on the immediacy and motivation of the natural sign.

In 'Holy Thursday' of *Songs of Innocence*, we are given a different species of thunder: the voices of the children are 'like harmonious thunderings the seats of heaven among' (E 13, K 122). Although this shift in orientation from the Ossianic and natural to the Biblical and divine does not of course disrupt the motivated character of thunder *qua* sign, the implicit change in the grounding for that motivation from a sensibilist to a theological sense of sign origins is most important. Blake's heavenly thunder suggests the unity of human, natural, and divine 'voice' that eighteenth-century Hebraists found to be a peculiar feature of the original language of the Old Testament. As Alexander Geddes pointed out in 1790, 'in the language which Moses spake, the word rendered *voice*, signifies, in general, every kind of sound, and . . . particularly the awful sound of thunder'.[1]

Blake's thunder returns to its natural home in the passage from *The Four Zoas* cited in Chapter 2 in connection with Urizen's unsuccessful attempt to communicate with the beasts. In that fallen context, the thunder loses its significance as an ideal sign and becomes the very image of the 'inarticulate' (E 347, K 315). With this bleak recognition of an inviolate gulf between natural sound and meaningful utterance also comes the development of natural sign theory into a theme in Blake's poetry. What began as a stylistic commonplace has become the representative of a fundamental concern in linguistic theory.

[1] Geddes, review of J. van Eyk, *Ledige Uuren* (1786–90), in *Analytical Review*, 7 (1790), 71.

The meaningless thunder of Urizen's voice is juxtaposed in *The Four Zoas* to a nostalgic recollection of the *Songs of Innocence*, those 'Climes . . . | Where the lamb replies to the infant voice' (E 348, K 315). Here we find Blake's least qualified celebration of language origins within the broad compass of eighteenth-century theories of the natural sign. Like Wordsworth's language of country folk and Herder's celebration of the 'language of nature' spoken by children, Blake's *Innocence* substitutes the life of the individual for the history of the race as a way of regaining access to the scene of original utterance.[2] Stylistically, the *Songs of Innocence* are as distant from Blake's Ossianic verses as are Wordsworth's poems from Macpherson's prose, but the implicit linguistic issues remain much the same.

The ideal form of signification in the world of innocence is founded on a concept of motivation with both expressive and mimetic components. The child responds to his environment with voice and bodily gestures. These spontaneously produced signs are linked through expressive causation to his emotions, but in some mysterious way they also embody or replicate the sense experiences that gave rise to those emotions. Shelley, in his *Defence of Poetry* of 1821, describes much the same concept of the motivated signs of childhood and, by proposing a basic similarity between them and the signs of 'the savage', demonstrates how such theories have their basis in eighteenth-century speculations about primitive languages:

> A child at play by itself will express its delight by its voice and motions; and every inflexion of tone and every gesture will bear exact relation to a corresponding antitype in the pleasurable impressions which awakened it; it will be the reflected image of that impression; and as the lyre trembles and sounds after the wind has died away, so the child seeks, by prolonging in its voice and motions the duration of the effect, to prolong also a consciousness of the cause. In relation to the objects which delight a child, these expressions are, what poetry is to higher objects. The savage (for the savage is to ages what the child is to years) expresses the emotions produced in him by surrounding objects in a similar manner; and language and gesture,

[2] See also Herder, *Essay on the Origin of Language*, p. 135: 'The human race in its childhood formed language for itself precisely as it is stammered by the immature: it is the babbling vocabulary of the nursery.'

together with plastic or pictorial imitation, become the image of the combined effect of those objects, and of his apprehension of them.[3]

By substituting Blake's 'Ecchoing' for Shelley's 'reflected', we can move closer to Blake's special variation on this general semiotic of play. The first stanza of 'The Ecchoing Green' offers a representative paradigm in which all acts—including utterance—bear a homologous relationship to all others.

The Sun does arise,
And make happy the skies.
The merry bells ring
To welcome the Spring.
The sky-lark and thrush,
The birds of the bush,
Sing louder around,
To the bells chearful sound.
While our sports shall be seen
On the Ecchoing Green.

(E 8, K 116)

The poem's symmetry is generated through a circle of responsiveness that immediately bridges the difference between those binary divisions (man/nature, man/God, act/word, *et al.*) upon which response is necessarily grounded. In this sense, the whole world becomes semiotic, with each act echoing, and thereby becoming a reference back to, every other. This at least is the innocent or primitive condition imagined by the speaker, who identifies himself as one of the children by referring in the second stanza to the 'old folk' laughing 'at our play'. He begins by presenting nature in terms of affective, rather than mechanical, response: the rising sun 'make[s] happy the skies'. The pattern is repeated, but with the introduction of sound and an implied human presence, when the bells 'welcome the Spring'. In turn, nature echoes back in the form of the birds—those traditional artists of the natural sign—who 'Sing louder' in accord with 'the bells chearful sound'. The children at play are introduced in the last couplet with a word ('While') that proposes only temporal congruence, but we have been given a sufficiently strong causal pattern in the prior eight lines to carry its echo into

3 *Poetry and Prose* (1977), 480–1.

the final two. As in the supposedly primitive verse of Ossian, we are prompted to take syntactic and temporal sequence as evidence for causality. At the same time, the lack of a transitional term specifying what is cause and what is effect leaves the line open to interpretations 'supplied by the reader's imagination', as Hugh Blair said of much the same situation in Ossian. For example, one reader has taken 'shall be' as a 'performative utterance' indicating that the echoing world of nature only exists 'While' the children call it into being through their play.[4] This extreme mentalist perspective has its sensibilist contrary in the view that the sights and sounds of nature are primary and the children's play is a response to them, just as the sun's descent precedes, and thus presumably brings about, the end of their 'sport' in the last stanza: 'The sun does descend, | And our sports have an end'. Yet, once again, only the order of the clauses indicates temporal succession, while the coordinating conjunction leaves the question of causal relationships completely open. It is as if we were placed within the echoing green without knowing which partner, the children or the environment, uttered the initial note now resounding between them. And that is exactly the condition of the children, innocent of absolute divisions between cause and effect, self and world. The state of consciousness embodied in the grammar of innocence has yet to be structured by the more abstract grammatical and logical categories of subordination and causation.

Blake's variant spelling of 'Ecchoing', archaic by his time, gives the word a motivated character by making the phenomenon present in its name. Visually and phonetically, the second 'c' echoes the first and implies a placement of the syllabic division such that the last letter of the first syllable is repeated by the first letter in the second.[5] The effect has not gone unnoticed by other readers, but it takes on its full linguistic significance only when we follow Herder's and Shelley's sense of children's speech and read Blake's *Innocence* as a return to an early stage in the evolution of language, much as the children's play in 'The Ecchoing Green' returns the 'old folk' in memory to their own 'youth-time'. The doubled 'c' is a trace of the

[4] H. Glen, *Vision and Disenchantment* (1983), 138. 'Performative utterance' is used in a very general way in this context and means little more than an obeyed command.

[5] To be a bit mechanical about the matter, the difference is between the now normative 'ech′o' (or Johnson's 'e′cho' in his *Dictionary*) and 'ec′cho'. Only in the last case does the word have an internal echo.

word's origin, that primal scene, imagined by theorists of the natural sign, when men first heard an echo and were moved to name it mimetically.[6]

We journey to an even earlier stage of naming in 'Infant Joy':

I have no name
I am but two days old.—
What shall I call thee?
I happy am
Joy is my name,—
Sweet joy befall thee!

Pretty joy!
Sweet joy but two days old,
Sweet joy I call thee;
Thou dost smile.
I sing the while
Sweet joy befall thee.

(E 16, K 118)

Blake can intimate the elementary speech of children through the monosyllabic words of lines 1, 2, and 5, and an inversion of standard syntax in line 4, but even these are obviously beyond the capacities of a two-day-old infant. In what special sense, then, does he 'speak'? The question is much the same as asking how mankind first spoke. Herder's playfully enthusiastic answer also centres on the act of naming—not a babe, but a lamb as it first comes to the notice of early man:

Let that lamb there, as an image, pass by under his eyes; it is to him, as it is to no other animal. . . . Not as it appears to any other animal to which the sheep is indifferent and which therefore lets it, clear-darkly, pass by because its instinct makes it turn toward something else!—Not so with man! As soon as he feels the need to come to know the sheep, no instinct gets in his way; no one sense of his pulls him too close to it or too far away from it. It stands there, entirely as it manifests itself in his senses. White, soft, woolly—his soul in reflective exercise seeks a distinguishing mark—the sheep bleats! His soul has found the distinguishing mark. The inner sense is at work. This bleating, which makes upon man's soul the strongest

[6] J. McKusick, in a review of T. McFarland's *Originality and Imagination*, in *Wordsworth Circle*, 12 (1986), 195, suggests the term *epanalepsis* (from the Greek for 'repetition' or 'return') as the proper name for the rhetorical strategy whereby a word's supposed origin becomes part of its meaning.

impression, which broke away from all the other qualities of vision and of touch, which sprang out and penetrated most deeply, the soul retains it. The sheep comes again. White soft, woolly—the soul sees, touches, remembers, seeks a distinguishing mark—the sheep bleats, and the soul recognizes it. And it feels inside, 'Yes, you are that which bleats.' It has recognized it humanly when it recognized and named it clearly, that is, with a distinguishing mark. . . . The sound of bleating perceived by a human soul as the distinguishing mark of the sheep became, by virtue of this reflection, the name of the sheep, even if his tongue had never tried to stammer it. . . . Language has been invented! Invented as naturally and to man as necessarily as man was man.[7]

The child of 'Infant Joy' speaks as does Herder's sheep. Babe and lamb first 'tell' their respective observers that they have 'no name', immediately prompting each 'soul' to seek out one 'mark', one natural sign, that distinguishes the creature from all others and will become its name. For Herder's generic 'man', this proto-nominative sign is bleating; for Blake's adult speaker, it is the child's smile (and perhaps other, implied gestures or noises) that signifies 'joy'. Thus, both Herder's non-linguistic sheep and Blake's pre-linguistic infant have named themselves in the eyes of their beholders through the motivated medium of natural, expressive signs preceding and underlying spoken language. The act of naming in 'Infant Joy' is not the imposition of a word on to something utterly non-semiotic, but the evolution of one form of semiosis ('smile' as a natural sign) into another ('joy' as a word). The lines spoken by the child are a translation into language of what the child 'says' through his expressive signs, just as Herder's 'you are that which bleats' transforms the expressive act of bleating into words. Blake takes us one step further, in the blessing ending each stanza, by using 'joy' as what Condillac called an 'abstract substantive', the name for a condition independent of the child. In the adult's speech and consciousness, the evolution toward abstraction has already begun.

The 'smile' of 'Infant Joy' is a visual companion to the host of auditory natural signs that resound through the *Songs of Innocence*: crying, laughing, weeping, sighing, shouting, sobbing, bleating, lamb's call, ewe's reply, birds' songs, beetle's hum, shriek, howl,

[7] *Essay on the Origin of Language*, pp. 116–18. Condillac makes a similar claim about animal sounds and their names—see ch. 2 n. 102.

growl, groan, crow, infant noise—and 'Ha, Ha, He'. These provide a background chorus of motivated utterance from which emerge the arbitrary signs of English. The designs provide a further environment of natural signs comprising both mimetic forms and expressive gestures. As coordinated accompaniments to the text, they suggest the 'hieroglyphic' form of semiosis, that combination of word and gesture which Warburton described as an early mode of communication underlying the figural language of the Bible.

After the birth of primary words (nouns and verbs) out of natural signs, eighteenth-century language theory proposed the secondary splitting-off of other grammatical forms, such as the derivation of adjectives from nouns. A language dominated by repeated adjective/noun pairings that imply a common root for both would thus indicate an early stage of linguistic development. Just such a pattern is a leading characteristic of the *Songs of Innocence*. As Gleckner has pointed out, 'just as the nouns emerge, as it were, from the adjectives ostensibly "modifying" them, so too do the adjectives emerge from the nouns—a kind of indissoluble grammatical and dictional unity that not only conveys the essentials of the state of innocence but dramatizes the condition of being that state represents'.[8] The Introduction poem is typical in this respect, containing at least three pleonastic pairs: 'pleasant glee' (is there any other sort?), 'merry chear', and 'happy chear' (E 7, K111). If we view these proximate verbal tautologies from the perspective of language evolution, as that was understood in Blake's time, then they situate the poem at an early stage of personal and cultural history. The five words in question are just beginning to proceed in different grammatical and semantic directions from a common root—ultimately, a natural sign expressive of a merry/happy/pleasant/gleeful/cheerful state of mind. We can also imagine a common source ('vale'?) for 'valleys wild' in the Introduction to *Innocence*, and another for 'sorrow sore' in 'The Little Girl Found',[9] with sound shifts as the mode of their etymological fission. A much simpler sound shift accounts for the etymological regression from 'sweep' to a fictive but pathetically

[8] 'Blake's Verbal Technique', in Rosenfeld, *Blake*, pp. 321–32 (quotation from p. 322). Gleckner makes his important observations without reference to 18th-century grammatical theory.

[9] E 22, K 114. 'The Little Girl Lost' and 'The Little Girl Found' were first written for and printed as part of *Songs of Innocence*, but were later placed in the *Songs of Experience* when Blake began issuing them as part of a single composite work.

appropriate root form, 'weep', in 'The Chimney Sweeper' (E 10, K 117). The child's speech, unable to pronounce the initial sibilant, returns us to an expressive, natural sign that becomes an implicit commentary on both linguistic and social institutions. The myth of return, played out in Blake's poems of children lost and found, is embodied in the trajectory of linguistic recovery shaping the language of the *Songs of Innocence*.

The verbal tendons unifying Blake's anthology extend well beyond single adjective/noun pairs. Adjectives form metonymic chains connected by related sounds or meanings (for example, *sweet*, *meek*, *mild*, *tender*, *soft*, *wooly*, *warm*, *white*, *clean*) that in turn link the various nouns they modify. One such cluster of nouns becomes thematic in several poems and provides an essential grounding for the language of innocence. The opening questions of origin in 'The Lamb' are answered in the second verse through a comparative, quasi-etymological, treatment of names:

Little Lamb who made thee
Dost thou know who made thee
Gave thee life & bid thee feed.
By the stream & o'er the mead;
Gave thee clothing of delight,
Softest clothing wooly bright;
Gave thee such a tender voice,
Making all the vales rejoice!
Little Lamb who made thee
Dost thou know who made thee

Little Lamb I'll tell thee,
Little Lamb I'll tell thee!
He is called by thy name,
For he calls himself a Lamb:
He is meek & he is mild,
He became a little child:
I a child & thou a lamb,
We are called by his name.
Little Lamb God bless thee.
Little Lamb God bless thee.

(E 8–9, K 115)

As for eighteenth-century etymologists from Michaelis to Tooke, this reply assumes that the relationships among words are keys to a knowledge of extra-linguistic, even ontological, origins. The reflected symmetry of 'He is called by thy name' and 'We are called by his name' indicates the common derivation and interchangeability of 'child', 'Lamb', and Christ, immanent throughout the *Songs* whenever these names for Him are spoken. 'Shepherd', 'father', and all their attendant adjectives and named qualities also gather about, and derive their meanings from, this central point of origin. Herder, who stresses how 'naturally' his scenario of naming unfolds in the passage quoted earlier, is clearly offering a secular substitute for Adam naming the beasts. In contrast, Blake's use of natural signs derives its innocence, its Adamic character, through the presence of the new Adam as the implied referent throughout the language of innocence. The patterns of secondary motivation in that language thereby recapitulate the primary motivation of Christ as incarnational sign; in both cases, spiritual meanings are immanent within the material signifiers. Names, an essential means for establishing differences within a taxonomic system, are in 'The Lamb' a way of discovering the common identity underlying such differences. Thus, these many names in one—or one name in many—are Adamic by being revelatory of true essences, but pre-Adamic in their return to a state before the processes of classification and desynonymization had begun. 'Christ' and 'Jesus' need not be spoken, for He is named by all other names in innocence. Individual words (*child*, *lamb*, *meek*, *tender voice*, *rejoice*, *He*, *I*, *thou*, and *name*) achieve their full meaning only in relation to Christ, conceived either as a shared origin and referent or as a universalized form of C. S. Peirce's 'interpretant', the companion sign providing the necessary context for realizing the meaning of a sign within a triadic model of signification.[10] Christ, as the sign of the father/origin, must be 'ever nigh' to keep the sign of the child from wandering forever in the 'lonely fen' of a wholly natural semiotic ('The Little Boy Found', E 11, K 121).

In 'The Divine Image', the immanence of the incarnational sign within the language of innocence becomes thematic. The poem achieves its 'virtues of delight' (E 12, K 117) because its physiognomic allegory and logical equations lead to 'the human form divine', the origin and telos of the poem's language, speaker, and implied

[10] See ch. 1 n. 52.

readers. This 'form' joining language, man, and God is performative rather than structural, for its presence is initiated by prayers made and answered, a spiritually transformed version of the echoes and other interchanges between natural signs and their referents elsewhere in *Innocence*. The same grammar and logic appear in 'A Divine Image', originally intended for the *Songs of Experience*:

> Cruelty has a Human Heart
> And Jealousy a Human Face
> Terror, the Human Form Divine
> and Secrecy, the Human Dress.
> The Human Dress, is forged Iron
> The Human Form, a fiery Forge.
> The Human Face, a Furnace seal'd
> The Human Heart, its hungry Gorge.[11]

But in this harshly contrary poem, there is no prayer, and the logic leads away from the human form divine, now reduced to the middle term in a series of equations (x = y, y = z) eliminated by the implied conclusion (x = z).

Without the transformative immanence of the incarnational sign, natural signs become for Blake all that we might expect from his opinions about nature conceived as an alterity granted ontological presence independent of mind. Blake's critique of the natural sign, and other hypostatizations of eighteenth-century rationalist linguistics, begins even before the etching of the *Songs of Innocence*. His three short tracts of about 1788, *All Religions are One* and the two series of *There is No Natural Religion*, attack the foundations of natural sign theory and suggest a very different conception of language. If a religion based on an *ab extra* nature merely repeats 'the same dull round' (E 2–3, K 97–8), then a language based on responses to that nature must be equally limited.[12] But man's desires are greater than the world created by organs of physical perception and reason—'the ratio of all we have already known'. Since language is capable of expressing those desires, it too must

[11] E 32, K 221. The poem appears in only one copy (BB) of the combined *Songs* printed by Blake. Copy BB also contains 'The Human Abstract', the replacement for 'A Divine Image' in all other complete copies.

[12] The point here is much the same as Blake's criticism of Locke for being misled into criticizing language because of his false metaphysics (annotations to Reynolds, E 659, K 474); see my discussion of this passage in ch. 2.

have an origin and a 'Poetic or Prophetic character' beyond the confines of nature and reason, those fundamental principles of eighteenth-century semiotics. To replace these, Blake offers two very different models for language: 'The Jewish & Christian Testaments' because they 'are An original derivation from the Poetic Genius' (E 1, K98), and Christ's body, the signifier with a motivated relationship to a spiritual—not a fallen or utterly natural—signified. As Blake writes at the conclusion of *There is No Natural Religion*, 'Therefore God becomes as we are, that we may be as he is'. These tantalizing hints toward an alternative semiotic would seem to lead in much the same direction as Boehme's language of incarnational signs, summarized in the previous chapter, but with a greater emphasis on poetry (for which the Bible is the great exemplar) as a derivative of the 'Poetic Genius . . . the true Man' that also created 'the forms of all things' (*All Religions are One*). By sharing the same origin with these forms, the secondary motivations of such a poetry manifest its primary motivation—not mimetically in direct relation to objects as referents, but to the shared ontological source of all form in spirit.

Blake presents a much bleaker picture of the history of language, its powers and its limits, in *Tiriel*. His concerns in that poem are focused more on practical consequences than underlying linguistic issues touching on matters metaphysical or epistemological. The world of the poem, for which the eponymous anti-hero is the central icon, is clearly in an advanced state of decline—political, ethical, even physical. It is as though Blake had turned Ossianic poetry upside-down to create a vision of man, nature, and language at once both primitive and decadent. The entire poem evokes a condition made explicit in the episodes concerning Har and Heva. They are Tiriel's parents, and thus (as Blake's illustrations confirm) even older than the aged tyrant, yet they act 'like two children' (E 277, K 100) in an infantile imitation of innocence. Something similar has happened to language—a collapse into a primitivism bearing a parodic relationship to eighteenth-century theories of linguistic origins and to the poetry, such as Ossian's, taken to be their representative.[13]

[13] For a somewhat different treatment of this thesis, see H. Ostrom, 'Blake's *Tiriel* and the Dramatization of Collapsed Language', *Papers on Language & Literature*, 19 (1983), 167–82. Ostrom does not relate his insights about the poem's linguistic themes to their 18th-century contexts.

The dominant form of utterance in *Tiriel* is the curse, a speech-act referred to by name some thirty-nine times in the poem's 354 lines. Cursing has displaced other forms of speech, including naming, that primary linguistic activity so essential to theories of linguistic origins and Blake's own language of innocence. In the first two words of his opening speech, Tiriel fulfils the patriarchal task of naming his people: 'Accursed race of Tiriel' (E 276, K 99). We learn, only four lines later, that his offspring are 'sons of the Curse', and later that the act rebounds against the cursing father: 'is not the curse now come upon your [Tiriel's] head' (E 277, K 100). In his capacity as Adamic progenitor and namer, Tiriel offers only curses. As ruler and lawgiver, his words are efficacious only when reduced to that same common denominator.

Another speech-act is implicated in the linguistic reductions of *Tiriel*. Cursing and prophesying have much in common. Both may be thought of as the first part of an event not yet completed, to borrow from Schleiermacher's definition of prophecy.[14] If and when that event is completed, then the speech-act constituting its first part takes on the character of a performative utterance. *Tiriel* might be included as one of Blake's 'Prophetic Works'[15] if construed as a dark vision of the future, but all proclamatory speech in the poem takes the form of cursing. As we have seen with Blake's painting of *Christ Blessing* (Plate 8), that mode of speech or gesture, in its ideal perfection, is also rendered a performative. In *Tiriel*, blessing is reduced either to the pathetically ineffectual gestures and prattle of Har (E 278, K 101) or to a confused equivalency with cursing. As his eldest son says of Tiriel, 'His blessing was a cruel curse. His curse may be a blessing' (E 276, K 99). Language, as simple reference to that which exists outside or prior to utterance, must remain largely intact for there to be a dialogue in *Tiriel*; but those proleptic forms of language, including not only prophecy and blessing but also laws and commands that precede the events to which they refer and constitute one of man's chief methods of extending linguistic into social and religious structures, have all degenerated into a wholly negative form of semiosis. As Tiriel pronounces in his

[14] See F. Schleiermacher, *On Religion* (1958, first pub. 1799), 89.

[15] E 276. A. C. Swinburne's note on the poem in his *Blake* (1868) appears in the section on 'The Prophetic Books', pp. 199–200. *Tiriel* is printed in *Prophetic Writings of Blake*, ed. D. J. Sloss and J. P. R. Wallis (1926), 2: 278–89.

final speech, 'Thy laws O Har & Tiriels wisdom end together in a curse' (E 285, K 109).

The Har and Heva episode adds to the sense of a breakdown in word/referent relationships. Their continual confusion over Tiriel's identity shows their inability to focus on a single 'distinguishing mark', as Herder calls it, which then becomes a person's or object's name. This failure in sensate perception, but one step away from Tiriel's literal blindness, has as its corollary a failure in sign recognition. In the Adamic ideal, the correspondence between name and nature permits knowledge of the former to reveal something about the latter. But Tiriel has little difficulty in disguising himself, for even after he refers to himself by name and Har announces 'thou art Tiriel' (E 279, K 102), his name and his identity continually draw apart in the speeches of Har and Heva. The person standing before them remains only a 'poor blind man' who 'takest the name of Tiriel' (E 278, K 101), as though it were not his own, and is 'so like Tiriel' (E 279, K 103), but never the man himself. In this context, the verb in Heva's act of denomination—'Then let thy name be Tiriel' (E 279, K 102) stresses how merely contingent and arbitrary naming has become, a parody of God's creative 'Let there be . . .' in the first chapter of Genesis.

The puerile state of nature into which Har and Heva have lapsed also bears a parodic relationship to semiotic ideals. The imagery of singing birds (Plate 6) or bleating sheep necessary for the primal scene of natural sign theory is confined to Heva's invitation to see 'our singing birds' and hear 'Har sing in the great cage' (E 279, K103), a location that marks his song as a substitute for, or imitation of, the birds' song. Much as a language limited to the senses follows 'the same dull round' in *There is No Natural Religion*, a language derived from natural signs is shown in *Tiriel* to be a prison house.[16]

When Tiriel leaves the company of Har and Heva, he encounters a more energetic, but more superstitious and malevolent, worshipper of nature in the person of Ijim. Name and identity again split apart, for Ijim believes Tiriel to be an 'Impudent fiend' whom he has 'at last . . . caught . . . in the form of Tiriel' (E 280–1, K 104–5). Ijim

[16] The sense of confinement and futility in this passage is sharpened by a recognition of its source in *King Lear*: 'Come, let's away to prison. | We two alone will sing like birds i' the cage' (5. 3. 8–9). On *Lear* as an influence on *Tiriel*, see K. Raine, 'Some Sources of *Tiriel*', *Huntington Library Quarterly*, 21 (1957), 1–36, esp. pp. 13–17.

believes that this fiend has a 'glib & eloquent tongue' (E 280, K 104) because of his supposed ability not only to assume Tiriel's voice, but also to roar like 'a dreadful lion' or 'whisper in [Ijim's] ears' like 'a toad or like a newt' (E 281, K 105). Thus, Tiriel is granted a voice like one of nature's own, but it is the wild and inarticulate cry of beasts or the invidious whisper of Satan when he becomes 'Squat like a Toad close at the ear of *Eve*'.[17] Ijim is in a sense right about Tiriel. After Ijim leaves, Tiriel uses a storm-tossed rhetoric of the sublime to call up the 'enormous voices' of nature (E 282, K 106), and later he conjures up the snakes that enfold around the 'madding brows' of his daughter, Hela (E 283, K 108). But in both cases, the text explicitly indicates that the medium of these performative conversions of word to world is a *curse*.

Tiriel leads us finally to an even lower stage of linguistic diminution. The destruction brought upon Tiriel's children through his curses leaves them in a condition even below inarticulate utterance: 'Desolate. Loathed. Dumb Astonishd' (E 282, K 107). A similar fate awaits Tiriel who, with his last words, pronounces the silence they have created—'my voice is past' (E 285, K 110). Here and elsewhere in Blake's poetry, silence is never the sign of the transcendence of language's materiality, but a descent below it. The silences of *Tiriel* are a precursor to the 'Dumb despair' that would have been Albion's lot in *Jerusalem* if Los had not built 'the stubborn structure' of language (Pl. 36; E 183, K 668).

My comments on *Tiriel* have focused on the fallen state of natural language imaged in the poem. The repeated curses embody that condition, but the rhetoric of the whole is dominated by an overwrought Ossianic sublimity. Whereas parataxis or semantic insufficiency are key elements in the *Songs of Innocence*, providing the 'space' for the reader to build interpretations, *Tiriel* offers a semantic surplus that would seem to overflow into what Swinburne was the first to call 'faint allegory'.[18] The exotic character names, supernatural events, exuberance of the rhetoric, and various *aporia* in the narrative require that, to take the poem seriously, one must assume the presence of more than simple denotative meanings, as

[17] Milton, *Paradise Lost*, bk. 4, line 800.

[18] *Blake*, p. 199. Sloss and Wallis, in their edn. of Blake's *Prophetic Writings*, call *Tiriel* an 'almost entirely dim allegory' (2: 275). On the theory of semantic surplus in relation to Ossian, see ch. 2 and n. 112.

though the manuscript were a relic whose meaning had disappeared along with the ancient culture that produced it.[19] Most readings of *Tiriel*, including mine, take it to be a metaphoric structure in search of a referent, one which the critic is eager to supply. My point is not to question such interpretations *en bloc*, but to indicate how Blake's language prompts such responses.

We can gain a surer sense of Blake's loose allegory and its evolution in the poems of the Lambeth period (1790–1800) through reference to two grammatical models suggested by Morton W. Bloomfield.[20] In personification allegory (e.g., 'Truth treads down Error'), the abstract substantives carry in themselves no figural displacement. The burden of metaphoricity rests on the simple predicate. 'Treads down' can only refer literally to an animate being, and thus its presence here converts the substantives into personifications. Interpretation, as a conversion back to an abstract but literal meaning, need only operate on the predicate. Blake uses this mode in the early experiments, 'then She bore Pale desire' and 'Woe cried the muse'; in both works, adjectives and adverbs also function as indices of figuration. Bloomfield contrasts this type of structure with what he calls 'symbolism' (without any suggestion of motivation), as in 'Jerusalem defeats Babylon'. In this case, the predicate is not figural but the substantives are. Interpretation operates on the substantives by converting them into abstractions. Blake's typical procedure in his so-called mythic poetry is to compound Bloomfield's two modes: 'Jerusalem treads down Babylon'. Works from 'The Song of Liberty' of *c.*1790–3 to *Jerusalem* (*c.*1804–18) are complex elaborations of this basic grammatical and figural strategy. If the interpreter takes such statements as an allegory, then he must transform both the substantives and the predicates to return to a literal and general statement (e.g., 'truth defeats error'), although these usually have some residual metaphoricity supplied by the critic's own rhetoric (as in 'defeats'). S. Foster Damon finds this kind of double-figuration even in the 'faint allegory' of *Tiriel*. He states, for example, that

[19] Some of the difficulties may be explained away as the results of incomplete revision, but there is no possibility that the manuscript is a draft for a realistic narrative or self-explanatory allegory like *Pilgrim's Progress*.

[20] 'A Grammatical Approach to Personification Allegory', *Modern Philology*, 60 (1963), 161–71. Although the examples I use suggest some of Blake's themes, they are taken from Bloomfield, who makes no reference to Blake (nor to the synthesis of the two categories I suggest here).

'*Har & Heva* symbolize poetry and painting in a degraded state'.[21] This view would lead us to interpret lines in the poem such as 'till thou hast . . . heard Har sing in the great cage' (E 279, K 103) to mean 'until you have seen poetry demonstrate its limitations'. Thousands of lines in Blake's poetry prompt those searching for conceptual meaning to produce similar translations. Consider, for example, the following:

> The Guardian Prince of Albion burns in his nightly tent
>
> (*America*, Pl. 3; E 52, K 197)
>
> Rahab triumphs over all she took Jerusalem | Captive . . .
>
> (*The Four Zoas*; E 385, K 356)
>
> I behold Babylon in the opening Street of London
>
> (*Jerusalem*, Pl. 74; E 229, K 714)

Of course no self-respecting Blake critic would ever produce, in response to *America* or *Jerusalem*, anything so leaden and mechanistic as my Damonesque reading of the lines from *Tiriel*, but the only way to avoid some fundamental transformation of the figural into the literal, or into some alternative figural construction, would be to give up interpreting such lines as forms of semantically displaced figuration—metaphor, allegory, symbol, myth, or what you will.

Oddly enough, Blake's species of allegory can carry us back full-circle to the literal—if, in the context of what he calls the 'fable', we take the substantives as literal references to animate creatures who could indeed tread on another, or triumph over her, or be seen in London's streets. If we allow Blake's tropologies this kind of freedom, then they tend to break down the interpretively useful but thin partitions between the literal and the figural, making them both portions of an expanded reality. To read the doubly-figural in this way may seem naive, but this literalization of figuration is precisely what Blake asks us to do in his definition of 'vision' in *A Vision of the Last Judgment*.[22] The conversion of 'Fable' into an 'Allegory' of abstract substantives is from this perspective the degradation of 'Vision . . . a Representation of what Eternally Exists' into

[21] *Blake* (1924), 307.

[22] E 554, K 604; see discussion in ch. 2.

an Abstract, which is a Negation
Not only of the Substance from which it is derived
A murderer of its own Body: but also a murderer
Of every Divine Member: it is the Reasoning Power
An Abstract objecting power, that Negatives every thing[23]

But as we shall see in *The Book of Urizen*, it is no easy matter to avoid objectification and abstraction when vision is a 'representation' in language—Blake's as much as a critic's.

Further complications accrue when the substantives in what we presume to be allegorical propositions are also historical figures, for they import into a text a whole world of acts and beings inscribed, as it were, in another 'text'. Blake first wrestled with this situation in *The French Revolution* of 1791. One of the two main rhetorical strategies is to convert historical events and personages into universal signs through predicates that act as metaphoric indices, a figural deformation often confirmed by subsequent Ossianic similes. This approach gives us lines such as 'Then the King glow'd: his Nobles fold round, like the sun of old time quench'd in clouds' (E 289, K 137). The predicate in the first clause deflects the human subject into an object reference implicit in his lineage from Louis XIV, *Le Roi-Soleil.* The figural treatment in Blake's text is thus motivated by the historical pre-text. The same type of semantic shift occurs in the next clause: 'fold round' forces 'Nobles' toward 'clouds', thereby supplementing the first displacement. Both are confirmed by the simile drawing out the implications of the preceding predicates. While these de-personifications convert discrete human events into cyclical and natural ones, the other main rhetorical device works in the opposite direction, humanizing natural objects and events to create a world where 'shady mountains | In fear utter voices of thunder', the 'Clouds of wisdom prophetic reply', and 'the morning prophecies to its clouds' (E 286, K 134).

These chiastic movements in the language of *The French Revolution* intersect at the conceptual nexus of its rhetoric, a point at which the usual semantic distinctions between the human and the non-human, cultural and natural history, collapse into a unity which, to a taxonomic grammarian, would seem more than a little indiscriminate.

[23] *Jerusalem*, Pl. 10; E 153, K 629. See also Blake's annotation to Reynolds: 'To Generalize is to be an Idiot' (E 641, K 451).

The precedents for Blake's figural strategies come from a very different realm. The example of similar tropes in Ossian is most important; but the belief that God becomes as we are so that we may be as He is, so clearly enunciated on the concluding plate of *There is No Natural Religion*, offers a parallel process with more than stylistic implications. The dynamics of this primary spiritual chiasmus are repeated in the secondary motivations of Blake's rhetoric as the double-movement of personification and de-personification. The union of nature and man where these two vectors cross also figures forth the original state of language and religion envisioned by eighteenth-century mythographers and speculative linguists. Blake offers his own straightforward summary of such views on Plate 11 of *The Marriage of Heaven and Hell*:

> The ancient Poets animated all sensible objects with Gods or Geniuses, calling them by the names and adorning them with the properties of woods, rivers, mountains, lakes, cities, nations, and whatever their enlarged & numerous senses could percieve.
>
> And particularly they studied the genius of each city & country. placing it under its mental deity.
>
> Till a system was formed, which some took advantage of & enslav'd the vulgar by attempting to realize or abstract the mental dieties from their objects: thus began Priesthood.[24]

These 'Gods or Geniuses' all 'reside in the human breast', as Blake tells us on the same plate, and are united with perceived objects through the linguistic activities of naming and poetic 'adorning'. In this sense, objects are humanized. This primal state of language and perception can be recapitulated, at least in part, through a tropology that tends to break down the conventional grammatical and logical distinctions between gods, men, and nature—that is, the rhetoric

[24] E 38, K 153. My comments on this passage are developed out of the excellent analysis in Adams, 'Blake and the Philosophy of Literary Symbolism', pp. 136–9. Many of his observations also appear in Adams, 'Blake, *Jerusalem*, and Symbolic Form', *Blake Studies*, 7 no. 2 (1975), 144–8. For the similarity between the historical narrative of *Marriage* Pl. 11 and Blake's sense of a decline from 'vision' to allegory, see ch. 2 n. 159. There are many precursors to Blake's account of the 'ancient Poets' and the fall of their language into 'system' and abstraction, including passages in Vico, *New System*, pp. 116–17, 127–8, 139; and Herder's *Essay on the Origin of Language*, pp. 133–4. Among the relevant texts that Blake may have known are W. Stukeley, *Stonehenge* (1740), 59; R. P. Knight, *An Account . . . of the Worship of Priapus* (1786), 45–6, 50–3, 173–5, 188, 192; and Swedenborg, *True Christian Religion*, 1: 300–3, sec. 203–5. This line of thinking finds its fullest development in G. F. Creuzer, *Symbolik und Mythologie der alten Völker* (1810–12).

Blake begins to develop in *The French Revolution*. Thus, when Blake wrote, many years later in *A Descriptive Catalogue*, that 'Mr. B. has in his hands poems of the highest antiquity' (E 542, K 578), he was referring to poems written by those same hands.

Blake's easily overlooked use of 'the', where we would expect 'their', in the passage quoted above hints at another dimension to the language of the ancient poets. Adam calls each beast by '*the* name' (Genesis 2: 19) and thus the habit of 'calling' things 'by *the* names' suggests a similar level of motivation. The Adamic character of this poetic naming is reinforced by Blake's reference, in the context of a similar mythologic history in *A Descriptive Catalogue*, to 'the eternal attributes, or divine names, which, when erected into gods, become destructive to humanity'.[25] In most theories of primary motivation, objects precede, and become the models for, words. Thus, Adam names the beasts according to *their* nature. But the primary motivation Blake suggests is just the reverse. The naming performed by the ancient poets animated objects with a divinity granted them by that performance, and thus the link between these names and their referents derived from the nature of language, not from the nature of objects prior to naming. The motivation flowed from word to object, as in the Logos and the performative or kerygmatic sign, and not from the object to the word, as in natural signs.[26] If indeed the ground for primary motivation was a shared linguistic spirit, then the relationship between names and objects was conterminous with motivated relationships among words. The now difficult juncture between primary and secondary motivation was then a seamless fabric because the 'secondary'—that is, the motivated structure of language—was the basis for the 'primary'. In these ancient circumstances, primal naming and verbal 'adorning' were one. To borrow from Shelley's *Defence of Poetry*, the 'vitally metaphorical' language of the ancient poets 'marks'—indeed, creates—'the before unapprehended relations of things' because those relations are brought into being by the animating power of Adamic poetry and its performative signs.[27]

[25] E 536, K 571. Later in the catalogue, in a discussion of what 'Jacob Bryant, and all antiquaries have proved', Blake refers to this same prelapsarian epoch when 'All [peoples] had originally one language' (E 543, K 579), indicating once again the residual Adamicism of 18th-century mythography.

[26] For a characterization of the performative sign in these terms, see ch. 1 n. 52.

[27] *Poetry and Prose*, p. 482.

Blake's description of the loss of the old animating powers focuses on the religious consequences, but these imply concomitant changes in the structure of language. For eighteenth-century rationalist grammarians, the progress of language followed the same course of increased systematization and abstraction criticized by Blake as a fall away from an original unity. His perspective shares common ground with those philologic speculators, from Warburton to Cleland, who posited a motivated original language in which words and things were united, and with the etymological politics of Horne Tooke, who also saw the progress of abstraction as the enslavement of 'the vulgar'. The tropes in Blake's poetry that intimate a more primitive and less abstract condition embody this same critique of grammatical structures, and the religious and political systems they support, that Blake presents on Plate 11 of *The Marriage of Heaven and Hell*.

The Book of Thel (1789) would seem to be a step back toward the original state of language imagined in *The Marriage* and evoked in the *Songs of Innocence*. Like Tiriel, Thel travels through 'the vales of Har',[28] but presumably before its fall into the decadent condition we witness in *Tiriel*. The creatures of nature speak in this pastoral world, much as in the old legends of animals conversing in Eden. The Lilly, Cloud, and Clod of Clay are natural signs raised to the level of articulate speech. The Worm cannot speak, presumably because of his tender years, but his weeping signifies none the less. All the beings Thel meets are animated with semiotic capabilities derived ultimately from a transcendental presence whom Thel calls, in an allusion to Genesis 3: 8, 'the voice | Of him that walketh in the garden in the evening time' (Pl. 1; E 3, K 127).

Blake may have written a now lost early version of *Thel* that maintained to its conclusion the vision of an articulate and benign world of natural signs. A preliminary sketch of two plates in the poem, the first showing the design etched on the penultimate plate and the second with a design not used in the book, suggests that Blake may have originally contemplated a very different final plate.[29] The

[28] *Tiriel*, E 277, K 100; *Book of Thel*, Pls. 2–4, 6 (E 4–6, K 128–30).

[29] Butlin no. 218, acquired by the British Museum in 1982. For discussions of the several possible implications of this pencil drawing, see R. N. Essick, review of Butlin in *Blake: An Illustrated Quarterly*, 16 (1982), 32–3; and G. E. Bentley, Jr., 'From Sketch to Text in Blake', *Blake: An Illustrated Quarterly*, 19 (1986), 128–41.

first through the penultimate text plates bear small cursive letters, whereas the preliminary plate containing 'Thel's Motto' and the last plate have much larger characters with a greater slant to the right. Further, the letter 'g' on both these plates shows a left-pointing serif not found in Blake's other etched writings before *c.*1791.[30] But even if the final plate is not a late addition, its sudden shift from pastoral pathos to the horrific sublime cannot fail to colour our reading of all that has come before.

Thel's journey ends at 'her own grave plot' where she listens to her own corpse restating in an altered tone the 'why' questions with which she began. But the 'eternal gates' through which Thel passes in the first line of the final plate and the 'voice of sorrow' she hears 'breathed from the hollow pit' (E 6, K 130) also belong to Tiriel, or at least to one of 'those whose mouths are graves whose teeth the gates of eternal death' (*Tiriel*, E 815, K 109). The lack of any explanation for this sudden change in vision and voice suggests that the 'Dolours and lamentations' Thel hears at the end were somehow implicit in the mild utterances of Thel's earlier instructors. A note Blake wrote in his copy of Henry Boyd's translation of Dante's *Inferno* indicates how this can be: 'Nature Teaches nothing of Spiritual Life but only of Natural Life'.[31] Thel had sought answers to her spiritual questions from natural signs, but these can provide information only about nature. Plate 11 of *The Marriage* explains historically, and the *Songs of Innocence* demonstrate poetically, how natural objects can be transformed into incarnational signs through divine and human action. Thel's interlocutors attempt just the reverse, treating natural phenomena as though they constituted a spiritual semiotic in their own right. This attempt fails for the very

[30] First pointed out in D. V. Erdman, 'Suppressed and Altered Passages in Blake's *Jerusalem*', *Studies in Bibliography*, 17 (1964), 52. The oft-repeated suggestion that the Motto and Pl. 8 are late additions was first made in Blake, *Prophetic Writings*, 2: 267–8.

[31] E 634, K 412. The annotations are generally dated *c.*1800 on the assumption that Blake received his copy of Boyd's translation, pub. 1785, from W. Hayley when Blake moved to Felpham in 1800. But just as the final plate of *Thel* may have been composed and etched somewhat later than the 1789 date on the title page, Blake could have written his annotations a good deal earlier than 1800. Although there are a considerable number of modern interpretations of *Thel*, the only one to take the same basic view I develop here is D. R. Pearce, 'Natural Religion and the Plight of Thel', *Blake Studies*, 8 no. 1 (1978), 23–35. The critique of natural religion also implies a criticism of the poetry with which *Thel* is often associated, such as J. Langhorne's popular *Fables of Flora* (1771), with its sentimentality and speaking flowers, and E. Darwin's versified natural philosophy, *The Loves of the Plants*, first pub. April 1789.

reason Blake proclaims with his title, *There is No Natural Religion*. Systems limited to natural signs, even in their mildest guises, provide no way to raise semiosis or consciousness above their systemic limitations. By listening only to 'the voices of the ground' (E 6, K 130), Thel is led inevitably to their undertones. Those voices are not only deadly but interrogative, for natural systems only reflect back to Thel the questions with which she began. Her own voiced response is a 'shriek', a return to that pre-articulate *cri du coeur* so important to the theorists of natural signification. If language began with an emotive cry of fear or pain, then a return to linguistic origins will also lead to a world stimulating those responses.

'Thel's Motto' offers related questions about signification:

> Does the Eagle know what is in the pit?
> Or wilt thou go ask the Mole:
> Can Wisdom be put in a silver rod?
> Or Love in a golden bowl?
>
> (E 3, K 127)

The rational, natural answer to the first question is 'no', followed by a turn to the sightless expert on the underground. But only the eagle, 'a portion of Genius',[32] provides answers that can release us from the mole's limitations. The problem of choosing which voice to attend to evolves into a more fundamental question, taken verbatim from a deleted passage in Tiriel's final speech (E 815, K 110), about the relationship between immaterial (or transcendental) signifieds (Wisdom and Love) and material signifiers (silver rod and golden bowl). The questions Thel hears from the pit, with their bleak view of the body and organs of sense, express a general fear of embodiment—in semiotic terms, a dread of the signifier. If material form is *ipso facto* a restriction, then even the incarnational sign may be compromised. How then can a poet use his medium without being caught like Thel in its restrictive trammels? But a lack of form, of outline and identity, can result in the evanescence and indefiniteness of the Cloud and of Thel's own self-conception:

[32] *Marriage of Heaven and Hell*, Pl. 9: 'When thou seest an Eagle, thou seest a portion of Genius' (E 37, K 152).

> Ah! Thel is like a watry bow. and like a parting cloud.
> Like a reflection in a glass. like shadows in the water.
> Like dreams of infants. like a smile upon an infants face,
> Like the doves voice, like transient day, like music
> in the air; . . . (E 3, K 127)

The progressive similes not only de-personify, and hence de-humanize, Thel, but they also drain her of substance and form.[33] Simile, as a substitute for and a deflection away from forms of 'to be', is itself implicated in this shrinking (and finally shrieking) away from identity. In her search for form-as-meaning, Thel is caught between the indefinite and a deadly materiality. The semiotic corollary to this plot is the problematic implicit in the Motto, the impossibility of communicating meaning except through a material medium.

The Devil boldly proclaims an answer to the quandaries of embodied meaning and material form in *The Marriage of Heaven and Hell*: 'Man has no Body distinct from his Soul for that calld Body is a portion of Soul discernd by the five Senses. the chief inlets of Soul in this age' (Pl. 4; E 34, K 149). In a manoeuvre typical of Blake's habits of thought, the Devil questions the ground of the troubling body/soul dichotomy, and thereby also undermines the basis of the division between material signifier and transcendental signified. The Devil offers a Kantian shift of the problem from metaphysics to epistemology and even hints that it is a matter of historical contingency 'in this age', much as Blake indicates on Plate 11 of *The Marriage*. But I wonder if the underlying issue of dualism can be overcome, even for Blake, by simply positing a prelapsarian unity. One plate earlier in *The Marriage*, we learn that 'Without Contraries is no progression' (E 34, K 149), and it is difficult to imagine contrariety without the very sorts of differences exemplified by the body/soul distinction and recorded everywhere in the structure

[33] What we might call 'de-substantiation', a variant of de-personification (discussed earlier), occurs whenever the concrete is compared to the immaterial, as in 'a quiver with its burning stores, a bow like that of night' (*America*, Pl. 1; E 51, K 196). Such structures reverse the sensibilist thrust of conventional 18th-century tropes. For a general study of the problem of identity in *Thel*, see C. Heppner, ' "A Desire of Being": Identity and *The Book of Thel*', *Colby Library Quarterly*, 13 (1977), 79–98. Although Heppner makes many interesting observations, I could not disagree more with his sense that Thel's interlocutors offer an appropriate model for *human* identity.

of our language. As we will see later in *The Book of Urizen*, the Devil in *The Marriage* does not sweep the problem of difference and its presence in semiosis from Blake's later writings.

The *Songs of Experience* (1794) continue and extend Blake's critique of the dominant sign theories of the eighteenth century. The differences between the linguistic landscape of innocence and of experience derive in large measure from the structural and functional distinction between two states of semiotic consciousness, one that unself-consciously perceives (and hence creates) incarnational signs as the embodiment and expression of the spirit immanent within the material, and another that is self-consciously aware of the differential nature of language. The Introduction to *Innocence* offers a free interchange between sky-borne child and earth-bound adult, between laughing and weeping, between singing and writing, and between the source of inspiration and the responses of the audience. In the Introduction to *Experience*, the Bard calls for a reunion of soul and body in the incarnate sign, 'The Holy Word' (E 18, K 210), but 'Earth's Answer' speaks only of division and bondage. 'Ah! Sun-Flower' (E 25, K 215) repeats a similar institution of unbridgeable difference in the very act of expressing the desire for union. Other speakers and characters in *Experience* respond to its inherent divisions with confusion, sorrow, fear, or even ghoulish delight. The common characteristic of their poems is a rhetoric that emphasizes the tension between terms defined in counterdistinction to each other. This pattern is clearly exemplified by 'The Clod & the Pebble' (E 19, K 211). Its major thematic structure, a division between two views of love, is repeated in the juxtapositions of terms within each perspective: itself/another, care/ease (and 'Joys'/'loss of ease' in the final stanza), and Heaven/Hell. Both versions of love are dominated by, and find expression only through, a matrix of semantic differences.

The speakers of several poems in *Experience* deploy combinations of paradigmatic logic and natural perception—that is, the machinery of eighteenth-century rationalist grammar—in doomed attempts to overcome the dualities built into their own strategies. The rhetorical questions in the second stanza of 'The Fly' suggest the same sort of chiasmic convergence of the human and the non-human we found in the tropology of *The French Revolution*:

Am not I
A fly like thee?
Or art not thou
A man like me?

(E 23, K 213)

The second question might initiate a process of humanization, but in the poem's concluding stanzas the speaker falls into a parody of syllogistic logic:

If thought is life
And strength & breath:
And the want
Of thought is death;

Then am I
A happy fly,
If I live,
Or if I die.

(E 24, K 213)

The first premiss reduces 'thought' to mere biological existence and the second to a near-tautology (i.e., the 'want' of life is death); the conclusion first reduces the 'I' to the condition of a fly, and finally both to dead objects. This pseudo-logical search for a common denominator, like a process of de-personification without the necessary counter-movement of personification, brings us to the same pit to which natural signs and their religion led Thel.

'The Tyger' presents a more ambitious attempt to move rationally from natural signs to spiritual conclusions:

Tyger Tyger, burning bright,
In the forests of the night;
What immortal hand or eye,
Could frame thy fearful symmetry?

In what distant deeps or skies.
Burnt the fire of thine eyes?
On what wings dare he aspire?
What the hand, dare sieze the fire?

And what shoulder, & what art,
Could twist the sinews of thy heart?

And when thy heart began to beat,
What dread hand? & what dread feet?

What the hammer? what the chain,
In what furnace was thy brain?
What the anvil? what dread grasp,
Dare its deadly terrors clasp!

When the stars threw down their spears
And water'd heaven with their tears:
Did he smile his work to see?
Did he who made the Lamb make thee?

Tyger Tyger burning bright,
In the forests of the night:
What immortal hand or eye,
Dare frame thy fearful symmetry?

(E 24–5, K 214)

The framing of the poem's many questions contains the method by which they can be answered. The speaker believes that the characteristics of a tiger signify the nature of the beast's creator. This god presumably expresses himself through his works; in turn, the observer of those works can interpret them as motivated signs and a pathway back to origins. Once these premisses are assumed, the logical coherence of the signifying system is assured and, like physiognomy, offers a way of determining personality from physical features.[34] The methodology also resembles that of a natural scientist when he attempts to derive unseen causes from the study of their effects, or of an etymologist as he derives the history and origin of a word from its present constituents. When elevated into a theological process, the association between creature and creator produces a tiger-god, a symmetry between material signifier and transcendental signified fearful enough to prevent the speaker from moving beyond the interrogative mode indicative of his sublime withdrawal from the conclusions of his own logic as much as from the tiger itself. That logic leads to further questions when we are offered another animal, the lamb, as the beginning of an argument over origins. Nature's diversity must lead to either polytheism (so many species,

[34] Some years earlier, in *An Island in the Moon*, Blake had associated physiognomy and the tiger in a brief satirical passage on man/animal comparisons: 'I think your face said he is like that noble beast the Tyger' (E 465, K 62).

so many gods), or a god so heterogeneous as to be self-contradictory, or the abandonment of the signifying system represented by 'The Tyger'. The speaker never considers that last alternative but returns to where he began, having moved only from awful questions about the tiger-god's ability ('Could frame . . .') to his audacity ('Dare frame . . .').[35]

The speaker of 'The Tyger' remains so enthralled by the logic of natural signs that he never reflects on the implications of his rhetoric. The god he creates is tigerish, but he is also a human artificer with hands and tools. These anthropomorphizing tendencies in the figural dynamics of mythology are also evident when lightning bolts and rain are converted into spears and tears in the penultimate stanza. While the speaker's argument follows a logical paradigm, the images in the poem evolve one from another through metonymy and synecdoche as the speaker progresses from hand to eye to wings to shoulder to hammer to anvil. This tropic matrix, even in a fragmented state, suggests a very different theory of origins, one capable of perceiving prosopopoeia and metonymically related synecdoches as the linguistic traces of the human form divine. With such perceptions, the speaker could learn that his god is a reification of his own being through language, for 'All deities reside in the human breast' (*Marriage of Heaven and Hell*, Pl. 11; E 38, K 153). The logical and figural orders complement each other in 'The Divine Image' of *Innocence*, but the domination of the figural by the logical results in their mutual distortion in 'The Tyger'. The poem remains suspended between the self-defeating logic of an 'idiot Questioner who is always questioning, | But never capable of answering',[36] and the fragments of a dismembered humanity.

In 'The Lamb', the naming of the animal unifies it with the speaker, God, audience, and author in that name. In 'The Tyger', the insistent naming of the beast initiates a centrifugal logic that divides and distances these same five presences. Yet, all are implicated in that process and are linked, like the tiger and its god, through analogy. Blake is, after all, the one who 'frame[s]' both tiger

[35] Pechey, '1789 and After: Mutations of "Romantic" Discourse', p. 59, interestingly characterizes the ending of 'The Tyger' as a 'deadlock' in which 'the logic of the allegorical signifier has carried the day against the misdirected search for a transcendental signified'.

[36] *Milton*, Pl. 41; E 142, K 533. See also 'Auguries of Innocence': 'The Questioner who sits so sly | Shall never know how to Reply' (E 492, K 433).

and lamb in the media of language and etching in copper.[37] The Hephaestian activities in 'The Tyger' further associate the creator in the poem with the metal-working creator of the poem. Both are as delimited as the speaker by the media in which they labour. When viewed from this self-reflexive perspective, the submergence of a humanizing tropology beneath a sensibilist logic in 'The Tyger' describes Blake's own historical situation. Claims made for the values of the primitive, the poetic, and the figural did not overthrow the dominant late eighteenth-century conception of language founded on a combination of taxonomic grammar and Tooke's reduction of all meanings to their supposed origin in sense impressions. The theological dilemma of the speaker in 'The Tyger' is couched in language embodying the author's semiotic dilemma, the inability to frame communicable meanings in anything other than a structure circumscribed by a limited and limiting consciousness of its nature.

'London' presents even more complex conflicts between semiotic systems and far more explicit bearings on the politics of language theory:

I wander thro' each charter'd street,
Near where the charter'd Thames does flow.
And mark in every face I meet
Marks of weakness, marks of woe.

In every cry of every Man,
In every Infants cry of fear,
In every voice: in every ban,
The mind-forg'd manacles I hear

How the Chimney-sweepers cry
Every blackning Church appalls,
And the hapless Soldiers sigh
Runs in blood down Palace walls

But most thro' midnight streets I hear
How the youthful Harlots curse
Blasts the new-born Infants tear
And blights with plagues the Marriage hearse

(E 26–7, K 216)

[37] Several readers (most recently Hilton, *Literal Imagination*, p. 184) have viewed 'The Tyger' as a text that comments self-reflexively on its own composition. A contrary interpretive tradition is represented by H. Bloom, *Visionary Company* (1961), 31: 'This questioner

As we have seen in Chapter 2, secular language theory in the eighteenth century recognized only two major varieties of signs, natural and conventional, the former a motivated response whether mimetic or expressive, and the latter an arbitrary social construct. 'London' presents the collapse of both types of sign system into disease, at once both social and biological. This semiotic crisis is one of the fundamental thematic issues in the poem and the vehicle for their dramatization in the language of the poem.

Sign theory is thematized by the first stanza of 'London'. Recent interpreters of the poem have quite rightly pointed out the Biblical resonances of the thrice-repeated 'mark[s]',[38] but its context in seventeenth- and eighteenth-century semiotics is equally significant. To 'mark' an object or event is to apprehend its identifying characteristic, its 'mark', by which it can be distinguished from all other objects or events. The primary motivation of this process, beginning with the physical senses, leads to a kind of mental marking/recording that precedes, and establishes the ground for, any secondarily motivated or arbitrary linguistic act of naming, as well as subsequent acts of oral remarking or the visual marking of paper or copper to form letters.[39] The initial apprehension and marking begin the chain of consciously constructed signs. When these in turn become objects of an interpreter's perceptions, he recapitulates, on a secondary level, the initial act of psychic marking, as Blake recognizes in his repeated injunction in *Milton* to 'Mark well my words! they are of your eternal salvation' (e.g., Pl. 2; E 96, K 482).

A host of linguistic theorists from Wilkins to Shelley used 'mark' to indicate all or some part of the fundamental process summarized

is of course not Blake; he is merely the Bard of Experience, and is trapped by the limitations of Experience. But Blake is not, and the purpose of his poem is to liberate us from such limitations.'

[38] Particularly Genesis 4: 15 (the mark of Cain), Ezekiel 9: 4–6 (the 'mark upon the foreheads of the men that sigh'), and the apocalyptic markings of Revelation 3: 16–17, 14: 9–11, 16: 2, 19: 20, 20: 4. For a useful summary and critique of major interpretations of 'London', see M. Ferber, ' "London" and its Politics', *ELH* 48 (1981), 310–38.

[39] Bacon, *Advancement of Learning*, bk. 2, fo. 50^{v}, describes '*Wordes*' as 'but the *Current Tokens or Markes of popular Notions of things*'. Locke, *Essay concerning Human Understanding*, writes that speakers must '*suppose their Words to be Marks of the Ideas in the Minds also of other Men*' (3. 2. 4) and refers to 'particles' (i.e., conjunctions and prepositions) as '*marks of some Action, or Intimation of the Mind*' (3. 7. 4). Warburton, *Divine Legation of Moses*, uses 'marks' to mean both 'signs' (2: 76) and the individual strokes of letters (2: 78). Hartley, *Observations on Man* (1791), 178, refers to written characters as 'marks'.

above.[40] Herder once again provides the most useful explanation of semiotic marking, briefly in his claim that man's original recognition of 'the first distinguishing mark'[41] was the beginning of language, and at greater length in his explanation of that process in the passage from his *Essay on the Origin of Language* quoted near the beginning of this chapter. Rousseau's remark that oral poems such as Homer's 'were [originally] written only in men's memories' (*On the Origin of Languages*, p. 24) presupposes a similar form of mental inscription prior to speech. And much earlier in the century, George Berkeley had proposed a semiotic theory of vision, a system of arbitrary but natural marks that operates on the mind prior to, but in a manner analogous to, linguistic signs. As he writes near the end of his *Essay toward a New Theory of Vision*, 'Upon the whole, I think we may conclude, that the proper Objects of Vision constitute the Universal Language of Nature, . . . And the manner wherein they signify, and mark out unto us the Objects which are at a distance, is the same with that of Languages and Signs of Human Appointment; which do not suggest the things signify'd, by any Likeness or Identity of Nature, but only by an Habitual Connexion, that Experience has made us to observe between 'em.'[42] These observations by Herder, Rousseau, and Berkeley are the eighteenth-century precursors to Derrida's 'grammatology', predecessors he ignores while setting his theory in opposition to Rousseau's valorization of speech over writing.[43]

The marks at the beginning of 'London' evoke the eighteenth-century concept of pre-linguistic, psychic or grammatological, inscription. The repetition of the word as both verb and noun, an action on the part of the perceiving subject and a characteristic of the perceived object, indicates the reciprocal and even constitutive

[40] See Wilkins, *Essay towards a Real Character*, p. 21 (quoted in ch. 2); Shelley, *Defence of Poetry*, in *Poetry and Prose*, p. 482 (quoted earlier in this chapter).

[41] Herder, *Essay on the Origin of Language*, p. 116. See also p. 132: 'From every sounding being echoed its name: The human soul impressed upon it its image, thought of it as a distinguishing mark.'

[42] Berkeley, *Essay toward a New Theory of Vision* (1709), 172–3.

[43] See Derrida, *Of Grammatology*, esp. the description of 'arche-writing', pp. 59–63, as the inscription of 'difference' (an elaboration of Herder's 'distinguishing'), and the critique of Rousseau, pt. 2, ch. 2. Foucault, *Order of Things*, p. 38, comments briefly on the theories of B. de Vigenère (*Traité des chiffres*, 1586) and C. Duret (*Thresor de l'histoire des langues*, 1613) that 'before Babel, before the Flood, there had already existed a form of writing composed of the marks of nature itself' which 'had always preceded the spoken, certainly in nature, and perhaps even in the knowledge of men'.

nature of meta-semiotic apprehension. Herder's 'distinguishing' marks do not exist as 'distinguishing' until they are marked by human consciousness.[44] The marking in 'London' functions in this same cyclical fashion, yet fails to perform its essential task of separating out and recording that characteristic of an object differentiating it from all others since 'every face' bears the same physiognomic marks of 'weakness' and 'woe'. This basic process lying at the heart of eighteenth-century sign theory thereby becomes reductive rather than usefully discriminate. The reciprocal nature of marking also insures that the speaker of the poem, as the subject who marks, will become implicated in weakness and woe as he transforms physical marks into their psychic inscriptions which are returned to visible presence in the words 'weakness' and 'woe'.[45]

To 'mark' something can mean to delimit it or inscribe boundaries upon it. This semantic association between 'mark' and 'charter'd' draws the latter term into the semiotic theme.[46] The cartographic charting or legal and economic chartering of streets and rivers presuppose an applicable semiotic system embodying those same structures. Before the streets of London can be marked out, chartered, and differentiated each from each, language must be marked and charted by a differential logic. We have already encountered these linguistically 'mind-forg'd manacles' in the taxonomic grammar of ideal language projectors like Wilkins and, more pervasively if less rigidly, in the whole tradition of rationalist linguistics from Bacon and Locke to Saussure. Languages, including the words of 'London', have been chartered and delimited by the very processes of marking that brought them into being. As in my negative or

[44] This aspect of semiotic marking would seem to stand behind the identification of 'mark' in 'London' as a performative utterance in G. Edwards, 'Repeating the Same Dull Round', in Hilton and Vogler, *Unnam'd Forms*, pp. 28–30. To do so requires such a broad definition of 'performative' as to include all acts of meta-semiotic apprehension while overlooking their dependence on the senses prior to any utterance. Both processes, however, are forms of primary motivation in all except Berkeley's formulation of the semiotics of vision.

[45] The speaker's self-generated involvement in a restrictive process of marking has been noted in Glen, *Vision & Disenchantment*, p. 210, and Larrissy, *Blake*, pp. 45–6, but without reference to the larger semiotic issues and their 18th-century context. Larrissy comments interestingly on how the speaker cannot find 'a point of pure perception' outside an ideological construct. I am suggesting here that the inclusive construct is present at an even more fundamental meta-semiotic level.

[46] As with 'mark', the semiotic implications of 'charter'd' underlie, but by no means exclude, the many other meanings of the word relevant to 'London'. For an exploration of some of the historical resonances of 'charter'd', see E. P. Thompson, 'London', in M. Phillips, ed., *Interpreting Blake* (1978), 5–31.

Derridean interpretation of *Adam Naming the Beasts* in Chapter 1, 'London' names semiosis itself as a fall into bondage. If one assumes a Berkelian view, even vision is circumscribed by a system of marks and their habitual associations.

While both 'mark' and 'charter'd' refer us to rigidifying structures, the mode of their meaning is antithetical to those structures. As we have seen in Chapter 2, the taxonomic grammars of seventeenth-century ideal languages sought univalent signs, essential to the one-to-one matching of signifier and signified. This tradition was continued into the politics of eighteenth-century language reform by Samuel Johnson and others who wished to tame the exuberance of words. But as modern interpreters of 'London' have so amply demonstrated, many meanings of 'mark' and 'charter'd' rise to semantic relevance in the context of the poem. Just below the surface marking and chartering of language into exclusionary categories resides a polysemy with the potential to transgress those categories in the act of their naming. Like the assonance and consonance associating the two key terms of the first stanza, this dynamic operates at the level of the signifiers and their secondary motivations that thwart attempts to harness words to single, denotative meanings. Similarly, Blake's design accompanying the text of 'London' breaks out of the conventional paradigms of direct illustration that require the artist to match his images to the poet's words. Neither of the major pictorial motifs—an old man led by a boy, and another child warming his hands by a fire—is named in the text, but both expand upon two of its marks, 'weakness' and 'woe'. Like the people who cry out in London's streets, words contain revolutionary powers never entirely effaced by the paradigmatic and syntagmatic manacles used to control them. These tensions in the language of 'London' are generated through a type of dialectic, inherent in the phenomenon of signification, which Blake explains in *The Marriage of Heaven and Hell* as the interdependent contrariety between polysemy and taxonomy, between 'the Prolific' and 'the Devouring':

> Thus one portion of being, is the Prolific. the other, the Devouring: to the devourer it seems as if the producer was in his chains, but it is not so, he only takes portions of existence and fancies that the whole.
>
> But the Prolific would cease to be Prolific unless the Devourer as a sea recieved the excess of his delights. (Pl. 16; E 40, K 155)

Taxonomic and grammatical structures take their own domain as the essence of language and hold that all other dimensions of the medium are delimited by those structures. But this is not to say that language can do without grammar, for the polysemous signifier needs multiple grammatical forms to achieve its own multiety. Only when one of these partners begins to dominate the other does language lose its full capabilities. 'The Tyger' and 'London' record just such an imbalance, a dominion of logical grammar over the prolific word, Blake found in the politics of language in his age.

The second stanza of 'London' shifts from visual to verbal 'marks'—the 'cry of every Man' in London's streets—to initiate a series of complex visual/aural interchanges. The precedent for such conversions was established by Blake's own profession of reproductive engraving. In 1760, the artist Paul Sandby published a group of twelve etchings depicting the wandering tradesmen and hawkers of London. Since these folk were known primarily by their individual cries identifying their goods or services, the prints were titled *The Cries of London*—that is, translations of those 'cries' into visual representations. Sandby's vigorous prints do not shy from the rough and tumble nature of life in the streets, but the genre was transformed to the picturesque and the prettified in Francis Wheatley's immensely popular *Cries of London*, published by Colnaghi as a series of fashionable stipple prints beginning in 1793.[47] Each pictures a pleasantly rumpled man or remarkably well-dressed and rosy-cheeked girl with the appropriate cry ('Turnips & Carrots ho', 'Round and Sound Five pence a Pound Duke Cherries', etc.) inscribed beneath. Needless to say, there are no lame old men or harlots in Wheatley's series; and while the architectural backgrounds in his prints feature some of London's more palatial edifices and church spires, none are blackened or bloodied. Blake's 'London', both text and design, bears a corrosively parodic relationship to such prints, cutting beneath their genteel surfaces to expose a very different meaning in their cries.

The first 'cry' we see and hear in 'London' is poised between the conventional (a hawker's trade cry) and the naturally expressive (a

[47] The production of the plates was directed by Louis Schiavonetti, later to become one of Blake's enemies when Robert Cromek took from Blake the commission to engrave his illustrations to Robert Blair's *Grave* and gave it to the Italian master. The draft of 'London' in Blake's *Notebook* has been dated to *c.*1793 by most authorities.

cry of pain). The next voice, 'every Infants cry of fear', returns us unambiguously to the *cri du coeur* standing at the origins of speech, personal and racial. What the speaker hears in that origin shared by 'every voice' is not the incarnational naming of *Innocence*, but rather the beginning of the 'mind-forg'd' signifying chain which both expresses and enforces the weakness and woe he sees in the first stanza.

The speaker's insistence on seeing, hearing, and interpreting the common meaning signified by all about him prompts the reader to attend to the marks (graphemes) and cries (phonemes) associating the words of the poem in a common note of woe. We can literally see and hear the 'Man' in the '*man*acles'. The 'Chimney Sweeper' poems of *Innocence* and *Experience* have taught us how to hear the natural cry of 'weep' lodged in his name and street cry. Slight, barely voiced additions allow us to hear the 'band' and the 'banns' in 'ban', thereby linking together marriage announcements, curses, and restrictions.[48] 'Appalls' resonates with a similar multiplicity as we hear and see in it the contrary notes of 'pall' (a dark covering over a corpse or hearse) and 'pale' in two senses, a whitish or weak colour and the name for yet another marked-out enclosure. As in Tooke's etymologies, these punning proliferations imply historical connections leading back to some ur-form of appalls/pall/pale before its division into separate signs. Other sight and sound effects connect one word in the poem with several others. Rhyme and consonance lead us on from 'appalls' to the 'Palace walls'. What we hear in 'hear' itself is both 'fear' and 'tear'. And is 'hearse' a plural of 'hear'? Even this seems possible as the signifiers create their own patterns of association and generate meanings that play beneath and transgress the poem's normative grammar and syntax. These eruptions of polymorphous secondary motivation threaten to disrupt arbitrary linguistic conventions and univalent meanings, much as those forms of primary expressive motivation, the sweeper's cry and the soldier's sigh, stain the institutions of church and state.[49]

[48] Through at least the 9th edn. (1806) of Johnson's *Dictionary*, 'ban' is defined as (1) 'Publick notice given of any thing, whereby any thing is publicly commended or forbidden,' including marriage banns; (2) 'A curse'; (3) 'Interdiction'. The last definition associates 'ban' with both 'charter'd' and 'mark' (in the sense of marking out the limits of something).

[49] In 'Criticism, Politics, and Style in Wordsworth's Poetry', *Critical Inquiry*, 11 (1984), 52–81, D. Simpson finds a similar juncture between linguistic and political issues in Wordsworth: 'The debates invoked by the linguistic and stylistic features of Wordsworth's poems are the great

The third stanza of 'London' is particularly rich in visual/aural transformations. The 'Chimney-sweepers cry' becomes visual because its effect on the 'Church' names colours through the epanalepsis of 'appalls'.[50] These complex, two-step transformations become a direct process in the sudden visualization of 'Soldiers sigh . . . in blood'. The synaesthetic conversions cut across conventional ways of categorizing sense experience and of representing it through matching semantic categories. At the same time, the language of the poem resists normalization through metaphor or allegory. The implied etymology of 'appalls', however fictive, still constitutes a concrete history that decompounds the word into names for things and their colours in a fully Tookean, anti-abstractionist, manner. A 'sigh' cannot 'run' down a wall, and thus the verb must be taken metaphorically. But 'blood' quickly returns the verb to the literal, leaving it in both categories in such a way as to shake their mutual exclusivity. Although this zeugmatic construction hinging on 'runs' creates an analogical relationship between 'sigh' and 'blood', neither becomes merely a figure for the other: the sigh does not run *like* blood but 'in blood'. Any attempt to rationalize the text by making absolute distinctions between literal and figural matrices is thwarted. At a more fundamental semiotic level, every thing functions as (and hence is) a sign; every sign functions as (and hence is) a thing.

In the last stanza of 'London', natural signs, reduced to their most fundamental and physical form, blast through the conventional schemata of church, state, and language. The 'harlots curse', unseen in the fashionable *Cries of London* prints and unheard in the approved discourse of London society, becomes the 'most' heard in 'London'. The final aural to visual transformation, from 'curse' as utterance to 'curse' as germs, affects not just objects but organs of sight, for the symptomatic marks of venereal disease will destroy the child's ability to perceive the semiotic marks that become the poem.[51] The

debates of contemporary legislation and social theory—about the relations of work and leisure, charity and relief, property and vagrancy, rich and poor' (p. 67). Simpson's general position—and mine—is not based on some notion of the free 'play' of the signifier that always disrupts all discourse, but specific and historically determined figural dislocations that transgress equally specific and historical norms.

[50] For 'epanalepsis', see n. 6. The black/white colour exchanges between the 'blackning Church' and the sweepers are nicely detailed in Ferber, ' "London" and its Politics', pp. 323–5.

[51] For an analysis of the pathology described by the final stanza, see G. C. Roti and D. L. Kent, 'The Last Stanza of Blake's "London" ', *Blake: An Illustrated Quarterly*, 11 (1977), 19–21.

ultimate natural signs, ones that require no social conventions or religious faith to achieve all the ideals of motivation, are the symptoms of a disease. Like expressive and mimetic natural signs, symptoms bear a direct and causal relationship to the disease they delineate. Like the incarnational sign and the Coleridgean symbol, they partake in the reality they render perceivable. And like performative utterance, they do what they signify. The production of signs has been reduced to pathogenesis, communication to a communicable disease. This explosion of nature into culture unites marriages and funerals, joins social classes, and overturns semantic categories. But the classless community thereby created is only the democracy of death. The whole doctrine of natural signs and Tooke's supposedly liberating return of all abstractions to sensations are revealed as essentially pathological. Like Thel, the speaker of 'London' leads us through a chain of natural signs to their underworld.

'London' records a terrible cultural crisis extending into the semiotic systems in which that crisis is both concealed and revealed. The politics of eighteenth-century language theory offer no perspective not already implicated in the fallen marks of 'London'. Neither the restrictive order of logical conventions, nor the revolutionary forces of secondary motivation and natural signs, rise above the world they all name. In *The Book of Urizen*, Blake carries this critique of the very sign systems he uses further into their meta-semiotic foundations. There he even rejects the concept of a prelapsarian origin, a language of Adam from which we have fallen but to which we may aspire to return. That great eighteenth-century pursuit, the recovery of origins, will in *Urizen* open up a void more profound than Thel's grave.

At the end of *The Marriage of Heaven and Hell*, Blake would seem to be announcing a forthcoming publication: 'I have also: The Bible of Hell: which the world shall have whether they will or no' (Pl. 24; E 44, K 158). *The* [*First*] *Book of Urizen* and its ancillary appendices, *The Book of Ahania* and *The Book of Los*, are Blake's extant works that come closest to fulfilling the concluding prophecy of *The Marriage*.[52] These three texts are unique among

[52] *The Book of Ahania* and *The Book of Los* are not narrative continuations of *The Book of Urizen*, but rather variations on its basic themes of division and conflict. Blake's change to intaglio etching for these two short works in itself indicates that they were not produced as additional 'Books' of the same single 'Bible'.

the illuminated books in their double-column format, like most Bibles, and division into chapters and numbered verses. *Urizen* is clearly a narrative of creation and fall, as in Genesis, and the beginning of an Exodus from 'Egypt' on its final plate. Thus, *Urizen* bears a close but parodic relationship to the Old Testament in the sense that it is written in direct and imitative response to this precursor text, but in such a way as to invert—or at least radically revise—the conventional understanding of the earlier work.[53] Like a devilish midrash, *Urizen* is written *sur la marge* of the Hebrew Bible.

Blake's praise of 'The Old & New Testaments' as 'the Great Code of Art' (E 274, K 777) does not necessarily exclude parodic responses to that code. Further, this famous declaration in the *Laocoön* inscriptions, written in the 1820s, is a less sure guide to Blake's opinions about the Old Testament in the 1790s than his annotations of *c.*1798 to Richard Watson's *Apology for the Bible*. In these comments, Blake opposes the New Testament to the Old and characterizes the latter as 'only an Example of the wickedness & deceit of the Jews & . . . written as an Example of the possibility of Human Beastliness in all its branches' (E 614, K 387). Blake also divided the God of the Old Testament into two deities, much as the Hebrew text of Genesis uses two names for God, 'Elohim' and 'Jahweh', in the first two chapters. In 1810, he told Henry Crabb Robinson that the creator of the material world 'was not Jehovah, but the Elohim', and this distinction seems also to have influenced Blake's revisions of the King James translation in the Genesis Manuscript he began in the last year or two of his life.[54] This illuminated manuscript contains illustrations of the joint creation

[53] A good case can be made for Pechey's suggestion ('1789 and After: Mutations of "Romantic" Discourse', p. 56) that the parodic is Blake's major literary mode in the 1780s and 1790s. The catalogue of parodies, when defined as a category larger than the comedic, would include *Poetical Sketches* (in their imitative but critical responsiveness to 18th-century lyric), *An Island in the Moon* (a comedic parody of contemporary intellectual chit-chat), *Tiriel* (a parody of Ossian), *The Book of Thel* (in its relations to the poetry of natural history and the doctrines of natural religion), *Songs of Experience* (as a parody of Blake's own *Songs of Innocence*), *The Marriage of Heaven and Hell*, and the 3 illuminated books discussed here. Thus *Urizen* may be viewed as a development out of *The Marriage* and some of the *Songs of Experience* (particularly 'The Tyger' because of its speculations on origins) as much as the poems of apocalyptic history and prophecy (*The French Revolution*, *America*, *Europe*, and *The Song of Los*).

[54] Robinson's *Reminiscences* in Bentley, *Blake Records*, p. 545. On the Genesis Manuscript, see R. N. Essick, *Works of Blake in the Huntington Collections* (1985), 88–115, esp. pp. 104, 114–15.

of Adam and Eve (leaf 6) and the emergence of Eve out of Adam (leaf 7), a pictorial doubling that underscores the presence of two creations of Eve in Genesis, 1: 27 and 2: 21–2. The dual creation plot in *The Book of Urizen*, one centring on the activities of Urizen and the other on Los, may also be a response to the composite structure of Genesis.[55] Taken together, this evidence suggests Blake's awareness of historical and textual studies of the Hebrew Testament that were calling into question its unity, authority, and primacy.

The historical study of the Bible in the late eighteenth century was given its fullest expression in the 'Higher Criticism' of German scholars such as Johann Jakob Griesbach, Johann Gottfried Eichhorn, and Johann Philipp Gabler. It is most unlikely that Blake had any direct knowledge of their work,[56] but some of their major conclusions about the historicity of Old Testament narrative had long been available to English readers. In the seventeenth century, Thomas Hobbes had claimed that the Pentateuch had been written long after the time of Moses, and Richard Simon had discussed the imbricated structure of Genesis.[57] These topics became urgent issues in the late 1780s, particularly in the pages of Joseph Johnson's *Analytical Review* and in the work of one of its theological contributors, Alexander Geddes. In the very first issue of the journal, Geddes reviewed G. B. de Rossi's *Variae lectiones* (1784–7), pointing out that 'the Bible hath undergone the destiny of all ancient writings: it hath not been handed down to us in its primitive integrity', and that 'it may even happen that not a single manuscript has preserved

[55] A point convincingly argued in Tannenbaum, *Biblical Tradition in Blake's Early Prophecies*, pp. 201–4.

[56] Several scholars have recently claimed that Blake could have learned about the Higher Criticism from members of the Joseph Johnson circle, notably Henry Fuseli and Alexander Geddes. See E. S. Shaffer, *'Kubla Khan' and the Fall of Jerusalem* (1975), 26–7; Tannenbaum, *Biblical Tradition in Blake's Early Prophecies*, pp. 13, 292–3; J. J. McGann, 'The Idea of an Indeterminate Text', *Studies in Romanticism*, 25 (1986), 303–24. My emphasis below on Johnson's *Analytical Review* is prompted by its role as a centre of the textual debate over the Bible. McGann notes that the journal reviewed 'all of the leading works being produced in Germany by scholars like J. D. Michaelis and Eichhorn' (p. 310), but this is not the case prior to 1794. Vol. 16 of 1793 contains an extensive review (pp. 304–10, 512–14) of Michaelis's *Introduction to the New Testament*, but this work was first pub. in German in 1750 and is at best a precursor to the Higher Criticism. The only notice given Eichhorn is a brief announcement of his *Commentaries on Apocalypse* (16 [1793], 105). For a general survey of the shift from reading the Bible as a transcendental text to treating it as an historical document, see H. W. Frei, *Eclipse of Biblical Narrative* (1974).

[57] Hobbes, *Leviathan* (1651), pt. 3, ch. 33; Simon, *Critical History of the Old Testament* (1682). The general perspective in these works was developed into a more thorough analysis by J. Astruc in his *Conjectures sur les mémoires originaux* (1753).

the true reading'.[58] Similar notes are struck in succeeding reviews of new translations of Genesis and other Books of the Bible. Some theologians, such as Henry Murray and Herbert Marsh, believed that textual scholarship was beginning to erode the authority of the Pentateuch, and thus felt called upon to defend Moses' authorship and his divine inspiration.[59] The revisionary school of thought culminated in England with Geddes's translation of the Bible (Pentateuch and Joshua published 1792) and Thomas Paine's *Age of Reason* (1794).[60] Geddes's view that the first compiler of the Pentateuch was an editor living in the reign of Solomon who worked with bits and pieces of earlier materials corresponds in major respects to Eichhorn's theories and the German tradition of *fragment-hypothese* fully developed by Johann Severin Vater, in part in response to Geddes's editorial theories.[61]

It may be difficult for us to imagine textual criticism and philology at the forefront of intellectual controversy, but this appears to have been the case in the early 1790s. In Germany, the scholarly recognition of the Old Testament as a work that evolved over a long time was elaborated into the concept of the Bible as a work still in progress. As Novalis asked, 'Who has declared the Bible completed? Should the Bible not be still in the process of growth?' Friedrich Schlegel's response to his friend's questions was an unrealized plan to write a new myth, a new Bible, for his age.[62] In England, the textual study of the Old Testament made possible a work as radical as *The Book of Urizen*. If, as Geddes claimed, the Bible should be placed in the same 'crucible of a severe rational critique' with the works of 'Homer, Virgil, Milton, and Shakspeare',[63] then the Bible

[58] *Analytical Review*, 1 (1788), 1, 6.

[59] See Murray, *Evidences of the Jewish and Christian Revelations* (1790); and Marsh, *Authenticity of the Five Books of Moses Considered* (1792). These were reviewed in the *Analytical Review*, 13 (1792), 37; and 14 (1792), 72.

[60] Both books were reviewed, with particular attention to their radical views on Genesis, in the *Analytical Review*, 17 (1793), 41–52; and 19 (1794), 159–65. In his annotations to Watson's *Apology for the Bible, in a Series of Letters, to Thomas Paine*, Blake indicates his familiarity with the latter's questions about the authorship of the Pentateuch (see esp. E 616, K 390–1), as well as his willingness to disagree with both men over how such questions might undermine the veracity of the Bible.

[61] See Vater, *Commentar über den Pentateuch* (1802–5).

[62] Novalis, 'Miscellaneous Fragments' no. 12, in *Hymns to the Night and Other Selected Writings* (1960); Schlegel, letter to Novalis of 20 October 1798, *Friedrich Schlegel und Novalis* (1957), p. 130.

[63] *Doctor Geddes's Address to the Public* (1793), 5. The passage is quoted in the *Analytical Review* (1793), 177.

could also become an object of devilish rewriting like that given *Paradise Lost* in *The Marriage of Heaven and Hell*. If the story of the fall of man in Genesis was 'simply a piece of Jewish mythology',[64] then it could be subjected to the same comparative analysis Bryant had applied to other Near Eastern and Classical myths. And if Genesis was only a syncretic narrative determined by the historical circumstances of its compilers, then questions about its predecessors could not be avoided. While scholars tried to recover these ur-texts by dissecting Genesis, Blake attempted in *Urizen* to slice through the textual impedimenta and directly create an ur-myth, one that could answer questions about what happened *before* the events related in Genesis. In its historical and parodic relationship to Genesis, *Urizen* is of course secondary; but Blake's primitive and fragmented narrative claims for itself an ontologically primary orientation toward all other creation stories. The language of the poem situates itself in an equally primordial state, in part by intimating what was then conceived to be the grammatical and rhetorical characteristics of ancient Hebrew.

In his 1778 translation of Isaiah, Robert Lowth attempted to recapture the rhythmic verse in which he believed the prophet's words had originally been arranged.[65] Lowth's versification is close to the prose of the King James Bible; in some cases, he merely had to print clauses on separate lines and substitute a few synonyms that added or subtracted syllables as needed for the rhythm. Two passages will indicate the considerable range of line lengths and accentual patterns:

> The ox knoweth his possessor;
> And the ass the crib of his lord:
> But Israel knoweth not Me;
> Neither doth my people consider.
>
> (1: 3)

> Hear ye the word of Jehovah, O ye princes of Sodom!
> Give ear to the law of our God, ye people of Gomorrah!
> What have I to do with the multitude of your sacrifices? saith Jehovah:
> I am cloyed with the burnt-offerings of rams, and the fat of fed beasts;
> And in the blood of bullocks, and of lambs, and of goats, I have no
> delight. (1: 10–11)

[64] Anon. review of the Geddes Bible, *Analytical Review*, 17 (1793), 43.

[65] R. Lowth, *Isaiah: A New Translation* (1778). J. Johnson pub. a new edn. in 1790. For an overview of late 18th-century verse translations of the Bible, see M. Roston, *Prophet and Poet* (1965), 126–42.

Beginning in *Tiriel* and *The Book of Thel*, Blake used a septenary line (or 'fourteener') with an extended cadence like Lowth's longer measures. The double-column format of *Urizen* required Blake to compress this metre into trimetre and tetrametre hemistichs similar to Lowth's lines of eight to ten syllables:

> So Fuzon call'd all together
> The remaining children of Urizen:
> And they left the pendulous earth:
> They called it Egypt, & left it.[66]

Blake's syllabic and accentual variability, like Lowth's, found contemporary justification in the theory that Hebrew versification was guided by the meaning of the words, not by a predetermined measure.[67] All these metrical experiments participated in the attempt to revive an ancient poetic mode from which the prose of the Hebrew Bible was supposed to have descended, much as Macpherson's prose claimed descent from Celtic verse.[68] Years later, in the second chapter of *Jerusalem*, Blake imagined just such a Biblical prototype in the form of Albion's tomb which, like the illuminated books, bears 'emblems & written verse'. From this 'Spiritual Verse, order'd & measur'd, . . . time shall reveal. | The Five books of the Decalogue, . . .' (Pl. 48; E 196, K 677).

Other characteristics of *Urizen* fit comfortably into a recognizably Hebraic context. As Condillac pointed out, examples of pleonasm 'occur very frequently in Hebrew'.[69] The simplest, most emphatic form of such redundancy is repetition of the same word, as in the incantatory 'Departing; departing; departing' of *Urizen* (3: 3). Only a few years after the publication of Condillac's treatise, Lowth widened the perspective on Hebrew pleonasm to discover parallelism.[70] Blake's frequent use of this technique in *Urizen* is

[66] *Book of Urizen*, Pl. 28 (ch. 11, ver. 8); E 83, K 237. Hereafter cited by ch. and ver. only.

[67] See J. Sturges, *Short Remarks on a New Translation of Isaiah* (1791). Sturges remarks that the 'verses' of Horace and Virgil 'are indubitably determined by measure, and hardly at all by the sense as in the Hebrew' (p. 12).

[68] Larrissy, *Blake*, p. 128, similarly comments that Lowth's *Isaiah* 'is the kind of resuscitation of Hebrew sacred poetry that Blake is imitating in *The Book of Urizen*'. But Lowth's long lines, not cited by Larrissy, suggest that any influence he may have had on Blake began *c.*1789 with the fourteeners of *Tiriel* and *Thel*.

[69] *Essay on the Origin of Human Knowledge*, p. 228.

[70] R. Lowth, *De sacra poesi Hebraeorum* (1753). First English translation pub. J. Johnson, 1787. Lowth briefly defines parallelism in the preface to his translation of Isaiah: 'The

underscored by epanaphora, the beginning of successive clauses with the same word:

> One command, one joy, one desire,
> One curse, one weight, one measure
> One King, one God, one Law.
>
> (2: 8)

Even on the purely grammatical level, the language of *Urizen* evokes Hebraic constructions. Contemporary Hebrew grammars comment on how 'the tenses are often used promiscuously, especially in the poetic and prophetic books' of the Bible. 'Instead of a present tense the participle of the present is used, hence called *benoni, between*, i.e. the past and future.'[71] As a result, the opening verses of Genesis contain only the past tense and present participles. This same combination gives *The Book of Urizen* its principal temporal division, not between past, present, and future, but between completed and continuing events.[72] Even Blake's oddly repetitive combination of an adverb and prepositional phrase—as in 'a roof, vast petrific around, | On all sides He fram'd' (3.7)—finds a precedent in Hebrew grammar.[73]

One can reasonably object that my somewhat laboured attempt to turn Blake's English into Hebrew has only indicated a commonality between *Urizen* and a late eighteenth-century sense of what constitutes any 'primitive' poetry and grammar. While the suspension of the Hebrew verb until the end of clauses matches the last line of the first verse of *Urizen* ('Brooding secret, the dark power hid'),

correspondence of one Verse, or Line, with another, I call *Parallelism*. When a proposition is delivered, and a second is subjoined to it, or drawn under it, equivalent, or contrasted with it, in Sense; or similar to it in the form of Grammatical Construction—these I call Parallel Lines; and the words or phrases, answering one to another in the corresponding Lines, Parallel Terms' (p. x). On Blake's use of parallelism in *Jerusalem*, see Paley, *Continuing City*, pp. 45–9.

[71] *Hebrew Grammar* (1792), 16. Like all 18th-century Hebrew grammars, this vol. derives ultimately from the *Sefer Miklol* of David Kimhi, first pub. Constantinople, 1532–4 (Latin edn., Paris, 1549).

[72] For the tense structure of Genesis, see J. Parkhurst's painfully literal translation of the first chapter, *Hebrew and English Lexicon* (1762). In *Hebrew Thought Compared with Greek* (1960), T. Boman points out that 'the Semitic notion of tense . . . views what happens principally from the standpoint of completed or incomplete action' (p. 144). For a discussion of the stylistic effects and conceptual implications of Blake's use of the 'progressive' tense in his later poetry, see R. C. Taylor, 'Semantic Structures and the Temporal Modes of Blake's Prophetic Verse', *Language and Style*, 12 (1979), 26–49; rpt. in Hilton, *Essential Articles for the Study of Blake*, pp. 237–70.

[73] See S. Willard, *Hebrew Grammar* (1817), p. 64: 'Many adverbs undergo certain changes of signification by means of a preposition going before them; as . . . "around" comes to mean "on all sides" . . .'.

surely the Latin and Miltonic precedents are more to the point. And while the disjointed narrative structure of *Urizen* may be compatible with the fragment hypothesis of Biblical composition, the same lack of temporal sequence and causal connectives is a leading characteristic of Macpherson's Ossian.[74] Such criticisms are helpful, for they indicate the syncretism motivating Blake's style and his attempt to recover the common origins of all the oldest known poetry—Greek, Hebrew, Celtic. This pursuit of a meta-poetic explains why, in a poem so closely related to the Bible, Blake begins with an invocation to his muses containing the unmistakably Homeric epithet, 'swift winged words', to which Horne Tooke had given linguistic currency through the Greek title of his *Diversions of Purley*. The emphasis on present participles also exhibits a grammatical synchrony that points back to a very early stage in the evolution of language. As we have seen, the eighteenth-century debate between mentalism and sensibilism often took the form of a question concerning the priority of the noun or the verb. As a verb, the present participle transforms completed action into ongoing event: 'Eternity roll'd wide apart | Wide asunder rolling' (3: 3). As a gerund, the same verbal form becomes a noun substantive: 'Why live in unquenchable burnings?' (2: 4) and 'the wrenching apart was healed' (3: 12). Thus the present participle/gerundive fulfils the dual role often granted the infinitive.[75] In addition, the form can serve as an adjective—'Hanging frowning cliffs' (3: 3)—or even as an adverb: 'Los wept howling around the dark Demon.'[76] Blake's ubiquitous use of '-ing' words implies that they are the root form underlying the four main grammatical categories which eighteenth-century theory claimed were the first to evolve. The language of *Urizen* thereby harkens back to a condition before those categories became separated through morphemic, and not merely syntactic, differences.

[74] See H. Blair's comments on Ossian, quoted in ch. 2. Condillac notes that, in 'the earliest poems . . . , the custom of leaving out words which are to be supplied, is very frequent. Of this the Hebrew is a strong proof; . . .' (*Essay on the Origin of Human Knowledge*, p. 234). Macpherson may have been influenced by Lowth's theories of Hebrew poetry—see Roston, *Prophet and Poet*, pp. 145–6.

[75] Beattie, *Theory of Language*, p. 264: 'some antient grammarians called it [the infinitive], *the verbal noun*, or, more properly, *the noun of the verb*'. See also the central importance of 'to be', the verb substantive, in Harris's *Hermes* and Coleridge's *Logic*.

[76] 3: 9. By inserting a comma between the verb ('wept') and quasi-adverb ('howling'), Keynes normalizes the latter into an adjective (K 224).

Urizen carries us even further toward apparently undifferentiated origins. The sounds named in the poem point the way. *Urizen* offers a full diapason of thunders, trumpet, voices, crash, roaring, howlings, cursing, 'Groaning! gnashing! groaning!' (3: 12). Some of these sounds rise to the level of 'Words articulate' (2: 3) and others can be taken for expressive natural signs, but the clatter is so extensive, random, and at times impersonal that we are plunged into a world of sounds more than signs. And even before these sounds we find Urizen's 'silent activity' and 'horrors silent' (1: 4, 6), both aural companions to the 'abominable void' (1: 1) his activities have created.

The theory and poetry of natural utterance are founded on words referring to particular objects of sense, but the utterances in *Urizen* lead us back to a strangely pre-sensate condition defined by negativity and absence: 'unknown, abstracted | Brooding secret, the dark power hid' (1: 1). It is as though the teleology of eighteenth-century rationalist semiotics had been turned upside-down, with the abstract terms coming before, rather than evolving out of, those naming things. This reversal implies a mentalist, verb-oriented bias concerning linguistic origins.[77] Things are invested with qualities, such as 'unknown', that presuppose a mind reflecting on its own functions and able to abstract from them the concept of their absence; actions are taken, such as dividing and measuring (1: 2), that require the prior existence of a mind already shaped by those categories. From this 'forsaken wilderness' of Urizenic consciousness are 'Bred' the 'shapes' of 'beast, bird, fish, serpent & element' (1: 3). For this Adam, the fall of language into abstraction precedes the naming—indeed, the being—of the beasts.

To follow further Blake's pursuit of linguistic origins in *Urizen* will require a continuation of the shift in perspective I have already begun, one that will take us from the actual language of the poem to the propositions about language it communicates. The opening verses of the Holy Bible presuppose the existence of an individual consciousness (God), semiosis (God's Word), and the void. Blake's Bible of Hell takes a step back from these givens and asks how they

[77] Blake's heavy use of participial adjectives shows a similar orientation toward the verb by attributing qualities to objects on the basis of function. J. Miles, *Renaissance, Eighteenth-Century, and Modern Language in English Poetry* (1960), 5, 8, calculates that 30 to 40% of Blake's adjectives are participial.

came to be. The surprising answer, unique in the history of linguistic speculation to Blake's day, is that they have a common genesis and essence.

The primal act in *Urizen* is the autotelic self-separation of the demiurge from his fellow 'Eternals'. This event immediately constitutes, and is constituted by, *difference* as the fundamental ontological category. The language in the first few plates of the poem traces this opening up of difference as a contraction and mutual withdrawal: 'spurn'd back', 'Self-closd, all-repelling', 'abstracted' (from *abstrahere*, to draw away from, to separate), 'divided', 'rifted', 'self-contemplating', 'solitude', 'set apart', 'condensing', 'I alone'. Like the typical eighteenth-century model for the origin of human speech in a cry expressing fear or pain, the meta-semiotic moment in *Urizen* is accompanied by 'fierce anguish' and 'howlings & pangs & fierce madness'.[78] The production of difference finds its primary epistemological embodiment in the 'Unknown' (1: 1), its metaphysical embodiment in the 'void' (1: 1), and its semiotic expression in the negative.[79] In all three of its extensions, difference becomes the interstices that define mutually exclusive identities, be they ideas, things, or words. Difference is 'unprolific' (1: 1), but by that very negativity it becomes 'Natures wide womb' (2: 5), the place where further contractions give birth to further separations. The nature thereby generated bears the mark of its paternity, the continual replication of difference.

The kind of semiosis, if any, Urizen falls away from is not described in the poem. (Blake will return us to that issue when we come to *Jerusalem*.) What he falls into, and institutes as the only possible form of semiosis in the world created by that fall, is the language described by the rationalist tradition of sign theory from

[78] 3:6. The pains of parturition echo through later verses of the poem, as when 'in anguish, | Urizen was rent from his [Los's] side' (3: 9), when 'pity divides the soul | In pangs' (5: 7), and when 'All Eternity shudderd at sight | Of the first female now separate' (5: 9). The link between pain and the origin of language is continued in Heidegger's *On the Way to Language*; see D. A. White, *Heidegger and the Language of Poetry* (1978), 83–8, 182.

[79] For a discussion of the negative as 'a particularly linguistic resource' and how 'there might even be a sense in which we could derive the linguistic faculty itself from the ability to use the Negative *qua* Negative', see K. Burke, 'A Dramatistic View of the Origins of Language and Postscripts on the Negative', in *Language as Symbolic Action* (1968), 419–79 (quotations from pp. 419–20). Burke's theory of the negative and the concept of difference I develop here have much in common, as *Urizen* itself demonstrates through its interweaving of terms of negation and absence (e.g., 'void') with verbs of differentiation (e.g., 'avoid').

the seventeenth-century grammarians to Derrida. By creating difference, Urizen creates the meta-semiotic ground for a language based on a differential matrix. The primary form of that schema is the difference between sign and referent, signifier and signified. The first substantive named in the opening chapter of *Urizen*, 'a shadow of horror' (1: 1), is a natural, motivated sign in that it bears a causal link to its referent, the object creating the shadow. Yet this is a curiously negative and insubstantial sign, one that records an absence (as in the expression, 'he is only the shadow of a man') while it claims a presence *somewhere else*. The shadow as sign indicates that the natural, no less than the conventional, sign is inscribed with difference. By penetrating to this common substrate, to the 'void immense' in the 'deep world within' the sign (2: 5), Blake reveals the radical inconsequence of the main eighteenth-century strategy for distinguishing the motivated from the arbitrary. A language constructed out of differential signs will, in its very attempts to bridge difference with reference, carry within itself the void, the absence, from which it sprung.

Language unfolds as a response to the breach opened up by Urizen's establishment of difference as the basis of identity. The first words spoken in the poem (as distinct from the words of the poem) are attributed to an unspecified 'Some'—presumably some of the Eternals—who identify Urizen as the creator of the 'abominable void' (1: 1). Blake brackets their comment, 'It is Urizen', with quotation marks, used nowhere else in the illuminated book. By enclosing the statement in this way, Blake emphasizes the separation of speech from being, even as it claims the existence of something other than language (i.e., the 'it' and 'Urizen') through a form of the verb 'to be'. This simplest of all copular structures, asserting the unity of 'it' and 'Urizen', presupposes their difference, for without the categorical division between subject and object (even in the form of a predicate nominative) there could be no statement. The proposition works against, but unavoidably replicates, the differential nature of the signs from which it is constructed. Derrida describes this phenomenon and its origin with admirable precision: 'Language could have emerged only out of dispersion. The "natural causes" [i.e., natural signs] by which one explains it are not recognized as natural except in so far as they accord with the state of nature, which is determined by dispersion. This dispersion should no doubt be overcome by language but, for that very reason, it determines the *natural condition* of language.'[80] The universality of this paradox makes it thematically insignificant in most contexts, but here it defines the 'natural' enclosure into which Urizen has forced all semiosis. Like the God of Genesis, the Eternals call a substantive ('Urizen') into being by naming it, but at the same time they reproduce the non-being Urizen institutes and Blake underscores with the language of absence and negativity: 'Unknown, unprolific', 'void', 'vacuum', 'secret', 'hid', 'unseen'.

Since the event called 'Urizen' is given self-presence as a character, his role as origin of difference/dispersion means that nature and semiosis are conterminous with a state of consciousness. That consciousness reveals itself through language when Urizen directly utters 'Words articulate' (2: 3), for the first and only time in the poem, through five verses in chapter 2. But even here, where the speaking 'I' posits itself as the source of language, it is equally true that language creates that 'I' by speaking itself seven times through Urizen.[81] The events and persons of the poem come into being as reifications of the grammar and syntax of their medium. We may suppose ourselves moving, in the first two chapters of *Urizen*, from a cluster of actions, the perpetrator of which is in doubt, through a series of divisions between characters and events, and finally to a speaking 'I' who asserts both his singularity and his will to universal dominance. Prompted by the medium-reflexivity of the poem itself, we can trace this same movement as a grammatical evolution from predicates with indeterminate subjects to the determination of those subjects through an emergence of grammatical categories that lead to the personal pronoun. The relevance of this plot to eighteenth-century language theory can be indicated through its parallels with Adam Smith's *Dissertation on the Origin of Languages*. For Smith, 'verbs must necessarily have been coeval with the very first attempts towards the formation of language'—that is, with the production of nouns. 'The first verbs, . . . made use of in the beginnings of

[80] *Of Grammatology*, p. 232. See also E. Jabès's comment that 'The object and the word which designates it take part in one and the same separation. The space they try to cross is the threshold which keeps them apart.' Jabès, *Book of Questions* (1973), 2: 155.

[81] The process is clearly set forth in G. W. F. Hegel, *Phenomenology of Mind* (1967), 530: '. . . in speech the self-existent singleness of self-consciousness comes as such into existence, . . .'. See also Benveniste, *Problems in General Linguistics*, p. 230: '. . . the subject is established by the instance of the utterance of its indicator (which is "I")'.

language would in all probability be . . . impersonal verbs. It is observed accordingly, I am told, by the Hebrew grammarians, that the radical words of their language, from which all the others are derived, are all of them verbs, and impersonal verbs.' The definition of the personal subject—or, in the language of *Urizen,* the change from 'An activity unknown' (1: 4) to structures such as 'I have sought . . .' (2: 4)—unfolds for Smith through an elaboration of difference, for 'mankind have learned by degrees to split and divide almost every event into a great number of metaphysical parts, expressed by the different parts of speech, variously combined in the different members of every phrase and sentence'.[82] The personal pronoun evolves only at a later stage in the progressive abstraction of language, for the word 'I' may 'be said to be, at once, both what the logicians call, a singular, and what they call, a common term; and to join in its signification the seemingly opposite qualities of the most precise individuality, and the most extensive generalization. This word, therefore, expressing so very abstract and metaphysical an idea, would not easily or readily occur to the first formers of language.'[83] By naming himself with the personal pronoun, Urizen names the grammatical abstraction enabling his self to come into being as an objectified generalization to itself.[84] Smith, like all eighteenth-century rational grammarians, assumes the priority of the 'metaphysical' distinctions that are 'expressed' in language. Blake makes no such assumption in the genesis plot of *Urizen* since primal difference, like a Kantian transcendental category, underlies both metaphysics and semiotics and is coextensive with them.

In his soliloquy in chapter 2, Urizen looks back upon the condition of the Eternals. By separating himself from them, Urizen has transformed the Eternals into a radical otherness. Much as the Eternals perceive Urizen as an 'abominable chaos' (1: 5), he sees them as living in the unorganized hell of 'unquenchable burnings' (2: 4). The difference in perspective reinstates the debate between the angel

[82] *Theory of Moral Sentiments . . . to which is Added, a Dissertation on the Origin of Languages* (1790), 2: 434, 436, 438.

[83] Smith, *Dissertation*, 2: 444. See also 2: 449 (the 'substantive verb, . . . *I am* . . . is . . . the most abstract and metaphysical of all verbs') and 2: 450 (the verb '*I have* . . . denotes an event of an extremely abstract and metaphysical nature').

[84] The same grammar constitutes the enabling paradigm for Coleridge's definition of 'a subject which becomes a subject by the act of constructing itself objectively to itself' (*Biographia Literaria*, 1: 273).

and the devil in *The Marriage of Heaven and Hell* at a deeper metaphysical and meta-linguistic level.[85] Urizen 'first . . . fought with the fire' (2: 5), a struggle that further establishes himself as subject (in both the psychological and grammatical senses), the fire as object, and his action as the verb that seeks to impose the desires of the subject on the object. The instrument of this desire is the logic of difference that seeks 'for a joy without pain, | For a solid without fluctuation' (2: 4). The semiotic basis of this logic is already present in Urizen's language, those 'words articulate' that maintain their articulation (from *articulare*, to separate into joints) through difference—for example, the phonemic and semantic differences between 'joy' and 'pain', 'solid' and 'fluctuation'. Urizen is building, and trying to organize his world according to, the 'one Law' (2: 8) of difference embedded in the paradigmatic grammar of the language giving him his separate being. Prior to or concomitant with his institution of 'Laws of peace, of love, of unity' (2: 8), Urizen must divide the chaos within and without into a taxonomy of signs and establish the laws by which they can be articulated into syntactic units. Thus, like a good seventeenth-century ideal language projector working under the aegis of 'One King' and his Royal Society, Urizen must force 'each' sign to 'chuse one habitation' (2: 8), one position within the semantic and grammatical network. And like Newton's calculus, this categorical language will impose a discontinuous system on the continuous flux of events. Urizen's only unity is the uniformity and universal application of the 'Law' itself, a schema dependent on oppositions (A/not A) that generate absences (/) and negatives (not). These are products of 'the Reasoning Power | An Abstract objecting power, that Negatives every thing' (*Jerusalem*, Pl. 10; E 153, K 629). In such a system, 'there are only differences *without positive terms*', as Saussure claims for all 'language'.[86]

Urizen proceeds rapidly through the early history of language, from uttering 'words articulate' (2: 3) to the more stable and permanent inscription of words in 'books formd of metals' (2: 6). In these he has 'written the secrets of wisdom | The secrets of dark

[85] See *Marriage*, Pl. 19, where the speaker claims that 'all that we saw was owing to your [the angel's] metaphysics' (E 42, K 156). And as Michaelis queries, 'Without abstract ideas, what would become of metaphysics?' (*Dissertation*, p. 52).

[86] *Course in General Linguistics*, p. 120.

contemplation' (2:6), as though these were intensely private journals never intended as a vehicle for communication with others. Urizenic writing thereby suggests the same psychic or grammatological form of inscription to which we were led by the noetic marking in 'London'. This first book of and by Urizen is not simply a satanic parody of the first book of Moses, but its hellish origin, the 'Laws' of language making all other writings possible. As Rousseau and others in the eighteenth century claimed, writing is a falling away from the immediacy and self-presence of speech. Monboddo even suggested that writing can be a 'hindrance' to knowledge when it replaces speech. The learning of 'the Pythagorean school, the most learned school of philosophy that ever was in Greece', was not 'committed to writing' until the community was 'broken and dispersed'.[87] As in *Urizen*, writing is perceived by Monboddo to be both cause and consequence of rupture and disengagement. But *Urizen* also shows that this descent into the book is an extension and condensation of the difference and absence already present in the form of semiosis instituted by Urizen's wilful falling away from his immediate co-presence with the other Eternals.

The concluding verse of Urizen's great speech, with its emphasis on laws, weight, and measure, brings to the fore the political and hegemonic dimensions of semiotic systems. Like any other rule of law, grammar and the representational powers of arbitrary signs depend upon consensus backed by enforcement. If Urizen is in some respects a seventeenth-century grammarian and mathematician, he is also an eighteenth-century lexicographical reformer who, like Johnson, struggles against what he perceives to be semantic chaos. The weapon for both Urizen and Johnson is a magisterial book establishing the 'one Law' of univocal meanings as the agency through which 'One King' and 'one God' (2: 8) can project their rule. The 'Oppression' of 'One Law for the Lion & Ox'[88] finds its conceptual ground and continual enforcement in the taxonomy distinguishing species of words.

[87] Monboddo, *Origin and Progress of Language*, 2: 259–60. For two recent and stimulating studies of Blake's attitudes toward books and writing, see P. Mann, '*The Book of Urizen* and the Horizon of the Book', in Hilton and Vogler, *Unnam'd Forms*, pp. 49–68; and W. J. T. Mitchell, 'Visible Language: Blake's Wond'rous Art of Writing', in M. Eaves and M. Fischer, eds., *Romanticism and Contemporary Criticism* (1986), 46–86. Mann writes in the shadows of Urizen and Derrida; Mitchell's view is wider and less bleak.

[88] *Marriage of Heaven and Hell*, Pl. 24 (E 44, K 158).

The taxonomic code spreads throughout and defines Urizen's world. Its temporal extension, forged by Los, is no less based on articulated difference, the 'links' of 'hours, days & years' (4b: 2). These divisions have their linguistic component in the syntagmatic structure of propositions, the 'chains of the mind' (4b: 4) formed by words that cannot free themselves from paradigmatic grammar any more than Los can rid himself of Urizen and what he has created. In his painful creation of the human body (4b: 5–12), Los gives literal embodiment to the differential system: conceptual and semiotic taxonomy congeals into anatomy. Elsewhere the semiotic network extends its rule through the imagery of 'nets & gins' (4a: 4) or webs or woven coverings. 'Science' is a 'woof wove' (5: 12) by Eternals whose 'infinite labour' would be impossible without a rationalized grammar of signs, verbal and mathematical.[89] As Urizen wanders through his world, a 'cold shadow follow'd behind him | Like a spiders web' (8: 6). This 'Web dark & cold' becomes separated from him and takes on its own identity as a 'Female in embrio' (8: 7). As in the extrusion from Los of 'the first female now separate' (5: 9), the sexual division recapitulates in the biological realm the differential schema that came into being with the genesis of Urizen's own separate identity. Finally, the web, 'twisted like to the human brain' (8: 8), is named: 'And all calld it, The Net of Religion' (8: 9). The literalizing movement of the figuration, from simile ('Like a spiders web') to independent entity ('a Web dark & cold'), dramatizes in the language of the poem its semiotic theme, the reification of a system of signs into physical nature. Part of the 'primeval Priests [i.e. Urizen's] assum'd power' ('Preludium') is the expropriation of the power of language to project a reality out of its own structures.[90]

[89] As S. Peterfreund has suggested, 'an understanding of Blake's response to the English empiricists' position on linguistic reform provides the necessary precedent and framework for understanding his response to Newton's position on the function of space and time'. *Urizen* shows that these two positions are conterminous and interdependent manifestations of the same schema—or, as D. D. Ault states the matter, 'the origin of language is the origin of the fallen world'. See Peterfreund, 'Blake on Space, Time, and the Role of the Artist', *STTH* 2 (1979), 248; Ault, *Visionary Physics* (1974), 167.

[90] As M. Rosenberg comments in 'Style and Meaning in *The Book of Urizen*', *Style*, 4 (1970), 198, the web 'simile has become a reality'. Rosenberg sees this as an instance of the constitutive powers of the imagination ('what can be imagined exists and is real', p. 202), but does not consider how these powers are directed and delimited by Urizen. As Blake states in *Jerusalem*, 'What seems to Be: Is: To those to whom | It seems to Be, & is productive of the most dreadful | Consequences to those to whom it seems to Be' (Pl. 32; E 179, K 663). The literalization of figuration will be discussed more fully in ch. 5.

In turn, that reality is allegorized into a natural religion whose god is a self-image of his priest's taxonomic consciousness and semiotic. This is the god Nietzsche will later fear 'we shall never rid ourselves of . . . , since we still believe in grammar'.[91]

It has become something of a commonplace in Blake studies to suggest that *The Book of Urizen*, printed from etched copper plates, is implicated in Blake's critique of Urizen's 'books formd of metals' (2: 6). This bibliographic parallel brings to the forefront a deeper level of linguistic involvement, for Blake's own signs and their grammar are descendants of what Urizen has wrought. Blake could write in some physical medium other than metal, but he could not avoid using a language with structures established outside and prior to his use of it. This belatedness, encumbent on all speakers everywhere, is figured forth in *Urizen* through the activities of the Eternals, particularly Los, whose response to Urizen's actions are unavoidably contingent upon those actions and reproduce their differential structure. How then can Blake, any more than Los, escape replicating the Urizenic in the language necessary for representing it?

One answer is offered by the celebration of the figural as a disruption of, and hence a release from, the taxonomic schema of meanings and grammatical categories. A proliferation of secondary motivation, from puns to extended metaphors, and the semantic excesses of polyvalent signifiers would seem to be the poet's best antidotes to the rigid matrices of Urizenic semiotics. This eighteenth-century and romantic tradition in tropology finds its modern advocates in philosophers such as Paul Ricoeur, who writes with elegant conviction of polysemy as 'the potential creativity contained in the word' and of 'the power of metaphor' as a way to 'break through previous categorization' because 'the dynamics of metaphor consist in confusing the established logical boundaries for the sake of detecting new similarities which previous categorization prevented our noticing'. Like Coleridge's symbol, Ricoeur's 'metaphor is no longer a rhetorical device, no longer a trope; it designates the general process by which we grasp kinship, break the distance between remote ideas, build similarities on dissimilarities'. Ricoeur's 'conclusion is that the strategy of discourse implied in metaphorical language is neither to

[91] F. W. Nietzsche, *Twilight of the Idols* (1968), 38.

improve communication nor to insure univocity in argumentation, but to shatter and to increase our sense of reality by shattering and increasing our language'.[92]

My own earlier comments on the figural strategies Blake begins to develop in *The French Revolution* accord well with Ricoeur's general theory. His perspective holds out the promise of discovering even in the language of *Urizen* an escape from Urizen's language. Consider, for example, the following passage:

And a roof, vast petrific around,
On all sides He fram'd: like a womb;
Where thousands of rivers in veins
Of blood pour down the mountains to cool
The eternal fires beating without
From Eternals; & like a black globe
View'd by sons of Eternity, standing
On the shore of the infinite ocean
Like a human heart strugling & beating
The vast world of Urizen appear'd. (3: 7)

This 'vast world' comes into verbal being through a trans-categorical series of figural and perspectival movements. The opening architectural image immediately violates the definition of 'roof' by extending on 'all sides', filling the lexical categories conventionally reserved for 'walls', 'floors', or their equivalents. The simile displaces this frame into anatomy. The ambiguity of 'Where' cuts across the normative differentiation I have just used between the (presumably) literal 'roof' and the figural 'womb': is this 'where' the building or an extension of the simile? 'Veins' and 'blood' indicate the latter; 'rivers' and 'mountains' point to neither, but lead to yet a third frame, the geographical.[93] Two successive similes—the 'black globe' viewed from without and the 'human heart' within—further disrupt the literal/figural dichotomy because the syntactically distant

[92] 'Creativity in Language: Word, Polysemy, Metaphor', in *Philosophy of Paul Ricoeur* (1978), 121, 132–3. For a technical study of 'sorts' (i.e., semantic categories) and many (but by no means all) metaphors as forms of 'sortal incorrectness', see S. Lappin, *Sorts, Ontology, and Metaphor* (1981).

[93] The body/earth compound has many precedents, including the myth of 'How the sons of Bore made heaven and earth' in the Icelandic Edda; see P. H. Mallet, *Northern Antiquities* (1770), 2: 22–3.

'roof' for which they are figures now seems equally metaphoric. All images are simultaneous manifestations of the same imaginative reality,[94] a 'strugling & beating' verbal plasma that expands and contracts through categorical distinctions (architectural, biological, geophysical) like the 'all flexible senses' of 'the Immortal' Urizen before his fall into singular being (2: 1). Much as Condillac, Blair, and Rousseau asserted the historical priority of the figural over the logical, the polysemous tropologies of *Urizen* would seem to carry us back to a condition prior to Urizen's origin and to preserve traces of the mobile fire his taxonomies never quite contain.[95]

Whatever insights might be gleaned from exegeses of the foregoing type depend upon a blindness to their own embedded categories—and Blake's. The very act of transgressing categorical distinctions presupposes the existence of such categories as the primary ground of the figural. Blake's phrase in *Urizen*, 'forms of deformity' (5: 5), nicely captures the dependency of figural deformation on its contrary. The 'structure' of language is 'stubborn', as Blake claims in *Jerusalem* (Pl. 36; E 183, K 668), because it refuses confinement in the 'rough basement' and insinuates itself throughout figural superstructures. The perception of similitude can even contribute to the aggrandizements of taxonomy by building general categories—e.g., the class of enclosed structures that includes buildings, globes, and hearts. Explanations of tropic transgressions must return to and name general categories, reinstituting them in the exegete's language even when only implicit in the poet's. When, for example, Hilton reveals with his usual insight all the 'layered' meanings in the word 'Urizen', he separates these meanings into layers or categories.[96] Urizen thereby gives birth to difference and taxonomy in more texts than his own. But the ways in which interpretation contributes mightily to the progress of abstraction are even more evident in these pages than in Hilton's.

[94] This collapse of tenor and vehicle into the same ontological status parallels, at the level of individual metaphors, Lowth's sense of the 'mystical allegory' of the Bible in which the literal and the figural are equally true and interdependent. See Lowth, *Lectures on the Sacred Poetry of the Hebrews* (1787), 1: 236–46.

[95] The extent to which etymological speculations in Blake's time also authorized the perception of original connections between words from diverse semantic categories is indicated by W. Whiter's proposal that the following all belong to the same family tree: cave, heaven (from cope of heaven and *coelum*), cloak, mantle, to collect, habitation, riches, desire, names of beasts of prey, to have power, to be eminent, the head, vestments of a priest, cup, tent, copper, couch, grave, engrave, to write. See Whiter, *Etymologicon magnum* (1800).

[96] 'Blakean Zen', *Studies in Romanticism*, 24 (1985), 196.

My best efforts to escape a differential semiotic have come full circle, a dull round of figural revolt and logical repression that effectively deconstructs many of my earlier claims about the anti-taxonomic successes of Blake's tropologies and the generative capabilities of a language unsubdued by grammatical prisons. Like the 'devourer' in *The Marriage of Heaven and Hell*, the structuralist and post-structuralist perspective *Urizen* has led us to has made it seem as though the 'producer'—the prolific signifier—'was in his chains'. The replication of difference that defeats Urizen's struggle for unity also defeats the age-old desire for a motivated sign. Even the incarnational sign, an ideal imagined through its differentiation from the differential, is inevitably decompounded into its constituent categories of being and meaning in our discourse about it. The dynamic contrariety of *The Marriage of Heaven and Hell* proposes to release us from static categories, but only by importing difference to the temporal axis as the interplay between freedom and necessity in any inherited medium. Like the fallen, natural man in *Milton* (Pl. 5; E 99, K 484), we seem to have no way of not 'conversing with the Void' if we converse at all, no way of not 'comprehending only Discord and Harmony' if we comprehend at all. In this world, Urizen's world, meaning itself is defined by what Derrida has called 'the primordial Difference of the absolute Origin'.[97] To overcome this legacy must we give up meaning? That would seem a self-defeating sacrifice, but at least we can move away from the equation of language with sign functions that has dominated most of this book. Such a major shift in perspective can be implemented by turning from the texts produced by Blake to his methods of production. This will also lead away from a concentration on devouring structures and toward a sense of language as prolific activity in which the desire to act encompasses, but overflows, the desire to mean. Even the words of *Urizen* are 'swift' and 'winged', for as Blake told Henry Crabb Robinson, 'the moment I have written, I see the Words fly about the room in all directions'.[98]

[97] *Edmund Husserl's Origin of Geometry: An Introduction* (1978), 153.
[98] Bentley, *Blake Records*, p. 547.

4. Language and Modes of Production

LET us begin with an innocent acceptance of Blake's own statements about how he created texts. In his guise as the shepherd-piper of the *Songs of Innocence*, Blake receives in the Introduction poem directions from a child on a cloud to play, sing, and write his songs. The 'Bard' in the Introduction to *Songs of Experience* is less explicitly prompted by a spiritual presence, but the special powers of his 'voice' seem to depend upon his having 'heard, | The Holy Word, | That walk'd among the ancient trees' (E 18, K 210). Gentle directives become an appeal for dictation at the beginning of *The Book of Urizen*: 'Eternals I hear your call gladly, | Dictate swift winged words, . . .' (E 70, K 222). *Europe* is dictated to Blake by 'a Fairy', at least according to the whimsical story of the poem's origin recounted on a preliminary plate (E 60, K 237–8) included in two of twelve copies printed by Blake. *The Song of Los* claims to be a song by Los, first 'sung' by him 'at the tables of Eternity' (E 67, K 245) and repeated in the illuminated book. The 'Daughters of Beulah' are the 'Muses who inspire the Poets Song' in *Milton* (Pl. 2; E 96, K481), while in the *Descriptive Catalogue* of 1809 Blake claims to have 'written' a 'voluminous' work 'under inspiration' (E 543, K 578). This may be a reference to *Jerusalem*, near the beginning of which we are told that the 'Verse' of the poem 'was first dictated to' its author/amanuensis and that at 'sun-rise' he can see 'the Saviour' who has been 'dictating the words of this mild song' (Pls. 3–4; E 145–6, K 621–2). One might suppose these passages to be traditional topoi having no substance outside literary conventions, but Blake claims otherwise in two letters of 1803 to Thomas Butts. Here he comments again on writing a 'Poem from immediate Dictation twelve or sometimes twenty or thirty lines at a time without Premeditation & even against [his] Will' (E 729, K 823). Thus, Blake 'dare not pretend to be any other than the Secretary' of the poem, for 'the Authors are in Eternity' (E 730, K 825). There is no reason to question these statements as anything other than what Blake really believed he was doing when he wrote some of his major poems. Even the method Blake used to publish these texts is granted an otherworldly origin in the story that he learned the technique of relief etching from his dead brother Robert in a vision.[1]

All these comments posit an otherness as origin, distinct from but in contact with the productive self. Elsewhere Blake suggests that this source, as the divine humanity or the universal poetic genius, is also a part of the self. Yet even in these gestures toward the romantic internalization of the muse, there remains a division between the faculty of imaginative invention and the means of physical reproduction. Such a distinction runs counter to Blake's central aesthetic and epistemological doctrine, the unity of conception and execution. As he wrote in his copy of Reynolds's *Discourses*, 'Invention depends Altogether upon Execution or Organization' (E 637, K 446). Several ringing statements in the *Public Address* of *c.*1810 strike the same note, first sounded in a letter of 1795 in which Blake announces his antipathy to 'the pretended Philosophy which teaches that Execution is the power of One & Invention of Another'.[2]

Can these contrary models of literary production be reconciled? Let me suggest one way of doing so, primarily for its heuristic possibilities. If the otherness at the origin of Blake's texts is language itself, then there can be no distinction between that source of conception and the medium of its execution: the medium *is* the origin. Blake's imagining of 'the Saviour' as the muse of *Jerusalem* hints at this unity of origins and means: the Word dictates the words. Language is the poetic genius within and without the individual, for it is simultaneously an extra-personal system by which he must allow

[1] Blake is in all probability the source for this tale, repeated by Smith in *Nollekens and his Times* (1828) and by A. Cunningham in his *Lives* (1830); see Bentley, *Blake Records*, pp. 460, 486. In a letter to Hayley of 6 May 1800, Blake wrote as follows about Robert: 'Thirteen years ago. I lost a brother & with his spirit I converse daily & hourly in the Spirit. & See him in my remembrance in the regions of my Imagination. I hear his advice & even now write from his Dictate' (E 705, K 797). In a letter to J. Trusler of 16 August 1799, Blake wrote that 'my Designs . . . are not Mine being of the same opinion with Milton when he says That the Muse visits his Slumbers & awakes and governs his Song . . .' (E 701, K 792). Years later, in his conversations with H. C. Robinson, Blake said that 'he acted by command' (Bentley, *Blake Records*, p. 311). For others who believed they were commanded to write, from King David (1 Chronicles 28: 19) to Boehme and Swedenborg, see Damon, *Blake*, pp. 206–7.

[2] E 699, K 790; see also *Public Address*, E 576, K 595–6. The importance of the unity of conception and execution to Blake's idea of artistic production is explored in M. Eaves, *Blake's Theory of Art* (1982), esp. pp. 79–91, 162–9.

himself to be guided,[3] and an intensely personal medium, a necessary means for becoming a fully human consciousness to himself and to others. This hypothesis also overcomes any shadow of an inconsistency between the 'dictation' theory of composition and Blake's commendations of the spontaneous in all matters ethical and aesthetic.[4] When he felt himself 'in fury of Poetic Inspiration', Blake was caught up in words, those 'Mental forms Creating'—not merely created by—the phenomena of textual production.[5] The more immediate and spontaneous these processes appear to the poet, the more they seem the product of inspiration. In such circumstances, 'all spontaneity is felt as receptivity',[6] and with good cause if the source is the medium of the poet's being *qua* poet. The internalized linguistic schemata and their generative potency are re-externalized into the persona of a dictating spirit. However studied and conscious Blake's efforts as a writer may be, they are erected on the foundation of a largely unconscious and spontaneous linguistic competency we all experience in the silent speech of thought. As Benjamin Heath Malkin wrote in his discussion of Blake's poetry, 'words and numbers present themselves unbidden, when the soul is inspired by sentiment, elevated by enthusiasm, or ravished by devotion'.[7] For this poet, listening to words as they speak their truths through him, 'language is Delphi'.[8]

[3] See Derrida, *Of Grammatology*, p. 158: '. . . the writer writes *in* a language and *in* a logic whose proper systems, laws, and life his discourse by definition cannot dominate absolutely. He uses them only by letting himself, after a fashion and up to a point, be governed by the system.'

[4] Blake's precedent for spontaneity is Jesus, who in Matthew 12: 34 states that 'out of the abundance of the heart the mouth speaketh', and who, according to Blake, 'was all virtue, and acted from impulse: not from rules' (*Marriage of Heaven and Hell*, Pls. 23–4; E 43, K 158). The spontaneous and the immediate also played a major role in Blake's conception of pictorial production. 'Enthusiasm is the All in All' (annotations to Reynolds, E 645, K 456) and prompts the artist to draw 'with a firm and decided hand at once. . . . Let a Man who has made a Drawing go on & on & he will produce a Picture or Painting but if he chooses to leave off before he has spoild it he will Do a Better Thing' (*Public Address*, E 576, K 595, 603). According to Gilchrist, Blake 'was wont to affirm:—"First thoughts are best in art, second thoughts in other matters" ' (*Life of Blake*, 1: 370).

[5] *Milton*, Pl. 30; E 129, K 519.

[6] E. Cassirer, *Language and Myth* (1946), 62. George Eliot makes a similar observation: 'And do we not all agree to call rapid thought and noble impulse by the name of inspiration? After our subtlest analysis of the mental process, we must still say . . . that our highest thoughts and our best deeds are all given to us.' *Adam Bede* (1859), 1: 210.

[7] *A Father's Memoirs* (1806) in Bentley, *Blake Records*, p. 427. Malkin's comment anticipates Shelley's famous image of 'a Poet hidden | In the light of thought, | Singing hymns unbidden, . . .' 'To a Sky-Lark', in *Poetry and Prose*, p. 227.

[8] Novalis, 'Miscellaneous Fragments' no. 21, in *Hymns to the Night and Other Selected Writings*.

Before I become too enraptured with the fury of my poetic theory, we should turn to its grounding in Blake's belief in the unity of conception and execution. Their relationship must at least become a two-way avenue for the medium to speak by allowing execution, in the form of linguistic performance, to generate conception in the form of meanings.[9] Before attempting to discover such a process in Blake's language, we must take a detour through Blake's methods of pictorial production. In these we can most readily observe the extent to which the ideal of free interchange between conception and execution is descriptive of actual practices.

Blake's ways of developing designs, from first thoughts on paper to finished watercolours or etchings, retain the possibilities for original conception throughout all stages of execution. Although the slavish copying of an image, in the mind's eye or on paper, might seem a way to preserve the original concept, such a procedure is actually antithetical to Blake's basic aesthetic position. The unity of conception and execution, when understood in the radical sense I am proposing here, requires continual revision as a form of reconception. The principle claims that there can be no conception without a medium of execution to conceive in, but it also prompts its adherents to promote the presence of conception in every act of execution. The principle is violated by either a *belief* in concepts (Blake would call them 'abstractions') that transcend all media, or by *processes* (such as reproductive engraving) that try to suppress eruptions of new conceptions within acts of execution. Thus, the unity of conception and execution goes hand in hand with a kind of creative revisionism—not the static maintenance of the same 'original' image, but its continual reconception each time it is executed.

Blake was an indefatigable reviser of his pictorial works. Two groups of related drawings reveal his methods and their consequences. From about 1780 to 1785, Blake drew at least eight versions of a design now known as *The Good Farmer*.[10] Each is a reconception

[9] To adopt the technical language of Saussure's *Course in General Linguistics*, I am suggesting that, however dependent *parole* may be on the pre-existent structures of *langue*, it is equally true that there would be no *langue* (structure) without *parole* (performance). Saussure himself emphasizes this interdependence, although he does not pursue the creativity of the diachronic axis, the ways in which *parole* shapes *langue* and brings new meanings to presence within language.

[10] Butlin nos. 120–4, including 3 recto/verso works.

of at least one of the figures or their groupings, with the major change in the central figure of Christ occurring between the recto and verso drawings on a single sheet. Eight designs on the theme of *Pestilence* show greater variations over a longer period of time.[11] The first two drawings, *c.*1779–80 and *c.*1780–4, are closely related, but the three composed in the 1790s are thorough revisions with minor but telling variants among them. Three figures appearing in the early set, but removed from the later group, re-emerge as central motifs in a *Notebook* emblem sketch of *c.*1792–3 and a full-page design in *Europe* (1794) with yet further differences in posture and expression. In about 1805, Blake executed a final version in watercolour, based fairly closely on the 1790s drawings but with changes in the background and the placement of one major figure. There is nothing extraordinary about this kind of continual revision of an image; many examples can be found in the careers of other artists. Yet the progress of *The Good Farmer* and *Pestilence* through their multiple versions does suggest how even standard procedures in the visual arts can prompt a theory that every execution is (or should be) a reconception. This same revisionary spirit seems to have motivated the differences between Blake's early and later sets of designs to Milton's poems.[12] As several Blake scholars have gone to considerable lengths to demonstrate, the different versions register changes in Blake's interpretive conceptions of the texts illustrated.[13]

Blake's late drawings evince a far less conventional procedure unifying conception and execution. The usual eighteenth- and early nineteenth-century method of producing a finished painting or watercolour established a fairly rigid barrier between preliminary sketching and final design. Evolving conceptions of an image resulted in a sequence of sketches, but these were stabilized into a drawing that was copied, sometimes through mechanical means, in the completed

[11] Butlin nos. 184–5, 190, 192–3, 201.25 (*Notebook* emblem), a pencil drawing of *c.*1793–7 recently discovered at the Huntington Library, and Pl. 10 (as numbered in Bentley, *Blake Books*) of *Europe*.

[12] Two sets of designs to *Comus*, *c.*1801 and *c.*1815 (Butlin nos. 527–8); two sets and the beginnings of a third for *Paradise Lost*, 1807, 1808, and 1822 (Butlin nos. 529, 536–7); two sets for 'On the Morning of Christ's Nativity', 1809 and *c.*1815 (Butlin nos. 538, 542). There are also important differences between the illustrations to The Book of Job of *c.*1805–6 and *c.*1821 (Butlin nos. 550–1), although there the matter is complicated by John Linnell's involvement in copying the outlines of the early set in preparation for the later.

[13] The book-length studies that pursue this thesis most assiduously are S. C. Behrendt, *The Moment of Explosion* (1983); and B. C. Werner, *Blake's Vision of the Poetry of Milton* (1986).

work. Thus, with his final execution, the artist attempted to avoid revision, much less reconception. There are of course some notable exceptions to this pattern, such as J. M. W. Turner repainting his oils even as they hung in an exhibition hall, but Blake takes such manœuvres to their limit by consolidating everything from first sketches to the finished image into the same physical object. Blake's drawing style in the 1820s is distinguished by many fine lines rapidly executed as though in pursuit of the single, appropriate outline. Each provisional stroke represents a conception of the image slightly different from its companions. This technique effectively collapses the usual sequence of multiple sketches into one. Several of Blake's more finished compositions indicate that such compound sketches underlie final versions. The 102 Dante illustrations, for example, exist in various stages of completion ranging from rough pencil sketches to highly finished watercolours.[14] The evolution of these images, all on the same size sheets of the same paper, indicates a continuous process of development with no physical separation between the design's first tentative conception in pencil and its final execution. The finished watercolour is one with its origins. The Genesis Manuscript, left only partially finished at Blake's death, shows the same method of developing both designs and letters, the latter begun as light pencil sketches and subsequently worked up with ink and watercolours. In *A Descriptive Catalogue*, Blake attacks 'those who separate Painting from Drawing' (E 538, K 573). In his own most typical practices, Blake physically and conceptually united them.

The conventional distinctions between stages of conception and of execution in the production of watercolours or oil paintings seem slight in comparison to what we find in the graphic arts of Blake's time. His own craft of reproductive engraving established a clear break between artistic conception and graphic execution, the former the province of the artist and the latter the province of the engraver who submitted his eye, hand, and medium to what the artist had wrought. This division is recorded in the customary way engravings were signed in the plate: in the lower left corner, the artist's name followed by *invenit* (usually abbreviated); in the lower right corner,

[14] Butlin no. 812. The illustrations to Bunyan's *Pilgrim's Progress* (Butlin no. 829) exhibit some of the same stages of development. I am grateful to Joseph Viscomi for pointing out to me these special characteristics of Blake's late drawing methods.

the engraver's name followed by *sculpsit*. The bondage of graphic style to the reproduction of images first conceived and executed in a different medium (oil paint, chalk, watercolours, etc.) is particularly evident in the eighteenth century. Almost all the technical innovations popular in Blake's era were developed specifically for their ability to imitate other media: mezzotint for oil paintings, aquatint for watercolours, 'chalk manner' stipple etching for drawings in chalk or crayon. Both traditional procedures, such as counterproofing, and newer tools like the parallelogram were dedicated to the mechanical transfer of the artist's image to the metal plate with a minimum of conceptual involvement on the part of the engraver.[15] The use of journeymen by the more successful engravers, a practice Blake roundly criticizes in his *Descriptive Catalogue* and *Public Address*, further anatomized production into discrete and mutually exclusive acts. The final stage of executing a print—the inking of the plate and its printing on paper—was generally placed in the hands of yet another craftsman, the professional plate-printer, whose sole duty was to turn out exact and uniform impressions of the lines and dots incised in the metal. Any revision on his part or deviation from exact repeatability was rejected as an error.

Blake's life as an engraver of his own designs and as a technically innovative printmaker was a revolt against the customary divisions I have briefly summarized. His revisionary habits as a draughtsman are again apparent in his graphic endeavours. In the 1780s and 1790s, Blake designed and engraved seven separate intaglio plates.[16] Rather than simply reprinting these throughout his career, Blake dramatically reworked all but two some time between *c.*1804 and the end of his life. *For Children: The Gates of Paradise* was similarly reconstituted into *For the Sexes: The Gates of Paradise* in about 1818. 'Chaucers Canterbury Pilgrims', first executed in 1810, was developed over the succeeding fifteen years through four very different states. 'Mirth', one of Blake's illustrations to Milton's 'L'Allegro', was originally engraved in stipple in about 1816, but this delicate image was later burnished away and almost entirely re-engraved in line. Most of these revisions go far beyond stylistic

[15] For descriptions of the graphic styles and processes mentioned here, see W. M. Ivins, *How Prints Look* (1943); and Essick, *Blake Printmaker*, pp. 8–28.

[16] For details on states, dating, and impressions, see R. N. Essick, *Separate Plates of Blake* (1983).

nuance and become new conceptualizations of the designs through the addition or elimination of inscriptions and major motifs.

Blake's unique method of relief etching provided a medium for his most radical experiments in the interweaving of graphic conception and execution within a seamless process of production.[17] Rather than transferring a design prepared in a different medium to the copper, the relief etcher can compose directly on the plate. Rough sketches in Blake's *Notebook* indicate that, for the earlier illuminated books in relief etching, Blake first executed the designs in pencil. These were not, however, mechanically counterproofed (and hence reversed) on to the plate: impressions have right and left the reverse of the sketches, and thus the images in the copper must have been in the same direction as the *Notebook* images.[18] The drawing of designs in acid-resistant varnish on the plate was a continuation of the sketching process. Neither the fact that there are no extant detailed mock-ups for any of the texts and designs in the illuminated books, nor the present absence of even the barest preliminaries for most of the relief-etched designs, can prove that such works never existed. But it is certain that the very nature of relief etching promotes the use of the copperplate as both sketching surface and graphic surface, for designs can be altered on the plate as freely as pencil on paper at any point prior to the application of acid. In *Jerusalem*, erasure extended even beyond the etching process, as scored-through lines of text on several plates indicate. When Blake returned to original line engraving for his series of Job illustrations, he continued the techniques of direct composition to create the border designs as drypoint sketches subsequently cut with the graver. As John Linnell tells us, 'the borders were an afterthought, and designed as well as engraved upon the copper without a previous drawing'.[19]

[17] My general comments on relief etching are based on the reconstructions of the process in Essick, *Blake Printmaker*, pp. 85–121; and J. Viscomi, *Art of Blake's Illuminated Prints* (1983). I am indebted to Professor Viscomi for discussing with me a forthcoming study of Blake's relief prints in which he offers detailed evidence for compositional development in the graphic medium and Blake's backwards writing of texts directly on plates.

[18] This however is not the case with Blake's technique of white-line etching, used extensively in *Milton* and *Jerusalem*, for that process requires counterproofing and thus results in impressions with right and left as in the preliminary drawing. See for example *Jerusalem* Pl. 26 and the sketch for it (Butlin no. 566) bearing glue-spots and a platemark, both evidence of counterproofing.

[19] Letter to C. W. Dilke of 27 September 1844 (Bentley, *Blake Records*, pp. 326–7). Since Linnell commissioned the Job engravings and helped Blake with their preparation and printing, he was in a good position to know how they were produced. Six early proofs of the Job central designs bear slight sketches for borders, but none is a direct or detailed preliminary for the engraved version.

In his *Public Address*, Blake insists that 'Painting is Drawing on Canvas & Engraving is Drawing on Copper & Nothing Else' (E 574, K 594). Nowhere is this more true than in Blake's special methods for uniting all three media.

The printing of a relief etching is a very different operation from printing in intaglio. The ink must cover a much larger proportion of the plate's surface and is more subject to variations, both accidental and purposeful, in density, reticulation, and tone. Blake's use of different ink colours—sometimes more than one on a single plate—further promoted the natural proclivity of his medium for creating differences among impressions. In some cases he also failed to ink, or masked or wiped clean, part of the relief surface, thereby eliminating part of the design or text.[20] Printing became a further opportunity for reconception.

Blake extended invention even further into what were, in conventional methods of publishing images and texts, mechanical repetitions of a conception completed at an earlier stage of production. His strikingly various hand colouring of the illuminated books was his most dramatic means for rethinking designs even after printing.[21] The addition or overpainting of pictorial motifs offers the most obvious examples of colouring as revising; but the mere presence of chromatic tone, particularly when washed right over texts, can have subtle effects on literary tone. The colouring in many copies of the illuminated books produced in Blake's later years is so rich and detailed that the pages become miniature paintings. For these, Blake printed the designs (but not contiguous texts) very lightly since he needed the etched image only as a guide for drawing and painting. The process makes a full circle: the conventional evolution from hand-drawn to graphic design is reversed, returning the printed plate to a unique image.

The arranging of a book's leaves is not generally thought of as an opportunity for the binder to exercise his creative abilities. The sequence is established by the author's text and announced by the

[20] The clearest example of the effect of printing variations on Blake's texts is the masking of the last four lines of *America* Pl. 4 (as numbered in Bentley, *Blake Books*) in 13 of the 18 extant copies of the illuminated book.

[21] By the end of the 18th century, the colour printing and hand colouring of prints had become a minor industry, but the processes were divided into discrete stages to achieve maximum uniformity and repeatability—values diametrically opposed to what we find in Blake's relief colour printing and hand tinting.

printer's page numbers and signatures in each gathering. But here again we find Blake disrupting this seemingly inviolable convention. An anthology like *Songs of Innocence and of Experience* permits Blake's multiple arrangements of its lyrics without disturbing their internal coherence. Nor do the various placements of full plate designs in *The Book of Urizen* and *The Song of Los* affect their textual sequence. But the two very different orderings of *Jerusalem* chapter 2, neither of which has clear authority over the other, are another matter entirely. No other major work of English literature displays such a radical reconceptualization of its structure introduced in the final stages of book production, the numbering and binding of its pages. In these circumstances, we are confronted with what Stephen Leo Carr has so aptly termed 'an invention always generated [and continually regenerated] by its execution'.[22]

Blake's use of relief etching to print texts as well as designs provides a bridge between graphic and verbal production. Much has been made of Blake's special medium as a way to etch designs and texts on the same plate; but this can be done with equal facility in intaglio engraving, as demonstrated by *The Book of Ahania* and *The Book of Los.* The distinguishing feature of relief etched texts is their autographic nature, the result of direct composition on the plate. An intaglio text must first be prepared as a fair copy on paper and counterproofed on to a varnished plate. The letters are then carefully traced with a sharp instrument that scratches through the varnish to expose the metal to acid subsequently applied. Typographic printing establishes an even clearer division between author's manuscript—like an artist's sketch, the medium of conceptual development—and a compositor's mechanical execution of a printed text. Relief etching joins manuscript and printable letters in one continuous operation. There are no extant manuscript fair copies for the poems in Blake's illuminated books, for these are unnecessary. Blake could, and in all probability did, proceed directly from working drafts, such as those appearing in his *Notebook*, to writing in reverse on the copperplate. The fair copy and the printing plate are one. Nor is there any evidence that Blake established details of format, such as line length, letter size, and number of lines per plate, prior to the

[22] 'Illuminated Printing: Toward a Logic of Difference', in Hilton and Vogler, *Unnam'd Forms*, p. 193.

seriatim writing out of the text in acid-resist on plates. The great variety of letter sizes in *Jerusalem*, and the way words are squeezed together toward the right margin (left on the copperplate), suggest that Blake became even freer in his compositional habits when writing his last extended text etched in relief. The result is best described with an almost oxymoronic composite term, a 'printed manuscript'.

Blake's illuminated books demonstrate his unification of the later stages of verbal publication—that is, of writing and printing. Does this pervasive attempt to marry conception and execution also extend back into the earlier phases of linguistic activity? The revisions in *The Four Zoas* suggest an affirmative reply. Some thirty-seven pages of the manuscript are written in fine script in ink. This formal lettering style must have necessitated copying from a preliminary draft in Blake's normal manuscript hand, the hand we see in the remainder of *The Four Zoas*. As Blake continued to work on the poem, he converted what began as a finished work of calligraphy into a working manuscript with a good many deletions and interlinear revisions. New passages added in the margins have all the physical qualities of first drafts. Yet, these hastily written lines have much the same texture in their language and versification as the most finished parts of the manuscript book. On page nine, for example, the following lines are in handsome script:

> Alternate Love & Hate his breast; hers Scorn & Jealousy
> In embryon passions. they kiss'd not nor embrac'd for shame & fear
> His head beamd light & in his vigorous voice was prophecy
> He could controll the times & seasons, & the days & years
> She could controll the spaces, regions, desart, flood & forest
>
> (E 305, K 270–1)

A passage scrawled sideways in pencil in the left margin of the same page includes these lines:

> Astonishd sat her Sisters of Beulah to see her soft affections
> To Enion & her children & they ponderd these things wondring
> And they Alternate kept watch over the Youthful terrors
> They saw not yet the Hand Divine for it was not yet reveald
> But they went on in Silent Hope & Feminine repose
>
> (E 305, K 270)

When these passages are printed together, as they are in Erdman's edition of *The Complete Poetry and Prose*, with only five intervening lines and no indication of their physical differences in the manuscript, we sense no sudden shift from preliminary jottings to a finished poem. The language is all of a piece. The roughest draft contains the same tone, diction, and rhythm of the fair copy: the fair copy preserves the language of the preliminary through whatever stages of revision may have come between. It is this seamless quality—a verbal equivalent to the physical union of sketching and painting, of drawing and etching, in Blake's pictorial productions—that allows editors to print, and critics to interpret, *The Four Zoas* as though it were a complete and finished work in spite of considerable physical evidence to the contrary.[23] Indeed, the differences between marginal drafts and sections in script, and the disruptions in conventional narrative sequence throughout *The Four Zoas*, are not much greater than what we find between contiguous passages in the long poems Blake published in relief etching, *Milton* and *Jerusalem*.

My pursuit of continuities in Blake's methods of language production might seem to end with his first drafts. But there is one further, difficult step to be taken. As we have seen, Rousseau, Monboddo, and others in the eighteenth century criticized writing as a secondary representation of the spoken word. Only through speech—'a thinking outwardly projected', as Friedrich Schlegel called it—could man experience the spontaneous power of language in its full intimacy with thought. The contrary view, proposed by rationalist grammarians like Johnson and Urizen, held that writing should be deployed to tame the ambiguities and inventive excesses of speech. Yet these two positions share common ground, for both force a gap between the spontaneous creativity of oral performance (whether thought of as good or ill) and reasoned execution in writing. In Shelley's *Defence of Poetry*, the gap becomes an abyss between conception and *any* mode of execution: '. . . when composition begins, inspiration is already on the decline, and the most glorious poetry that has ever been communicated to the world is probably a feeble shadow of the original conception of the poet'.[24] Blake's

[23] Most interpretations of the poem were published after G. E. Bentley, Jr., demonstrated in detail that the manuscript did not represent a finished work. See Bentley, 'Failure of Blake's *Four Zoas*', *Texas Studies in English*, 37 (1958), 102–13; and Blake, *Vala or The Four Zoas* (1963).

[24] *Poetry and Prose*, p. 504.

methods of pictorial production are an attempt to bridge, and thereby deny the inevitability of, such distinctions. If he extended this same effort and its concomitant aesthetic values throughout all stages of verbal production, then we should find yet another syncretic form within his printed manuscripts—an oral writing.

The original oral nature of most ancient poetry, Biblical and Classical, became a commonplace among its students by the second half of the eighteenth century.[25] The attempt to transcribe oral verse not previously written down began with Macpherson's *Fragments of Ancient Poetry, Collected in the Highlands of Scotland*, first published in 1760. He too claimed, in effect, that these poems, as well as his slightly later Ossianic inventions, were 'dictated' to him. But the culture of late eighteenth-century Britain, not just the Highlands, seems to have been far more oral and aural than our vision-dominated world today. This was particularly true in religious activities such as ecstatic and unconscious utterance in the Pentecostal tradition of speaking in tongues,[26] Methodist witnessing, and of course the sermon. Schleiermacher elevated this intimacy between faith and utterance into a theological principle, claiming that even 'in the written communication of piety, everything needs to be twice or thrice repeated, the original medium [of speech] requiring to be again exhibited'.[27] Christopher Smart's antiphonal poem, *Jubilate Agno*, is the most dramatic example of an attempt to preserve this orality of religious expression in a written text.[28] On the secular side, the spoken word played a central role in everything from the *conversaziones* of the sort Blake satirizes in *An Island in the Moon* to the street cries he evokes and interprets in *Songs of Innocence and of Experience*. Reading aloud from books—a literal return of the written back into speech—still played an important role as evening entertainment, as it did for Blake and Hayley when together

[25] See the views of Blackwell, Wood, Lowth, and Pinkerton cited in ch. 2. Pinkerton ('On the Oral Tradition of Poetry', in *Scottish Tragic Ballads*, p. xiii) describes Homer, Moses, and the Druid bards as founders of the oral tradition. Lowth, *Isaiah*, p. 5, claims that 'the prophets in the first place delivered their inspired instructions, verbally to the people'.

[26] Late 18th-century interest in glossolalia is indicated by J. G. Herder, *On the Gift of Tongues*, reviewed in *Analytical Review*, 20 (1794), 326–30.

[27] *On Religion*, p. 150. See also p. 151: 'On the highest subject with which language has to deal, it is fitting that the fullness and splendour of human speech be expended.'

[28] Smart may have also been influenced by Lowth's studies of the (originally spoken or sung) structures of Hebrew verse; see Smart, *Jubilate Agno* (1954), Introduction, p. 20. Paley makes some telling comparisons between *Jubilate Agno* and *Jerusalem* in *Continuing City*, pp. 47–9.

at Felpham.[29] Several of the major poets of Blake's time tried various strategies for preserving the spoken in the written: Robert Burns's attempt to retain the intonations of spoken border English in his poetry; Wordsworth's theory of poetic diction based on the speech of common men; Coleridge's 'conversation' poems; Byron's attempt, in *Beppo* and *Don Juan*, to join the art of the *improvisatore* with a highly structured verse form.[30] There are good reasons to include Blake in this tradition.

The emphasis in recent Blake criticism on verbal/visual interactions in the illuminated books has tended to obscure how often the poetry evokes an aural world.[31] A glance at the word count in the *Concordance* shows that Blake may be our noisiest poet, at least in the number and variety of human utterances he names. 'Voice' appears more frequently than any other human attribute or activity, more even than 'see' or 'human'. Forms of 'weeping' are commoner than 'God', 'heaven', and 'light'. We hear 'groans' more than we see 'visions', 'howling' as much as 'moon', 'cries' more than 'stone', 'song' as much as 'sin'. The 'curse' is elemental, appearing as often as 'air' and 'waters'. 'Said' is of course very frequent, but is named only one more time than 'heard'. Many of these sounds are 'loud', but they are still present when 'silent'; we encounter the first adjective more than 'soul', the second more than 'heart'. Sometimes the noises cluster together and overwhelm all other senses. 'The howlings gnashings groanings shriekings shudderings sobbings burstings | Mingle together to create a world for Los', and a cacophony for the reader, in Night the Sixth of *The Four Zoas* (E 346, K 313).

The oral is more than a motif in Blake's writings, for the attempt to preserve the spoken word lies behind some of his most characteristic poetic forms. Articulate utterances extend into dialogues, although these often decay into talking at humorous cross-purposes, as in *An Island in the Moon*, or the self-enclosing monologues of *The Four Zoas*. The recognition of loss is a dominant motif in many poems, but it takes the primitive and oral form of lamentation, not the

[29] See Bentley, *Blake Records*, p. 95; and W. Hayley, *Memoirs* (1823), 2: 42, 44.

[30] On Burns's orality, see D. B. Morris, 'Burns and Heteroglossia', *The Eighteenth Century: Theory and Interpretation*, 28 (1987), 3–27. For a detailed study of how Coleridge tried 'to reproduce in his verse the natural cadences of speech,' see M. F. Schulz, *Poetic Voices of Coleridge* (1963), quotation from pp. 1–2.

[31] A notable exception is T. R. Frosch, *Awakening of Albion* (1974), 103–23. My comments on orality as a motif in Blake's poetry are indebted to Frosch's cogent observations.

literary modes of epitaph or elegy. When we hear Blake's own voice among the many speakers, it is the hortatory and declamatory speech of the prophet, the bard, and the 'true Orator' to whom Blake implicitly compares himself at the beginning of *Jerusalem* (Pl. 3; E 146, K 621). Blake's rhetorical versification, responsive to emotional tone and cadence more than a predetermined measure,[32] is complemented by idiosyncratic punctuation that indicates vocal pauses and emphases more than logical divisions. His use of internal exclamation marks, sometimes two or three within a single sentence to emphasize the immediately preceding word or phrase, is the most obvious form of this oratorical approach to pointing. More generally, Blake's relief-etched books continue into that bibliographic form some characteristics usually associated with spoken 'publication'. Just as effective oral performance requires gesture as a visual accompaniment, the illuminated book permitted Blake a pictorial component through illustration. Unlike an author who must place his words in the hands of printers and booksellers, the orator delivers his words directly to the public. By being his own etcher, printer, and bookseller, Blake retained a similar level of production control over his written words. When an orator gives the same speech more than once, no two performances are identical in tone and pacing. The proliferation of variety in colour and texture through multiple printings of the illuminated books insured an equivalent performative diversity.

Scholars in the eighteenth century recognized patterns of repetition as the leading characteristic of oral poetry. Lowth's concept of parallelism in the Bible is by far the most sophisticated analysis of such structuring, but Pinkerton suggests something more pervasive in his comments on 'the frequent returns of the same sentences and descriptions expressed in the very same words, . . . of which we meet with infinite examples in Homer, and some, if I mistake not, in Ossian'.[33] Thanks to the studies of Milman Parry, Albert B. Lord, and their cohorts, we now recognize formulaic phrases as a basic building-block of oral poetry, the technique that allows the unlettered

[32] As Damon points out (*Blake*, p. 57), Blake's 'septenaries . . . are to be poured out in a great flood of oratory, stressing the natural accents, and passing rapidly over the unaccented syllables. . . . Each line represents a breath; and this breath is the real metrical unit, around which all the variations are formed.'

[33] 'On the Oral Tradition of Poetry', in *Scottish Tragic Ballads*, p. xx.

bard to become absorbed in his medium and simultaneously create and deliver poems of great length.[34]

The repetitions of phrases and verse paragraphs in Blake's poetry have long been recognized, but the surprising extent to which they match the characteristics of oral-formulaic verse has perhaps seemed too extravagant a comparison to merit attention. In *Visions of the Daughters of Albion* (1793), formulaic patterns become not simply evident, but a dominant *modus operandi*, through the insistent anaphora of Oothoon's lamentations. Lines 30–1 on the second text plate initiate the process of beginning two or more consecutive lines with the same words: 'They told me that . . .' (E 47, K 191). The form is extended on the next plate through lines 2–4 ('With what sense . . .') and 22–4 ('Tell me what is . . .'), with the latter followed by a modified version of the formula ('And in what . . .'). Another variant, dropping the key word ('what') but continuing its initial phoneme/grapheme and picking up 'Tell me', shapes lines 3–4 on Plate 4 ('Tell me where . . .'). Strict anaphora ends on this plate ('And are there . . .' lines 20–3), but the rhetorical technique alerts us to somewhat looser parallelisms. Lines 7 and 10 on Plate 5 begin questions with 'Does', a pattern to which we are returned in the last verse paragraph on the plate ('Does the . . .' lines 33, 37; 'Does not . . .' lines 39, 41) and again in the last line on Plate 7 and three times in the middle of lines (1, 2, 4) in the final plate. A more tightly knit but various anaphoric structure dominates lines 12–19 on Plate 5. The sequence opens with 'How' repeated thrice, followed by a shift to 'Who' that requires a minimal change in sounds, followed by a return to 'How'. With the variant now established, the last three lines in the group shift to *W* words: 'With', 'What', 'With'. The process also creates a visual pattern in the autographic script, an interplay of *W* and *H* letter forms, both upper and lower case, sustained through the first word in all eight lines. In all these examples, the form is triggered by a key word or sound, as in oral-formulaic verse.[35] Even the isocolon (noun, adjective, present participle) in lines 4 and 5 on Plate 6 begins with an aural echo:

[34] The classic studies are Lord, *Singer of Tales* (1960); and Parry, *Making of Homeric Verse* (1971).

[35] See Parry, *Making of Homeric Verse*, pp. 302–3, on how 'essential ideas' are prompted in the oral poet by a single word or sound that 'is, as it were, the bridge between idea and sound'.

Infancy, fearless, lustful, happy! nestling . . .
. . . Innocence! honest, open, seeking . . .

(E 49, K 193)

In *Visions of the Daughters of Albion*, Blake would seem to be consciously deploying oral techniques to establish the speaking presence of a voice other than his own. Like the most primitive forms of ululation, the insightful lamentations of Oothoon derive part of their momentum from repeated sounds that stimulate patterns of meaning. We can hear the residual *W*ails and *H*owls in her voice, those natural utterances imagined to be at the origin of words. Her repetitions can also be explained as imitations and moderate extensions of Biblical parallelism, for most operate at the level of contiguous or nearly contiguous lines. In Blake's later poetry, however, we find less concentrated but more pervasive patterns of repetition that extend well beyond parallelism and anaphora and into the realm of oral-formulaic poetry.

The smallest formulaic unit is the single sound repeated as a phonetic intensive through semantically distinct passages. These are generally accompanied by far more obvious patterns in oral poetry, much as in the anaphora of *Visions of the Daughters of Albion* and elsewhere in Blake's verse. Searches for single-sound patterns are generally successful, since they occur spontaneously in all language, and thus are not very useful indicators of an underlying oral structure in written texts. Nonetheless, the prominence of such patterns, particularly alliteration, is typical of oral verse. There are a vast number of examples in Blake's poetry, but perhaps the most telling instances are those in which a particular word very frequently appears with alliterative companions. In twenty-nine out of thirty-seven appearances of 'bow' (the weapon, not the act or place) in *America*, *The Book of Ahania*, *The Four Zoas*, *Milton*, and *Jerusalem*, the word alliterates with at least one other term in the same or an immediately contiguous line. The literal sound of the bow sparks its repetition in other words and thereby helps form the parameters of meaning in these texts. In a few passages, a single sound identified with a particular character or theme would also seem to act as a motivating presence in Blake's poetry. Aaron Fogel has demonstrated, for example, how *ru* operates as 'the organizing sound motif' in lines 14–26 on Plate 6 of *Milton*.[36] As in oral-formulaic poetry, this pattern relates directly to narrative content and theme.[37] The action described, the scattering of Je*ru*salem's fragments, is presented phonetically as the dispersal of *ru* through the passage.

The repeated use of the same word as an intensifier in a wide variety of contexts, like the presence of composite terms, does not necessarily depend on the aural dimension of words. Yet, both are common in oral-formulaic verse.[38] The first verse paragraph of *Europe* Plate 10 (E 63, K 241) reveals Blake's propensity for the noun-participle and adverb-participle compound: 'serpent-form'd', 'high-towering', 'oak-surrounded', 'earth-born', and 'ever-varying' all appear within thirteen lines. The word occurring more than any other in Blake's poetry is 'all'—at 1007 times, almost twice that of the next most common term. 'Every' is the twenty-fourth most common. In 32 out of its 269 appearances, 'every' is followed by 'thing'; in 46 instances the word immediately precedes 'one', 'human', or 'man'. The totalizing thrust of Blake's mythologies has its microcosmic analogue—perhaps even its verbal seed—in the repeated appearances of 'all' and 'every'.

Larger formulaic units play important roles throughout Blake's longer poems. Here again, *Visions of the Daughters of Albion* is a harbinger. 'The Daughters of Albion hear her woes, & eccho back her sighs' echoes three times through the poem, including the final line (E 51, K 195). But, like 'Mark well my words . . .' repeated eight times in *Milton*, formulae that approach the character of a refrain in a single poem are not as indicative of oral composition as less emphatic patterns extending through more than one work. The phrase 'head or heart or reins' appears twice in *The Four Zoas*,

[36] Fogel, 'Pictures of Speech', pp. 230–32. The focus throughout this excellent essay on the phonemic/graphemic dynamics of Blake's language is relevant to my arguments here, but Fogel does not attempt to relate his topic to an oral mode of composition. For a description of similar phonetic and 'word-root' patterns in the Bible, see R. Alter, *Art of Biblical Narrative* (1981), 90, 93–5.

[37] On the congruity of the 'subject unit' (or 'theme') and oral formulae, see Parry, *Making of Homeric Verse*, pp. 68, 73, 410–11. The repeated image clusters in *The Four Zoas* show this same synchrony with thematic patterns; see the computer analysis summarized in N. M. Ide, 'Image Patterns and the Structure of William Blake's *The Four Zoas*', *Blake: An Illustrated Quarterly*, 20 (1987), 125–33.

[38] Composite terms were recognized as a component of oral composition in the 18th century; see Rousseau's comments on this device in the earliest forms of sung verse in his *Essay on the Origin of Languages*, p. 15, and T. Percy's description of what we now call 'kennings' in the unnumbered introduction to his edition of *Five Pieces of Runic Poetry* (1763).

once in *Milton*, and once in *Jerusalem*. 'Amalek, Canaan and Moab' and its variations occur eight times in these same three poems. Alliteration, consonance, and assonance provide the aurally mnemonic prompting for formulae of this type. Other repeated phrases, such as 'Which is the Divine Body of the Lord Jesus. blessed for ever' on Plate 3 of *Milton* and Plate 5 of *Jerusalem*, depend less on sounds than on incantatory rhythms and linguistic habits shaped by the life-long reading (and hearing) of the Bible. Character formulae—that is, the repeated use of the same epithet for a character—are another hallmark of oral poetry we find in Blake's verse. The composite term 'age-bent' appears seven times in *The Four Zoas*, 'The Mental Traveller', and *Jerusalem*. In each instance, Blake added the same alliterative companion to create a formulaic epithet, 'blind & age-bent'. In all but two of their occurrences, these words describe the character Enion. Her name evokes the formula which then becomes a significant part of what 'Enion' means within Blake's allegory.

The most obvious repetitions in Blake's poems are among *The Four Zoas*, *Milton*, and *Jerusalem*. A few are as long as the 'twelve or sometimes twenty or thirty lines' Blake told Butts he composed 'without Premeditation'.[39] In the case of Blake's barely modified borrowings of lines from *The Book of Urizen* (Pls. 10–11) in Night the Fourth of *The Four Zoas* (pp. 54–5), one can only assume direct copying, but the subsequent revisions of these same lines and their interpolation with others on Plate 3 of *Milton* bespeak a less mechanical mode of composition. The shift from verbatim repetition to lexical variation brings Blake's method closer to the orally formulaic.[40] Many of the repeated root phrases have a distinctly formulaic character: 'in chains of the mind lock'd up', 'red round Globe hot burning', 'And a first [second, third, etc.] Age passed over & a State of dismal woe' (E 96–7, K 482). Further, there are more repetitions between *Milton* and *Jerusalem* than between either poem and *The Four Zoas*, and hence all of their lines in common cannot be explained away as Blake's cannibalization of an unfinished

[39] E 729, K 823. In his edition of *Blake's Writings* (1978), G. E. Bentley, Jr., conveniently notes these repetitions of one or more lines (but not the shorter formulaic phrases I discuss here).

[40] Throughout *The Making of Homeric Verse*, Parry makes a distinction between the 'formulary' character of verbatim repetition, rare in oral poetry, and the more common 'formulaic' process that includes a continual evolution of small differences within the basic lexical pattern.

manuscript for which he had no other use. The two epics in relief etching were in the main written during the same years; both bear the date of 1804 on their title pages.[41] The compositional process and its implicit aesthetic clearly did not exclude, and even seems to have promoted, the sharing of passages. Thus the process contributed to the synchronic and mosaic structure of *Milton* and *Jerusalem*,[42] one in which formulaic text units could be shifted about within and between the poems without disrupting some underlying principle of dynamic form. Like the Bible, *Milton* and *Jerusalem* appear to have been produced by assembling, repeating, and reshaping a multitude of fragments. But Blake was his own redactor, and thus, like the oral-formulaic poet, he could extend the evolution of original conception through to the final stages of execution.

There is ample evidence to support Thomas Frosch's observation that Blake attempted 'to reconstitute poetry as an auditory medium'.[43] To do so required Blake to reintroduce orality at the most fundamental levels of composition, just as his reconstitution of reproductive graphics into original printmaking required a radical change in production methods. This is not to claim that Blake could magically become a Homer or Ossian, sing oral-formulaic verses, and then switch to his literate self and write them down. But it also seems highly unlikely that Blake's poetry is the product of a calculated process of imitation by a poet who consistently praised the spontaneous, claimed that he wrote freely and quickly under inspiration, and damned the imitative. Both these compositional models merely reinstate a division between oral conception and autographic execution. The best explanation of how Blake's auditory structures were generated is offered by a method of writing that does not silence the tongue and stop the ears, a writing that gathers oral composition into itself by uniting ear and hand as completely as Blake

[41] This may be the year Blake finished a draft of the poems and began etching them, but it is demonstrably not the date he finished his etching labours or first printed complete copies.

[42] The form of *Jerusalem* is discussed in these terms by Paley, *Continuing City*, pp. 278–314. For a study of the 'manifold repetitions of key incidents and images' in the two books of *Milton*, see S. Fox, *Poetic Form in Blake's* Milton (1976), quotation from p. xii. Although Fox's thesis centres on the elaborate symmetries between the two books of the poem, she cites Blake's letter to Butts about 'Dictation' and is careful 'not [to] argue that Blake consciously devised the structure of *Milton* according to the principles delineated in [her] study' (p. xiii).

[43] *Awakening of Albion*, p. 122. See also Mitchell's somewhat tentative suggestion that 'Blake's visible language heals the split between speech and writing' in 'Visible Language', p. 62.

the painter and engraver joined eye and hand. Although no single feature of his poetry can prove that Blake was that paradoxical compound, an oral-formulaic writer,[44] the variety and complexity of his formulae go well beyond what was known about oral verse patterns in his time. Thus, however prompted by ancient precedents or contemporary theories, the orality of Blake's poetry would seem the unselfconscious and inevitable result of an oral method of writing in which 'The living voice is ever living in its inmost joy' (*The Four Zoas*, E 324, K 289).

The technique of oral writing helps explain more in Blake's poetry than the auditory and formulaic features indicative of that procedure. Oral compositions tend to be accumulative, additive, and paratactic. Blake's poetry, like Smart's, exhibits these characteristics both in its emphasis on coordinate clauses and in the more encompassing sense of simultaneous activity with no event subordinated to any other. Particular examples are legion, ranging from the sequence of 'and' clauses spoken by the child in 'The Chimney Sweeper' of *Songs of Innocence* to the grammatical parallelisms of Blake's own bardic voice:

> The citizens of New-York close their books & lock their chests;
> The mariners of Boston drop their anchors and unlade;
> The scribe of Pensylvania casts his pen upon the earth;
> The builder of Virginia throws his hammer down in fear.[45]

Paratactic verse of this type generates metonymic structures—that is, patterns of association built up along the syntagmatic axis as distinct from metaphoric operations across the paradigmatic matrix. Citizens, mariners, scribe, and builder are joined through their identical grammatical roles and syntactic positions; closing, locking, dropping, casting, and throwing become linked actions. Oral writing, the means of execution, gives rise to an important mode of figuration that in turn becomes the foundation of conception.

The influence of orality on Blake's basic intellectual positions may be even more pervasive, if less easily demonstrated. In *The Presence*

[44] In 'The Literary Character of Anglo-Saxon Formulaic Poetry', *PMLA* 81 (1966), 334–41, L. D. Benson argues for a similar composite form in medieval literature.

[45] *America*, Pl. 14; E 56, K 201. See also the predominance of 'and' and 'while' clauses in *Jerusalem*. In *Allegory* (1964), 166, A. Fletcher remarks that Blake did 'not write oral poetry', but then quotes these same lines from *America* to exemplify the parataxis of oral-formulaic verse.

of the Word, Walter J. Ong conveniently summarizes a good deal of theorizing about the epistemic dispositions of oral cultures. 'Oral modes of existence are synthetic rather than analytic', according to Ong, and tend to promote the sense of a profoundly animate universe filled with warring forces that are psychic and human, not simply physical.[46] Thus the dynamics of myth, for which Blake's poetry has become the paradigmatic representative in English literature, are conterminous with orality. Ong further contends that 'the oral-aural individual . . . does not find himself simply situated somewhere in neutral, visual-tactile, Copernican space. Rather, he finds himself in a kind of vast interiority' (p. 164). At the very least, such speculations hint at an underlying compatibility between Blake's methods of creating poems and his critique of objective space and time and their Newtonian quantifications. The interiority of auditory space, and its associations with a lost but recoverable ideal, are given anatomical presence in Blake's identification of 'the Auricular Nerves of Human life' with 'Eden' at the beginning of *The Four Zoas* (E 301, K 264).

The model of verbal production I have been assembling is consistent with Blake's statements about his compositional practices, cited at the beginning of this chapter, and with the few scattered comments on his writing habits made by those who knew him. Cunningham reports that Blake composed tunes while he was writing his lyrics and drawing the accompanying designs; all three were 'the offspring . . . of the same moment'.[47] This unity of music and word at their point of origin, each the enabling companion of the other, recapitulates in Blake's production processes the supposed original unity of the arts.[48] According to Gilchrist, Blake's conversation and the imaginative range of his writings shared a similar intimacy. His speech was 'copious and varied, the fruit of great, but not morbid, intellectual activity, it was, in its ordinary course, full of mind, sagacity, and varied information. Above all, it was something quite

[46] *Presence of the Word* (1967), 264. Even more far-reaching models of the oral universe and contrasts with modern spatio-temporal structures are elaborated in M. McLuhan's once heralded but now generally ignored book, *Gutenberg Galaxy* (1962).

[47] Bentley, *Blake Records*, p. 482. J. T. Smith also notes that Blake 'composed tunes' for his lyrics which 'he would occasionally sing to his friends' (*Blake Records*, p. 457).

[48] Rousseau sums up this 18th-century tradition with his comment that 'verse, singing, and speech have a common origin. . . . the first discourses were the first songs' (*Essay on the Origin of Languages*, p. 50).

different from that of other men: conversation which carried you "from earth to heaven and back again, before you knew where you were".'[49] Fragmentary evidence for Gilchrist's description is provided by the bits and pieces of Blake's speech recorded by Henry Crabb Robinson. As Damon has pointed out, these records show that 'Blake was simply extending his symbolism to his conversation'.[50] The orality of Blake's symbolic writings allows one to claim with equal justice that he extended his conversation to his poetry.

The congruence of the auditory and the visual, the oral and the written, characteristic of Blake's production methods finds explicit expression in the texts thereby created. Blake often granted to imaginative 'vision' an aural dimension that provides the basis for the visual/auditory transformations essential to poems like 'London'. In a parenthetical interjection in Night the Third of *The Four Zoas*, Blake asks us to 'listen to [his] Vision' (E 328, K 294). On Plate 34 of *Jerusalem*, he recalls that 'In Felpham' he both 'heard and saw the Visions of Albion' (E 180, K 665). Near the end of the poem, he follows a dramatic speech with 'So spake the Vision of Albion' (Pl. 97; E 256, K 744). And when, at the conclusion of *A Vision of the Last Judgment*, Blake transforms the material metaphor of the 'Sun . . . somewhat like a Guinea' into spiritual vision, he not only *sees* 'an Innumerable company of the Heavenly host' but *hears* their articulate cry, 'Holy Holy Holy is the Lord God Almighty'.[51]

The synaesthetic nature of vision continues into Blake's scenes of inspired writing. The Introduction to *Songs of Innocence* provides a simple yet compelling example:

[49] *Life of Blake*, 1: 311. Gilchrist states that 'all speak of [Blake's] conversation' in these terms, but as usual does not identify his sources. Gilchrist also notes 'the "wild and whirling words" [Blake] would utter in conversation' (1: 327). F. Tatham briefly describes Blake's 'entertaining & pleasant' conversation 'possessing . . . novel thoughts & . . . eccentric notions' (Bentley, *Blake Records*, p. 253; see also p. 526).

[50] *Blake*, p. 199.

[51] E 565–6, K 617. Blake presents a symmetrically reversed conversion in a letter to Hayley of 27 January 1804. Blake's memories of the 'verses' of Edward Garrard Marsh that 'still sound upon [his] Ear' proceed through a series of similes to the visual image 'of the Glorious & far beaming Turret' of Hayley's house (E 741, K 835). For the tradition that St John's vision of Revelation was both seen and heard, as Blake states in Night the Eighth of *Four Zoas* (E 385–6, K 356), see J. A. Wittreich, Jr., 'Painted Prophecies: The Tradition of Blake's Illuminated Books', in Essick and Pearce, *Blake in his Time*, pp. 101–15.

Piping down the valleys wild
Piping songs of pleasant glee
On a cloud I saw a child.
And he laughing said to me.

Pipe a song about a Lamb;
So I piped with merry chear,
Piper pipe that song again—
So I piped, he wept to hear.

Drop thy pipe thy happy pipe
Sing thy songs of happy chear,
So I sung the same again
While he wept with joy to hear

Piper sit thee down and write
In a book that all may read—
So he vanish'd from my sight.
And I pluck'd a hollow reed.

And I made a rural pen,
And I stain'd the water clear,
And I wrote my happy songs
Every child may joy to hear

(E 7, K 111)

The shepherd-piper sees the child and hears his directions to play the pipe, sing 'songs of happy chear' in accord with the child's own 'laughing' speech, and write them 'In a book that all may read'. The sequence unfolds without consciousness of any discontinuities among the media. In the last line, we are returned to the auditory via the written, for the piper's book contains 'happy songs | Every child may joy to hear'. Writing has not replaced voice but has, in this innocent context, continued and preserved it for recreation by the audience.

Blake intimates a similar continuity between hearing and the act of writing in his opening invocation to the 'Daughters of Beulah' in *Milton* (E 96, K 481). They 'inspire the Poets Song', but they are also invited to 'Come into' the 'hand' of the writer-etcher and descend 'down the Nerves of [his] right arm | From out the Portals of [his] Brain'. A more direct but complex interweaving of the spoken and the written dominates the address to the reader on the first text plate of *Jerusalem*:

Reader! [*lover*] of books! [*lover*] of heaven,
And of that God from whom [*all books are given*,]
Who in mysterious Sinais awful cave
To Man the wond'rous art of writing gave,
Again he speaks in thunder and in fire!
Thunder of Thought, & flames of fierce desire:
Even from the depths of Hell his voice I hear,
Within the unfathomd caverns of my Ear.
Therefore I print; nor vain my types shall be:
Heaven, Earth & Hell, henceforth shall live in harmony[52]

Blake implies that God's gift of writing was one with His speaking, for Blake once 'again' hears Him speak 'in thunder and in fire' as the poet in his hearing regains contact with the origin of writing. These natural signs of thunder and fire, spiritualized by the character of their source, are motivated in their oneness with 'Thought' and 'desire'. The place of motivated writing, 'Sinais awful cave', expands into the 'depths of Hell' and contracts dramatically to the poet's own sounding chamber, 'the unfathomd caverns of [his] Ear'. With the force of a logical conclusion, Blake responds by returning sound to vision through his printed 'types'.[53] The divine voice unites heaven, hell, and earthly caverns by resounding through all three, just as God unites visual and auditory media. By preserving that voice in his types, Blake claims the power to include those same realms in the aural and visual 'harmony' of his illuminated books. He thereby attempts to avoid the destructive opposition between the spoken and the written imaged later in *Jerusalem* as the bondage of the organs of speech and hearing to the stony tablets of the law:

Malah come forth from Lebanon: & Hoglah from Mount Sinai:
Come circumscribe this tongue of sweets & with a screw of iron
Fasten this ear into the rock! (Pl. 68; E 221, K 705)

Blake's scenes of ideal writing are openly susceptible to ironic interpretations or Derridean deconstructions.[54] But we need not

[52] E 145, K 621. The italic words in brackets were partly deleted from the copperplate by Blake before printing all extant impressions.

[53] By 'types' Blake no doubt means his relief-etched plates that look a good deal like the recently perfected stereotype plates, even though the process used to make them is very different from Blake's non-mechanical methods. He refers to his first relief etching as a 'Stereotype' in *Ghost of Abel*, Pl. 2 (E 272, K 781).

[54] For an ironic and sceptical reading of the Introduction to *Songs of Innocence*, see Mitchell,

marshal modern strategies to generate such readings, for, as we have seen, Blake established their perspective in *The Book of Urizen*. However internally consistent such interpretations may be, once their premisses are granted, their concentration on the differential structure of linguistic signs tends to ignore the felt experience of language performance. In rapid or ecstatic speech, we enter unselfconsciously into the medium and do not sense a gap between thoughts and the words that seem to issue 'from out the Portals' of our brains in a fully motivated union with our thoughts.[55] Thus spoken language, more than any other semiotic medium, generates and almost seems to achieve that illusive and perhaps illusory ideal, the Adamic sign. Blake carried this same absorption in language, this same marriage of conception and execution, into acts of writing that he felt to be motivated even if the signs he used were arbitrary. In this light, the visions of inspired hearing/speaking/writing in Blake's poetry can be apprehended as idealizations of the actual activities that produced them. His muse is a personification of the medium as lived experience.

My claim that Blake was absorbed in his linguistic medium in a peculiarly intense way, and in a sense allowed himself to be taken over by it, goes hand in hand with his emphasis on active execution rather than introspection and detached conception. In a verse fragment Blake wrote in his *Notebook c.*1808–11, beginning 'You dont believe I wont attempt to make ye', he insists on the superiority of faith to doubt. That faith has a profoundly religious basis, but it is also the faith of the artist/poet in his own activities. The poem concludes not with a state of mind but with a call to action: 'Try Try & never mind the Reason why' (E 501, K 536). Through the voice of Los, Blake makes much the same point in *Jerusalem*: 'I will not Reason & Compare: my business is to Create' (Pl. 10; E 153, K 629). Almost all readers of *Jerusalem* have taken Los to be an avatar of the poet's imagination, but this identification must be accompanied by a recognition that he is presented in the poem as ever labouring,

'Visible Language', pp. 55–6. Mitchell (pp. 60–2) also comments intelligently on the address to the reader in *Jerusalem*.

[55] For a study of this kind of linguistic experience and an argument 'that the arbitrariness of the sign is alien to the experience of normal people and can exist only in the minds of linguists', see D. Panhuis, 'The Arbitrariness of the Lingual Sign as a Symptom of Linguistic Alienation', *Studies in Language*, 5 (1981), 343–60.

building, working. To cease is to fall into 'despair and ever brooding melancholy' (Pl. 13; E 157, K 633). The temptation to do so is figured forth in *Jerusalem* as Los's Spectre, a self-alienated and alienating 'Reasoning Power' (Pl. 10; E 153, K 629) that abstracts conception from execution.[56] To overcome this divided consciousness thwarting creative acts, Los must reintegrate the Spectre back into the production process:

> Therefore Los stands in London building Golgonooza
> Compelling his Spectre to labours mighty; trembling in fear
> The Spectre weeps, but Los unmovd by tears or threats remains
>
> (Pl. 10; E 153, K 629)

The inactive or self-reflective mind, the Wordsworthian 'Soul by contemplation sanctified',[57] is antithetical to all that Los does and represents through that doing. Golgonooza, the city of art, is not a transcendental category of aesthetic consciousness, for it exists only in the continual activities of the artist. As Blake wrote in his *Laocoön* inscriptions, 'Without Unceasing Practise nothing can be done[.] Practise is Art[.] If you leave off you are Lost' (E 274, K 777).

Frederick Tatham indicates that Blake's life demonstrated a similar emphasis on the indivisibility of mental and physical activity: 'Mrs Blake has been heard to say that she never saw [her husband] except when in conversation or reading; with his hands idle, he scarcely ever mused upon what he had done. Some men muse & call it thinking, but Blake was a hard worker, his thought was only for action, as a man plans a House, or a General, consults his Map, & arranges his forces for a Battle.'[58] Yet Blake did have periods of melancholy musing, and these he associated with a breakdown in the unity of conceiving and doing. As he wrote to Butts in September 1801, 'I labour incessantly & accomplish not one half of what I intend because my Abstract folly hurries me often away while I am at work,

[56] This is of course only one dimension of a remarkably polyvalent image that extends into many manifestations of psychic division. However, H. Adams's characterization of the conflict between Los and his Spectre as 'the struggle of Blake with his medium' ('Blake, *Jerusalem*, and Symbolic Form', p. 161) is misleading, for it assumes the Urizenic or spectrous conception of language (or any medium) as an extrinsic structure. This is the very state of consciousness that must be overcome by the artist so that he may become one with his media. See my comments below on the Selfhood.

[57] '1810', in *Poetical Works*, 3: 138.

[58] Bentley, *Blake Records*, p. 526. Tatham's concluding image echoes Blake's idea of 'Mental Fight' (*Milton*, Pl. 1; E 95, K 481), another compound of interdependent thought and deed.

carrying me over Mountains & Valleys which are not Real in a Land of Abstraction where Spectres of the Dead wander' (E 716, K 809). The concluding clause suggests that such experiences are one of the biographical matrices forming the image of the Spectre in *Milton* and *Jerusalem*. In this same period, Blake was residing in Felpham under the intrusive patronage of William Hayley, who attempted to direct Blake toward essentially commercial engraving tasks and away from original composition. Hayley thereby became a separate presence, like the Spectre, appropriating the powers of conception and leaving to Blake only repetitious tasks of execution. In *Milton*, Blake transforms this separation into the contentions between the craftsman Palamabron and Satan, whose usurpations dramatize Hayley's. Los mistakenly gives Satan control over 'the Harrow of the Almighty' (Pl. 7; E 100, K 486) and Palamabron acquiesces, much as Blake allowed Hayley to direct his engraving and printing tools. The result is anger, accusation, and chaos.

The conflict between Blake and Hayley, like its mythic expansions in *Milton*, was fraught with psychological tensions, but the events also had a social and linguistic dimension. The economic distinctions inherent in the artist/patron relationship were reinforced by the fact that Hayley had been educated at Eton and Cambridge, had travelled on the Continent, and had at least a good reading knowledge of several languages ancient and modern. Blake came from the very different class of London artisans, a product of the master/apprentice system and largely self-educated in all but engraving. He attempted to rise above that station through original art and poetry, but also by trying to make up for his lack of a classical education. As he told his brother in a letter of January 1803, 'I go on Merrily with my Greek & Latin: am very sorry that I did not begin to learn languages early in life as I find it very Easy. am now learning my Hebrew: . . . I read Greek as fluently as an Oxford scholar . . .'.[59] But even if Blake did attain the expertise he claims, the class barriers—delineated in part by differences in linguistic competency—could not be so easily hurdled. Blake's difficult relationship with Hayley centred on the graphic arts, but it at least touched upon the politics of language.

[59] E 727, K 821. The generic comparison to an 'Oxford scholar' may have been prompted by the classical pretensions of Hayley's friend, the Oxford student Edward Marsh. Blake's division of men into 3 classes (the Reprobate, the Redeemed, and the Elect) in *Milton* hints at his consciousness of class distinctions brought to the fore by his relationship with the Hayley circle.

Hayley was a member of the same class that attempted, through instruments such as Johnson's *Dictionary*, to establish the meanings of words and determine what constituted educated discourse. This effort at uniformity only served to underscore class distinctions, much as Hayley's direction of Blake's graver divided conception from execution and emphasized the difference between their respective classes—social, economic, and linguistic.

After Blake's return to London in 1803, distance from Hayley did not mean a release from the trade of reproductive engraving. Blake still had to earn his daily bread, but at least he was more his own man and could write his poetry 'no Longer Pesterd with [Hayley's] Genteel Ignorance & Polite Disapprobation'.[60] According to Tatham, Blake 'was very much accustomed to get out of his bed in the night to write for hours, & return to bed for the rest of the night, after having committed to paper pages & pages of his mysterious Phantasies'.[61] Blake alludes to these nocturnal habits in his recollection of that time 'When God commanded this hand to write | In the studious hours of deep midnight' ('The Grey Monk', E 489, K 430), and in his comment at the beginning of *Jerusalem* that its 'theme calls me in sleep night after night' (Pl. 4; E 146, K 622). He probably began writing at night during his apprentice years, for that may well have been the only time Blake had some freedom from his duties in Basire's engraving shop. The continuation of this schedule into his later years also served a practical purpose, for an eighteenth-century engraver needed the light of day to practise those parts of his craft requiring precise and delicate workmanship. But the night also offered an absence of worldly sights and sounds, and thus could assist the poet's merging with his medium, listening only to his own 'all-powerful Human Words', and 'Hearing the march of long resounding strong heroic Verse' as it carried him forward in his labours.[62]

My pursuit of orality in Blake's poetry has led us beyond that demonstrable characteristic and to some far more general observations

[60] Letter to Butts, 6 July 1803 (E 730, K 825).

[61] Bentley, *Blake Records*, p. 525. Gilchrist, relying on information probably supplied by Tatham, tells a similar story of Blake 'sketching and writing' late 'in the night, when he was under his very fierce inspirations' with his wife 'motionless and silent' at his side (*Life of Blake*, 1: 316). See also Blake's reference to Milton's nocturnal muse in the letter to Trusler quoted in n. 1 above.

[62] *Jerusalem*, Pl. 24 (E 169, K 646); *Four Zoas*, E 300, K 264.

on Blake's active engagement with language. My initial hypothesis that the medium was Blake's muse has evolved into the linked propositions that the poet allowed his medium to speak its own multifarious being, and to do so he had to abnegate his independent will and become only one among many forces within an undivided production process. The concept of the poet as a channel through which language speaks has had a certain philosophical currency in our century, particularly in schools of thought associated with the works of Martin Heidegger,[63] but it is anticipated by Blake's methods of oral writing and manuscript printing. The values implicit in those practices led him to question conventional assumptions about texts, including a poem's unity and the role of the poet's intentions.

In his brief tract of *c.*1820, *On Homers Poetry* [and] *on Virgil*, Blake attacks the principles of classical aesthetics (E 269–70, K 778). Chief among these is a concept of unity based on 'Mathematic Form', a product of 'the Reasoning Memory'. This he juxtaposes to 'Living Form' and a 'Unity' which 'is as much in a Part as in the Whole'. Consequently, 'the Torso [i.e., the Farnese Torso] is as much a Unity as the Laocoon'. We have already observed this sort of unity in Blake's own heroic fragment, *The Four Zoas*. It is a unity based not on the static form of the completed text, but rather on the unified methods of its conception/execution that produced every part as much as the whole. Blake's 'unity' describes the temporal phenomena of creating or experiencing a work of art, not its spatial structure. His comments on aesthetic form are compatible with, and may be yet another conceptualization of, his own methods of composition.

Blake gives expression to the submergence of the artist in the means of production with his comment about writing 'even against [his] Will' in the letter to Butts, quoted earlier, and through the critique of the 'Selfhood' in his poetry. For Boehme, from whom Blake may have borrowed this term, giving up a wilful and separate ego is

[63] G. Steiner presents a sweeping summary of these modern views in his comments on an 'ontological difficulty' in poetry that 'seems to point to a hypostasis of language such as we find, precisely, in the philosophy of Heidegger. It is not so much the poet who speaks, but language itself: *die Sprache spricht*. The authentic, immensely rare, poem is one in which "the Being of Language" finds unimpeded lodging, in which the poet is not a *persona*, a subjectivity "ruling over language", but an "openness to", a supreme listener to, the genius of speech. The result of such openness is not so much a text, but an "act", an eventuation of Being and literal "coming into Being". . . . We bear witness to [the poem's] precarious possibility of existence in an "open" space of collisions, of momentary fusions between word and referent.' 'On Difficulty', in *On Difficulty and Other Essays* (1978), 45–6. See also Derrida's comment quoted in n. 3 above.

essential for spiritual enlightenment.[64] This mystical tradition provides the context for Blake's unqualified assertion, in his annotations of *c.*1789 to Swedenborg's *Wisdom of Angels Concerning Divine Love and Divine Wisdom*, that 'Will is always Evil' (E 602, K 89). And much as Coleridge claimed that a temporary 'suspension of disbelief . . . constitutes poetic faith',[65] Blake found that a temporary suspension of the will is necessary for poetic composition. Thus, as part of his invocation to the muse of *Jerusalem*, Blake asks the 'Saviour' to 'Annihilate the Selfhood' in him and to 'Guide' his 'hand which trembles' as he 'write[s] of the building of Golgonooza' (Pl. 5; E 147, K 623). The self-instituted presence of an intentionality existing prior to and outside the artist's medium, graphic or linguistic, replicates Urizen's divisive self-substantiation. Like the Spectre, an image with which the Selfhood is allied in *Jerusalem*, an independent will takes unto itself the powers of conception and separates them from execution. The Selfhood is the Spectre within, much as Hayley was the Spectre without. Blake's method of composition, one in which he felt himself the recipient of dictated words, required him to give up something of his own intentional presence so that the language could express its own will. *The Book of Urizen* led us to conceive of language structure as an otherness imprisoning the desires of the self. Blake's way of producing texts leads us to view language performance as the liberation of an inherently limited self.

The sharing of creative responsibility between artist and medium blurs conventional distinctions between what is intended by the artist and what is an unintended 'accident' or 'error'. Blake had little direct control over the reticulated patterns caused by his innovative colour printing technique. Rather than struggling against such displays of a medium's inherent properties, Blake allowed them to flourish.[66] He used pen and ink to give definition and outline to his colour prints, but their accidental features were thereby incorporated into, not eliminated from, the final image. Even Blake's monochrome

[64] See for example *Signatura rerum*, ch. 15, para. 22 (quoted in ch. 2). A similar but secular theme in the literature of Blake's era, and its associations with attempts to return to a naive or primitive state of mind, are discussed in G. H. Hartman, 'Romanticism and Anti-Self-Consciousness', *Beyond Formalism* (1970), 298–310.

[65] *Biographia Literaria*, 2: 6.

[66] This attitude, and its contrast with the attempt to suppress the intrinsic qualities of graphic media in the reproductive technologies of Blake's time, is a central thesis in Essick, *Blake Printmaker*.

relief prints are filled with ink droplets in white areas, variations in ink density, and other features that would be accounted errors in intaglio printmaking and lead to the rejection of any impressions showing them. This is not to say that Blake accepted any impression no matter how flawed,[67] but clearly he expanded the circumference of the acceptable far beyond the limitations standard in his craft.

An equivalent willingness to incorporate the contingent in verbal production is not so easily observed, particularly if we take linguistic signs as intentional structures by definition. Yet, one can still ask, 'Intended by whom?' Blake claimed, in his dictation theory of composition, that the words he wrote down had their intentional origin outside his own self. If we doubt this, as a literal truth in regard to the signifiers, we must still acknowledge its validity on the level of the signifieds. None of us can determine what our words mean without reference to a common body of definitions established within the language we speak. The medium dictates the meanings of the signs we select. Nor is there any guarantee that these meanings are unitary or stable, no matter what our intentions. Rationalist grammarians from Wilkins to Johnson believed with some justification that it was more difficult to control accident and variation in speaking than in writing. In rapid conversation, we all say things we don't mean, either to our regret or—in the case of clever but unintended puns—our pleasure. Oral writing brings to a printed text something of this same increased presence of the accidental productions of spoken language. These include Blake's punning and other types of wordplay explored at length in Hilton's *Literal Imagination*, for the formulaic character of oral writing prompts aural repetitions of the very sort underlying wordplay. Attempts to determine which of these phonetic homologies and the meanings they generate were specifically intended by Blake, and which were not, are thwarted by a compositional method based on the merging of authorial intention with the accidents of the medium. For a reader like Hilton to discover meanings in those accidents simply continues

[67] One of the few pieces of evidence we have about what sorts of prints Blake rejected is a misaligned impression of *The Book of Urizen* Pl. 4, originally printed as part of copy G. Blake did not reprint the plate, but simply left it out of the finished volume. See R. N. Essick, 'Variation, Accident, and Intention in Blake's *Book of Urizen*', *Studies in Bibliography*, 39 (1986), 230–5. I also discuss the interplay between the intentional and the accidental in Blake's graphics in 'How Blake's Body Means'.

into the process of interpretation the possibilities for continual (re)conception Blake dispersed throughout the process of production. Just as Blake claimed, he is not the sole source of the linguistic experiences embodied in the texts he wrote.

As a reader, Blake was well aware of the pleasures and significance of chance. In August 1807, he wrote in his *Notebook* that his 'Wife was told by a Spirit to look for her fortune by opening by chance a book which she had in her hand it was Bysshes Art of Poetry'. Pleased 'with her Luck', Blake tried the same.[68] This playful attempt at stichomancy suggests that the Blakes at least entertained the notion that the fortuitous could be an extension of spiritual dictation. By reversing this line of reasoning, Blake concluded that the unintended and unhappy results of some of his experiments in painting with gum or glue-based tempera were caused by 'blotting and blurring demons'. These held temporary sway over Blake because he allowed himself to be influenced by 'that infernal machine, called Chiaro Oscuro', as practised by 'Venetian and Flemish Demons' such as Titian.[69] A similar response to structures of sound and sense arising without conscious effort in the execution of his writings—the creations, as it were, of what Coleridge called 'the blessed machine of language'[70]—may have led Blake to believe that these effects had been dictated by spiritual presences. The arbitrary is thereby converted into the transcendentally motivated.

The foregoing would seem to violate one of Blake's boldest and most frequently cited statements about his writings. On the first text plate of *Jerusalem*, he announces that 'Every word and every letter is studied and put into its fit place: the terrific numbers are reserved for the terrific parts—the mild & gentle, for the mild & gentle parts, and the prosaic, for inferior parts.'[71] How can a poem be both 'studied' and written with enthusiastic abandon to the muse? How can it have every word in its 'fit place' and also permit two different

[68] E 696, K 440–1. E. Bysshe, ed., *Art of English Poetry* (first pub. 1702), was a popular anthology of passages from English poems arranged by subject.

[69] *Descriptive Catalogue*, E 546–7, K 581–2.

[70] *The Friend* (1969), 1: 108.

[71] E 146, K 621. Traditional defences of the Bible's authority rested on similar claims about its verbal structure. See for example J. Edwards, *Discourse concerning the Authority . . . of the Old and New-Testament* (1693), 1: 34: 'We have reason therefore to assert that every Word of Scripture is endited by God, and that every Letter and Syllable of it is exact, and that there is nothing wanting, nothing superfluous, no Fault nor Blemish in the Stile and Phraseology of it.'

arrangements of its second chapter? Any conflicts between Blake's statement about *Jerusalem* and my theories of how Blake wrote the poem are far less serious than his own apparent contradiction of those claims. But the perception of such inconsistencies rests upon an assumed antithesis between inspiration and study, another version of the distinction between conception and execution Blake found to be false and struggled against in his working methods. A writing and printing dedicated to constant revision requires more continual thought and labour, even in those inspired and 'studious hours of deep midnight', than the mechanical reproduction of the same image. Reconception throughout production will lead to many structures, all equally 'fit' so long as they are the direct products of the unity of conception and execution at the heart of Blake's aesthetic theories and practices. Fit places, like fit meanings, are multiple, not singular.[72] This sense of appropriate 'Living Form' becomes explicit in the near-tautologies following the colon in the lines from *Jerusalem*: the 'numbers', the sounds and rhythms in which each part of the poem is executed, are one with—indeed, are productive of—its emotive and conceptual character. Further, the passive construction of Blake's statement makes no claim that he is the only party doing the studying and fitting. As Blake asks in *Milton*, 'how can I with my gross tongue that cleaveth to the dust, | Tell of the Four-fold Man, in starry numbers fitly orderd'? He cannot, and thus he turns to his muse for assistance: 'O Lord | Do with me as thou wilt! for I am nothing, and vanity' (Pl. 20; E 114, K 502). The one Lord the poet must submit himself to is his medium, a language which had undergone its own complex evolution through many voices before Blake ever began to use it. That historical effort established the forms of English syntax and orthography determining in large measure where the author/scribe can place his words and letters. Urizen sees, and in that seeing creates, these necessary forms as imposed and tyrannic structures. Blake's inspiration lies in his ability to see these same forms as his muse, the tools and helpmates of his labours in language.

* * *

[72] In *Inventions* (1982), G. L. Bruns finds a similar interplay of the determinate and the multiple in the Hebraic tradition of interpretation. In the Torah, 'the fixity of the letter does not produce a corresponding fixity of meaning; on the contrary, the hermeneutical function of the Oral Torah [Mishnah, Talmud, Midrash] is precisely to maintain the openness of what is written to that which is unforeseen or which is yet to come' (p. 29). Blake, in effect, incorporates this 'hermeneutical function' into his means of production.

The revolt against dualism central to Blake's way of creating texts returns us to the Adamic themes with which this book began. The unity of conception and execution in his means of production is a phenomenal equivalent to the structural ideal of the unity of signified idea and material signifier defining the motivated sign. Like Humboldt's diffusion of motivation throughout language as an historical and cultural phenomenon, Blake strove to disperse a motivated relationship between conception and execution through the entire production process. The original conception thereby maintained is not a matter of individual novelty, for its origin includes but extends beyond the author's separate self and gives to his words an authority beyond his private means.[73] This sense of a poet's originality as depending on a return to origins suggests a further point of contact between compositional modes and the concept of the motivated origins of language itself. By embracing the accidental as part of textual production, the poet gains access to the dynamic of language evolution—those unplanned changes in the pronunciation and meanings of words tracked by etymologists. These difficult junctures between the phenomenal and the structural, and between the poet's linguistic acts and the greater history of language, become thematic issues in Blake's epic ventures, particularly *Jerusalem*. The next chapter will centre on these themes and how they offer an alternative to those rationalist formulations of language that for Blake (and for us in the previous chapter) had reached a dead-end in Urizen's double bind.

[73] In *The Political Theory of Painting from Reynolds to Hazlitt* (1986), 222–57, J. Barrell argues convincingly that a similar preservation of extra-personal origins is central to Blake's theories of pictorial art. As Blake claims in *A Descriptive Catalogue*, he was 'taken in vision into the ancient republics, monarchies, and patriarchates of Asia', has 'seen those wonderful originals called in the Sacred Scriptures the Cherubim', and 'has endeavoured to emulate the grandeur of those [works] seen in his vision' (E 531, K 565).

5. The Return to Logos

LIKE the city of Golgonooza, Blake's later poetry encompasses within its wide embrace all that has come before in his earlier works: 'not lost not lost nor vanishd . . . all remaining still' (*Jerusalem*, Pl. 13; E 157–8, K 634). His method of formulaic and mosaic writing, combined with a desire to compose a syncretic myth containing the seeds of all others, could result in nothing other than a poetry of recapitulation and reformation. Urizenic consciousness in all its many shapes haunts even the concluding pages of *The Four Zoas*, *Milton*, and *Jerusalem*. To trace Blake's strategies for releasing language from that consciousness will require a brief consideration of how the differential and taxonomic paradigm of *The Book of Urizen* continues as a motif in its successor poems.

The major actions and images of *The Four Zoas* have semiotic resonances half-submerged in the general tumult. The division of Zoas into masculine Spectres and feminine Emanations follows the same trajectory as the sundering of the motivated into the arbitrary sign. In the 'mild fields of happy Eternity', the two 'in undivided Essence walkd about | Imbodied' (Night the Seventh, E 359, K 326–7). This original unity is torn by centrifugal forces—'a dread repulsive power'—that cast Emanations 'Into Non Entity' (Night the First, E 304, K 270). This opening up of difference, both metaphysical (existence/non-existence) and semiotic (material signifier/immaterial signified), is one with the fall into the world of nature and natural signs:

> Thro the Confusion like a crack across from immense to immense
> Loud strong a universal groan of death louder
> Than all the wracking elements deafend & rended worse
> Than Urizen & all his hosts in curst despair down rushing
>
> (Night the Third, E 329, K 295–6)

The echoes of Genesis and *Paradise Lost* in this plot and its attendant imagery reinforce the parallels between *The Four Zoas* and the traditional history of language from Eden to Babel. The story of Albion's fall and dismemberment, not fully developed until

Jerusalem, offers a slightly different corollary to the fragmentation and dispersal of Adamic language. The point of contact between the Albion myth and language history is indicated by the identification of 'Babel' as 'The Spectre of Albion' (*Milton*, Pl. 6; E 100, K 486).

Again and again in *The Four Zoas*, the interiority of existence as the 'undivided' co-presence of self and other falls into the distinction between perceiving selves and a projected exteriority: 'they behold | What is within now seen without' (Night the Second, E 314, K 281). This action lays the foundation for a displacement of an incarnational semiotic into the language of reference. In turn, this language solidifies into taxonomic structures and their allegorical matching to the perceived order of nature. We have arrived at the conception of word and world represented historically and epistemically by Blake's Satanic trinity, Bacon, Locke, and Newton.[1] The universe they create, particularly as envisioned in Night the Second of *The Four Zoas*, bears the imprint of the rationalist semiotic from which it sprang, the biaxial fabric of the taxonomic grid:

> For measurd out in orderd spaces the Sons of Urizen
> With compasses divide the deep; they the strong scales erect . . .
> And weigh the massy Cubes, then fix them in their awful stations . . .
> The enormous warp & woof rage direful in the affrighted deep
>
> (E 318–19, K 283–4)

In *Milton*, this same cloth is woven by 'the Shadowy Female' from threads of natural utterance:

> My Garments shall be woven of sighs & heart broken lamentations . . .
> I will have Writings written all over it in Human Words
> That every Infant that is born upon the Earth shall read
> And get by rote as a hard task of a life of sixty years[2]

The linearity of the foregoing summary violates Blake's own mode of presentation, one in which causes and effects are mingled and repeated as part of an eternal yet instantaneous psychomachia.

[1] First named together in *Milton*, Pl. 41 (E 142, K 533), but the world-view they personify is fully present in *The Four Zoas*.

[2] Pl. 18; E 111, K 499. Much the same woven structure is intimated on Pl. 4 through 'the Woof of Locke' (E 98, K 483); see also the 'woof . . . called . . . Science' in *The Book of Urizen* (Pl. 19; E 78, K 231). As a reproductive line engraver, Blake executed his own cloth-like patterns of crosshatching.

Individual sentences in this drama rarely violate normative grammar and syntax, but conventional narrative sequence is generously overthrown. The Zoas and their Emanations are continually threatened by a false and rigid order, on the one hand, and on the other by its contrary companions, chaos and the indefinite. The language of *The Four Zoas* is fraught with similar tensions—and with uncertain results. Where can we locate in that language a freedom that is not chaotic, an order that is not a limitation? An answer that seemed decisive for many years was offered in 1947 by the exposition of Blake's mythic constructs in Frye's *Fearful Symmetry*. Metonymies and metaphors associate each Zoa with different senses, body parts, planets, and a host of other items that extend in Frye's reckoning to a vertical list with twenty-nine entries. By adding the four Zoas (Luvah, Urizen, Tharmas, Urthona) as a horizontal axis, Frye produces a grid with 145 slots. The structuralist dynamic in this approach is indicated by Frye's admission that two of the items on the vertical axis 'have been added to complete the pattern' and that three others 'are guesses'.[3] Blake criticizes this type of extrapolation from taxonomic hierarchies to fill an empty position in a table of correspondences in his dismissive comments on those for whom 'God is only an Allegory of Kings & nothing Else'.[4] This is not to say that the interpretive tradition represented by Frye has imposed an altogether alien system on Blake's poetry, for there is no denying the presence of such structures lurking within his Zoaic myth. As with *The Book of Urizen*, we are again confronted with the inability of the figural to escape a differential schema embedded at a far deeper level of semiotic activity than the distinctions between mythic and non-mythic, or figural and literal, modes of discourse. The very tensions in Blake's language, its struggles to exceed the network of linguistic conventions without plunging through the boundaries of meaning, evince the presence of quandaries that remain unresolvable when couched in structuralist terms.[5] Further, there is no inherent

[3] *Fearful Symmetry*, pp. 277–8, 445 n. 13. Drawing up charts of Zoaic correspondences has a long history in Blake scholarship, beginning with the commentary by E. J. Ellis and W. B. Yeats in *Works of Blake* (1893), 1: 340, and continuing in S. F. Damon, *Blake Dictionary* (1965), 212.

[4] Annotations to Thornton's *New Translation of the Lord's Prayer*, E 669, K 789.

[5] In 'Re-Visioning *The Four Zoas*' (Hilton and Vogler, *Unnam'd Forms*, pp. 105–39) D. Ault begins by suggesting that the poem is 'saturated with . . . strategies . . . [Blake] developed . . . to combat and subvert the form of explanatory storytelling that can be labeled generically

principle of closure in the mythic system, for either the poet or his reader can add words along the vertical axis and extend the table of correspondences until it covers every conceivable category. Perhaps a growing awareness of these fundamental difficulties led Blake to abandon *The Four Zoas*, leaving us not simply an incomplete, but an incompletable, poem. On the penultimate page of the manuscript, Blake reflects on his own nocturnal compositions and recognizes the sad burden of structures they cannot cast off:

> And Men are bound to sullen contemplations in the night
> Restless they turn on beds of sorrow. in their inmost brain
> Feeling the crushing Wheels they rise they write the bitter words
> Of Stern Philosophy & knead the bread of knowledge with tears &
> groans (E 406, K 379)

Even if Blake could not literally escape Urizen's 'deadly words',[6] he could at least use them to propose ideal modes of signification. Some of these alternatives harken back to the language of the *Songs of Innocence*; all strive toward a non-differential semiotic in which the signified is immediately present within, or bears a motivated relationship to, the signifier. Blake's pastoral epic, *Milton*, is particularly rich in its evocations of natural signs transformed into a medium for spiritual messages. The motivated character of such signs is expressive, not mimetic, and is grounded in the proposition that 'every Natural Effect has a Spiritual Cause' (Pl. 26; E 124, K 513). The songs of the nightingale and lark I previously associated with Blake's painting of Eve and the birds are only the most dramatic instances of spiritualized natural signs in *Milton*. They are accompanied by 'every Bird of Song', by 'Flowers' that 'put forth their precious Odours', and finally by 'every Tree, | And Flower & Herb' as they 'fill the air with an innumerable Dance' (Pl. 31; E 131, K 520–1). Taken together, these constitute a semiotic similar to, but more emotively expressive and less codified than, the 'signatures' in Boehme's 'Language of Nature' and Swedenborg's

as ''Newtonian narrative'' ' (p. 106). While Ault offers a compelling argument for this view of narrative (de)constructions in *The Four Zoas*, his concluding charts of events in the poem (each appropriately titled an 'Abstract', pp. 132–6) are more daunting, but no less schematic, than Frye's graph of figural associations. Ault represents the syntagmatic, and Frye the paradigmatic, ends of the structuralist spectrum.

[6] *Four Zoas*, Night the Eighth; E 375, K 344.

doctrine of correspondences.[7] For Blake, this divine language, occluded by the fall, is less an objective presence than a product of an alteration in our perceptions that returns to nature its human attributes, as in the old legends of creatures conversing in Eden. Under these conditions, even 'Natural Religion'—and its associated doctrine of natural signs Blake attacks in his early tractates—'is the voice of God'. 'All the Wisdom which was hidden in caves & dens, from ancient | Time; is now sought out from Animal & Vegetable & Mineral', for even 'the Trees on mountains' are 'Uttering prophecies & speaking instructive words to the sons | Of men'.[8]

The chorus of birds on Plate 32 of *Milton* is set in Beulah, a dream-like state of consciousness associated with the poetry of sexual love and pastoralism and, in Blake's own life, with the more pleasant aspects of his three-year sojourn 'upon mild Felpham shore' (Pl. 38; E 139, K 529). Beulah offers 'windows into Eden', but remains a step removed from the 'Perfect harmony in Eden'.[9] The language of Beulah is similarly close to, but not fully one with, the Adamic ideal. Beulah's spiritually charged signs save the natural semiotic of *The Book of Thel* from its disastrous consequences in that poem, but such signs are not without inherent limitations. To posit a motivated relationship between natural beings (including the sounds they make) and divinity results in a system with at best a tangential association with the languages of men. Even if our language evolved out of similarly 'natural' expressions, and is still able to return us onomatopoeically to that origin through the 'trill, trill, trill, trill' of the lark on Plate 31 of *Milton*, the connections between the semiotic of Beulah and the vast majority of the poet's words remains arbitrary. The divine may reveal itself to the inspired perceiver through the literal presence of natural objects and events, but this does not in itself constitute a 'Divine Revelation in the Litteral expression' of human language (*Milton*, Pl. 42; E 143, K534).

[7] See the discussion of Boehme in Ch. 2 and Swedenborg, *Angelic Wisdom concerning the Divine Love and the Divine Wisdom*, p. 205, sec. 374, on the 'correspondence between things spiritual and things natural'. Blake's emphasis on birds may have been influenced by Swedenborg's frequent references to them as divine symbols (see, e.g., *Divine Love and Divine Wisdom*, p. 206, sec. 374: 'the spiritual . . . is like a bird of paradise, which flies near the eye, even touching the pupil with its beautiful wings longing to be seen').

[8] Annotations to Watson's *Apology*, E 614, K 388; *Milton*, Pls. 25 (E 121, K 510) and 26 (E 123, K 512). Natural signs are similarly charged with spiritual meaning in 'Auguries of Innocence' of *c.*1803: 'The Bleat the Bark Bellow & Roar | Are Waves that Beat on Heavens Shore' (E 491, K 432).

[9] *Four Zoas*, Night the First; E 304, 311, K 270, 277.

The traditional mediatory role of Christ, both the incarnate Word and a speaker of human words, offers a more direct bond between Logos and language. This semiotic ideal, immanent in the *Songs of Innocence*, accompanies His increasing importance in Blake's nineteenth-century writings, beginning with what are probably late additions to *The Four Zoas* manuscript. The identification of 'the Divine Body of the Lord Jesus' with 'the sports of Wisdom in the Human Imagination' situates Him as a universal presence within the personal source of artistic expression.[10] Blake also associates Christ with the historical origins of language. In *A Descriptive Catalogue*, he writes that 'All had originally one language, and one religion, this was the religion of Jesus, the everlasting Gospel' (E 543, K 579). Blake makes this claim in the midst of his description of a now lost painting, *The Ancient Britons*. This implicit connection between Patriarchal Christianity and the history of Britain is explained in the prose introduction to the second chapter of *Jerusalem*. If 'All things'—including 'The Religion of Jesus'—'Begin & End in Albions Ancient Druid Rocky Shore' (Pl. 27; E 171, K 649), then the 'one language' must also have its source in that realm. Taken together, these comments link the linguistic theories of eighteenth-century Celticists and the myth of an ancient British Christianity of the sort proposed by William Stukeley.[11] That civilization and its language effectively replace, or become the immediate successors to, the more conventional Adamite myth of cultural origins. This shift has several important consequences. Those two representatives of the linguistic and poetic tradition in which Blake saw himself to be working—the oral Bards of ancient Britain and the prophets of the Old Testament—are joined together under the aegis of Christianity. And while in Blake's poetry Adam became more completely identified with a fallen and divided state of nature, Christ began to assume Adam's traditional function as a nexus of language origins and ideals. Much as in Blake's series of tempera paintings (Plates 1, 6–8), the

[10] *Milton*, Pl. 3; E 96, K 482. See also *Vision of the Last Judgment*: 'All Things are comprehended in their Eternal Forms in the Divine body of the Saviour the True Vine of Eternity The Human Imagination' (E 555, K 605–6).

[11] Stukeley, *Stonehenge*, p. 2: 'Therefore they [the Druids] brought along with them the patriarchal religion, which was so extremely like Christianity, that in effect it differ'd from it only in this; they believed in a Messiah who was to come into the world, as we believe in him that is come.' For the influence of such theories on Blake's Job designs, see B. Lindberg, *Blake's Illustrations to the Book of Job* (1973), 85–7.

Old Adam is replaced by the New. Even the fall and fragmentation of language were reconceived as the loss of the words that embodied the original Christian vision. As Jerusalem laments, 'Babel mocks saying, there is no God nor Son of God' (*Jerusalem*, Pl. 60; E 211, K 693).

The role Blake grants Christ in the history of speech is complemented by His redemption of writing in *Milton*. The story works itself through Blake's cloth and garment imagery, beginning with his apparently unique version of the story of Joseph:

> . . . thou rememberest when Joseph an infant;
> Stolen from his nurses cradle wrapd in needle-work
> Of emblematic texture, was sold to the Amalekite,
> Who carried him down into Egypt . . .[12]

When considered in light of Blake's theory that all heathen art was copied from Patriarchal originals, these lines would seem to suggest that Joseph's 'emblematic' swaddling bands were the origin of Egyptian hieroglyphics. We can further assume that the original meaning of these emblems was lost, much as hieroglyphics descend from a motivated and universally intelligible form of writing into a secret code in Warburton's account of Egyptian history. Near the end of *Milton*, these original spiritual meanings are restored by Christ's garment:

> . . . with one accord the Starry Eight became
> One Man Jesus the Saviour. wonderful! round his limbs
> The Clouds of Ololon folded as a Garment dipped in blood
> Written within & without in woven letters: & the Writing
> Is the Divine Revelation in the Litteral expression:
> A Garment of War, I heard it namd the Woof of Six Thousand Years
> (Pl. 42; E 143, K 534)

The Starry Eight and Ololon are characters in Blake's mythic representation of his understanding of Milton's life and writings. Thus, Blake's fellow English poet serves as the historical and literary experience from which emerges the vision of Jesus. That revelation is accompanied by a transformation of the corpus of Milton's writings ('The Clouds of Ololon') into Christ's flesh in Jesus, the living garment of His body, without loss of its textual nature. The 'Garment dipped in blood' resonates typologically with the account

[12] Pl. 24; E 120, K 508. In *A Blake Dictionary*, p. 224, Damon notes that he too has 'found no source' for this tale.

of Joseph's coat in Genesis 37: 31,[13] but its written character also connects it to the emblematic cloth in Blake's rendering of the Joseph story on Plate 24 of *Milton* and to their shared antithesis, the garment of sighs and lamentations woven by the Shadowy Female on Plate 18. Jesus' raiment, a text that is one with His body, achieves that union of being and meaning defining the incarnational sign: Jesus *is* the 'Divine Revelation' as well as its 'Litteral expression'. The double character of this expression through letters 'Written within & without' further indicates its union of outer, material signifiers and inner, spiritual signifieds. This image of the Saviour's garment as a motivated text fulfils Boehme's typological interpretation of 'Joseph's *party-coloured Coat*' as a symbol of 'how the inward Power of God would again be revealed through the outward Man' in the person of Jesus.[14]

By assuming the garment of flesh as the semiotic medium through which He makes Himself known to us, Christ enters historical time and battles to save us from it. Thus His flesh is 'a Garment of War' woven from the 'War[p]' of His divinity and 'the Woof of Six Thousand Years', the record of human mortality He takes upon Himself to suffer and to redeem as the man Jesus.[15] The Saviour's garment/body is 'namd' this history, for 'All Things are comprehended in their Eternal Forms in the Divine body of the Saviour'.[16] Hence this naming is a fully motivated act that indicates the Saviour's role as the extravagantly polyvalent signifier of all

[13] Damrosch, *Symbol and Truth in Blake's Myth*, p. 328, notes parallels with Isaiah 63: 3 ('and their blood shall be sprinkled upon my garments') and Revelation 19: 13 ('he was clothed with vesture dipped in blood: and his name is called The Word of God'), but does not associate the passage on Pl. 42 with either Blake's or the Bible's version of Joseph's raiment. For a brief discussion of false coverings in *Milton* as images of obscuring rhetoric, see J. Rieger, ' "The Hem of their Garments": The Bard's Song in *Milton*', in S. Curran and J. A. Wittreich, Jr., eds., *Blake's Sublime Allegory* (1973), 278–9.

[14] *Mysterium Magnum*, 64. 35 (*Works of Behmen*, 3: 395). Boehme's interpretation of the Joseph story, one in which the coat functions as an emblem of Joseph's '*Words* and *Doctrine*' (*Mysterium Magnum*, 64. 49), may have directly influenced Blake's associations between writing and the garments of both Joseph and Jesus. The identification of Christ with written scripture is traditional; see for example John Donne's sermon preached 1 April 1627: '. . . so Christ was *loquens Scriptura*; living, speaking Scripture. . . . Christ was the *Word*; not onely the Essentiall Word, which was alwayes with God, but the very written word too . . .'. *Sermons of Donne* (1954), 7: 400.

[15] Blake also describes this act in Night the Seventh of *The Four Zoas*:'. . . behold the Lamb of God | Clothed in Luvahs robes of blood descending to redeem' (E 369, K 330).

[16] *Vision of the Last Judgment*, E 555, K 605–6. See also the description of 'the Divine image' as one who 'must be All | And comprehend within himself all things both small & great' in a deleted marginal insertion in Night the First of *The Four Zoas* (E 825, K 272).

human experience. But that history also names the Saviour, for when rightly understood it is the prophecy of His first coming in the person of Jesus and His second coming at the end of time. In the body of the incarnational sign, time and eternity, humanity and divinity, unite in a reciprocally motivated semiotic, each both signifier and signified to each other.

Blake's naming of the incarnational sign near the end of *Milton* is his most complete and complex imagining of the semiotic ideal proposed by the mystical tradition in language theory. As such, the passage draws to a conclusion an important strand in Blake's linguistic thought. Yet the dynamic syntax of these lines directs us to another way of looking at language. As is often the case with Blake's multiply compounded images, it is nearly impossible to visualize them as a stable entity. We are given instead a series of transformations, stated or implied, with each assimilating into itself those that have come before. The Saviour's garment becomes a body, a text, and all of history, but never ceases to be a garment. Nouns and adjectives predominate, yet the thrust of the whole subordinates objects to events, concluding with the absolute temporality of the 'Six Thousand Years' that the tropological circumference expands to include and thereby converts into an eternal present. The Divine reveals itself in the 'expression' of the literal, in the acts of writing, hearing, naming—and not, as Boehme would have it, in the structures of sounds or written letters. Blake comes to this revelation through his reading of Milton, his contentious identification with his great predecessor, and his writing of *Milton*. Poetic election and composition thereby become metonymic avenues to the incarnation of the Word within the Saviour's textual body. This shift toward a phenomenological perspective on language, one I earlier defined through a brief summary of Humboldt's linguistics and tentatively proposed as an alternative to the self-defeating structuralisms of Urizen, becomes more clearly evident in Blake's development of three key semiotic concepts in his later poetry: articulation, conversation, and community.[17]

[17] As his title indicates, two of these concepts are at issue in L. W. Deen's *Conversing in Paradise: Poetic Genius and Identity-as-Community in Blake's Los* (1983). Deen's perspective, however, is not essentially linguistic; his major concern is tracing the development of the character Los through Blake's poetry. 'Conversation' is briefly discussed in M. Ferber, *Social Vision of Blake* (1985), 205–9. The ontological consequences of community in *Milton* are explored in M. Bracher, *Being Form'd* (1985).

The Book of Urizen has already introduced us to Blake's first allusion to the important eighteenth-century debate over the emergence of articulate speech out of natural utterance. In that fallen context, Urizen's 'Words articulate' (Pl. 4; E 71, K 223) lie at the heart of his taxonomic matrix. Beginning in *The Four Zoas*, articulation, as a physical activity, becomes a far more positive measure of a speaker's perceptual and conceptual status. A descent down the scale of consciousness is indicated by a concomitant fall into the inarticulate and incoherent. Luvah identifies the 'Primeval Chaos' he fears as a 'concourse of incoherent | Discordant principles' (*The Four Zoas*, Night the Second; E 318, K 282). Near the beginning of *Jerusalem*, the fragments of Albion's human form are 'scatter'd upon | The Void in incoherent despair' (Pl. 5; E 147, K 623), a confusion at once anatomical, geographical, and semiotic. Albion's original state of coherence is matched by Blake's theories of a grand antediluvian culture from which man fell into a beastly condition. The latter is characterized by the inarticulate mode of signification posited by natural sign theory:

> In pain he [man] sighs in pain he labours in his universe
> Screaming in birds over the deep & howling in the Wolf
> Over the slain & moaning in the cattle & in the winds
>
> (*The Four Zoas*, Night the Eighth; E 385, K 355)

The natural history of speech continues through intermediate stages, the 'articulate howlings' of the Shadowy Female and the 'scarcely articulate' voices of the Spectres,[18] as language evolves toward its present condition. For eighteenth-century rationalist linguistics, the progression of articulation concludes with human language as we know it. For Blake, this record is only one small segment of the total spectrum. When Ololon descends into Blake's garden at Felpham, she speaks with a 'voice . . . more distinct than any earthly' (*Milton*, Pl. 37; E 137, K 527). Just as a 'Spirit and a Vision . . . are organized and minutely articulated beyond all that the mortal and perishing nature can produce', so too are the words of a spirit heard in vision more articulate, more distinctly sculpted, than the 'rough basement' of Blake's own English.[19]

[18] *Milton*, Pl. 18 (E 111, K 499); *Jerusalem*, Pl. 42 (E 190, K 671).
[19] *Descriptive Catalogue*, E 541, K 576; *Jerusalem*, Pl. 36 (E 183, K 668).

Blake's concept of articulated vision leads us to the pictorial equivalent of coherent words, the 'distinct, sharp, and wirey . . . bounding line' the true artist draws 'with a firm and decided hand at once' to produce 'an Original Invention' that is 'Organized & minutely Delineated & Articulated'.[20] Blake also suggests a musical analogue, the line of 'Melody' he juxtaposes to the 'Harmonies of Concords & Discords', those auditory equivalents to the system of categorical similitudes and differences constituting taxonomic grammar.[21] By these articulations—verbal, visual, musical—consciousness establishes the 'Outline of Identity' (*Jerusalem*, Pl. 18; E 162, K 640) by which we distinguish one signifying form from another. The articulate outline, a Blakean version of the proto-semiotic 'mark' of apprehension so important to eighteenth-century sign theory, also expresses the human identity of its creator.[22] Conversely, 'the want of this determinate and bounding form evidences the want of idea in the artist's mind' (*Descriptive Catalogue*, E 550, K 585). Blake shares this sense of line and articulation as definitive of human consciousness with several of his distinguished contemporaries. Schiller, for example, claims that 'Genius delineates its own thoughts at a single felicitous stroke of the brush with an eternally determined, firm, and yet absolutely free outline.' Humboldt concurs with his comment that 'only the strength of self-consciousness forces upon material, physical nature that sharp division and definite boundary line that we call articulation'.[23] This 'bounding line and its infinite inflexions and movements . . . distinguishes honesty from knavery', the 'horse from the ox', and the 'lineaments of universal human life' from 'chaos' (*Descriptive Catalogue*, E 533, 550, K 567, 585).

Through his ideas about articulation, when understood in relationship to his theory of line, Blake would seem to be searching for a principle of identity—including the identity or meaning of the

[20] *Descriptive Catalogue*, E 550, K 585; *Public Address*, E 576, K 595.

[21] *Jerusalem*, Pl. 74; E 229, K 715. Rousseau, *Essay on the Origin of Languages*, p. 53, claims an even more direct equivalency between melody and line: 'The role of melody in music is precisely that of drawing in a painting. This is what constitutes the strokes and figures, of which the harmony and the sounds are merely the colors.'

[22] For the semiotics of marking, see the discussion of 'London' in ch. 3.

[23] F. Schiller, *Naive and Sentimental Poetry* (1966; first pub. 1795–6), 98; Humboldt, *On Comparative Linguistics* (1820), in *Humboldt: Humanist without Portfolio*, pp. 240–1. Eaves, *Blake's Theory of Art*, discusses Blake's sense of line as the expression of identity; see esp. pp. 40–4, 160, 196, 205.

linguistic sign—that incorporates, but is not delimited by, difference.[24] 'Articulation' would then move outward from its etymological origins in paradigmatic difference to become an activity along the syntagmatic axis, the cohering (from *cohaerere*, to stick together) of phonemes into words, words into propositions, propositions into poems. The identifiable meaning of each element depends upon its role in this verbal community, much as in Peirce's contextualist and triadic theory of signification in which each sign must relate to another to be a sign.[25] Textual production, in contrast to grammatical analysis, thus becomes a process akin to reconstructing Albion, 'Collecting up the scatterd portions of his immortal body' and rearticulating its members.[26] From a structuralist and object-oriented perspective, there is no way to discriminate between such a semiosis of identities and differential signification, much as there is no objective distinction between Urizen's articulate words and Blake's, or between the line 'form'd' by Urizen 'To divide the Abyss' and 'the line of the almighty' that 'must be drawn out upon it [chaos] before man or beast can exist'.[27] Given this difficulty, similar to the paradoxes of embodied form we encountered in *The Book of Thel* and to the inability to escape difference as a categorical absolute in *The Book of Urizen*, it is not surprising that Blake delineates the ideal of non-differential articulation primarily through contrast with its antitheses. When Los, the labourer in metals and words in Blake's nineteenth-century poetry, explores the interior of Albion in *Jerusalem*, he finds a place where unknown villains

> . . . take up
> The articulations of a mans soul, and laughing throw it down
> Into the frame, then knock it out upon the plank, & souls are bak'd
> In bricks to build the pyramids of Heber & Terah.
>
> (Pl. 45; E 194, K 656–7)

[24] For a study distinguishing between Blake's 'logic of identity' and a 'logic of difference', see D. Stempel, 'Blake, Foucault, and the Classical Episteme', *PMLA* 96 (1981), 388–407. Although Stempel makes a number of acute observations, his attempt to accommodate Blake to Foucault's 'classical' (i.e., 17th- and 18th-century) episteme prevents Stempel from investigating how Blake challenges the structuralist perspective and searches for phenomenological alternatives.

[25] For Peirce's theory, see ch. 1 n. 52.

[26] *Four Zoas*, Night the Eighth; E 385, K 355. Compare to Enion's lament at the beginning of *The Four Zoas*: 'Why wilt thou Examine every little fibre of my soul [?] . . . The infant joy is beautiful but its anatomy | Horrible Ghast & Deadly . . .' (E 302, K 265).

[27] *Book of Urizen*, Pl. 20 (E 80, K 233); *Descriptive Catalogue*, E 550, K 585.

We learn from an earlier passage who some of these brickmaking grammarians are:

> For Bacon & Newton sheathd in dismal steel, their terrors hang
> Like iron scourges over Albion, Reasonings like vast Serpents
> Infold around my limbs, bruising my minute articulations
>
> (Pl. 15; E 159, K 635)

Immediately following these lines, Blake turns 'to the Schools & Universities of Europe' and sees in them naught but the machinery of rationalist ideology, 'the Loom of Locke whose Woof rages dire | Washd by the Water-wheels of Newton'. These are the 'Systems' Los strives with 'to deliver Individuals'—including the articulated identities of individual signs—'from those Systems' and their 'Abstract objecting power, that Negatives every thing'.[28] The language of *Jerusalem* is of course implicated in the semiotic incursions of these systems, and thus Los's struggle reflects Blake's own attempt to deliver his medium from its seventeenth- and eighteenth-century captors.

Two of Blake's most striking images of textual production and interpretation suggest how rationalist machinery can be reversed. Toward the end of the first book of *Milton*, the 'Wine-press of Los' is converted into

> . . . the Printing-Press
> Of Los; and here he lays his words in order above the mortal brain
> As cogs are formd in a wheel to turn the cogs of the adverse wheel.
>
> (Pl. 27; E 124, K 513)

As a structure, the cogged wheel of Los, like the articulated order of Blake's words, is identical to the wheels of the mind limited to the natural world and its attendant semiotic. If this were not the case, Los's wheel could not mesh with 'the adverse wheel', just as the poet's words must be determined in part by inherited paradigms if it is going to affect an audience. Yet the action of these gears, when Los's words are the driving wheel, reverses the motion of the mortal brain. The words that issue from Blake's own rolling press are intended to have the same result, changing the motions of mortality

[28] *Jerusalem*, Pls. 10, 11; E 153–4, K 629–30. 'Deliver' here means both to rescue (as in the delivery of the Jews out of Egypt, Exodus 18) and to give birth to.

to visions of immortality.[29] The passage is remarkable for its double perspective on language, similar to those prompted by *Adam Naming the Beasts*. Blake admits that even Los, the active imagination, cannot avoid differential structures, embodied in the shape of successive cogs and the spaces between. At the same time, the passage offers a model for articulated actions and counter-actions that release the experience of language from the dominion of those structures. Much the same sense of including differential grammar within a wider phenomenological perspective is signalled by the presence of 'Bacon & Newton & Locke', as well as 'Milton & Shakspear & Chaucer', riding in 'The innumerable Chariots of the Almighty' near the conclusion of *Jerusalem* (Pl. 98; E 257, K 745). Like Humboldt, Blake is reaching beyond the paradigms of rationalist sign theory to consider language in the totality of its making and doing.

In *Jerusalem*, Blake offers another perceptual reversal in his comparison of two ways of interpreting a text:

> The Spectre builded stupendous Works, taking the Starry Heavens
> Like to a curtain & folding them according to his will
> Repeating the Smaragdine Table of Hermes to draw Los down
> Into the Indefinite, refusing to believe without demonstration[.]
> Los reads the Stars of Albion! the Spectre reads the Voids
> Between the Stars; . . .[30]

The Spectre creates the heavens known to science, the one we see with our fallen vision. He shapes this sky according to the 'Smaragdine Table' of Hermes Trismegistus.[31] The tabular and allegoric form of Hermes' alchemical laws also manifests

[29] Blake owned an engraver's rolling press and used it to print his illuminated books. The top roller moves counter-clockwise as the inked plate passes below it; the lower roller moves in the adverse direction. Neither roller is cogged, but by the early nineteenth century some presses may have been fitted with reduction gears linking the top roller to the spoked wheel worked by the pressman. See Essick, *Blake Printmaker*, p. 25 and Figs. 10 (press with gear drive) and 11 (direct drive).

[30] Pl. 91; E 251, K 738. The stars/text metaphor is traditional; see, for example, Plotinus, *Enneads* (1969), 96 (2. 3. 7): 'We may think of the stars as letters perpetually being inscribed on the heavens or inscribed once for all and yet moving as they pursue the other tasks allotted to them.'

[31] For a text of this 'Table', see Damon, *Blake Dictionary*, pp. 182–3. The first Smaragdine principle is the correspondence between 'what is above' and 'that which is below', similar to Swedenborg's doctrine of correspondence. Blake's critique of the Table may also be a veiled criticism of Swedenborg's allegoric matching of heavenly signifieds and earthly signifiers.

itself in the taxonomic semiotics historically and conceptually identified with the development of the physical sciences in the late seventeenth century. Rather than a replacement for Hermeticism, Blake sees these newer sciences as a continuation of a basic biaxial and reductive paradigm common to both. The doctrine of 'demonstration' at the heart of scientific method is limited to the universe already constructed according to its rules. The Spectre's starry heaven is not the absolute reality and neutral ground on which science can prove its theories, for that heaven is merely a 'repeating' of science's own presuppositions. Their tabular framework, like the brickmaking frames of the pyramid builders, is essentially empty—a structure without content, a void without identities. The Spectre attempts to drag Los into an acceptance of this universal 'Indefinite'.

In the last two lines of the passage, what had begun as a text (the Smaragdine Table) is returned to a text. Its first reader takes each sign as a self-sustaining positivity within a community of such identities. For Los, words are 'Things', perhaps even 'living Things', as Coleridge said in allusion to the realist tradition in linguistics extending from Cratylus to Boehme and Swedenborg.[32] The second reader perceives the whole text as a system of differences without positive terms—to paraphrase Saussure's famous crystallization of the nominalist and conventionalist tradition in linguistics. The distinction between the articulation of identities and the empty grid of taxonomy could not be more succinctly evoked. And as with Los's wheels, his starry text is structurally the same as the Spectre's. Their opposition resides in the way each perceives that common text and conceives of the reading process. The Spectre's composition of the heavens and his parallel reading of them reduce every individual sign (and reader) to the Urizenic 'one Law' of an abstraction detached from substantial and individual being. Los's reading allows each sign to achieve its meaning out of its identity, however various and incommensurable with the articulations of others.[33] The Spectre's

[32] Letter of 22 September 1800 to William Godwin (*Collected Letters of Coleridge*, 1: 626).

[33] For a study of the incommensurable in Blake's narrative patterns and its opposition to the reductive systems of the physical sciences, see D. Ault, 'Incommensurability and Interconnection in Blake's Anti-Newtonian Text', *Studies in Romanticism*, 16 (1977), 277–303, rpt. in Hilton, *Essential Articles for the Study of Blake*, pp. 141–73. My sense of the paradigmatic connections between the Smaragdine Table and rationalist science follows Ault's insightful reading, but he does not consider the semiotic implications. Incommensurable identity is one of Blake's methods of absorbing difference and diluting its hegemony over meaning.

system restrains polyvalence and variant readings; Los's vision, like Blake's methods of producing texts, promotes semantic plenitude and multiple readings.

Blake's story of the Spectre and Los as readers places the burden of meaning on their respective methodologies, there being no objective presence, no text, outside the perceptions generated by those methodologies. We are led once again to a process-oriented perspective on language, but more specifically to a heightened consciousness of the productive struggle between freedom and necessity in all articulation, at least as we know it in this world beneath the Spectre's starry heaven. Working, as he must, within an inherited medium, Blake's individual words are determined by its lexicon. There is, however, one avenue back to an almost Adamic originality in linguistic invention. Eighteenth-century grammarians believed that proper nouns lay just outside the periphery of their subject. As Harris states, rather uneasily, 'proper names . . . may be unknown to those, who know the language perfectly well, and can hardly therefore with propriety be considered as parts of it'.[34] This small opening in the taxonomic net allowed Blake a way of escaping at least some of its restrictions without disrupting the linguistic competency necessary for communicating with an audience. By creating unconventional names for his fictive characters and places, a poet can step outside the conventional lexicon and experiment with how new words are formed in ways that suggest how all words originated. Through acts of naming, Blake explores how phonemes (and their graphemic representations) can cohere, how names can emerge from natural signs, and how other words can evolve from primal names. These activities around the outer margins of articulation recapitulate, in concentrated form, the dynamics of language history.[35]

Outside the articulated consciousness giving identity to existence lies a realm that can only be named as the unnameable. This is the habitation of the active but 'Unnam'd forms' in the 'Printing house in Hell' in *The Marriage of Heaven and Hell* (Pl. 15; E40, K 155)

[34] *Hermes*, pp. 345–6.

[35] This approach to Blake's names is compatible with, and in part developed out of, two recent studies: V. A. De Luca, 'Proper Names in the Structural Design of Blake's Myth-Making', *Blake Studies*, 8 no. 1 (1978), 5–22, rpt. (with a few unfortunate misprints) in Hilton, *Essential Articles for the Study of Blake*, pp. 119–39; and Ferber, *Social Vision of Blake*, esp. pp. 202–5.

and of the 'nameless shadowy Vortex' in Night the Seventh of *The Four Zoas* (E 363, K 336). One character half emerges from 'the margin of non-entity', the 'nameless female' of *America* who becomes the 'nameless shadowy female' of *Europe* and *The Four Zoas*, and finally the 'nameless Shadowy Mother' in *Milton*.[36] Although this evolving figure begins without 'voice or sound' in *America*, her later maternal nature and membership in the Siren-like chorus who sing 'songs of amorous delight' in *Milton* suggest that she is the auditory *materia prima* from which names can be formed.

In a few instances, Blake follows eighteenth-century natural sign theory on how articulated names were first formed. 'Rintrah roars' in the first line of *The Marriage of Heaven and Hell* (E 33, K 148), and from that roaring issue the sounds initiating his naming. The process accords with Herder's scene of naming sheep: Rintrah is that which roars.[37] As we learn later in *The Marriage*, 'The roaring of lions' is one of those 'portions of eternity too great for the eye of man' (Pl. 8; E 36, K 151), but by extracting a name from such sublime noises they are accommodated to the tongue and ear of man. 'Oothoon' may be composed in part from the natural sounds of lamentation, a phonemic doubling and orthographic quadrupling of the 'O' interjection so prominent in Blake's diction.[38] 'Bowlahoola' rumbles with the natural and involuntary sounds of what it names, 'the Stomach in every individual man' (*Milton*, Pl. 24; E 121, K 509).

Onomatopoesis does not explain most of Blake's coinages. Nor have several generations of Blake scholars been able to convert all of them into punning combinations of conventional words and thereby give his names discursive import. In some passages, the act of naming seems to have its own internal and non-referential momentum, as detached from any meaning-granting context as Harris believed all names to be from grammar. Take, for example, the following from Night the Eighth of *The Four Zoas*:

[36] *Visions of the Daughters of Albion*, Pl. 7 (E 50, K 194); *America*, Pl. 1 (E 51, K 195); *Europe*, Pl. 1 (E 60, K 238); *Milton*, Pl. 34 (E 134, K 524).

[37] See the discussion of naming in *Songs of Innocence* in ch. 3 and the passage from Herder's *Essay on the Origin of Language*, pp. 116–18, quoted therein.

[38] 'Ololon' in *Milton* may have the same genesis, with a subsidiary pun on 'all alone'. P. F. Fisher, *Valley of Vision* (1961), 248, points out the similarity between 'Ololon' and a Greek word 'which signified the crying of women to the gods'. According to *OED*, 'ululate' also has an 'imitative origin'. For further speculations on these echoes and their thematic significance, see D. H. Reiman and C. S. Kraus, 'The Derivation and Meaning of "Ololon" ', *Blake: An Illustrated Quarterly*, 16 (1982), 82–5.

> And these are the Sons of Los & Enitharmon. Rintrah Palamabron
> Theotormon Bromion Antamon Ananton Ozoth Ohana
> Sotha Mydon Ellayol Natho Gon Harhath Satan
> Har Ochim Ijim Adam Reuben Simeon Levi Judah Dan Naphtali
> Gad Asher Issachar Zebulun Joseph Benjamin David Solomon
> Paul Constantine Charlemaine Luther Milton
> These are our daughters Ocalythron Elynittria Oothoon Leutha
> Elythiria Enanto Manathu Vorcyon Ethinthus Moab Midian
> Adah Zillah Caina Naamah Tamar Rahab Tirzah Mary[39]

The lack of punctuation contributes to an auditory and visual density of the sort V. A. De Luca has aptly called 'a wall of words'.[40] More precisely, we seem to be presented with pure signifiers without signifieds, a name-crazy Adam with no animals before him, a lingual materiality with reference only to an oral formulaic mode of composition aspiring to the condition of onomastic glossolalia. The incantatory staccato, playing initially on *o*, *m*, and *n* sounds, carries over from the invented to the borrowed names, draining from the latter (Satan, Adam) something of their familiarity, while at the same time suggesting a link between the *outré* inventions and names at the heart of Western culture.

Our responses to Blake's impacted naming, and to a lesser extent even to isolated coinages, are similar to those we feel when confronted with a congeries of sounds we recognize as a language having a few cognates with our own but for the most part foreign to our understanding. Perhaps it is for this reason that several scholars have suggested that Blake's invented names are meant to be fragments of a lost *Ursprache*.[41] As we have seen, positing the existence of such an original tongue is an essential feature of traditional linguistic Adamicism and its eighteenth-century descendants, the mythographers and etymologists. The Celticists and speculators, such as Jacob Bryant, in Greek-Semitic relations were particularly concerned

[39] E 380, K 350. De Luca, 'Proper Names', pp. 7–10, uses the first three lines of this passage to substantiate one of his major theses, 'the autonomy of the mythic name'.

[40] 'A Wall of Words: The Sublime as Text', in Hilton and Vogler, *Unnam'd Forms*, pp. 218–41.

[41] Stempel, 'Blake, Foucault, and the Classical Episteme', p. 390 ('Blake's naming is founded on the premise of a perfectly transparent original language of unfallen man'); Ferber, *Social Vision of Blake*, pp. 202, 204. Stempel, p. 395, makes some particularly interesting comparisons (not repeated here) between Blake's names and the Celticist theories of language origin held by Jones and Cleland.

with the names of places, persons, and gods as routes to the recovery of cultural origins. Blake suggests a similar emphasis in his narrative of the 'ancient Poets' and their motivated naming according to 'mental' deities in *The Marriage of Heaven and Hell* (Pl. 11; E 38, K 153), and in his reference in *Jerusalem* to 'the Daughters of Albion' as 'Names anciently rememberd, but now contemn'd as fictions' (Pl. 5; E 148, K 624). Blake's habit of giving two names to some of his characters, such as Los, whose name was Urthona 'In Eden' (*The Four Zoas*, Night the First; E 301, K 264), enacts the division between prelapsarian and later languages.

The hypothesis that Blake's invented names are meant to be taken as shards from one or more ancient languages opens up the possibility that some of these nouns are the roots of their cognates in known languages. This view helps explain some of the peculiarities of Blake's coinages and associates the processes of their articulation with the free-wheeling etymological pursuits of the late eighteenth century. His names function more like eponyms than personifications, and their present semantic opacity is a measure of how far we have fallen from an original transparency. Their supposed historical priority accounts for the ordering of the lists from *The Four Zoas* quoted above. The names of the sons begin with nine invented by Blake, followed by a name (Mydon) from Homer, followed by four more inventions, the first (Ellayol) with a distinctly Hebraic phonation and the last (Harhath) only slightly displaced from the Biblical place name, 'Hareth' (1 Samuel 22: 5). Further integrations of the invented and the inherited follow: Satan, Adam, and the less familiar Ochim (translated as 'doleful creatures' in Isaiah 13: 21) from the Bible; Har and Ijim from Blake's own *Tiriel*—the former claimed by Bryant to be the word for 'mountain' in an unspecified Near Eastern tongue, the latter Hebrew for 'the people inhabiting the wilderness' (Psalms 74: 14).[42] The remainder of the list proceeds over more familiar linguistic ground until the mythic chronology that began with a recreated original culture and its names emerges into recorded history.

The notion that Blake's names are a linguistic reconstruction parallels his own claim that his pictorial works are a form of

[42] Bryant, *New System*, 1: 107. Raine, *Blake and Tradition*, 1: 53, also suggests precedents for Har in W. Stukeley, *Abury* (1743), and the Icelandic Edda. For Ochim and Ijim, see Swedenborg, *True Christian Religion*, 1: 67–8, sec. 45 (cited in Frye, *Fearful Symmetry*, p. 243).

archaeology, a return to lost originals by means of the universal imagination. The relationship between invented but supposedly ancient names and known languages need operate only at the level of the signifier, for sound shifts and the dispersal of 'radicals'—that is, discrete phonemes repeated through the words of two or more languages—were the means employed by eighteenth-century etymologists to discover original tongues. In many cases, those discoveries were hardly less fanciful than Blake's inventions. Further, phonetic similarities can be of the most general sort to make a word, such as 'Ellayol', sound like a representative of the original form of a language. Blake began using this technique as early as *Tiriel* (*c.*1789), the first poem in which exotic names take centre stage. Tiriel's sons, three of whom are mentioned only once and serve no narrative purpose, are named Heuxos, Yuva, Lotho, Clithyma, and Makuth. By adopting the loose standards of speculative philology in Blake's time, one can find a considerable range of ethno-linguistic associations for these names. 'Heuxos' echoes with the Aramaic 'Huzoth' (as in 'Kirjath-huzoth', Numbers 22: 39), the 'Hyksos' invaders of ancient Egypt, and perhaps the Greek 'hex'. 'Yuva', a phonetic predecessor of 'Luvah' in Blake's later poetry, sounds almost as typically Hebraic as 'Yehovah'. 'Makuth' has near homonyms in both Hebrew ('makkah', a wound) and Persian tribal and place names (e.g., 'Maku'). 'Lotho' is as Germanic as 'Otho' and 'Lothar', but could also be the root of the Greek 'Clotho'. 'Clithyma' might serve as a common source for both Greek ('Clytie', 'chlamys') and Celtic ('Elythness', 'Glamis') forms. Tiriel's sons are the imagined linguistic forebears of several ancient cultures, the representatives of a phonetic generation before Semitic, Greek, German, and Celtic languages split apart and developed along separate paths.

I have not added more odd words to Blake's own lists in an attempt to prove that he rifled through dictionaries and carefully constructed imaginary roots. According to Samuel Palmer, Blake '*was* mad about languages'.[43] Given that predilection, coupled with a good auditory memory and an oral formulaic method of writing, Blake could very probably produce with little effort as many ancient-sounding names as necessary. The spontaneity of their articulation would have

[43] Letter of September 1862 to Anne Gilchrist, *Letters of Palmer*, ed. R. Lister (1974), 2: 669. Palmer knew Blake in his last few years and acquired several books from Blake's library.

validated their genuineness, perhaps even their motivated character, for a poet who believed that whole poems were dictated to him by superior presences speaking through his imagination. And if to us such a production method seems more than a little random and *ad hoc*, that only implicates Blake's linguistic inventions in the same kinds of accidents driving the historical evolution of all languages.

Some of Blake's names have more than general phonetic ties to known languages, including homophonic relationships with specific words that indicate what the name represents in Blake's poetry. Thus the use of such names can function as a form of metalepsis, the substitution of a remote but original cause for present effects, both linguistic and extra-linguistic. Urizen is the best-known case in point, the creator of the fallen world whose name is the etymological ur-form of several terms particularly descriptive of that world. 'Urizen' has been variously described as a pun on 'your reason', the Greek 'ourizein' (from which the English 'horizon' is derived), 'is risen' in the first line of *The Book of Urizen* chapter 1, 'your eyes in', 'ur reason', and 'err-reason'.[44] If we consider each conventional word or phrase as the source for 'Urizen', we must either choose among them or take Blake's name for his arch-villain to be thoroughly overdetermined. But no matter what sparked the invention of the word, Urizen's role as a polysemous etymon, one of Blake's linguistic 'Giant forms',[45] is only strengthened by our discovery (or invention) of further punning plays upon his name. Blake sometimes provides his own clues as to how English words were derived from his reconstructed roots. One plate after introducing 'Bowlahoola' in *Milton*, he points out one of its derivatives: 'Bowlahoola is namd Law. by mortals' (Pl. 24; E 120, K 509). This startling assertion is not explained or elaborated. Its primary justification would seem to lie in the body's natural laws governing our lives, but the presence of the letters of 'Law' in the middle of 'Bowlahoola' backs such conceptual extrapolations with etymological evidence. We are encouraged to find other homophones on the same plate, including 'Golgonooza', the flute's 'lula lula', and the 'bellowing' furnaces,

[44] I take the last three possibilities from Hilton, *Literal Imagination*, p. 255. McGann, 'Idea of an Indeterminate Text', pp. 317–18, points out that Blake could have learned of the derivation of 'horizon' from the Greek word for '*bound* or *terminate*' from a note in the Geddes Bible.

[45] *Jerusalem*, Pl. 3; E 145, K 620.

the last also associated with the stomach whose sounds echo through the passage.

The link between formulaic habits of composition and Blake's naming practices is particularly evident in the lists quoted from *The Four Zoas*. The second through the fourth names of the sons are familiar from *Visions of the Daughters of Albion*. Their formulaic '-on' ending propels the onomasticon forward into 'Antamon', first introduced in *Europe*, and then to the echoing nonce word 'Ananton'. The aural key changes to a play on initial and internal *o* sounds for the next three names. Such permutations, common to oral formulaic patterns, match in miniature the slow historical process of sound shifts. We are returned to the '-on' group by Mydon, whose presence as the only clearly Greek name in the list may have been motivated by the key phoneme alone. Names based on the '-on' radical form the largest family group among Blake's coinages, centred around the important figure of Enitharmon.[46] It is as though these words come from an ancient language in which all proper names end with the same sound, as is the case with surnames in Armenian. Alternatively, all '-on' names suggest genetic descent from that single radical. This is precisely the way Bryant treats the same terminal morpheme, which he believed was 'another title of the Sun among the Amonians', and its continuation through words such as 'Amon', 'Abelion', and 'Abaddon'.[47]

Place names, so important to eighteenth-century Celticists, play a particularly prominent role in *Jerusalem*. Albion and his Emanation each join places and people into one name. Somewhat looser connections between these two typcs of proper nouns are suggested by wordplay: 'O melancholy Magdalen [prounouced 'Maudlen'] behold the morning over Malden break' (Pl. 65; E 217, K 700). Such lines accord with Bryant's guiding principle 'that most ancient names, not only of places, but of persons, have a manifest analogy'.[48] But

[46] De Luca, 'Proper Names', p. 10, notes a smaller family, also descending from Enitharmon, based on the 'th' radical. Blake's interest in name families is most clearly indicated by his decompounding of 'Enitharmon' to create the names of her parents, Enion and Tharmas. See also De Luca, 'Proper Names', pp. 18–20, for an excellent analysis of the 4 name families in *Jerusalem*.

[47] Bryant, *New System*, 1: 16–18. Blake sometimes associates Enitharmon with the moon, another '-on' word that an imaginative etymologist like Bryant could consider a derivative from her name.

[48] *New System*, 1: xv. There are also numerous Biblical precedents for treating the same name as both a person and a place.

Blake's major attempts at analogizing place names exceed even Bryant's generous methodology or the etymological speculations of Celticists who could find significance in the phonetic resemblance between 'Babel' and a village in Norfolk. The most striking feature of Blake's alignment of Jerusalem's 'Gates' with the counties of Great Britain is the sheer arbitrariness of the system. Even a brief selection will indicate why most readers pass quickly over these passages:

> Of Reuben Norfolk, Suffolk, Essex. Simeon Lincoln, York Lancashire
> Levi. Middlesex Kent Surrey. Judah Somerset Glouster Wiltshire.[49]

Neither geographical parallels, as in transparent map overlays, nor phonetic conjunctions can explain the individual assignments. It is as though Blake found in incantatory naming a way to bring the absolutely arbitrary full circle back to the motivated and to construct a grammar of willed identifications that could replace the poet's usual grammar of metaphor. We can perceive, at least with our fallen senses, no way in which Levi is 'like' Middlesex. Yet language can bring them together in the temporality of their saying and the topography of their writing. Language serves as the vehicle for the imagining of a post-apocalyptic synchrony, a reconstruction of the geographic schema through the reordering of the place names representing it. As Blake wrote of 'divine names' in *A Descriptive Catalogue*, 'They ought to be the servants, and not the masters of man, or of society' (E 536, K571).

Blake's more exotic articulations have led us both back to the issue of origins and forward to how words are connected historically and, more immediately, in propositional and metonymic structures. Conversation is the primary interpersonal extension of these interverbal exchanges and is, in turn, an activity promoting change in both the language and its users. This social product of articulate performance, a formal characteristic of works as early as *An Island in the Moon* (*c.*1784–5), becomes thematic in Blake's later poetry, particularly *Jerusalem*. The central linguistic concern moves away from what language is to what men can do with it—and what it does

[49] Pl. 16; E 160, K 637. Damon, *Blake*, p. 442, comments that 'this assignment of the various counties of Great Britain among the twelve Sons of Israel is not too important in the understanding of *Jerusalem*'. Paley, *Continuing City*, pp. 269–70, sensibly concludes that 'what the specific analogies are is less important than the fact that a general analogical relationship can be envisaged'.

to them. As is so often the case with Blake's dramatizations of a concept, he implies an ideal condition by presenting it in a decayed or parodic form. Urizen's unsuccessful attempt in *The Four Zoas* to converse with animals is taken a step further in the image of fallen man 'conversing with the Void' in *Milton*.[50] The phrase embraces two senses: a pointless attempt to gain a response from utter absence; but also the process of conversing by means of a differential semiotic, the same one we encountered with the Spectre's proclivity for reading 'the Voids | Between the Stars' in *Jerusalem*. It is obvious that silent partners make poor conversationalists, but verbal interchange is also stopped if we become overly conscious of the empty matrix of grammar and treat words as anything less than articulated positivities. As Blake emphasizes in his ideas about artistic creation, abstract contemplation inhibits performance.

In more positive contexts, Blake builds upon, but expands far beyond, the celebration of everyday conversation of the sort we encountered with Herder and Humboldt.[51] In *A Vision of the Last Judgment*, Blake describes 'Poetry Painting & Music' as the media for 'conversing with Paradise' because they are the remnants of the original semiotic 'which the flood did not Sweep away' (E 559, K 609). Blake's energetic annotating of books suggests that he perceived reading as yet another conversational mode. In his own rather mechanical way, Harris established this concept of conversing with the written word: 'For what is Conversation between Man and Man?—'Tis a mutual intercourse of Speaking and Hearing. . . . The same may be said of a *Writer* and a Reader; as when anyone reads today or tomorrow, or here or in Italy, what Euclid wrote in Greece two thousand years ago' (*Hermes*, p. 398). Visionary dictation could also become dialogue: at the beginning of *Jerusalem*, Blake claims 'to converse with' the Spirit of Jesus 'daily, as man with man'.[52]

[50] Pl. 5; E 99, K 484. Much the same passage appears in *Jerusalem*, with the phrase altered to 'conversing with the ground' (Pl. 49; K 680). Oddly, Erdman takes this as an 'error in copying *Milton*' (E 811) rather than a purposeful revision. Whether void or ground, the 'conversing' is only a soliloquy.

[51] This tradition continues in modern theological studies of language; see for example G. Ebeling, *God and Word* (1966), 19: 'It is not the concept of signification but far more profoundly the concept of answerability that points us to that which is fundamental in language.'

[52] Pl. 3; E 145, K 621. See also Blake's letter to Butts of 25 April 1803 in which he says he is returning to London so that he 'may converse with [his] friends in Eternity' (E 728, K 822). Blake told H. C. Robinson that he 'must have had conversations' with Socrates and Jesus (Bentley, *Blake Records*, p. 310).

If Blake's media were indeed his muses, as I have argued in the previous chapter, then the give and take between an individual poet and the ancestral voices speaking through his language may have prompted Blake's sense of engaging in imaginary conversations which to him were, like all imaginative acts, as real as material objects. Given these psychological conditions, those 'who converse in the spirit' believe they 'converse with spirits', as Blake proclaims in his annotations to Lavater's *Aphorisms* (E 600, K 88).

At the same time that he expands the circumference of what constitutes conversation, Blake envisions an ideal form—we might call it 'hyper-conversation'—by literalizing those very qualities Herder and Humboldt found so appealing in the activity. As Los tells us in *Jerusalem*,

> When in Eternity Man converses with Man they enter
> Into each others Bosom (which are Universes of delight)
> In mutual interchange. and first their Emanations meet
> Surrounded by their Children. if they embrace & comingle
> The Human Four-fold Forms mingle also in thunders of Intellect
> But if the Emanations mingle not; with storms & agitations
> Of earthquakes & consuming fires they roll apart in fear
> For Man cannot unite with Man but by their Emanations
> Which stand both Male & Female at the Gates of each Humanity
>
> (Pl. 88; E 246, K 733)

In our world, the closest we can come to such interchanges is through language, for only words can flow freely back and forth between us, entering into and building our consciousness of self and of other selves. Conversely, that common experience is the foundation—again, the 'rough basement'—for conversations in which male and female Emanations replace verbal mediation. Semiosis becomes not simply literal but physical, a triumph of the body over abstraction that reaches beyond even the powers of the signifier in Boehme's linguistic alchemy. In Los's eternity, verbal and sexual intercourse merge into a single engendering act at once biological and intellectual. The ancient dream of the union of words and things in the Adamic sign is reestablished in an ideal of conversation. Thus, much as we found in Humboldt's writings, linguistic motivation is transported from the structural inter-objectivity of the signifier/signified relationship to the phenomenal intersubjectivity of communication.

The family groups in Los's description lead us beyond the conversations of one person with another to larger social units. Here and elsewhere Blake would seem to be moving toward a conception of language as the social Logos, the creator of communities based on an actively shared linguistic competency. The traditional language in which Blake frames his sense of speech communities indicates the commonality between images of Christian brotherhood, established by the kerygmatic signs of the type pictured in *Christ Blessing* (Plate 8), and enthusiastic proposals by Humboldt and like-minded philologists about language as the cement of social constructs. When language fails as a medium of intercourse, as it does so disastrously in *Tiriel*, the social order also collapses. Blake's image of a restored community centres on the body of Christ as defined by St Paul: 'So we, being many, are one body in Christ, and every one members one of another' (Romans 12: 5). Blake repeats this formula in his *Laocoön* inscriptions and extends it by equating 'The Divine Body' of Jesus with 'The Eternal Body of Man' which 'is The IMAGINATION'.[53] Although Blake never explicitly adds language to this line of identities, it is implicit as one of the chief means of bodying forth the imagination. Further, this communal body preserves the structure of the propositions defining its linguistic outline, an articulated unity in which the members retain their distinct identities. Any attempt to organize this body politic according to abstract, differential schemata is tantamount to dismemberment:

> Till Brotherhood is changd into a Curse & a Flattery
> By Differences between Ideas, that Ideas themselves, (which are
> The Divine Members) may be slain in offerings for sin
> (*Milton*, Pl. 35; E 135, K 525)

Blake's model of community, like Humboldt's, argues against those Urizenic reformers who would 'seek the consummation of humanity in attainment of a general, abstractly conceived perfection, rather than in the development of a wealth of great individual forms'.[54]

[53] E 273, K 776. See also *Milton*, Pl. 3: 'the Human Imagination | . . . is the Divine Body of the Lord Jesus' (E 96, K 482). At the beginning of *The Four Zoas*, Blake further identifies 'The Universal Man' with 'the Universal Brotherhood of Eden' (E 300, K 264). The importance of the human form throughout Blake's poetry is demonstrated by Frosch, *Awakening of Albion*. The body as an image of community is nicely summarized in Deen, *Conversing in Paradise*, pp. 8–13. See also M. Ferber, 'Blake's Idea of Brotherhood', *PMLA* 93 (1978), 438–47.

[54] Humboldt, *Observations on World History* (1814), in *Humanist without Portfolio*, p. 76.

Simply put, community in human form is an extended conversation manifesting itself as the social body, just as Christ in the body of Jesus is the Word incarnate. In *A Vision of the Last Judgment*, Blake resolves this synthesis of Jesus/conversation/community into an image strikingly like his painting of *The Virgin and Child in Egypt* (Plate 7): 'I have seen when at a distance Multitudes of Men in Harmony appear like a single Infant sometimes in the Arms of a Female' (E 557, K 607).

As John Barrell has recently demonstrated, the social role of the artist was a major issue in late eighteenth- and early nineteenth-century England.[55] Blake participated directly in this debate through works such as the *Descriptive Catalogue* of 1809 and the *Public Address* of *c.*1810. Here and elsewhere he focuses on the public responsibilities of the pictorial artist, but these also apply to poets who place themselves in a tradition of social conscience extending back to the Bards of ancient Britain, to 'Jesus & his Apostles & Disciples' who 'were all Artists' (*Laocoön*, E 274, K 777), and to the prophets of the Old Testament. Such poets need not directly address social issues at every turn to contribute to the community, for 'Art is the glory of a Nation' and 'Genius and Inspiration are the great Origin and Bond of Society'. Hence, 'Nations are Destroy'd, or Flourish, in proportion as Their Poetry Painting and Music, are Destroy'd or Flourish!'[56]

The relationship any linguistic performance establishes with its audience must determine in large measure its immediate contribution to the community in which it was produced. This issue clearly concerned Blake, for he made ambitious statements about the public importance of his work. In the prospectus 'TO THE PUBLIC' of 1793, he claims to have already 'engaged the attention of many persons of eminence and fortune' and to have 'been regularly enabled to bring before the Public works (he is not afraid to say) of equal magnitude and consequence with the productions of any age or country' (E 692, K 207). This bit of puffery is exceeded by Blake's indignant letter of 23 August 1799 to Dr. John Trusler. Blake points out to the man who had rejected one of his paintings that 'What is Grand is necessarily obscure to Weak men. That which can be made Explicit

[55] Barrell, *Political Theory of Painting from Reynolds to Hazlitt*.
[56] Advertisement to the Exhibition of 1809, E 528, K 561; *Jerusalem*, Pl. 3 (E 146, K 621).

to the Idiot is not worth my care' (E 702, K 793). This implication that his work will select its own audience by rejecting those incapable of understanding it would also seem relevant to the words Blake scratched into the upper corners of his address 'To the Public' at the beginning of *Jerusalem*, 'SHEEP' and 'GOATS', in allusion to Christ's parable of their apocalyptic separation.[57] Yet, in the text below, Blake asks from his audience a far more sympathetic response: '[Dear] Reader, [forgive] what you do not approve, & [love] me for this energetic exertion of my talent.'[58] This appeal accords with Friedrich Schlegel's definition of an ideal writer/reader relationship in his *Lyceum* aphorisms of 1797:

> The analytical writer observes the reader as he is; accordingly, he makes his calculation, sets his machine to make the appropriate effect on him. The synthetic writer constructs and creates his own reader; he does not imagine him as resting and dead, but lively and advancing toward him. He makes that which he had invented gradually take shape before the reader's eyes, or he tempts him to do the inventing for himself. He does not want to make a particular effect on him, but rather enters into a solemn relationship of innermost symphilosophy or sympoetry.[59]

Schlegel's 'synthetic' writer is matched by Schleiermacher's ideal reader: 'In interpretation it is essential that one be able to step out of one's own frame of mind into that of the author'.[60] Los's description of conversations in eternity, and Blake's invitation in *A Vision of the Last Judgment* to 'Enter into' the images of his painting (E 560, K 611), are more dramatic expressions of this same hermeneutic, then evolving in Germany out of Boehme's beliefs in mystical identification with the Word and into the historicism of the Higher Criticism.[61] This shared model of reading requires a

[57] *Jerusalem*, Pl. 3; E 145, K 620. In Matthew 25: 33, the sheep are 'on his right hand, but the goats on the left'. These positions were preserved in Blake's copperplate, but are of course reversed in impressions from it.

[58] E 145, K 621; the words in square brackets were partly deleted from the plate. For further observations on Blake's concept of his public that stress a personal poet/reader union, see M. Eaves, 'Romantic Expressive Theory and Blake's Idea of the Audience', *PMLA* 95 (1980), 784–801.

[59] *Dialogue on Poetry and Literary Aphorisms* (1968), 131–2. For predecessors to Schlegel's idea of allowing the reader to do part of the 'inventing', see my comments on Blair and Ossian in ch. 2.

[60] 'The Aphorisms of 1805 and 1809–10', in F. Schleiermacher, *Hermeneutics* (1977), 42.

[61] J. A. Ernesti's *Institutio interpretis Novi Testamenti* (1762) is an important transition between Boehme and the Higher Criticism because it preserves the concept of sympathetic

suspension of our independent and judgmental selves that repeats, in the reception of a text, the sacrifice of the Selfhood so important to Blake's dictation theory of textual production. The author and his readers ideally meet and converse together in and through a text which thereby becomes the motivation for a hermeneutic community whose members share a common language. The essential paradigm shifts from dyadic signification (signifier/signified) to triadic interchanges among author, text, and reader, as in the kerygmatic sign. The *telos* of motivation is not abandoned, but sought for in a different dimension of linguistic activity. This attempt to replicate the structure of the Adamic sign in the larger phenomenon of reading is one way Blake hoped 'to Restore what the Ancients calld the Golden Age'.[62]

Have Blake's works created a hermeneutic community, even if far from golden? The question cannot be answered by any feature intrinsic to the language of his texts, but only by the history of their reception. If we look at Blake's own time, the answer is 'no'. The audience he imagined in his poetry bears little resemblance to the one he actually had, a disparity he recognized in the last year of his life with the admission that he 'is not likely' to 'get a Customer for' the beautifully hand-coloured copy of *Jerusalem*. In these circumstances it is difficult not to view Blake's claims about laying up 'treasures in heaven' as a compensatory gesture, the invention of a transcendental audience to fill the absence of an earthly one.[63] His chief patrons for his paintings and prints, Thomas Butts and John Linnell, showed little beyond curiosity about Blake's writings and seem to have appreciated the illuminated books primarily as works of graphic art. Even the 'Ancients', that group of young artists who gathered about Blake in his last years, were brought together through their admiration of the man and a few of his pictorial efforts, not his writings. The selectivity enacted by Blake's language, its

identification within a rationalist and historicist framework. For an impressive modern revision of this hermeneutic, one that stresses 'a reading which is psychological and divinatory rather than grammatical and structuralist', see T. Rajan, 'The Supplement of Reading', *New Literary History*, 17 (1986), 573–94. Rajan makes a distinction between a 'hermeneutic' reading that tries to reconstruct an original meaning and a 'heuristic' reading productive of new meanings. For Blake, this is a distinction without a difference because of his belief in the unity of origin and originality.

[62] *Vision of the Last Judgment*, E 555, K 605.

[63] Letter of 12 April 1827 to Cumberland, E 784, K 878; letter of 10 January 1803 (misdated 1802) to Butts, E 724, K 812.

tendencies toward a private idiom even while in pursuit of the kerygmatic and universal, thwarted its ability to become the nexus and medium of even a small community.

If we turn to the present and repeat my earlier question, the answer changes. I may be breaking scholarly decorum by using the reader as a way of making a point, but surely anyone who has read this far in this book must be a member of something very like a hermeneutic community generated by Blake's works. Within this sodality—even if small, academic, and inconsequential in the greater scheme of things—there is a shared language of images, verbal and pictorial, a dictionary, canonical texts, a wealth of commentaries, a pantheon of mythic figures, and sporadic gatherings to discuss common concerns. Blake has even made an impact outside this community of dedicated Blakeans. 'The Tyger' is one of the best known lyrics in English; 'And did those feet in ancient time' has been set to music and become one of the Church of England's most popular hymns. Blake's reputation as a visual artist is higher with the general museum-going public than with art historians. *The Ancient of Days* has become one of the most recognizable icons of Anglo-American culture. And 'Urizenic', a modern extension of Blake's invented articulations, has almost entered the general lexicon.

The study of Blake's texts as culturally effective phenomena necessarily ends with the history of their modern audience. This does not, however, exhaust Blake's dramatization of the power of words over the world. His *Adam Naming the Beasts* led us to speculations, as old as Genesis and as modern as the philosophy of Martin Heidegger, on how being itself is constituted by semiotic activity. We must now return to a more detailed consideration of that theme, including its enactment in Blake's figural strategies, as a way of approaching his reconstitution of the relationship between meaning and being.

Several times in this book I have referred to Blake's 'literalization of figuration'—that is, how he (or one of his characters) grants substantial being to what we would usually take to be only a figure of speech. The technique emerges out of conventional extensions of a key metaphor through several metonymically related images, as in Blake's own 'King Edward the Third':

> . . . Our names are written equal
> In fame's wide trophied hall; 'tis ours to gild
> The letters, and to make them shine with gold
> That never tarnishes: . . . (E 424, K 18)

The metaphor of writing in fame's hall is treated, in the images of the letters, as an actual event. But gilding and shining the letters of one's name relate metaphorically to the concept of fame, and thus each image becomes an alternative vehicle for the single guiding tenor. We can normalize the lines into a conceit and avoid the oddity of constructing a hall and its contents with a fictive reality equivalent to that of the king who speaks these lines. The distinction between the 'real' referents of the language and the figures of rhetoric is maintained. That barrier becomes a little less certain in 'The Human Abstract' and 'A POISON TREE' of *Songs of Experience*. In the former, 'Humility takes . . . root' and from it grows the tree of 'Mystery' (E 27, K 217). The 'Catterpiller and Fly', which we can imagine feeding on a tree, instead feed on its tenor, 'Mystery'. Our first attempt at rationalizing the lines might be to convert the insects into concepts, so that they operate in the same sphere as 'Mystery', but this goal can also be accomplished by giving Blake's metaphorical tree the substantial presence of a real one which can indeed fall prey to insects. Our usual distinctions between literal and figural, the substantial and the conceptual, are further confounded by Blake's return of his by now fully realized tree to 'the Human Brain' in the last line of the poem.[64] Have the tree and its inhabitants been an allegory all along, or are real trees productions of mental states? The first alternative reinstitutes the comforting distinction between thought and being, but the second is implied by Blake's famous dictum that 'Mental Things are alone Real' (*A Vision of the Last Judgment*, E 565, K 617).

The sinister uses of literalization are particularly evident in *The Book of Urizen*. There the strategy dramatizes the aggrandizements of the differential structures defining Urizen's semiotic consciousness,

[64] P. J. Gallagher, 'The Word Made Flesh: Blake's "A Poison Tree" and the Book of Genesis', *Studies in Romanticism*, 16 (1977), 237–49, offers some similar observations on 'A POISON TREE', finding that 'tenor and vehicle are completely interconvertible, or rather the one becomes the other as the poem proceeds . . .' (p. 239).

as for example in the shift of his 'web' from trope to material object and religious law.[65] But the process is not in itself restrictive. Everything depends on *what* is transformed from the figural to the literal, and whether the result is a prison or the realization of desires imagined in language. The technique is pervasive in *Jerusalem*, where it becomes most apparent in the hypostatization of simile:

> Then Mary burst forth into a Song! she flowed like a River of
> Many Streams in the arms of Joseph & gave forth her tears of joy
> Like many waters, and Emanating into gardens & palaces upon
> Euphrates & to forests & floods & animals wild & tame from
> Gihon to Hiddekel, & to corn fields & villages & inhabitants
> Upon Pison & Arnon & Jordan. And I heard the voice among
> The Reapers Saying, . . .[66]

Mary and her song and tears are posited as literal presences—that is, as signifieds within the referential matrix. The river and waters to which they are compared act in this context as second-order signifiers within the tropic matrix. Suddenly, with the word 'Emanating', simile is carried beyond itself and the song and tears emanate into a well-populated landscape with known place names and figures capable of speech. The key verb takes Mary or her song as its subject, but the intervening terms of comparison make possible its objects. The figures of speech (song is 'like' a river, tears are 'like' many waters) are literalized back into the referential, giving their metonymic extensions through forests, floods, and villages the same status as signifieds, the same substantial being, as Mary and her song and tears. The process is a rhetorical analogue to Coleridge's stated method of composing 'Kubla Khan' in a dream, one 'in which all the images rose up before him as *things*', and to Blake's sense of his words becoming objects that 'fly about the room'.[67]

The underlying dynamic of literalization also finds expression in Blake's conversions of evanescent phenomena, particularly utterances, into more permanent objects. Los forges just such 'condens'd thoughts' on *Jerusalem* Plate 9:

[65] Pl. 25; E 82, K 235 (see discussion in ch. 3).

[66] Pl. 61; E 212, K 695. For a similar conversion of the human into a landscape by means of literalized simile, see *Four Zoas*, Night the Fifth, p. 61, lines 24–31 (E 341–2, K 308).

[67] Prefatory note to 'Kubla Khan', *Poetical Works of Coleridge*, 1: 296; in Bentley, *Blake Records*, p. 547. Coleridge also claims for his opium-induced dream consciousness an Adamic unity of '*things*' and their 'correspondent expressions'.

> I saw terrified; I took the sighs & tears, & bitter groans:
> I lifted them into my Furnaces; to form the spiritual sword.
> That lays open the hidden heart: I drew forth the pang
> Of sorrow red hot: I workd it on my resolute anvil: . . .
> (E 152, K 628)

Paley has commented that these lines 'make us uneasily aware of how (just barely) the imagery of the smithy accommodates the tenor'.[68] Indeed, it may be wrong to treat such passages in terms of conventional metaphoric structures since Blake's language calls into question the very differences between the literal and the figural in which such structures are grounded, just as his basic principles of artistic creation tear down the usual barriers between execution and conception. Los's 'sword' is intensely physical, but at the same time 'spiritual'. Blake's most characteristic tropologies are thus a peculiarly radical form of sortal transgression, for they cross the primary boundaries between the ontological, established by the language of reference, and the poetic, established by the language of tropes.[69] This feature of his rhetoric would seem to be the unacknowledged prompting for Karl Kroeber's observations on the anti-metaphorical thrust of *Jerusalem*, and for Geoffrey Hartman's recent comment that 'we cannot be sure of the referentiality of [Blake's] figures—of the links between metaphor and concept, or between literal and figurative in his poems'.[70] I suspect that most of us share Hartman's uncertainty when confronted by texts that recognize his categorical distinctions only to subvert and overwhelm them.

Steven Knapp has pointed out that, in late eighteenth-century discourse, 'the symbol must be saved by allegory from its innate gravitation toward the literal'.[71] This is precisely what Blake refuses

[68] *Continuing City*, p. 62.

[69] For 'sorts' in reference to lexical categories, see ch. 3 n. 92. For a similar, fundamental questioning of the literal/figural distinction (but without reference to ontological implications), see S. D. Ross, 'Metaphor, the Semasic Field, and Inexhaustibility', *New Literary History*, 18 (1987), 517–33.

[70] Kroeber, 'Delivering *Jerusalem*', in Curran and Wittreich, *Blake's Sublime Allegory*, pp. 347–67; Hartman, 'Envoi: "So Many Things" ', in Hilton and Vogler, *Unnam'd Forms*, p. 243.

[71] *Personification and the Sublime* (1985), 22. See also G. L. Bruns, 'The Problem of Figuration in Antiquity', in G. Shapiro and A. Sica, *Hermeneutics* (1984), 148: '. . . recourse to the notion of figure, or to some equivalent concept such as allegory, symbol, or even catachresis, was for the ancients a way of normalizing the Scriptures. For once you have identified a scandal as a figure, you have already turned it into something you can deal with.'

to do. When, for example, Reynolds in his *Discourses* declares that 'to understand literally . . . metaphors or ideas expressed in poetical language' is 'absurd', Blake reacts sharply:

> The Ancients did not mean to Impose when they affirmd their belief in Vision & Revelation Plato was in Earnest. . . . How very Anxious Reynolds is to Disprove & Contemn Spiritual Perception[72]

In his own works, Blake not only allows but encourages the tendency of the figural to create its own world and, taking the process even a step further, pronounces that world to be the reality hidden within the allegories of fallen time and space. We can also observe this gravitational pull in Blake's visual art. His 'Visionary Heads' convert the imaginative recreation of a personality, historical or fictive, into the literality of pencil portraits. As an illustrator of works by other poets, Blake habitually takes metaphors, even if only implied by the text, as the basis for fully fleshed human forms in his designs. Edward Young's personifications in *Night Thoughts* become in Blake's illustrations of 1795–7 a world of men and women who walk, soar, and even swim around the poem.[73] When criticized for similar procedures in his designs for Robert Blair's *The Grave*, Blake defended himself in his *Descriptive Catalogue* by pointing out that artists had for centuries been 'representing spirits with real bodies' and that 'The Prophets describe what they saw in Vision as real and existing men'.[74] This last observation, like the response to Reynolds, hints at how the literalization of the figural or imaginative delineates Blake's distinction between 'allegory' and 'Vision' in *A Vision of the Last Judgment*.[75]

It is difficult to overemphasize the importance of the literalization of figuration in Blake's later works, or to summarize adequately how it embodies his fundamental beliefs about the constitutive powers of semiosis. The 'Divine Revelation' of the Bible, so often rationalized into figural expression by the exegetes of Blake's time,

[72] Reynolds, *Works*, 1: 195; Blake's annotations, E 658, K 473.

[73] For complete reproductions of the watercolours and engravings, see Grant, *et al.*, *Blake's Designs for Young's* Night Thoughts (1980).

[74] E 541, K 576. This response was probably prompted by Robert Hunt's review of *The Grave* illustrations; see R. N. Essick and M. D. Paley, *Robert Blair's* The Grave (1982), esp. pp. 26–7.

[75] E 554, K 604. For the literality of vision, see discussion in chs. 2 and 3. For some brief suggestive comments on 'vision' as 'apostrophe . . . literalized', see G. Pechey, '*The Marriage of Heaven and Hell*: A Text and its Conjuncture', *Oxford Literary Review*, 3 (1979), 70–1.

undergoes a similar transformation into 'Litteral expression' in Blake's unfolding of Christ's textual garment at the end of *Milton* (Pl. 42; E 143, K 534). Like Los, the figural has 'kept the Divine Vision in time of trouble' (*Jerusalem*, Pl. 44; E 193; K 655); its literalization will again reveal its hidden truths. This apocalyptic movement also enacts, within the secondary motivations of Blake's language, the movement from word to thing defining the primary motivation of the Logos and Christ's incarnation. But the impact of language on being can be extended well beyond these special cases. If language is the medium of thought, as Schlegel, Coleridge, Humboldt, and others among Blake's contemporaries argued, then it is also the medium of existence if we concur with Blake's implied affirmative answers to his questions, 'Where is the Existence Out of Mind or Thought Where is it but in the Mind of a Fool'.[76] We have already witnessed a foolish mind reifying itself into a world in *The Book of Urizen*. There the initial act of self-separation established difference as the enabling structure within language and its concomitant distinctions between subject and object, self and world. But Urizen's structuralist conception of the medium of being is not the only way to think language into its being. From Blake's compositional practices and ideas about articulation, conversation, and community evolves a phenomenological view of language with transactional events instead of difference as its essence. Rather than rigidly objectivist, grammatical, and spatial, this language is expansively subjectivist, instrumental, and temporal. If being were reconceived not on the basis of what language is as a structure but what it does as an event, then 'being' would be returned to its etymological root as a present participle of a verb, a continual coming-into-being in which the verb substantive articulates a conversation between subject and object giving communal identity to both.[77] What if this

[76] *Vision of the Last Judgment*, E 565, K 617. See also *Jerusalem*, Pl. 71: '. . . in your own Bosom you bear your Heaven | And Earth, & all you behold, tho it appears Without it is Within' (E 225, K 709).

[77] As this etymological excursion suggests, my route into Blake's ontological linguistics has been shaped by similar considerations in Heidegger's *Introduction to Metaphysics* (1959), *Being and Time* (1962), and *On the Way to Language* (1971). See also the discussion of *hayah*, 'to be' in Hebrew, in Boman, *Hebrew Thought Compared with Greek*, p. 45: '. . . the meaning of *hayah* is as much "become" as "be", sometimes one and sometimes the other. Sometimes it fluctuates between them, and at other times it encompasses both "becoming" and "being" and contains yet a third active motif; in this motif of *effecting* is apparently to be sought the arch that spans the gap between "becoming" and "being".'

language, the language of the poet and his figural explorations of the full range of the conceivable, were literalized into a world? What if that world could be as receptive to desire as language, and we could move bodily from heaven to earth, from earth to heaven, as easily as you have just done linguistically? *Jerusalem*, especially its concluding plates, provides some answers.

At the beginning of the ninety-sixth plate, Blake writes his last, half-hidden simile in *Jerusalem*: 'As the Sun & Moon lead forward the Visions of Heaven & Earth | England who is Brittannia entered Albions bosom rejoicing' (E 255, K 743). The destiny of such tropes is indicated five lines later: 'And the Divine Appearance [Jesus] was the likeness & similitude of Los.' The figural productions of the linguistic imagination manifest themselves in the actual appearances of the incarnate Word. Accordingly, the personal relationship between Jesus and Los, as they 'conversed as Man with Man' in 'Eternity', is itself a simile. Our own conversations produce figures of comparison; those in eternity produce human figures of similitude. The difference between saying 'Jesus is like Los' and 'Jesus is a simile of Los' may seem trivial, but if we attend to the precise literal meaning of the latter, and to the difference between a statement of comparison ('is like') and a proposition of identity ('is a'), we can grasp something of the difference between our world and the alternative Blake constructs in *Jerusalem*. Most readers, particularly those who also feel compelled to write about the poem, tend to re-allegorize it to accommodate it to a language grounded in a disjunction between being (the signifier) and meaning (the signified). Albion's bow, 'loud sounding', 'Murmuring', and shooting 'Arrows of Intellect' in the ninety-eighth plate (E 257, K 744–5), can be taken as a metaphor for speech without disrupting what it means, but its being *as a bow* is cast into the immateriality of the figural. Blake's language asks us to resist such conversions, however useful, and imagine a bow that is the literal incarnation of a speech act. Blake's 'vision', a mode of seeing, hearing, and writing antithetical to allegory, demands nothing more nor less than a language of direct reference, just as we might describe a view before our eyes. What we perceive in Blake's words has been characterized by Hazard Adams as a 'world *made into* words', and by Leonard Deen as 'speech' that 'transforms itself into act'.[78] Each

[78] Adams, 'Blake and the Philosophy of Literary Symbolism', p. 137; Deen, *Conversing in*

of these readers has described half of a chiasmus. At its crossing point, we find simple and reversible copular propositions where thoughts are things: 'My Streets are my, Ideas of Imagination | . . . My Houses are Thoughts: my Inhabitants; Affections' (Pl. 34; E 180, K 665). As Deen suggests, language has been given the ontological status of 'real' events. Yet the objects in this world made of words continue to behave as though they were parts of a language, as Adams's cogent phrase implies. Events in this world are limited only by Blake's generous sense of English syntax and grammar and his ability to form propositions. The medium of representation and the things represented operate on the same principles. This condition is achieved not, as in the schemes of ideal language projectors, by constructing a language isomorphic with its own prior reifications into fallen nature, but by reconstituting nature according to man's experience of language. Whatever can be imagined in language can be described as an occurrence in fact. Urizen and his historical allies, the rationalist grammarians and scientists, had turned their language and the world it invents into a prison house. Blake turns both into a poem.

Not surprisingly, the world of words in *Jerusalem* seems more than a little odd. Some of its strangeness lessens if we keep in mind that transactions among persons and things accord with transactions among words. Language permits any noun to be substituted for any other in a proposition; it is only our sense of a 'real' distinction between one thing and another that prohibits their interchange. Once free of such encumbrances, instituted by fallen perceptions, Blake explores a number of categorical transferrals. His many place/person conjunctions are his most obvious disruptions of conventional distinctions, but these are far less radical than his habit of interchanging time and space in ways perfectly acceptable to the rules of language yet resisted by our most basic ontological instincts. 'Space' can be pluralized, so why not 'time', or even 'eternity'? Blake answers with 'Times on times' as early as *The Book of Urizen*; *Jerusalem* expands multiple temporality into 'Ages of Eternity'.[79]

Paradise, p. 236. A similar perspective is suggested by Stempel's observation that 'language and representation become one' at the end of *Jerusalem* ('Blake, Foucault, and the Classical Episteme', p. 398) and by Paley's comment that 'we sense' on Pl. 98 'the effort of the language to abandon its function as mediator and to become meaning itself' (*Continuing City*, p. 64).

[79] *Book of Urizen*, Pl. 3 (E 70, K 222); *Jerusalem*, Pl. 96 (E 255, K 743). Taylor, 'Semantic Structures and the Temporal Modes of Blake's Prophetic Verse', pp. 31–2, discusses the plural 'times' as an example of how Blake is 'playing with linguistic boundedness'. That

Further, our ability to move through space is transferred to eternal time as we move 'forward irresistible from Eternity to Eternity' (Pl. 98; E 257, K 745). The nature of this movement is not extrapolated from the spatial activity of things in our world, but from the movement of words in our conversations. That phenomenon must once again become our principal concern.

It will be helpful to recall Humboldt's sense of man's linguistic transactions before plunging into their apotheosis on the final two text plates of *Jerusalem*. His description of language as an interchange between the subjective and objective realms is especially pertinent:

> In thinking, a subjective activity forms itself an object. For no type of imaginative representation may be considered a merely receptive apperception of an already existent object. The activity of the senses must be synthetically joined with the inner action of the spirit. From their connection the imaginative representation tears itself loose, becomes objective in relation to the subjective energy, and then returns to it, having first been perceived in its new, objective form. For this process language is indispensable. For while the spiritual endeavor expresses itself through the lips, its products return through the very ears of the speaker. The representation is therefore truly transformed into actual objectivity without therefore being withdrawn from subjectivity. Only language can accomplish this, and without this constant transformation and retransformation in which language plays the decisive part even in silence, no conceptualization and therefore no true thinking is possible.[80]

For Humboldt, language is itself a grand sortal transgression. As his student G. J. Adler points out, 'the most general and characteristic function of language' is that 'it constitutes, in the first place, the connecting link between the finite and infinite nature of man. In language . . . the subjective unites itself with the objective. By the act of speech the external world becomes converted into an internal one'.[81] In one of his more speculative flights, Humboldt himself offers a vision of these semiotic transformations become a metaphysic:

boundedness is in these examples a good deal more flexible than the fallen world of time and space.

[80] Introduction to the study of Kawi, *Humanist without Portfolio*, p. 289.

[81] *Wilhelm von Humboldt's Linguistic Studies* (1866), 16.

. . . the language-creating energy in mankind will not rest until it has brought forth, whether in one place or everywhere, whatever accords most perfectly with its demands. . . . To express it in another way, one can see in language the striving of the archetypal idea of linguistic perfection to win existence in reality.[82]

We have been tracing the pursuit of this same *telos* of language through *Jerusalem*, and have arrived at a vision of its consummation in a place/time Blake calls 'Eternity' in the twenty-seventh line of the penultimate text plate. In the next line, Blake describes the eternal relationship between the Four Living Creatures—the four aspects of divine humanity—as linguistic performance: 'And they conversed together in Visionary forms dramatic . . .' (E 257, K 746). The medium of this communal conversation, its articulated 'forms', unites the signifying precision of vision with the action of drama. We have encountered this same combination in the kerygmatic signs of Christ and His followers and in Warburton's theories of the hieroglyphic combination of linguistics and kinesics by the Old Testament prophets.[83] Blake's own idea of poetic composition as a union of conception and execution, of the artist's vision and his labour, can also be described as a form both dramatic and visionary. Yet these important precedents, cultural and personal, capture neither the full ontological potency nor the conversational dynamic of language in eternity.

At the beginning of the second book of *Milton*, Blake equates 'the breath of the Almighty', the 'words of man to man | In the great Wars of Eternity', and the 'fury of Poetic Inspiration' with 'Mental forms Creating' (Pl. 30; E 129, K 519). 'Visionary forms dramatic' enact this same integration of human conversation, poetic composition, and divine Logos:

And they conversed together in Visionary forms dramatic which bright
Redounded from their Tongues in thunderous majesty, in Visions
In new Expanses, creating exemplars of Memory and of Intellect
Creating Space, Creating Time according to the wonders Divine
Of Human Imagination, . . . (E 257–8, K 746)

[82] Introduction to the study of Kawi, *Humanist without Portfolio*, p. 258.

[83] See discussion of Warburton in ch. 2 and *Divine Legation of Moses*, 2: 84–5, on the dual use of 'significative *Action*' and '*Vision*'. For some precedents in commentaries on Revelation, including the concept of 'visionary theatre' in 17th-century works by John Lightfoot

As the Living Creatures converse, their words are, like ours, 'exemplars of Memory and of Intellect'. Like the poet's, their words act 'according to the wonders Divine | Of Human Imagination'. And like God's, their words are continually 'Creating Space, Creating Time'. Humboldt's sense of language as an objectivity that is not withdrawn from subjectivity becomes in these lines the process in which *all* objectivity and subjectivity share their perpetual and participial coming-into-being.

The mediatory action of language, so important to Humboldt's theory of discourse, becomes an essential and literal event in Blake's eternity. When 'England who is Brittannia entered Albions bosom' (Pl. 96; E 255, K 743), she follows the same course from objective and external to subjective and internal presence that Humboldt traces for words. As in language, the process is reversible. Urizen's self-reifications are a one-way avenue. The cohesive pluralism of the eternal and internal empties itself into a heterogeneous objectivity and becomes trapped in it, like a speech act without an auditor. In contrast, the Living Creatures 'walked | To & fro in Eternity as One Man reflecting each in each & clearly seen | And seeing' (Pl. 98; E 258, K 746). This ideal conversation, with its back and forth movement and mutual understanding, varies 'According to the subject of discourse'. The senses and the things they perceive also function in accord with the perfected responsiveness of conversations in eternity; even 'Time & Space | . . . vary according as the Organs of Perception vary'. With this reification of discourse into a mode of perception, Blake returns us to a condition briefly glimpsed in *The Book of Urizen*, that time when 'The will of the Immortal expanded | Or contracted his all flexible senses' (Pl. 3; E 71, K 223). This seamless intercourse between semiotic conception and ontological execution, and its absolute symmetry with desire, expands to become the movement of being in and out of time on the final text plate of *Jerusalem*. There Blake asks us to envision a world in which all 'Forms'—not just words—are at will 'going forth . . . | Into the Planetary lives of Years Months Days & Hours' (E 258, K 747). And from that exteriority all forms may return, like words heard

and David Pareus, see J. A. Wittreich, 'Opening the Seals: Blake's Epics and the Milton Tradition', in Curran and Wittreich, *Blake's Sublime Allegory*, pp. 23–58; and Paley, *Continuing City*, pp. 285–7.

and understood, into the interiority of Albion's 'Bosom', there to awaken to the 'Life of Immortality' Blake saw and heard in his linguistic imagination.

The alternative reality Blake conceives in *Jerusalem* is shaped by his experience of the medium of its execution. As so many philosophers of language from Herder to Humboldt insisted, that medium is profoundly human. Indeed, language is the activity that creates a being as human. Through the trope of personification, language can also be used to grant human qualities to the non-human or to the abstractions language itself produces. Blake takes such merely figural and provisional extensions to their radical conclusion. His projection of phenomenological linguistics into an ontology is the vehicle for the humanization of all being. At the same time, this language joins man to divinity. The 'Words of the Mutual Covenant Divine' revealed to Blake near the end of *Jerusalem* are themselves the covenant, the medium establishing the mutuality of man and God (Pl. 98; E 258, K 749). This covenant calls forth, on the final text plate, the replacement of categorical difference with incommensurable and immutable identities.[84] Yet just as words acquire meaning through their participation in a community of other words, the articulated forms of eternity take on their identities by participating in a human community. 'All Human Forms identified'—that is, all forms identified *as* human—'even Tree Metal Earth & Stone' (E 258, K 747). The human forms of these things in our world are the names we give them, the words by which they can be identified and made part of human subjectivity. In Blake's imagined world, the linguistic consciousness grounded in these words becomes the ground of being for the things they name. The generative power of language, available to Blake and to us through our ability to create propositions never before heard, has become the generation of ontological out of verbal identities.

The desire of language to win existence in reality has carried Blake's poem beyond the dream of the Adamic sign, even beyond the animating powers of the 'ancient Poets' in *The Marriage of Heaven and Hell*, to a vision of language reclaiming its power as the Logos. The culminating act of this revivified language is to name

[84] As Blake states in *A Vision of the Last Judgment*, 'In Eternity one Thing never Changes into another Thing' (E 556, K 607).

the community of things it creates: 'And I heard the Name of their Emanations they are named Jerusalem' (E 259, K 747). This is also the name of the community of words constituting Blake's poem. Thus we are returned, in the final sentence of the poem, to the simple yet necessary event of its author hearing the word 'Jerusalem' before naming *Jerusalem*. The objective and communal presence of a single word has entered the consciousness of a poet who returns it to objective presence in a written text so that it may enter through the senses into the consciousness of readers whose shared linguistic experience creates the foundation for a community. In these common but miraculous acts lies the world imagined as the words of *Jerusalem*.

Afterword: Romantic Languages and Modern Methodologies

MY concentration on Blake's language practices and concepts has tended to suppress more general historical and methodological concerns. Let me raise a few of these wider issues by briefly making my text its own object.

As I indicated in the Introduction, interchanges between conception and execution have been both a subject for investigation and a procedural assumption in this book. We have all learned to be sceptical of organicist proposals about perfect articulation between concept and form or intention and production. Most models of unmediated symmetry, like concepts of motivated signification, imply a causal superiority of one member of the linked pair over the other. Historically, but by no means inevitably, the conceptual and intentional have been granted control over the substantial and the performative. One of the clearer manifestations of this tendency is the hegemony of linguistic structure over linguistic activity in philosophical grammar from Port-Royal to Saussure. Historical linguistics takes a very different bearing on its subject to assert the influence of performances on structures by their disruptions of those structures. Even if these disruptions are slight and trivial, when repeated over a long period of time their effect can be enormous—for example, the evolution of one language into another. This view of language was beginning to come into focus in the late eighteenth century. Accordingly, I have tried to invest my medium-oriented perspective with a similar consciousness of the temporality of language as it works its influence even within the production of a single text. Methods of production, in their multiple and even contentious intersections with the requirements of the medium, affect propositional structures, and hence the meanings, of the texts produced. If, for example, a poet employs a formulaic compositional technique, his poems will emphasize repeated patterns of motifs and the concepts they express. These interactions between conception and execution establish a ground for motivation even if the signs by which we apprehend both are arbitrary. It is for these reasons that I have extrapolated Blake's proposals about the unity of conception and execution into a heuristically useful principle for the general study of how texts are shaped by and give shape to the medium of their being.

In the spirit of Schleiermacher's hermeneutic, I have frequently identified my interpretive orientation with what I take to be Blake's own linguistic suppositions. The failure of this approach to overcome an inherent circularity may be less dangerous than its apparent successes. The final chapter has occasionally treated *Jerusalem* as a dialectical subsumption of the problems of sign structure raised by *The Book of Urizen*. But a phenomenological theory does not so much solve as avoid structuralist perplexities. Blake's confrontations with rationalist grammar and his development of a very different way of thinking about language delineate an historical debate, not a transcendental solution. That debate demonstrates, finally, the historicity of language itself. The understanding of how linguistic performances are shaped by ideas about their medium must be responsive to shifting ideas about language's essential character. The modern interpreter of literary texts can gain the power of intellectual conviction by deciding (or simply assuming) that language has always been and will always be one particular conception of it. Those who believe, in the tradition of Locke, Saussure, and Derrida, that language is fundamentally differential can find evidence for that paradigm in *Jerusalem* as easily as in *The Book of Urizen*. But the universality of this method is its greatest limitation, for it fails to discriminate among the different ways texts respond to different conceptions of language. A deconstructive reading of *Urizen* is grounded in the same schema and its inherent ironies at issue in the poem, and thus tells us something about the text's self-reflections on its medium as well as its historical relationship to seventeenth- and eighteenth-century grammatical theory. The same approach to *Jerusalem* obscures both, for the linguistic reflections in that text are grounded in the very different tradition nascent in Boehme, emergent in Humboldt, and continued by Heidegger. Like two other great works of the early nineteenth century that construct ontologies modelled on discourse, Hegel's *Phenomenology of Mind* and Shelley's *Prometheus Unbound*, *Jerusalem* asks its readers to abandon synchronic reductions and follow an apocalyptic quest through the diachronic activities of the linguistic mind. When such texts engage transcendence as a product of linguistic performance, they do so not to deconstruct the transcendental but to celebrate the engendering powers of language. Readers of these and other linguistic romances might take *Adam Naming the Beasts* as their emblem, for the silence of Blake's painting speaks to the grammatical and the phenomenological, the differential and the constitutive, ways of making language conscious of itself and the historical struggles among them.

Bibliography

AARSLEFF, HANS, 'Leibniz on Locke on Language', *American Philosophical Quarterly*, 1 (1964), 165–88.

—— *The Study of Language in England, 1780–1860* (Princeton, NJ: Princeton Univ. Press, 1967).

—— *From Locke to Saussure: Essays on the Study of Language and Intellectual History* (Minneapolis: Univ. of Minnesota Press, 1982).

ABRAMS, MEYER H., *The Mirror and the Lamp: Romantic Theory and the Critical Tradition* (New York: W. W. Norton, 1958).

ADAMS, HAZARD, 'Blake and the Philosophy of Literary Symbolism', *New Literary History*, 5 (1973), 135–46.

—— *Philosophy of the Literary Symbolic* (Tallahassee: Univ. Presses of Florida, 1983).

—— 'Blake, *Jerusalem*, and Symbolic Form', *Blake Studies*, 7 no. 2 (1975), 143–66.

ADLER, GEORGE J., *Wilhelm von Humboldt's Linguistic Studies* (New York: Wynkoop and Hallenbeck, 1866).

AGRIPPA VON NETTESHEIM, HEINRICH CORNELIUS, *Three Books of Occult Philosophy*, trans. J.F. (London: G. Moule, 1651).

ALLEN, DON C., 'Some Theories of the Growth and Origin of Language in Milton's Age', *Philological Quarterly*, 28 (1949), 5–16.

ALTER, ROBERT, *The Art of Biblical Narrative* (New York: Basic Books, 1981).

ANON., *The Hebrew Grammar, with Principal Rules; Compiled from Some of the Most Considerable Hebrew Grammars* (London: G. Terry, 1792).

ANON., Review of the Geddes Bible, *Analytical Review*, 17 (1793), 41–52.

ANON., Review of T. Paine, *The Age of Reason, Analytical Review*, 19 (1794), 159–65.

ANON., *The School of Raphael; or, the Student's Guide to Expression in Historical Painting* (London: J. Boydell, *c.*1800).

ANSARI, ASLOOB AHMAD, 'Blake and the Kabbalah', in Rosenfeld, *Blake*.

AQUINAS, St THOMAS, *Basic Writings of St. Thomas Aquinas*, 2 vols., ed. Anton G. Pegis (New York: Random House, 1945).

ARISTOTLE, *The Basic Works of Aristotle*, ed. Richard McKeon (New York: Random House, 1941).

ARNAULD, ANTOINE, and CLAUDE LANCELOT, *Grammaire générale et raisonnée, ou, l'art de parler* (Paris, 1660).

ASTRUC, JEAN, *Conjectures sur les mémoires originaux dont il paroît que Moyse s'est servi pour composer le livre de la Genèse* (Brussels: Fricx, 1753).

AUBREY, BRYAN, *Watchmen of Eternity: Blake's Debt to Jacob Boehme* (Lanham, Md.: Univ. Press of America, 1986).

AUGUSTINE, St, *Basic Writings of Saint Augustine*, 2 vols., ed. Whitney J. Oates (New York: Random House, 1948).

AULT, DONALD D., *Visionary Physics: Blake's Response to Newton* (Chicago: Univ. of Chicago Press, 1974).

—— 'Incommensurability and Interconnection in Blake's Anti-Newtonian Text', *Studies in Romanticism*, 16 (1977), 277–303.

—— 'Re-Visioning *The Four Zoas*', in Hilton and Vogler, *Unnam'd Forms*.

AUSTIN, GILBERT, *Chironomia; or a Treatise on Rhetorical Delivery* (London: Cadell and Davies, 1806).

AUSTIN, J. L., *Philosophical Papers* (Oxford: Clarendon Press, 1961).

BACON, FRANCIS, *The Two Bookes of Francis Bacon: Of the Proficience and Advancement of Learning, Divine and Humane* (London: H. Tomes, 1605).

BARRELL, JOHN, *The Political Theory of Painting from Reynolds to Hazlitt* (New Haven, Conn.: Yale Univ. Press, 1986).

BEATTIE, JAMES, *The Theory of Language* (London: Strahan, Cadell, and Creech, 1788).

BECK, CAVE, *The Universal Character* (London: W. Weekley, 1657).

BEHRENDT, STEPHEN C., *The Moment of Explosion: Blake and the Illustration of Milton* (Lincoln: Univ. of Nebraska Press, 1983).

BENSON, LARRY D., 'The Literary Character of Anglo-Saxon Formulaic Poetry', *PMLA* 81 (1966), 334–41.

BENTHAM, JEREMY, *The Works of Jeremy Bentham*, 11 vols., ed. John Bowring (Edinburgh: W. Tait, 1838–42).

BENTLEY, GERALD E., JR., 'The Failure of Blake's *Four Zoas*', *Texas Studies in English*, 37 (1958), 102–13.

—— *Blake Records* (Oxford: Clarendon Press, 1969).

—— *A Bibliography of George Cumberland* (New York: Garland, 1975).

—— *Blake Books* (Oxford: Clarendon Press, 1977).

—— 'The Triumph of Owen', *National Library of Wales Journal*, 24 (1985), 249–61.

—— 'From Sketch to Text in Blake: The Case of *The Book of Thel*', *Blake: An Illustrated Quarterly*, 19 (1986), 128–41.

BENVENISTE, EMILE, *Problems in General Linguistics*, trans. Mary Elizabeth Meek (Coral Gables, Fla.: Univ. of Miami Press, 1971).

BERKELEY, GEORGE, *An Essay toward a New Theory of Vision* (Dublin: Jeremy Pepyat, 1709).

BEWELL, ALAN J., 'Wordsworth's Primal Scene: Retrospective Tales of Idiots, Wild Children, and Savages', *ELH* 50 (1983), 321–46.

BIBLE, *The Holy Bible*, 2 vols., trans. Alexander Geddes (London: for the author, 1792–7). Vol. 1 (1792) contains the Pentateuch and Joshua only.

— *The Christian's Complete Family Bible* (Liverpool: Nuttall, Fisher, and Dixon, 1808).

— *The Holy Bible* (London: R. Edwards, 1811).

— *The Holy Bible . . . with . . . Copious Marginal References by Thomas Scott*, 2nd American edn. based on the 2nd London edn. (Philadelphia: W. Woodward, 1811).

BLACKWELL, THOMAS, *An Inquiry into the Life and Writings of Homer* (London, 1735).

BLAIR, HUGH, *A Critical Dissertation on the Poems of Ossian* (London: T. Becket and P. de Hondt, 1763).

— *Lectures on Rhetoric and Belles Lettres*, 2 vols. (London: Strahan, Cadell, and Creech, 1783).

BLAIR, ROBERT, *The Grave, a Poem* (London: R. Cromek, 1808).

BLAKE, WILLIAM, *The Works of William Blake*, 3 vols., ed. Edwin John Ellis and William Butler Yeats (London: B. Quaritch, 1893).

— *The Prophetic Writings of William Blake*, 2 vols., ed. D. J. Sloss and J. P. R. Wallis (Oxford: Clarendon Press, 1926).

— *Vala or The Four Zoas*, ed. G. E. Bentley, Jr. (Oxford: Clarendon Press, 1963).

— *Blake: Complete Writings with Variant Readings*, ed. Geoffrey Keynes, 1966, rpt. with corrections (Oxford: Oxford Univ. Press, 1979).

— *The Notebook of William Blake*, ed. David V. Erdman (New York: Readex Books, 1977).

— *William Blake's Writings*, 2 vols., ed. G. E. Bentley, Jr. (Oxford: Clarendon Press, 1978).

— *The Complete Poetry and Prose of William Blake*, rev. edn., ed. David V. Erdman (Berkeley: Univ. of California Press, 1982).

BLOOM, HAROLD, *The Visionary Company* (Garden City, NY: Doubleday, 1961).

BLOOMFIELD, MORTON W., 'A Grammatical Approach to Personification Allegory', *Modern Philology*, 60 (1963), 161–71.

BOASE, T. S. R., *The York Psalter* (London: Faber and Faber, 1962).

BOEHME, JACOB, *The Works of Jacob Behmen, the Teutonic Theosopher*, 4 vols., ed. G. Ward and T. Langcake, mostly from the translations of John Sparrow (London: M. Richardson and G. Robinson, 1674–81).

BOMAN, THORLIEF, *Hebrew Thought Compared with Greek*, trans. Jules L. Moreau (Philadelphia: Westminster Press, 1960).

BOND, DONALD F., ed., *The Spectator*, 5 vols. (Oxford: Clarendon Press, 1965).

BORST, ARNO, *Der Turmbau von Babel: Geschichte der Meinungen über Ursprung und Vielfalt der Sprachen und Völker*, 4 vols. in 6 (Stuttgart: A. Hiersemann, 1957–63).

BRACHER, MARK, *Being Form'd: Thinking through Blake's* Milton (Barrytown, NY: Station Hill Press, 1985).

BROSSES, CHARLES DE, *Traité de la formation mécanique des langues et des principes physiques de l'étymologie*, 2 vols. (Paris: Saillant, 1765).

BROWN, JOHN, *A Dissertation on the Rise, Union, and Power, the Progressions, Separations, and Corruptions, of Poetry and Music* (London: Davis and Reymers, 1763).

BRUNS, GERALD L., *Inventions: Writing, Textuality, and Understanding in Literary History* (New Haven, Conn.: Yale Univ. Press, 1982).

—— 'The Problem of Figuration in Antiquity', in Gary Shapiro and Alan Sica, eds., *Hermeneutics: Questions and Prospects* (Amherst: Univ. of Massachusetts Press, 1984).

BRYANT, JACOB, *A New System, or, an Analysis of Ancient Mythology*, 3 vols. (London: Payne, Elmsley, White, and Walter, 1774–6).

BULTMANN, RUDOLF, *Jesus Christ and Mythology* (New York: Scribner's Sons, 1958).

BULWER, JOHN, *Chirologia: Or the Naturall Language of the Hand* (London: R. Whitaker, 1644).

BURKE, KENNETH, *Language as Symbolic Action* (Berkeley: Univ. of California Press, 1968).

BUTLIN, MARTIN, 'A New Portrait of Blake', *Blake Studies*, 7 no. 2 (1975), 101–3.

—— *The Paintings and Drawings of William Blake*, 2 vols. (New Haven, Conn.: Yale Univ. Press, 1981).

BYSSHE, EDWARD, ed., *The Art of English Poetry* (London: Knaplock, Castle, and Tooke, 1702).

CARR, STEPHEN LEO, 'Illuminated Printing: Toward a Logic of Difference', in Hilton and Vogler, *Unnam'd Forms*.

CASSIRER, ERNST, *Language and Myth*, trans. Susanne K. Langer (New York: Harper, 1946).

CHARLES, R. H., ed., *The Apocrypha and Pseudepigrapha of the Old Testament in English*, 2 vols. (Oxford: Clarendon Press, 1913).

CHRISTENSEN, JEROME, *Coleridge's Blessed Machine of Language* (Ithaca, NY: Cornell Univ. Press, 1981).

CLELAND, JOHN, *The Way to Things by Words, and to Words by Things; Being a Sketch of an Attempt at the Retrieval of the Ancient Celtic* (London: Davis and Reymers, 1766).

COHEN, MURRAY, *Sensible Words: Linguistic Practice in England 1640–1785* (Baltimore, Md.: Johns Hopkins Univ. Press, 1977).

COLERIDGE, SAMUEL TAYLOR, *Aids to Reflection*, ed. Henry Nelson Coleridge (London: W. Pickering, 1839).

—— *The Complete Poetical Works of Samuel Taylor Coleridge*, 2 vols., ed. Ernest Hartley Coleridge (Oxford: Clarendon Press, 1912).

—— *The Table Talk and Omniana*, ed. T. Ashe (London: Bell and Sons, 1923).

—— *Miscellaneous Criticism*, ed. Thomas Middleton Raysor (London: Constable, 1936).

—— *Collected Letters of Samuel Taylor Coleridge*, 6 vols., ed. Earl Leslie Griggs (Oxford: Clarendon Press, 1956–71).

—— *The Notebooks of Samuel Taylor Coleridge*, 3 vols. in 6 to date, ed. Kathleen Coburn (Princeton, NJ: Princeton Univ. Press, 1957–73).

—— *The Friend*, 2 vols., ed. Barbara E. Rooke (Princeton, NJ: Princeton Univ. Press, 1969).

—— *Shakespearean Criticism*, 2 vols., ed. Thomas Middleton Raysor (London: Dent, 1960).

—— *Lay Sermons*, ed. R. J. White (Princeton, NJ: Princeton Univ. Press, 1972).

—— *Essays on his Times*, 3 vols., ed. David V. Erdman (Princeton, NJ: Princeton Univ. Press, 1978).

—— *Marginalia*, 2 vols. to date, ed. George Whalley (Princeton, NJ: Princeton Univ. Press, 1980–4).

—— *Logic*, ed. J. R. de J. Jackson (Princeton, NJ: Princeton Univ. Press, 1981).

—— *Biographia Literaria*, 2 vols., ed. James Engell and Walter Jackson Bate (Princeton, NJ: Princeton Univ. Press, 1983).

COMENIUS, JOHN AMOS, *Via Lucis* (Amsterdam: C. Conradum, 1668).

—— *The Way of Light*, trans. E. T. Campagnac (Liverpool: Liverpool Univ. Press, 1938).

CONDILLAC, ETIENNE BONNOT DE, *Essai sur l'origine des connaissances humaines* (Amsterdam: P. Mortier, 1746).

—— *An Essay on the Origin of Human Knowledge Being a Supplement to Mr. Locke's Essay on the Human Understanding*, trans. Thomas Nugent (London: J. Nourse, 1756).

CORNELIUS, PAUL, *Languages in Seventeenth- and Early Eighteenth-Century Imaginary Voyages* (Geneva: Libraire Droz, 1965).

COULSON, JOHN, *Newman and the Common Tradition* (Oxford: Clarendon Press, 1970).

COWPER, WILLIAM, *Poetical Works*, 4th edn., ed. H. S. Milford (London: Oxford Univ. Press, 1934).

CREUZER, GEORG FRIEDRICH, *Symbolik und Mythologie der alten Völker, besonders der Griechen*, 4 vols. (Leipzig: Leske, 1810–12).

CUNNINGHAM, ALLAN, *Lives of the Most Eminent British Painters, Sculptors, and Architects*, 6 vols., 2nd edn. (London: J. Murray, 1830–8).

CURRAN, STUART, and JOSEPH ANTHONY WITTREICH JR., eds., *Blake's Sublime Allegory: Essays on* The Four Zoas, Milton, *and* Jerusalem (Madison: Univ. of Wisconsin Press, 1973).

DALGARNO, GEORGE, *Ars signorum, vulgo character universalis et lingua philosophica* (London: J. Hayes, 1661).

DAMON, S. FOSTER, *William Blake: His Philosophy and Symbols* (London: Constable, 1924).

—— *A Blake Dictionary* (Providence, RI: Brown Univ. Press, 1965).

DAMROSCH, LEOPOLD, JR., *Symbol and Truth in Blake's Myth* (Princeton, NJ: Princeton Univ. Press, 1980).

DANTE ALIGHIERI, *A Translation of the Inferno*, 2 vols., trans. Henry Boyd (Dublin, 1785).

DARWIN, ERASMUS, *The Loves of the Plants* (Part 2 of *The Botanic Garden*). (Lichfield, 1789).

—— *The Botanic Garden*, 1791, 4th edn., 2 vols. (London: J. Johnson, 1799).

—— *The Temple of Nature; or, the Origin of Society: A Poem* (London: J. Johnson, 1803).

DAVIES, EDWARD, *Celtic Researches, on the Origin, Traditions & Language, of the Ancient Britons* (London: J. Booth, 1804).

DEEN, LEONARD W., *Conversing in Paradise: Poetic Genius and Identity-as-Community in Blake's Los* (Columbia: Univ. of Missouri Press, 1983).

DEFOE, DANIEL, *Mere Nature Delineated: or, a Body without a Soul* (London: T. Warner, 1726).

DE LUCA, VINCENT A., 'Proper Names in the Structural Design of Blake's Myth-Making', *Blake Studies*, 8 no. 1 (1978), 5–22.

—— 'A Wall of Words: The Sublime as Text', in Hilton and Vogler, *Unnam'd Forms*.

DEMETZ, PETER, 'The Elm and the Vine: Notes toward the History of a Marriage Topos', *PMLA* 73 (1958), 521–32.

DE MOTT, BENJAMIN, 'The Sources and Development of John Wilkins' Philosophical Language', *Journal of English and Germanic Philology*, 57 (1958), 1–13.

DERRIDA, JACQUES, *Of Grammatology*, trans. Gayatri Chakravorty Spivak (Baltimore, Md.: Johns Hopkins Univ. Press, 1976).

—— *Edmund Husserl's Origin of Geometry: An Introduction*, trans. John P. Leavey (Stony Brook, NY: N. Hayes, 1978).

DERRIDA, JACQUES, *Writing and Difference*, trans. Alan Bass (Chicago: Univ. of Chicago Press, 1978).

DONNE, JOHN, *The Sermons of John Donne*, 10 vols., ed. Evelyn M. Simpson and George R. Potter (Berkeley: Univ. of California Press, 1953–62).

DU BARTAS, GUILLAUME, *Du Bartas his Divine Weekes and Workes*, trans. Joshua Sylvester (London: H. Lounes, 1611).

DUBOS, JEAN BAPTISTE, *Réflexions critiques sur la poésie et sur la peinture* (Paris: J. Mariette, 1719).

DURET, CLAUDE, *Thresor de l'histoire des langues de cest univers* (Cologne: La Societé Caldoriene, 1613).

EAVES, MORRIS, 'Blake and the Artistic Machine: An Essay in Decorum and Technology', *PMLA* 92 (1977), 903–27.

—— 'Romantic Expressive Theory and Blake's Idea of the Audience', *PMLA* 95 (1980), 784–801.

—— *William Blake's Theory of Art* (Princeton, NJ: Princeton Univ. Press, 1982).

EBELING, GERHARD, *God and Word* (Philadelphia: Fortress Press, 1966).

EDWARDS, CHARLES, *Hebraismorum Cambro-Britannicorum specimen* (London, 1675).

EDWARDS, GAVIN, 'Repeating the Same Dull Round', in Hilton and Vogler, *Unnam'd Forms*.

EDWARDS, JOHN, *A Discourse concerning the Authority, Stile, and Perfection of the Books of the Old and New-Testament*, 3 vols. (London: R. Wilkin, 1693–5).

EICHHORN, JOHANN GOTTFRIED, *Commentarius in Apocalypsin Joannis*, 2 vols. (Gottingen, 1791).

ELIOT, GEORGE, *Adam Bede*, 3 vols. (Edinburgh: Blackwood and Sons, 1859).

ELIOT, THOMAS STEARNS, 'The Post-Georgians', *Athenaeum*, No. 4641 (11th April 1919), 171–2.

ELLIOTT, RALPH W. V., 'Isaac Newton's "Of An Universall Language" ', *Modern Language Review*, 52 (1957), 1–18.

EPICURUS, 'Letter to Herodotus', in Diogenes Laertius, *Lives of Eminent Philosophers*, 2 vols., trans. R. D. Hicks (Cambridge, Mass.: Loeb Library, 1950).

ERDMAN, DAVID V., 'The Suppressed and Altered Passages in Blake's *Jerusalem*', *Studies in Bibliography*, 17 (1964), 1–54.

—— ed., *A Concordance to the Writings of William Blake*, 2 vols. (Ithaca, NY: Cornell Univ. Press, 1967).

ERNESTI, JOHANN AUGUST, *Institutio interpretis Novi Testamenti* (Leyden: J. Le Mair, 1762).

ESSICK, ROBERT N., *William Blake Printmaker* (Princeton, NJ: Princeton Univ. Press, 1980).

—— Review of M. Butlin, *Paintings and Drawings of Blake*, in *Blake: An Illustrated Quarterly*, 16 (1982), 22–65.

—— *The Separate Plates of William Blake: A Catalogue* (Princeton, NJ: Princeton Univ. Press, 1983).

—— *The Works of William Blake in the Huntington Collections* (San Marino, Calif.: Huntington Library, 1985).

—— 'William Blake, William Hamilton, and the Materials of Graphic Meaning', *ELH* 52 (1985), 833–72.

—— 'How Blake's Body Means', in Hilton and Vogler, *Unnam'd Forms*.

—— 'Variation, Accident, and Intention in William Blake's *The Book of Urizen*', *Studies in Bibliography*, 39 (1986), 230–5.

—— and MORTON D. PALEY, *Robert Blair's* The Grave *Illustrated by William Blake: A Study with Facsimile* (London: Scolar Press, 1982).

—— and DONALD PEARCE, eds., *Blake in his Time* (Bloomington: Indiana Univ. Press, 1978).

EVANS, JOHN M., Paradise Lost *and the Genesis Tradition* (Oxford: Clarendon Press, 1968).

EVELYN, JOHN, *Sculptura: or the History, and Art of Chalcography* (London: Beedle, Collins, and Crook, 1662).

FERBER, MICHAEL, 'Blake's Idea of Brotherhood', *PMLA* 93 (1978), 438–47.

—— ' "London" and its Politics', *ELH* 48 (1981), 310–38.

—— *The Social Vision of William Blake* (Princeton, NJ: Princeton Univ. Press, 1985).

FERGUSON, FRANCES, *Wordsworth: Language as Counter-Spirit* (New Haven, Conn.: Yale Univ. Press, 1977).

FISH, STANLEY EUGENE, *Surprised by Sin: The Reader in* Paradise Lost (Berkeley: Univ. of California Press, 1971).

FISHER, PETER F., *The Valley of Vision: Blake as Prophet and Revolutionary*, ed. Northrop Frye (Toronto: Univ. of Toronto Press, 1961).

FLETCHER, ANGUS, *Allegory: The Theory of a Symbolic Mode* (Ithaca, NY: Cornell Univ. Press, 1964).

FLUDD, ROBERT, *Mosaicall Philosophy: Grounded upon the Essential Truth or Eternal Sapience* (London: H. Moseley, 1659).

FOGEL, AARON, 'Pictures of Speech: On Blake's Poetic', *Studies in Romanticism*, 21 (1982), 217–42.

FOUCAULT, MICHEL, *The Order of Things* (New York: Vintage Books, 1973).

FOX, SUSAN, *Poetic Form in Blake's* Milton (Princeton, NJ: Princeton Univ. Press, 1976).

FRAIN DU TREMBLAY, JEAN, *Traité des langues* (Amsterdam: E. Roger, 1709).

—— *A Treatise of Languages*, trans. M. Halpenn (London: D. Leach, 1725).

FRASER, RUSSELL A., *The Language of Adam* (New York: Columbia Univ. Press, 1977).

FREI, HANS W., *The Eclipse of Biblical Narrative: A Study in Eighteenth and Nineteenth Century Hermeneutics* (New Haven, Conn.: Yale Univ. Press, 1974).

FROSCH, THOMAS R., *The Awakening of Albion: The Renovation of the Body in the Poetry of William Blake* (Ithaca, NY: Cornell Univ. Press, 1974).

FRYE, NORTHROP, *Fearful Symmetry: A Study of William Blake* (Princeton, NJ: Princeton Univ. Press, 1947).

FUNK, ROBERT W., *Language, Hermeneutic, and Word of God: The Problem of Language in the New Testament and Contemporary Theology* (New York: Harper and Row, 1966).

GALLAGHER, PHILIP J., 'The Word Made Flesh: Blake's "A Poison Tree" and the Book of Genesis', *Studies in Romanticism*, 16 (1977), 237–49.

GEDDES, ALEXANDER, Review of G. B. De Rossi, *Variae Lectiones*, in *Analytical Review*, 1 (1788), 1–12.

—— Review of Johannes van Eyk, *Ledige Uuren*, in *Analytical Review*, 7 (1790), 70–4.

—— *Doctor Geddes's Address to the Public, on the Publication of the First Volume of his New Translation of the Bible* (London: J. Johnson, 1793).

GENETTE, GÉRARD, *Mimologiques: voyage en Cratylie* (Paris: Editions du Seuil, 1976).

GILCHRIST, ALEXANDER, *Life of William Blake, Pictor Ignotus*, 2 vols. (London: Macmillan, 1863).

GLECKNER, ROBERT F., 'Blake's Verbal Technique', in Rosenfeld, *Blake*.

—— 'Most Holy Forms of Thought: Some Observations on Blake and Language', *ELH* 41 (1974), 555–77.

—— *Blake and Spenser* (Baltimore, Md.: Johns Hopkins Univ. Press, 1985).

GLEN, HEATHER, *Vision and Disenchantment: Blake's Songs and Wordsworth's* Lyrical Ballads (Cambridge: Cambridge Univ. Press, 1983).

GOMBRICH, ERNEST H., '*Icones Symbolicae*: The Visual Image in Neo-Platonic Thought', *Journal of the Warburg and Courtauld Institutes*, 11 (1948), 163–92.

GOODMAN, NELSON, *Languages of Art* (Indianapolis, Ind.: Hackett, 1976).

GRANT, JOHN E., EDWARD J. ROSE, MICHAEL J. TOLLEY, and DAVID V. ERDMAN, eds., *William Blake's Designs for Edward Young's* Night Thoughts, 2 vols. (Oxford: Clarendon Press, 1980).

HANDELMAN, SUSAN A., *The Slayers of Moses: The Emergence of Rabbinic Interpretation in Modern Literary Theory* (Albany: State Univ. of New York Press, 1983).

HARRIS, JAMES, *Hermes; or, a Philosophical Inquiry concerning Language and Universal Grammar* (London: Nourse and Vaillant, 1751).

HARTLEY, DAVID, *Observations on Man*, 2nd edn. (London: J. Johnson, 1791).

HARTMAN, GEOFFREY H., *Beyond Formalism: Literary Essays 1958–1970* (New Haven, Conn.: Yale Univ. Press, 1970).

—— 'Envoi: "So Many Things" ', in Hilton and Vogler, *Unnam'd Forms.*

HAYLEY, WILLIAM, *Memoirs of the Life and Writings of William Hayley*, 2 vols., ed. John Johnson (London: Colburn, Simpkin, and Marshall, 1823).

HAZLITT, WILLIAM, *The Spirit of the Age: Or Contemporary Portraits* (London: H. Colburn, 1825).

HEGEL, GEORG WILHELM FRIEDRICH, *The Phenomenology of Mind*, 2nd edn., trans. J. B. Baillie (New York: Harper, 1967).

HEIDEGGER, MARTIN, *An Introduction to Metaphysics*, trans. Ralph Manheim (New Haven, Conn.: Yale Univ. Press, 1959).

—— *Being and Time*, trans. John Macquarrie and Edward Robinson (New York: Harper and Row, 1962).

—— *On the Way to Language*, trans. Peter D. Hertz (New York: Harper and Row, 1971).

HEPPNER, CHRISTOPHER, ' "A Desire of Being": Identity and *The Book of Thel*', *Colby Library Quarterly*, 13 (1977), 79–98.

HERDER, JOHANN GOTTFRIED, *Über die neuere deutsche Litteratur*, 3 vols. in 2 (Riga, 1767).

—— *The Spirit of Hebrew Poetry*, 2 vols., trans. James Marsh (Burlington, Vt.: E. Smith, 1833).

—— *Essay on the Origin of Language*, in *On the Origin of Language*, trans. John H. Moran and Alexander Gode (New York: F. Ungar, 1966).

HILTON, NELSON, *Literal Imagination: Blake's Vision of Words* (Berkeley: Univ. of California Press, 1983).

—— 'Blakean Zen', *Studies in Romanticism*, 24 (1985), 183–200.

—— ed., *Essential Articles for the Study of William Blake* (Hamden, Conn.: Archon Books, 1986).

—— and THOMAS A. VOGLER, eds., *Unnam'd Forms: Blake and Textuality* (Berkeley: Univ. of California Press, 1986).

HOBBES, THOMAS, *Leviathan: Or the Matter, Forme and Power of a Commonwealth* (London: A. Crooke, 1651).

HODGSON, JOHN A., 'Transcendental Tropes: Coleridge's Rhetoric of Allegory and Symbol', in Morton W. Bloomfield, ed., *Allegory, Myth, and Symbol* (Cambridge, Mass.: Harvard Univ. Press, 1981).

HORAPOLLO, *Hieroglyphica* (Venice: A. Manutius, 1505).

HUMBOLDT, WILHELM VON, *Humanist without Portfolio: An Anthology of the Writings of Wilhelm von Humboldt*, trans. Marianne Cowan (Detroit, Mich.: Wayne State Univ. Press, 1963).

—— *Linguistic Variability & Intellectual Development*, trans. George C. Buck and Frithjof A. Raven (Coral Gables, Fla: Univ. of Miami Press, 1971).

IDE, NANCY M., 'Image Patterns and the Structure of William Blake's *The Four Zoas*', *Blake: An Illustrated Quarterly*, 20 (1987), 125–33.

IVERSEN, ERIK, *The Myth of Egypt and its Hieroglyphs* (Copenhagen: Gec Gad Publishers, 1961).

IVINS, WILLIAM M., JR., *How Prints Look* (Boston: Beacon Press, 1943).

JABÈS, EDMOND, *The Book of Questions*, 3 vols. in 2, trans. Rosmarie Waldrop (Middleton, Conn.: Wesleyan Univ. Press, 1972–3).

JACOB, NOAH JONATHAN, *Naming-Day in Eden* (New York: Macmillan, 1958).

JOHNSON, SAMUEL, *A Dictionary of the English Language*, 2 vols. (London: Knapton, *et al.*, 1755), and 9th edn. (London: J. Johnson, *et al.*, 1806).

JONES, ROWLAND, *The Origin of Language and Nations* (London: J. Hughs, 1764).

—— *Hieroglyfic; or, a Grammatical Introduction to an Universal Hieroglyfic Language* (London, 1768).

—— *The Philosophy of Words, in Two Dialogues between the Author and Crito* (London: Dodsley, *et al.*, 1769).

—— *The Circles of Gomer, or, an Essay towards an Investigation of the English, as an Universal Language* (London: Cowder, *et al.*, 1771).

—— *The Io-Triads; or, the Tenth Muse* (London: for the author, 1773).

JOSEPHUS, FLAVIUS, *The Genuine and Complete Works of Flavius Josephus*, trans. George Henry Maynard (London: J. Cooke, *c.*1785).

KAMES, HENRY HOME, Lord, *Elements of Criticism*, 6th edn., 2 vols. (Edinburgh: Bell, *et al.*, 1785).

KAYSER, WOLFGANG, '*Böhmes Natursprachenlehre und ihre Grundlagen*', *Euphorion*, 31 (1930), 521–62; French trans., *Poétique*, 3 (1972), 337–66.

KEYNES, GEOFFREY, *The Complete Portraiture of William & Catherine Blake* (London: Trianon Press, 1977).

KIRCHER, ATHANASIUS, *Arca Noë* (Amsterdam: J. Janson, 1675).

—— *Turris Babel* (Amsterdam: J. Janson, 1679).

KNAPP, STEVEN, *Personification and the Sublime: Milton to Coleridge* (Cambridge, Mass.: Harvard Univ. Press, 1985).

KNIGHT, RICHARD PAYNE, *An Account of the Remains of the Worship of Priapus* (London: T. Spilsbury, 1786).

KNOWLSON, JAMES, *Universal Language Schemes in England and France 1600–1800* (Toronto: Univ. of Toronto Press, 1975).

KONOPACKI, STEVEN A., *The Descent into Words: Jacob Böhme's Transcendental Linguistics* (Ann Arbor, Mich.: Karoma Publishers, 1979).

KRISTEVA, JULIA, ed., *La Traversée des signes* (Paris: Editions du Seuil, 1975).

—— 'Signifying Practice and Mode of Production', *Edinburgh Magazine*, 1 (1976), 64–76.

KROEBER, KARL, 'Delivering *Jerusalem*', in Curran and Wittreich, *Blake's Sublime Allegory*.

LAND, STEPHEN K., *From Signs to Propositions: The Concept of Form in Eighteenth-Century Semantic Theory* (London: Longman, 1974).

—— *The Philosophy of Language in Britain: Major Theories from Hobbes to Thomas Reid* (New York: AMS Press, 1986).

LAPPIN, SHALOM, *Sorts, Ontology, and Metaphor: The Semantics of Sortal Structure* (Berlin: W. de Gruyter, 1981).

LARRISSY, EDWARD, *William Blake* (Oxford: B. Blackwell, 1985).

LAVATER, JOHN CASPAR, *Aphorisms on Man*, trans. Henry Fuseli (London: J. Johnson, 1788).

—— *Essays on Physiognomy, Designed to Promote the Knowledge and Love of Mankind*, 3 vols. in 5, trans. Henry Hunter (London: J. Murray, *et al.*, 1789–98).

LAYCOCK, DONALD C., *The Complete Enochian Dictionary: A Dictionary of the Angelic Language as Revealed to Dr. John Dee and Edward Kelley* (London: Askin Publishers, 1978).

LE BRUN, CHARLES, *A Method to Learn to Design the Passions*, trans. John Williams (London: for the author, 1734).

LESSING, GOTTHOLD EPHRAIM, *Anti-Goeze* (Brunswick, 1778).

—— *Laokoon*, ed. Hugo Blümmer (Berlin: Weidmannsche Buchhandlung, 1880).

LINDBERG, BO, *William Blake's Illustrations of the Book of Job* (Acta Academiae Aboensis, ser. A, vol. 46; Abo: Abo Akademi, 1973).

LOCKE, JOHN, *An Essay concerning Human Understanding*, ed. Peter H. Nidditch (Oxford: Clarendon Press, 1975).

LODOWYCK, FRANCIS, *A Common Writing* (London: for the author, 1647).

—— *The Ground-Work or Foundation Laid, or so Intended, for the Framing of a New Perfect Language; and an Universall or Common Writing* (London, 1652).

LORD, ALBERT B., *The Singer of Tales* (Cambridge, Mass.: Harvard Univ. Press, 1960).

LOWTH, ROBERT, *De sacra poesi Hebraeorum* (Oxford: Clarendon Press, 1753).

LOWTH, ROBERT, *Isaiah: A New Translation* (London: J. Dodsley, *et al.*, 1778).

—— *Lectures on the Sacred Poetry of the Hebrews*, 2 vols. (London: J. Johnson, 1787).

MCGANN, JEROME J., 'The Idea of an Indeterminate Text: Blake's Bible of Hell and Dr. Alexander Geddes', *Studies in Romanticism*, 25 (1986), 303–24.

MCKUSICK, JAMES C., *Coleridge's Philosophy of Language* (New Haven, Conn.: Yale Univ. Press, 1986).

—— Review of Thomas McFarland, *Originality and Imagination*, in *Wordsworth Circle*, 12 (1986), 194–6.

MCLUHAN, MARSHALL, *The Gutenberg Galaxy: The Making of Typographic Man* (Toronto: Univ. of Toronto Press, 1962).

MACPHERSON, JAMES, *Fragments of Ancient Poetry, Collected in the Highlands of Scotland* (Edinburgh: G. Hamilton and J. Balfour, 1760).

—— *Fingal, an Ancient Epic Poem, . . . Translated from the Galic Language, by James Macpherson* (London: Becket and De Hondt, 1762).

MALKIN, BENJAMIN HEATH, *A Father's Memoirs of his Child* (London: Longman, *et al.*, 1806).

MALLET, PAUL HENRI, *Northern Antiquities*, 2 vols. (London: T. Carnan, 1770).

MAN, PAUL DE, *Blindness and Insight: Essays in the Rhetoric of Contemporary Criticism* (Minneapolis: Univ. of Minnesota Press, 1983).

MANN, PAUL, '*The Book of Urizen* and the Horizon of the Book', in Hilton and Vogler, *Unnam'd Forms*.

MARSH, HERBERT, *The Authenticity of the Five Books of Moses Considered* (Cambridge: for the author, 1792).

MASSEY, WILLIAM, *The Origin and Progress of Letters* (London: J. Johnson, 1763).

MELLOR, ANNE K., 'Physiognomy, Phrenology, and Blake's Visionary Heads', in Essick and Pearce, *Blake in his Time*.

MERCURIUS, FRANCISCUS, Baron van Helmont, *Alphabeti verè naturalis Hebraici* (Sulzbach: A. Lichtenthaler, 1657 [i.e., 1667]).

MERSENNE, MARIN, *Harmonie universelle*, 2 vols. (Paris: S. Cramoisy, 1636–7).

MICHAEL, IAN, *English Grammatical Categories and the Tradition to 1800* (Cambridge: Cambridge Univ. Press, 1970).

MICHAELIS, JOHANN DAVID, *A Dissertation on the Influence of Opinions on Language and of Language on Opinions* (London: Owen and Bingley, 1769).

—— *Introduction to the New Testament*, 4 vols., trans. Herbert Marsh (Cambridge: J. Merrill, *et al.*, 1793–1801).

MILES, JOSEPHINE, *Renaissance, Eighteenth-Century, and Modern Language in English Poetry: A Tabular View* (Berkeley: Univ. of California Press, 1960).

MILEUR, JEAN-PIERRE, *Vision and Revision: Coleridge's Art of Immanence* (Berkeley: Univ. of California Press, 1982).

MILTON, JOHN, *Complete Poems and Major Prose*, ed. Merritt Y. Hughes (New York: Odyssey Press, 1957).

MITCHELL, W. J. T., *Iconology: Image, Text, Ideology* (Chicago: Univ. of Chicago Press, 1986).

—— 'Visible Language: Blake's Wond'rous Art of Writing', in Morris Eaves and Michael Fischer, eds., *Romanticism and Contemporary Criticism* (Ithaca, NY: Cornell Univ. Press, 1986).

MONBODDO, JAMES BURNET, Lord, *Of the Origin and Progress of Language*, 2nd edn., 6 vols. (Edinburgh: Balfour and Cadell, 1774–92).

MORRIS, DAVID B., 'Burns and Heteroglossia', *The Eighteenth Century: Theory and Interpretation*, 28 (1987), 3–27.

MÜLLER, MAX, *Lectures on the Science of Language*, 2 vols. (London: Longman, *et al.*, 1861).

MURRAY, HENRY, *The Evidences of the Jewish and Christian Revelations* (Dublin: for the author, 1790).

NELME, L. D., *An Essay toward an Investigation of the Origin and Elements of Language and Letters* (London: S. Leacroft, 1772).

NEWTON, ISAAC, *Theological Writings*, ed. H. MacLachlan (Liverpool: Liverpool Univ. Press, 1950).

NIETZSCHE, FRIEDRICH WILHELM, *Twilight of the Idols, and the Anti-Christ*, trans. R. J. Hollingdale (Harmondsworth: Penguin, 1968).

NOVALIS (FRIEDRICH VON HARDENBERG), *Hymns to the Night and Other Selected Writings*, trans. Charles E. Passage (New York: Liberal Arts Press, 1960).

ONG, WALTER J., *The Presence of the Word* (New Haven, Conn.: Yale Univ. Press, 1967).

OSTROM, HANS, 'Blake's *Tiriel* and the Dramatization of Collapsed Language', *Papers on Language & Literature*, 19 (1983), 167–82.

OWEN, A. L., *The Famous Druids* (Oxford: Clarendon Press, 1962).

PAGE, THOMAS, *The Art of Painting in its Rudiments, Progress, and Perfection* (Norwich: W. Chase, 1720).

PAINE, THOMAS, *Rights of Man: Being an Answer to Mr. Burke's Attack on the French Revolution* (London: J. Johnson, 1791).

—— *The Age of Reason* (Paris: Barrois, and London: D. Eaton, 1794).

PALEY, MORTON D., ' "A New Heaven is Begun": William Blake and Swedenborgianism', *Blake: An Illustrated Quarterly*, 13 (1979), 64–90.

PALEY, MORTON D., *The Continuing City: William Blake's* Jerusalem (Oxford: Clarendon Press, 1983).

—— 'The Fourth Face of Man: Blake and Architecture', in Richard Wendorf, ed., *Articulate Images: The Sister Arts from Hogarth to Tennyson* (Minneapolis: Univ. of Minnesota Press, 1983).

PALMER, SAMUEL, *Letters of Samuel Palmer*, 2 vols., ed. Raymond Lister (Oxford: Clarendon Press, 1974).

PANHUIS, DIRK, 'The Arbitrariness of the Lingual Sign as a Symptom of Linguistic Alienation', *Studies in Language*, 5 (1981), 343–60.

PARKHURST, JOHN, *Hebrew and English Lexicon* (London: W. Faden, 1762).

PARRY, MILMAN, *The Making of Homeric Verse: The Collected Papers of Milman Parry*, ed. Adam Parry (Oxford: Clarendon Press, 1971).

PEARCE, DONALD R., 'Natural Religion and the Plight of Thel', *Blake Studies*, 8 no. 1 (1978), 23–35.

PECHEY, GRAHAM, '*The Marriage of Heaven and Hell*: A Text and its Conjuncture', *Oxford Literary Review*, 3 (1979), 52–76.

—— '1789 and After: Mutations of "Romantic" Discourse', in Francis Barker, *et al.*, eds., *1789: Reading Writing Revolution* (Colchester: Univ. of Essex, 1982).

PEIRCE, CHARLES SANDERS, *Collected Papers*, 8 vols., ed. Charles Hartshorne and Paul Weiss (Cambridge, Mass.: Harvard Univ. Press, 1931–58).

—— *Semiotic and Significs*, ed. Charles S. Hardwick (Bloomington: Indiana Univ. Press, 1977).

—— *Writings of Charles S. Peirce*, 3 vols. to date, ed. Max H. Fisch, *et al.* (Bloomington: Indiana Univ. Press, 1982–6).

PERCY, THOMAS, ed., *Five Pieces of Runic Poetry Translated from the Islandic Language* (London: R. and J. Dodsley, 1763).

PETERFREUND, STUART, 'Blake on Space, Time, and the Role of the Artist', *STTH: Science/Technology and the Humanities*, 2 (1979), 246–63.

PHILO JUDAEUS, *Philo*, 10 vols., trans. F. G. Colson and G. H. Whitaker (London: W. Heinemann, 1929–42).

—— *Questions and Answers on Genesis*, 2 vols., trans. Ralph Marcus (Cambridge, Mass.: Harvard Univ. Press, 1953).

PINKERTON, JOHN, ed., *Scottish Tragic Ballads* (London: J. Nichols, 1781).

PLATO, *The Cratylus, Phaedo, Parmenides and Timaeus of Plato*, trans. Thomas Taylor (London: B. and J. White, 1793).

—— *The Dialogues of Plato*, 2 vols., trans. Benjamin Jowett (New York: Random House, 1937).

PLOTINUS, *The Enneads*, 4th edn., trans. Stephen MacKenna, rev. B. S. Page (London: Faber and Faber, 1969).

PLUTARCH, *Moralia*, 15 vols., trans. Frank Cole Babbitt, *et al.* (London: W. Heinemann, 1928–69).

PRESTON, THOMAS R., 'Biblical Criticism, Literature, and the Eighteenth-Century Reader', in Isabel Rivers, ed., *Books and their Readers in Eighteenth-Century England* (Leicester: Leicester Univ. Press, 1982).

PRICKETT, STEPHEN, 'The Living Educts of the Imagination: Coleridge on Religious Language', *Wordsworth Circle*, 4 (1973), 99–110.

QUARLES, FRANCIS, *Hieroglyphikes of the Life of Man* (London: J. Marriot, 1638).

RAINE, KATHLEEN, 'Some Sources of *Tiriel*', *Huntington Library Quarterly*, 21 (1957), 1–36.

—— *Blake and Tradition*, 2 vols. (Princeton, NJ: Princeton Univ. Press, 1968).

RAJAN, TILOTTAMA, 'The Supplement of Reading', *New Literary History*, 17 (1986), 573–94.

REIMAN, DONALD H., and CHRISTINA SHUTTLEWORTH KRAUSS, 'The Derivation and Meaning of "Ololon" ', *Blake: An Illustrated Quarterly*, 16 (1982), 82–5.

REYNOLDS, JOSHUA, *The Works of Sir Joshua Reynolds*, 3 vols. (London: Cadell and Davies, 1798).

RICHARDSON, ALEXANDER, *The Logicians School-Master; or, a Comment Upon Ramus Logicke* (London: J. Bellamie, 1629).

RICOEUR, PAUL, *The Philosophy of Paul Ricoeur*, ed. Charles E. Reagan and David Stewart (Boston: Beacon Press, 1978).

RIEGER, JAMES, ' "The Hem of their Garments": The Bard's Song in *Milton*', in Curran and Wittreich, *Blake's Sublime Allegory*.

ROBINS, ROBERT HENRY, *Ancient & Medieval Grammatical Theory in Europe* (London: Bell, 1951).

ROE, ALBERT S., 'The Thunder of Egypt', in Rosenfeld, *Blake*.

ROSENBERG, MARC, 'Style and Meaning in *The Book of Urizen*', *Style*, 4 (1970), 197–212.

ROSENFELD, ALVIN H., ed., *William Blake: Essays for S. Foster Damon* (Providence, RI: Brown Univ. Press, 1969).

ROSS, STEPHEN DAVID, 'Metaphor, the Semasic Field, and Inexhaustibility', *New Literary History*, 18 (1987), 517–33.

ROSTON, MURRAY, *Prophet and Poet: The Bible and the Growth of Romanticism* (Evanston, Ill.: Northwestern Univ. Press, 1965).

ROTI, GRANT C., and DONALD L. KENT, 'The Last Stanza of Blake's London', *Blake: An Illustrated Quarterly*, 11 (1977), 19–21.

ROUSSEAU, JEAN JACQUES, *Essay on the Origin of Languages*, in *On the Origin of Language*, ed. John H. Moran and Alexander Gode (New York: F. Ungar, 1966).

SALMON, VIVIAN, *The Works of Francis Lodwick: A Study of his Writings in the Intellectual Context of the Seventeenth Century* (London: Longman, 1972).

—— *The Study of Language in 17th-Century England* (Amsterdam: J. Benjamins, 1979).

SAUSSURE, FERDINAND DE, *Course in General Linguistics*, ed. Charles Bally and Albert Sechehaye, trans. Wade Baskin (New York: McGraw-Hill, 1966).

SCHILLER, FRIEDRICH, *Naive and Sentimental Poetry and On the Sublime*, trans. Julius A. Elias (New York: F. Ungar, 1966).

SCHLEGEL, AUGUST WILHELM, *A Course of Lectures on Dramatic Art and Literature*, trans. John Black, rev. A. J. W. Morrison (London: H. Bohn, 1846).

SCHLEGEL, FRIEDRICH, *The Philosophy of Life, and Philosophy of Language*, trans. A. J. W. Morrison (London: H. Bohn, 1847).

—— *Friedrich Schlegel und Novalis: Biographie einer Romantikerfreundschaft in ihren Briefen*, ed. Max Preitz (Darmstadt: H. Gentner, 1957).

—— *Dialogue on Poetry and Literary Aphorisms*, trans. Ernst Behler and Roman Struc (University Park: Pennsylvania State Univ. Press, 1968).

SCHLEIERMACHER, FRIEDRICH, *On Religion: Speeches to its Cultured Despisers*, trans. John Oman (New York: Harper, 1958).

—— *Hermeneutics: The Handwritten Manuscripts*, ed. Heinz Kimmerle, trans. James Duke and Jack Forstman (Missoula, Mont.: Scholars Press, 1977).

SCHOLEM, GERSHOM G., *Major Trends in Jewish Mysticism* (New York: Schocken Books, 1941).

—— *On the Kabbalah and its Symbolism*, trans. Ralph Manheim (London: Routledge and Kegan Paul, 1965).

SCHULZ, MAX F., *The Poetic Voices of Coleridge* (Detroit, Mich.: Wayne State Univ. Press, 1963).

SHAFFER, ELEANOR S., *'Kubla Khan' and the Fall of Jerusalem: The Mythological School in Biblical Criticism and Secular Literature 1770–1880* (Cambridge: Cambridge Univ. Press, 1975).

SHELLEY, PERCY BYSSHE, *Shelley's Poetry and Prose*, ed. Donald H. Reiman and Sharon B. Powers (New York: W. Norton, 1977).

SIMON, RICHARD, *A Critical History of the Old Testament*, trans. H.D. (London: J. Tonson, 1682).

SIMPSON, DAVID, 'Criticism, Politics, and Style in Wordsworth's Poetry', *Critical Inquiry*, 11 (1984), 52–81.

SINGER, ISIDORE, ed., *The Jewish Encyclopedia*, 12 vols. (New York: Funk and Wagnalls, 1910).

SLAUGHTER, M. M., *Universal Languages and Scientific Taxonomy in the Seventeenth Century* (Cambridge: Cambridge Univ. Press, 1982).

SMART, CHRISTOPHER, *Jubilate Agno*, ed. W. H. Bond (Cambridge, Mass.: Harvard Univ. Press, 1954).

SMITH, ADAM, *The Theory of Moral Sentiments . . . to which is Added, a Dissertation on the Origin of Languages*, 6th edn., 2 vols. (London: Strahan, *et al.*, 1790).

SMITH, GABRIEL, *The School of Art; or, Most Compleat Drawingbook Extant* (London: J. Bowles, *et al.*, 1765).

SMITH, JOHN THOMAS, *Nollekens and his Times*, 2 vols. (London: H. Colburn, 1828).

SMITH, OLIVIA, *The Politics of Language 1791–1819* (Oxford: Clarendon Press, 1984).

SOUTH, ROBERT, *Sermons Preached upon Several Occasions*, 5 vols. (Oxford: Oxford Univ. Press, 1842).

SPRAT, THOMAS, *The History of the Royal-Academy of London* (London: J. Martyn, 1667).

STACKHOUSE, THOMAS, *Reflections on the Nature and Property of Languages in General, and on the Advantages, Defects, and Manner of Improving the English Tongue in Particular* (London: J. Batley, 1731).

STAM, JAMES H., *Inquiries into the Origin of Language: The Fate of a Question* (New York: Harper and Row, 1976).

STEINER, GEORGE, *After Babel: Aspects of Language and Translation* (London: Oxford Univ. Press, 1975).

—— *On Difficulty and Other Essays* (New York: Oxford Univ. Press, 1978).

STEMPEL, DANIEL, 'Blake, Foucault, and the Classical Episteme', *PMLA* 96 (1981), 388–407.

STUKELEY, WILLIAM, *Stonehenge: A Temple Restor'd to the British Druids* (London: Innys and Manly, 1740).

—— *Abury, a Temple of the British Druids* (London: for the author, 1743).

STURGES, JOHN, *Short Remarks on a New Translation of Isaiah* (London: T. Cadell, 1791).

SWEDENBORG, EMANUEL, *A Treatise concerning Heaven and Hell*, 2nd edn. (London: R. Hindmarsh, 1784).

—— *Angelic Wisdom concerning the Divine Love and the Divine Wisdom* (New York: American Swedenborg Society, 1915).

—— *The True Christian Religion*, 2 vols. (New York: American Swedenborg Society, 1915).

—— *Arcana coelestia*, 12 vols., ed. John Faulkner Potts (New York: Swedenborg Foundation, 1928–38).

—— *The Apocalypse Revealed*, 2 vols. (New York: Swedenborg Foundation, 1949).

SWIFT, JONATHAN, *Gulliver's Travels*, ed. Herbert Davis (Oxford: B. Blackwell, 1959).

SWINBURNE, ALGERNON C., *William Blake: A Critical Essay* (London: J. Hotten, 1868).

TANNENBAUM, LESLIE, *Biblical Tradition in Blake's Early Prophecies: The Great Code of Art* (Princeton, NJ: Princeton Univ. Press, 1982).

TAYLOR, ANYA, 'Blake's Moving Words and the Dread of Embodiment', *Cithara*, 15 (1976), 75–85.

TAYLOR, RONALD CLAYTON, 'Semantic Structures and the Temporal Modes of Blake's Prophetic Verse', *Language and Style*, 12 (1979), 26–49.

THOMPSON, E. P., 'London', in Michael Phillips, ed., *Interpreting Blake* (Cambridge: Cambridge Univ. Press, 1978).

TODD, RUTHVEN, *Tracks in the Snow* (London: Grey Walls Press, 1946).

TODOROV, TZVETAN, *Theories of the Symbol*, trans. Catherine Porter (Ithaca, NY: Cornell Univ. Press, 1982).

TOOKE, JOHN HORNE, *A Letter to John Dunning* (London: J. Johnson, 1778).

—— *"Επεα πτερόεντα: Or, the Diversions of Purley*, 2nd edn., 2 vols. (London: J. Johnson, 1798–1805).

ULLMAN, STEPHEN, 'Natural and Conventional Signs', in Thomas A. Sebeok, ed., *The Tell-Tale Sign: A Survey of Semiotics* (Lisse: P. de Ridder, 1975).

VATER, JOHANN SEVERIN, *Commentar über den Pentateuch . . . mit Einleitung zu den einzelnen Abschnitten, der eingeschalteten Übersetzung von Dr. Alexander Geddes's merkwürdigeren, critischen, und exegetischen Anmerkungen, und einer Abhandlung über Moses und die Verfasser des Pentateuchs*, 3 vols. in 2 (Halle: Waisenhaus-Buchhandlung, 1802–5).

VICO, GIAMBATTISTA, *The New Science*, trans. Thomas Goddard Bergin and Max Harold Fisch (Ithaca, NY: Cornell Univ. Press, 1968).

VIGENÈRE, BLAISE DE, *Traité des chiffres, ou secretes manieres d'escrire* (Paris: Abel, 1586).

VISCOMI, JOSEPH, *The Art of William Blake's Illuminated Prints* (Manchester: Manchester Etching Workshop, 1983).

VOGLER, THOMAS A., 'Re: Naming in *MIL/TON*', in Hilton and Vogler, *Unnam'd Forms*.

WARBURTON, WILLIAM, *The Divine Legation of Moses*, 2 vols. in 3 (London: F. Giles, 1738–41).

WARD, SETH, *Vindicae Academiarum; Containing Some Briefe Animadversions upon Mr Websters Book, Stiled, The Examination of Academies* (Oxford: T. Robinson, 1654).

WARNER, JANET A., *Blake and the Language of Art* (Kingston, Ont.: McGill-Queen's Univ. Press, 1984).

WATSON, RICHARD, *An Apology for the Bible, in a Series of Letters, Addressed to Thomas Paine* (London: T. Evans, 1797).

WEBSTER, JOHN, *Academiarum Examen; or, the Examination of Academies* (London: G. Calvert, 1654).

WEISKEL, THOMAS, *The Romantic Sublime: Studies in the Structure and Psychology of Transcendence* (Baltimore, Md.: Johns Hopkins Univ. Press, 1976).

WEITZMANN, KURT, *Late Antique and Early Christian Book Illumination* (New York: Braziller, 1977).

WELLBERY, DAVID E., *Lessing's Laocoon: Semiotics and Aesthetics in the Age of Reason* (Cambridge: Cambridge Univ. Press, 1984).

WELLEK, RENÉ, *A History of Modern Criticism: 1750–1950* (New Haven, Conn.: Yale Univ. Press, 1955–86).

WERNER, BETTE CHARLENE, *Blake's Vision of the Poetry of Milton* (Lewisburg, Pa.: Bucknell Univ. Press, 1986).

WHITE, DAVID A., *Heidegger and the Language of Poetry* (Lincoln: Univ. of Nebraska Press, 1978).

WHITER, WALTER, *Etymologicon Magnum; or, Universal Etymological Dictionary on a New Plan* (Cambridge: J. Deighton, *et al.*, 1800).

WILKINS, JOHN, *An Essay towards a Real Character, and a Philosophical Language* (London: Gellibrand and Martin, 1668).

WILLARD, SIDNEY, *A Hebrew Grammar* (Cambridge, Mass.: University Press, 1817).

WITTREICH, JOSEPH ANTHONY, JR., 'Opening the Seals: Blake's Epics and the Milton Tradition', in Curran and Wittreich, *Blake's Sublime Allegory*.

—— 'Painted Prophecies: The Tradition of Blake's Illuminated Books', in Essick and Pearce, *Blake in his Time*.

WOOD, ROBERT, *An Essay on the Original Genius and Writings of Homer* (London: privately printed, 1769).

WORDSWORTH, JONATHAN, 'As with the Silence of the Thought', in Lawrence Lipking, ed., *High Romantic Argument: Essays for M. H. Abrams* (Ithaca, NY: Cornell Univ. Press, 1981).

WORDSWORTH, WILLIAM, *The Poetical Works of William Wordsworth*, 2nd edn., 5 vols., ed. Ernest de Selincourt and Helen Darbishire (Oxford: Clarendon Press, 1940–54).

—— *The Prelude*, 2nd edn., ed. Ernest de Selincourt, rev. Helen Darbishire (Oxford: Clarendon Press, 1959).

—— *The Prose Works of William Wordsworth*, 3 vols., ed. W. J. B. Owen and Jane Worthington Smyser (Oxford: Clarendon Press, 1974).

YEATS, WILLIAM BUTLER, 'William Blake and his Illustrations to *The Divine Comedy*', *Savoy*, no. 3 (1896), 41–57.

Index

Plate numbers of Blake's illuminated books are printed in italic.